SHINOBU OHTAKA

*Magi volume 33 is
momentous!*

MAGI

Volume 33

Shonen Sunday Edition

Story and Art by
SHINOBU OHTAKA

MAGI Vol.33
by Shinobu OHTAKA
© 2009 Shinobu OHTAKA
All rights reserved.
Original Japanese edition published by SHOGAKUKAN.
English translation rights in the United States of America, Canada, the United Kingdom,
Ireland, Australia and New Zealand arranged with SHOGAKUKAN.

ORIGINAL COVER DESIGN / Yasuo SHIMURA+Bay Bridge Studio

Translation & English Adaptation 🔷 John Werry

Touch-up Art & Lettering 🔷 Stephen Dutro

Editor 🔷 Mike Montesa

Printed in Canada

Published by VIZ Media, LLC
P.O. Box 77010
San Francisco, CA 94107

10 9 8 7 6 5 4 3 2 1
First printing, December 2018

PARENTAL ADVISORY
MAGI is rated T for Teen. This volume
contains fantasy violence and
suggestive themes.

WWW.SHONENSUNDAY.COM

MEDIA
viz.com

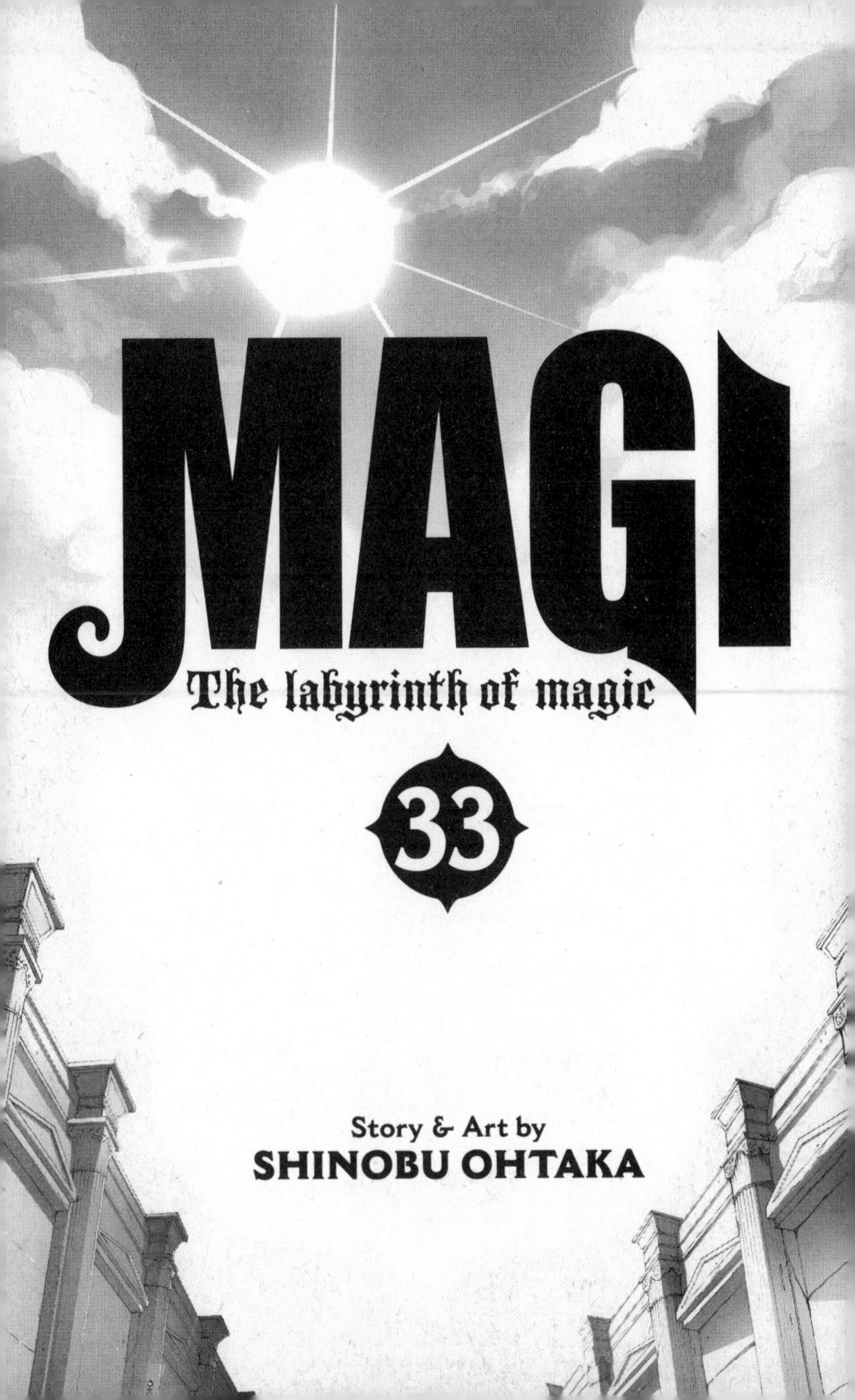

MAGI

The labyrinth of magic

33

Story & Art by

SHINOBU OHTAKA

MAGI
The labyrinth of magic

33

CONTENTS

Night 319: Kogyoku's Thankfulness

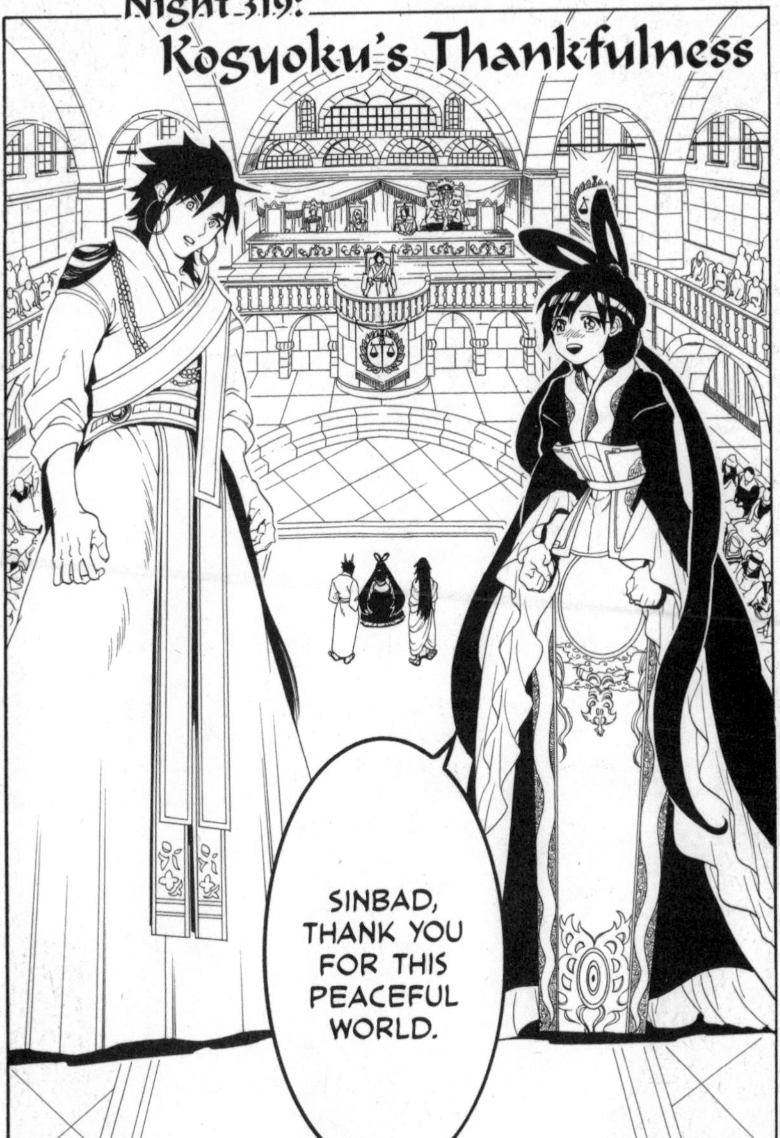
SINBAD, THANK YOU FOR THIS PEACEFUL WORLD.

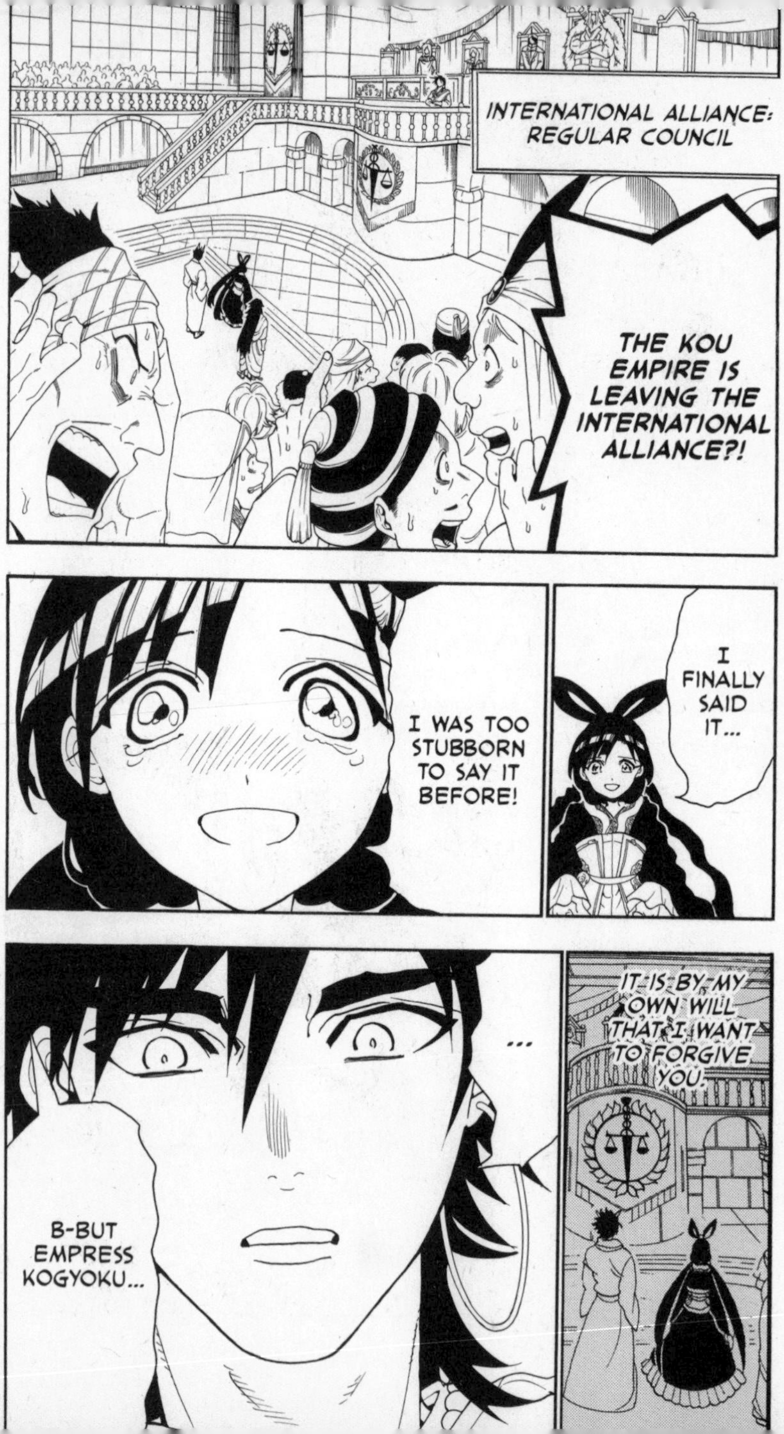
INTERNATIONAL ALLIANCE: REGULAR COUNCIL
THE KOU EMPIRE IS LEAVING THE INTERNATIONAL ALLIANCE?!
I FINALLY SAID IT...
I WAS TOO STUBBORN TO SAY IT BEFORE!
IT IS BY MY OWN WILL THAT I WANT TO FORGIVE YOU.
...
B-BUT EMPRESS KOGYOKU...

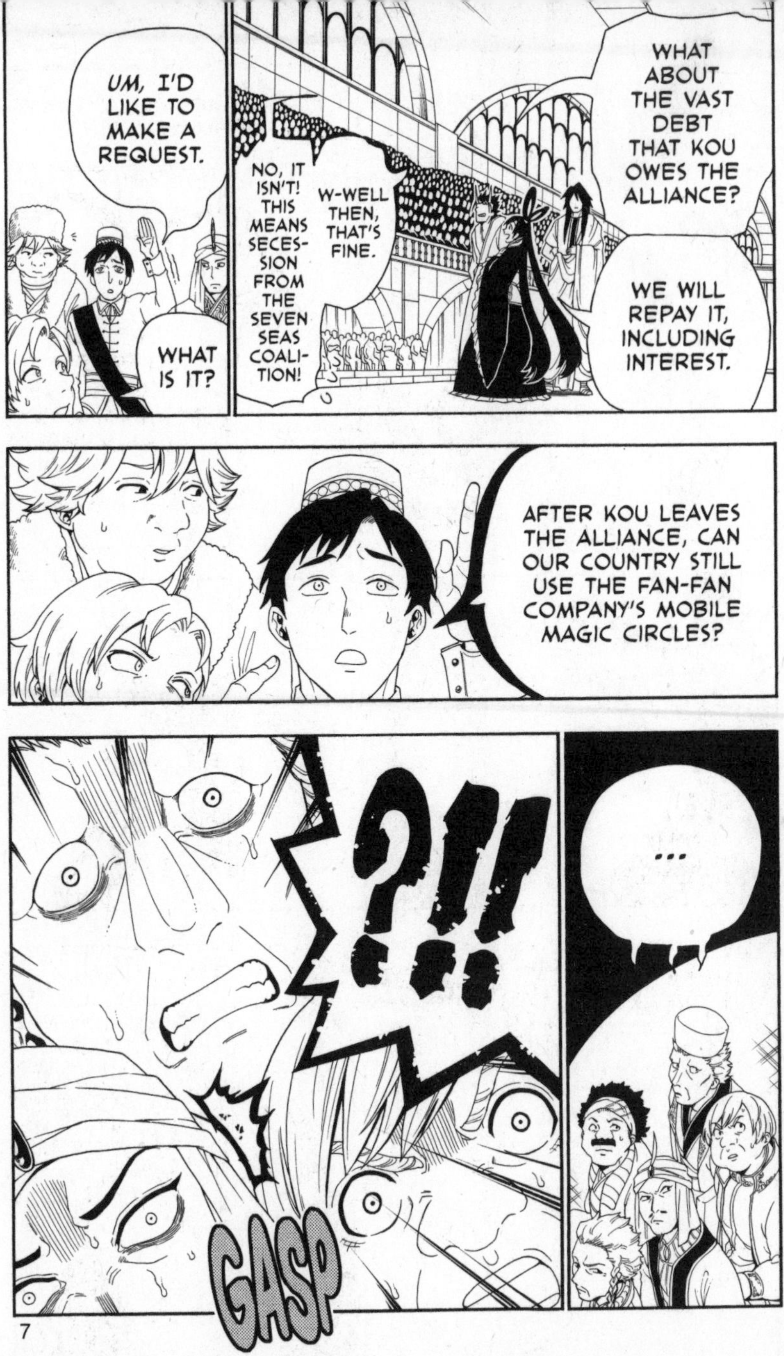
WHAT ABOUT THE VAST DEBT THAT KOU OWES THE ALLIANCE?
WE WILL REPAY IT, INCLUDING INTEREST.
W-WELL THEN, THAT'S FINE.
NO, IT ISN'T! THIS MEANS SECES-SION FROM THE SEVEN SEAS COALI-TION!
UM, I'D LIKE TO MAKE A REQUEST.
WHAT IS IT?
AFTER KOU LEAVES THE ALLIANCE, CAN OUR COUNTRY STILL USE THE FAN-FAN COMPANY'S MOBILE MAGIC CIRCLES?
...
?!!
GASP

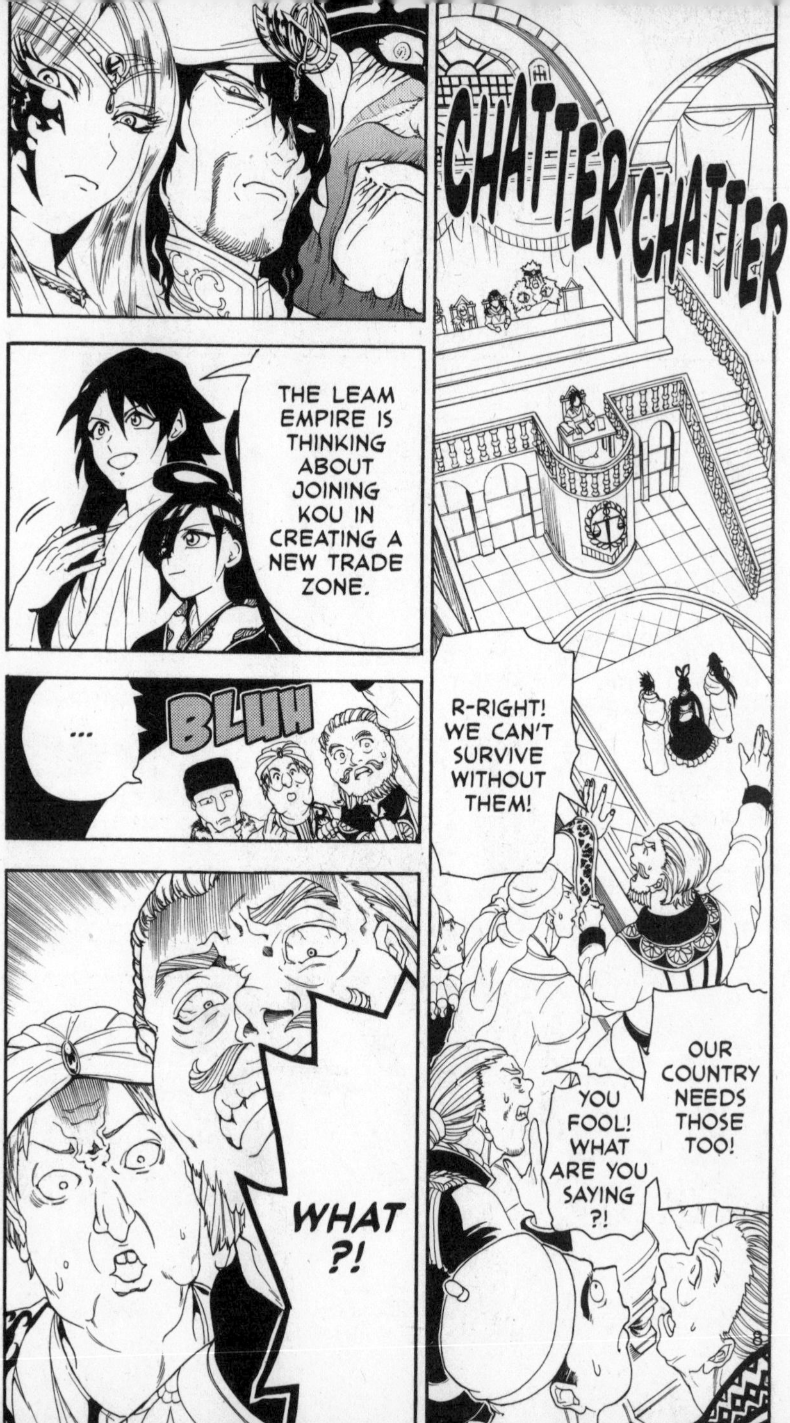
CHATTER CHATTER
R-RIGHT! WE CAN'T SURVIVE WITHOUT THEM!
OUR COUNTRY NEEDS THOSE TOO!
YOU FOOL! WHAT ARE YOU SAYING ?!
THE LEAM EMPIRE IS THINKING ABOUT JOINING KOU IN CREATING A NEW TRADE ZONE.
...
BLUH
WHAT ?!

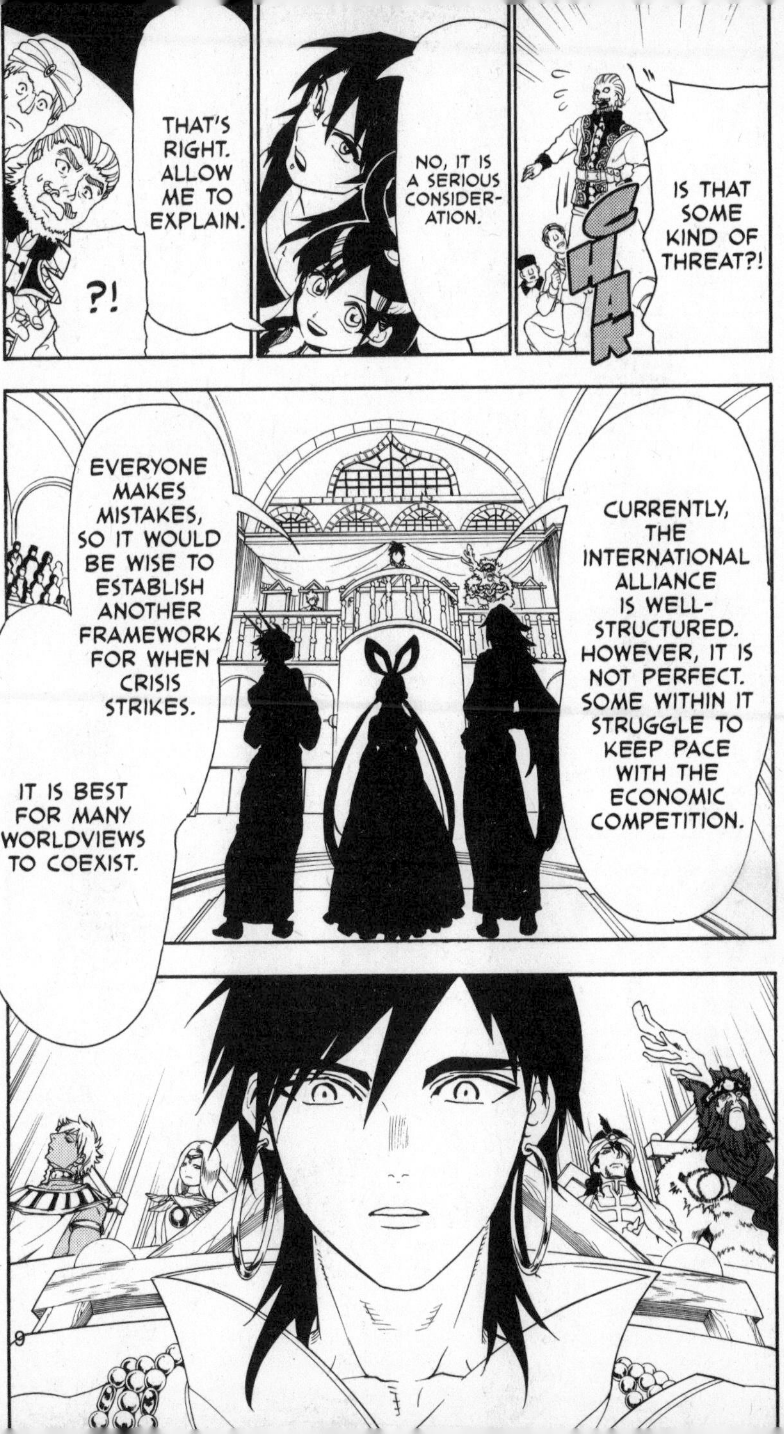
IS THAT SOME KIND OF THREAT?!
CHAK
NO, IT IS A SERIOUS CONSIDER-ATION.
THAT'S RIGHT. ALLOW ME TO EXPLAIN.
?!
CURRENTLY, THE INTERNATIONAL ALLIANCE IS WELL-STRUCTURED. HOWEVER, IT IS NOT PERFECT. SOME WITHIN IT STRUGGLE TO KEEP PACE WITH THE ECONOMIC COMPETITION.
EVERYONE MAKES MISTAKES, SO IT WOULD BE WISE TO ESTABLISH ANOTHER FRAMEWORK FOR WHEN CRISIS STRIKES.
IT IS BEST FOR MANY WORLDVIEWS TO COEXIST.

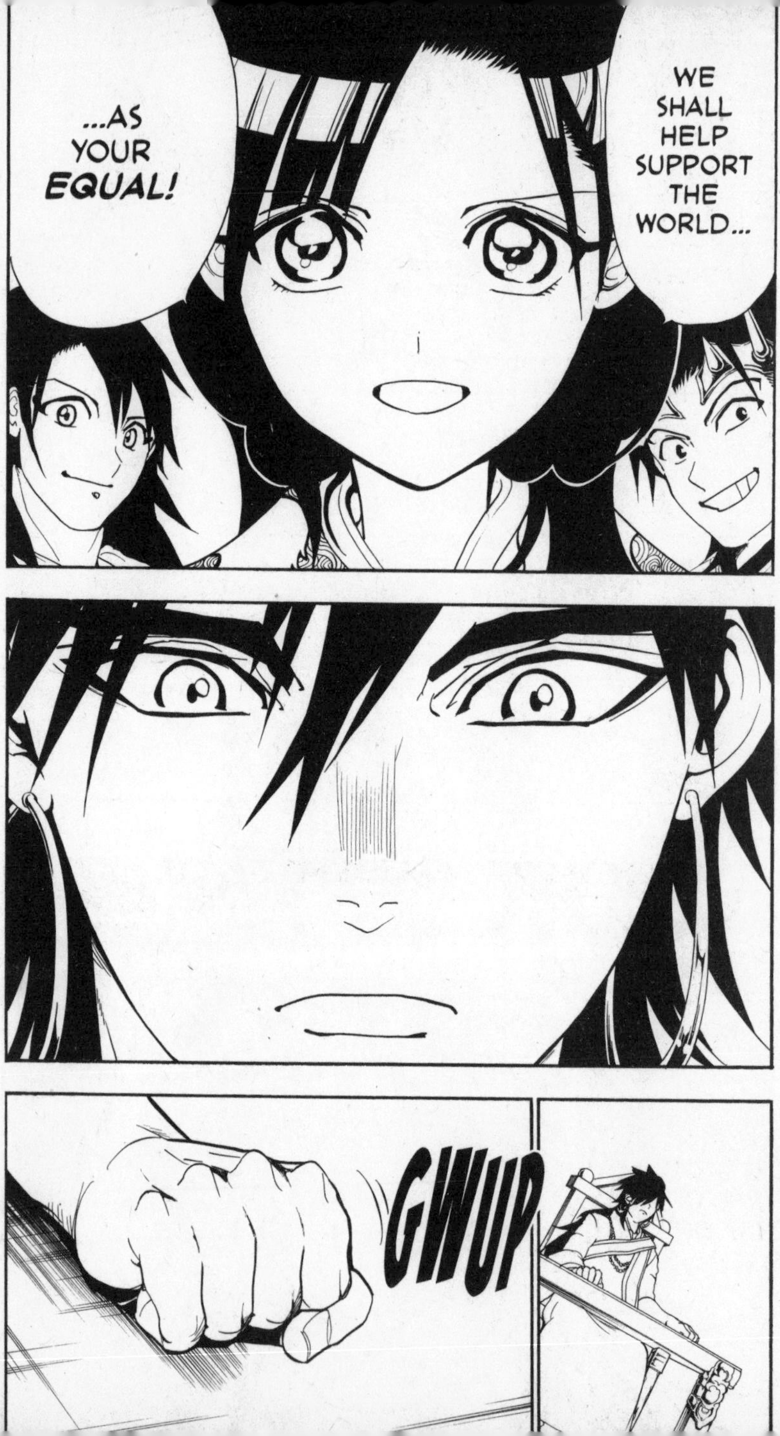
WE SHALL HELP SUPPORT THE WORLD...
...AS YOUR EQUAL!
GWUP

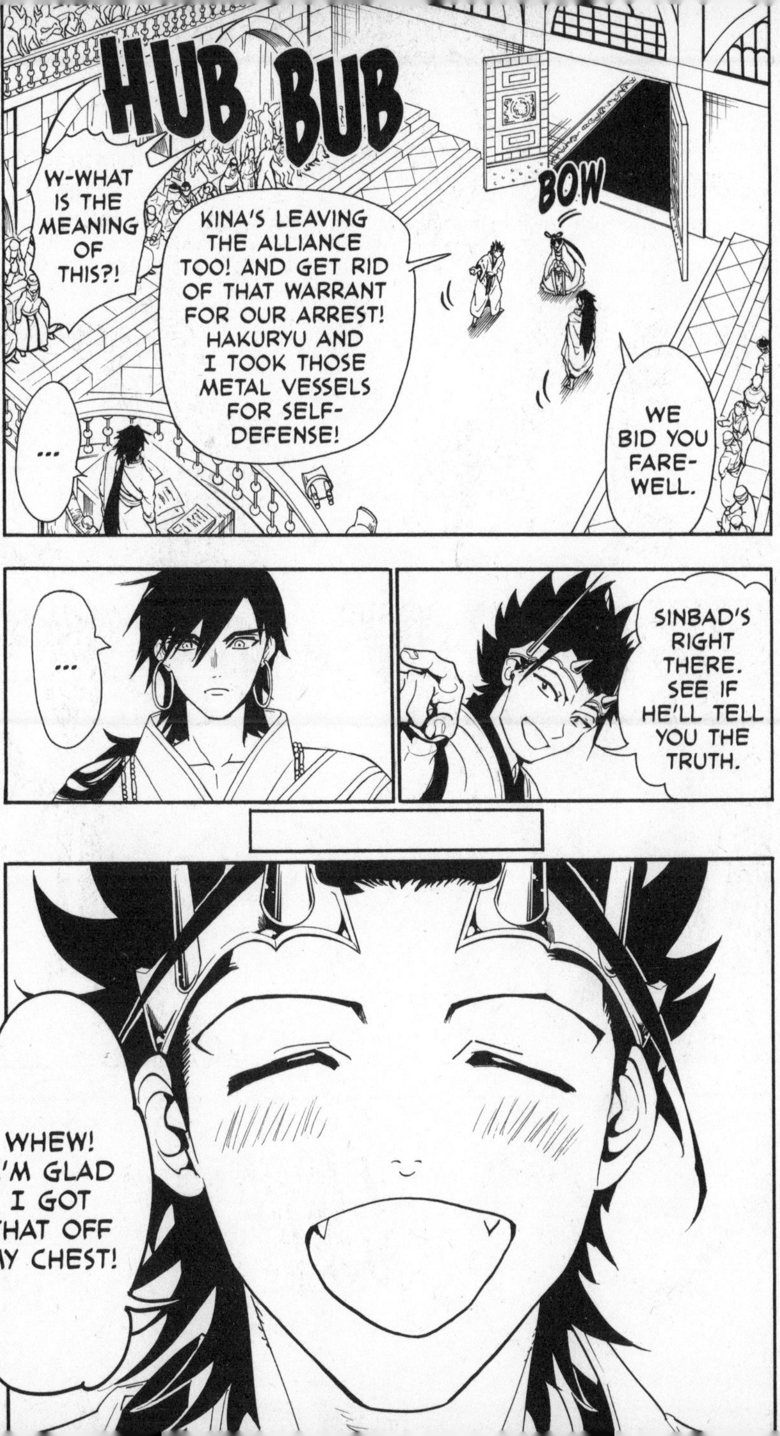
HUB BUB
BOW
KINA'S LEAVING THE ALLIANCE TOO! AND GET RID OF THAT WARRANT FOR OUR ARREST! HAKURYU AND I TOOK THOSE METAL VESSELS FOR SELF-DEFENSE!
WE BID YOU FAREWELL.
W-WHAT IS THE MEANING OF THIS?!
...
SINBAD'S RIGHT THERE. SEE IF HE'LL TELL YOU THE TRUTH.
...
WHEW! I'M GLAD I GOT THAT OFF MY CHEST!

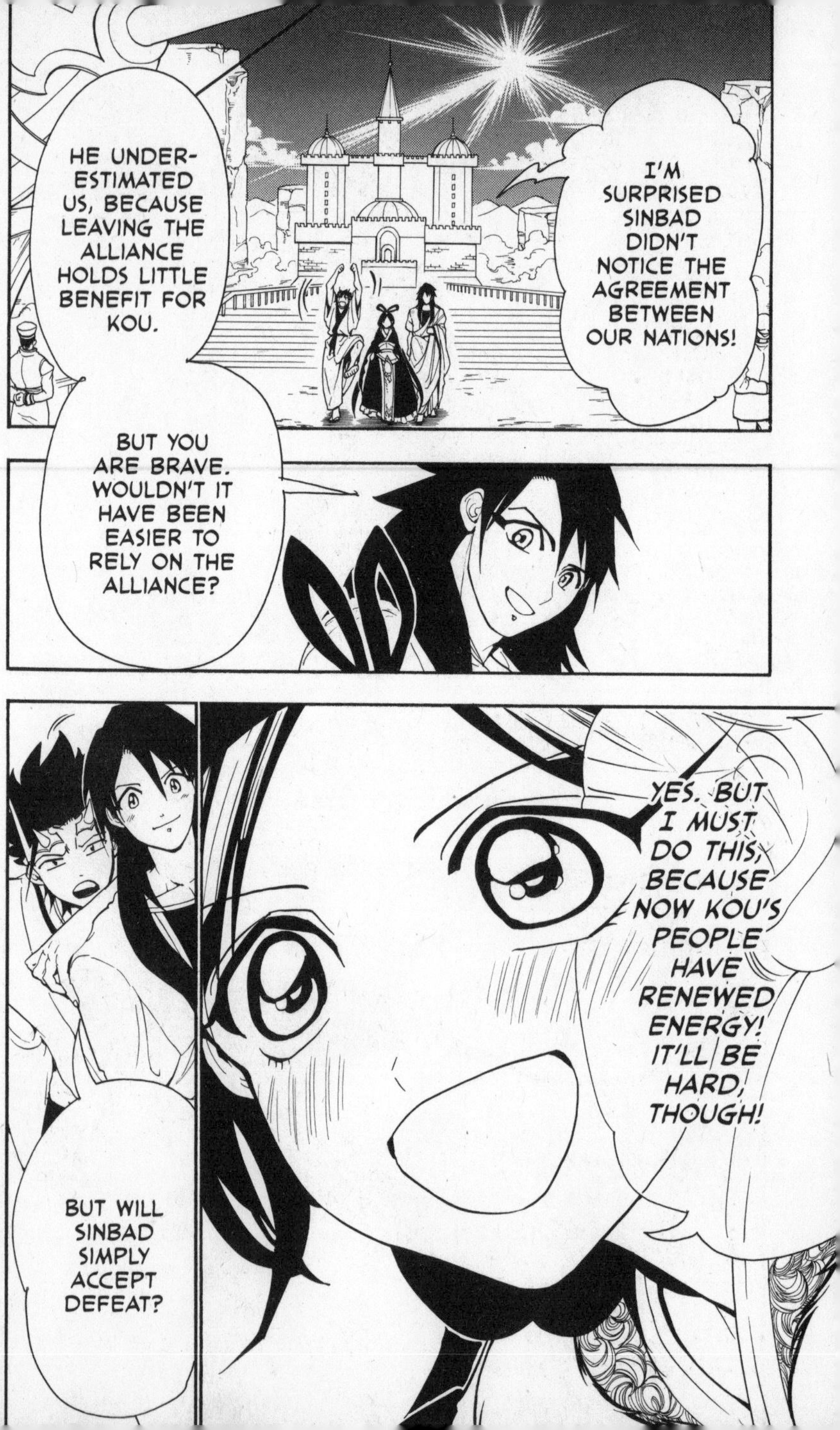
I'M SURPRISED SINBAD DIDN'T NOTICE THE AGREEMENT BETWEEN OUR NATIONS!
HE UNDER-ESTIMATED US, BECAUSE LEAVING THE ALLIANCE HOLDS LITTLE BENEFIT FOR KOU.
BUT YOU ARE BRAVE. WOULDN'T IT HAVE BEEN EASIER TO RELY ON THE ALLIANCE?
YES. BUT I MUST DO THIS, BECAUSE NOW KOU'S PEOPLE HAVE RENEWED ENERGY! IT'LL BE HARD, THOUGH!
BUT WILL SINBAD SIMPLY ACCEPT DEFEAT?

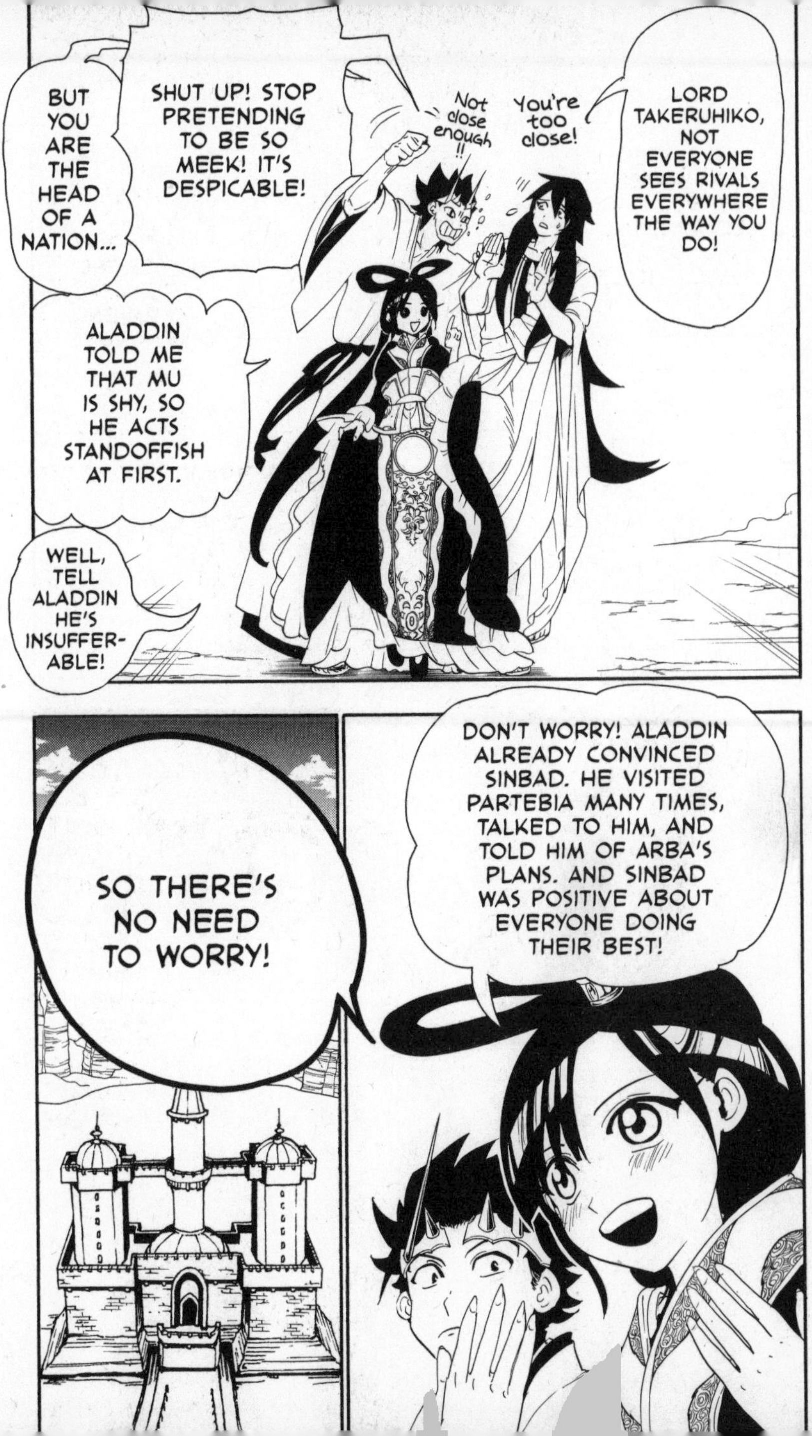
LORD TAKERUHIKO, NOT EVERYONE SEES RIVALS EVERYWHERE THE WAY YOU DO!
You're too close!
Not close enough!!
SHUT UP! STOP PRETENDING TO BE SO MEEK! IT'S DESPICABLE!
BUT YOU ARE THE HEAD OF A NATION...
ALADDIN TOLD ME THAT MU IS SHY, SO HE ACTS STANDOFFISH AT FIRST.
WELL, TELL ALADDIN HE'S INSUFFER-ABLE!
DON'T WORRY! ALADDIN ALREADY CONVINCED SINBAD. HE VISITED PARTEBIA MANY TIMES, TALKED TO HIM, AND TOLD HIM OF ARBA'S PLANS. AND SINBAD WAS POSITIVE ABOUT EVERYONE DOING THEIR BEST!
SO THERE'S NO NEED TO WORRY!

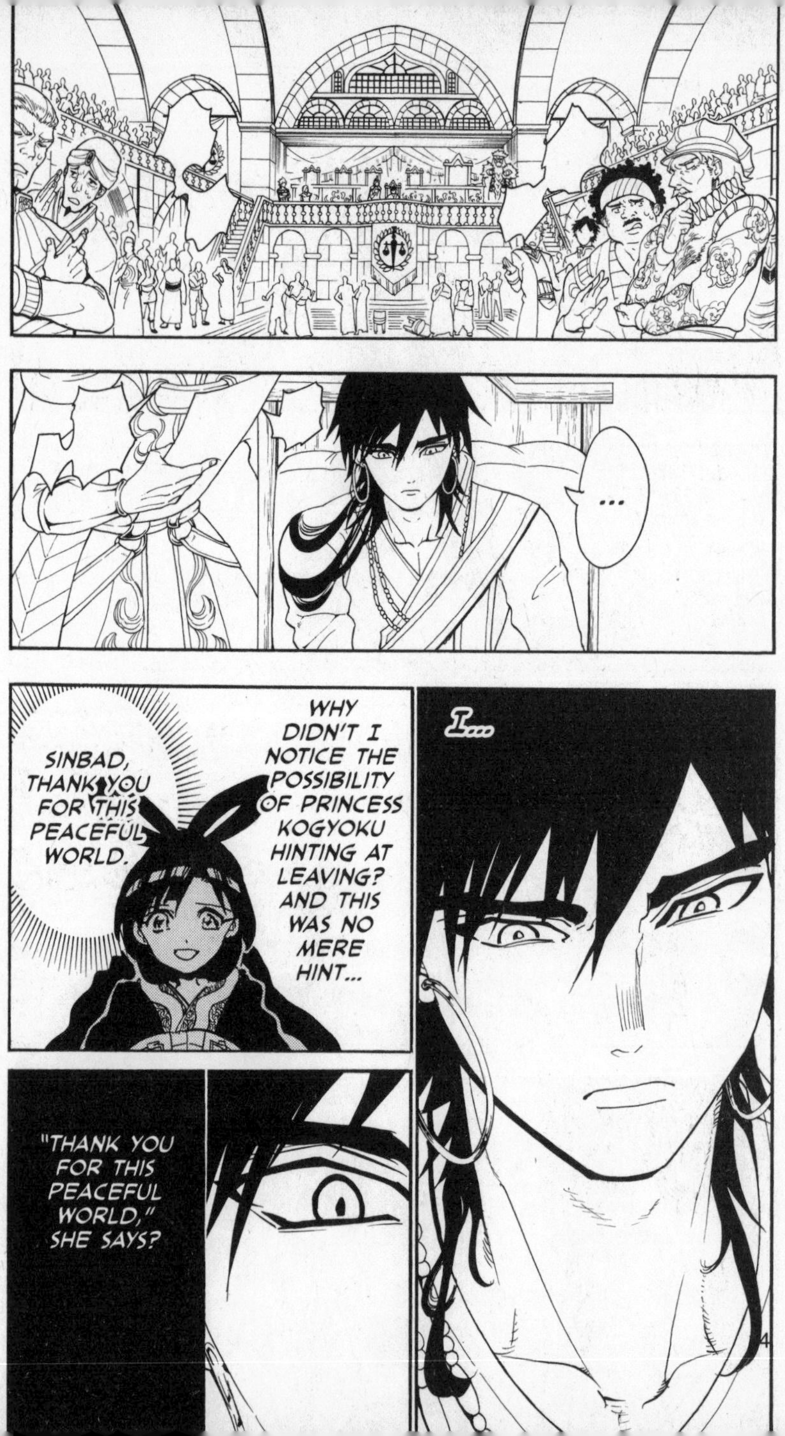
...
I...
WHY DIDN'T I NOTICE THE POSSIBILITY OF PRINCESS KOGYOKU HINTING AT LEAVING? AND THIS WAS NO MERE HINT...
SINBAD, THANK YOU FOR THIS PEACEFUL WORLD.
"THANK YOU FOR THIS PEACEFUL WORLD," SHE SAYS?

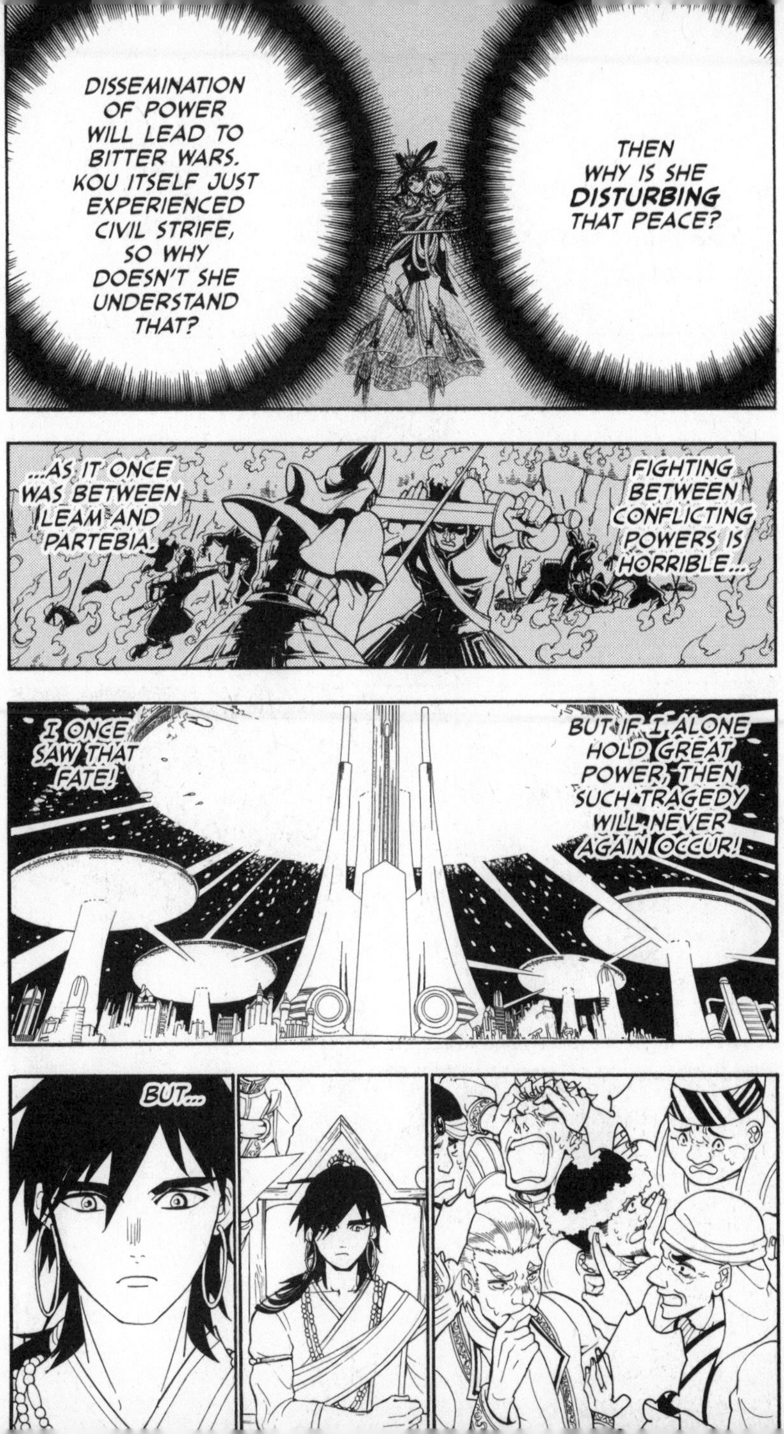
THEN WHY IS SHE DISTURBING THAT PEACE?
DISSEMINATION OF POWER WILL LEAD TO BITTER WARS. KOU ITSELF JUST EXPERIENCED CIVIL STRIFE, SO WHY DOESN'T SHE UNDERSTAND THAT?
FIGHTING BETWEEN CONFLICTING POWERS IS HORRIBLE...
...AS IT ONCE WAS BETWEEN LEAM AND PARTEBIA.
BUT IF I ALONE HOLD GREAT POWER, THEN SUCH TRAGEDY WILL NEVER AGAIN OCCUR!
I ONCE SAW THAT FATE!
BUT...

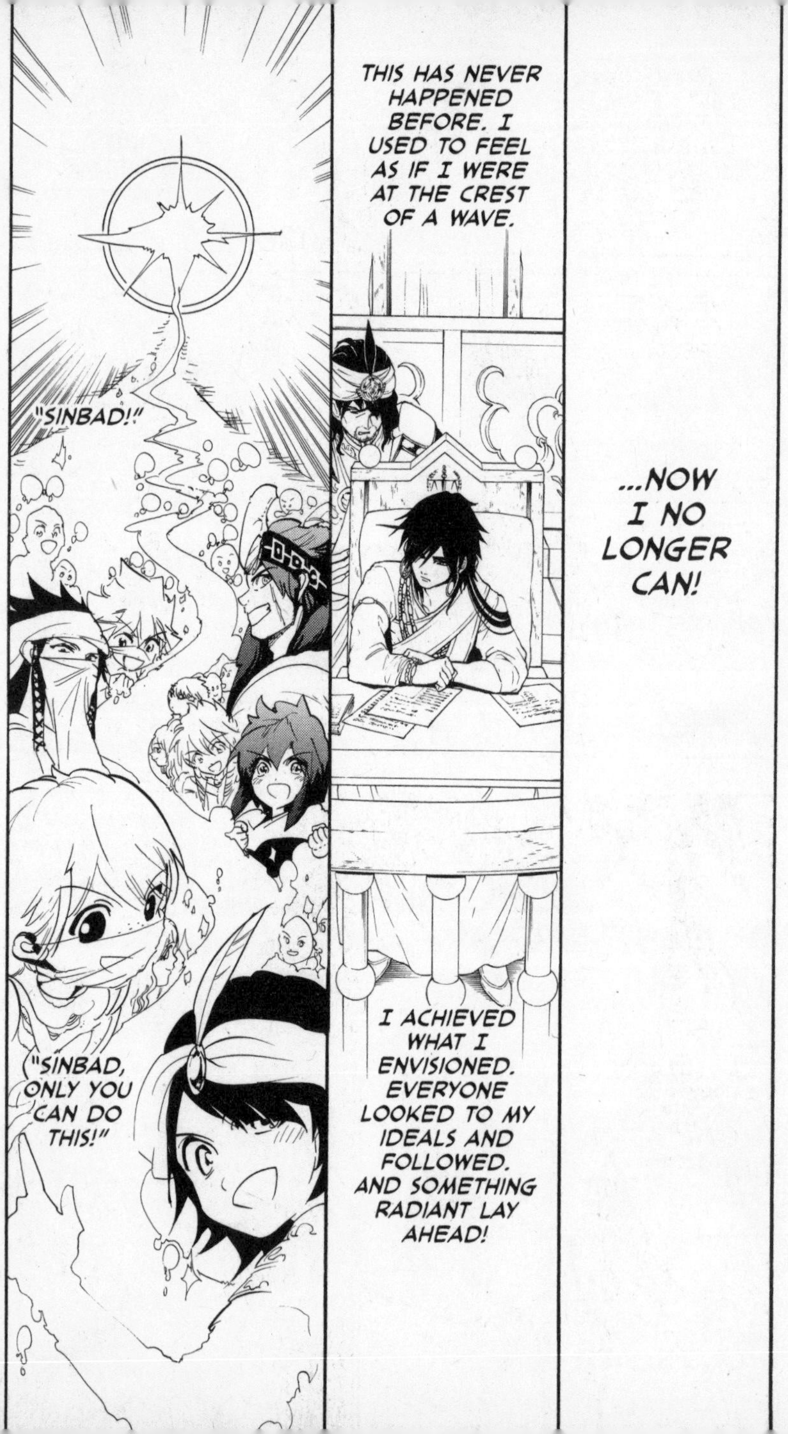
...NOW I NO LONGER CAN!
THIS HAS NEVER HAPPENED BEFORE. I USED TO FEEL AS IF I WERE AT THE CREST OF A WAVE.
I ACHIEVED WHAT I ENVISIONED. EVERYONE LOOKED TO MY IDEALS AND FOLLOWED. AND SOMETHING RADIANT LAY AHEAD!
"SINBAD!"
"SINBAD, ONLY YOU CAN DO THIS!"

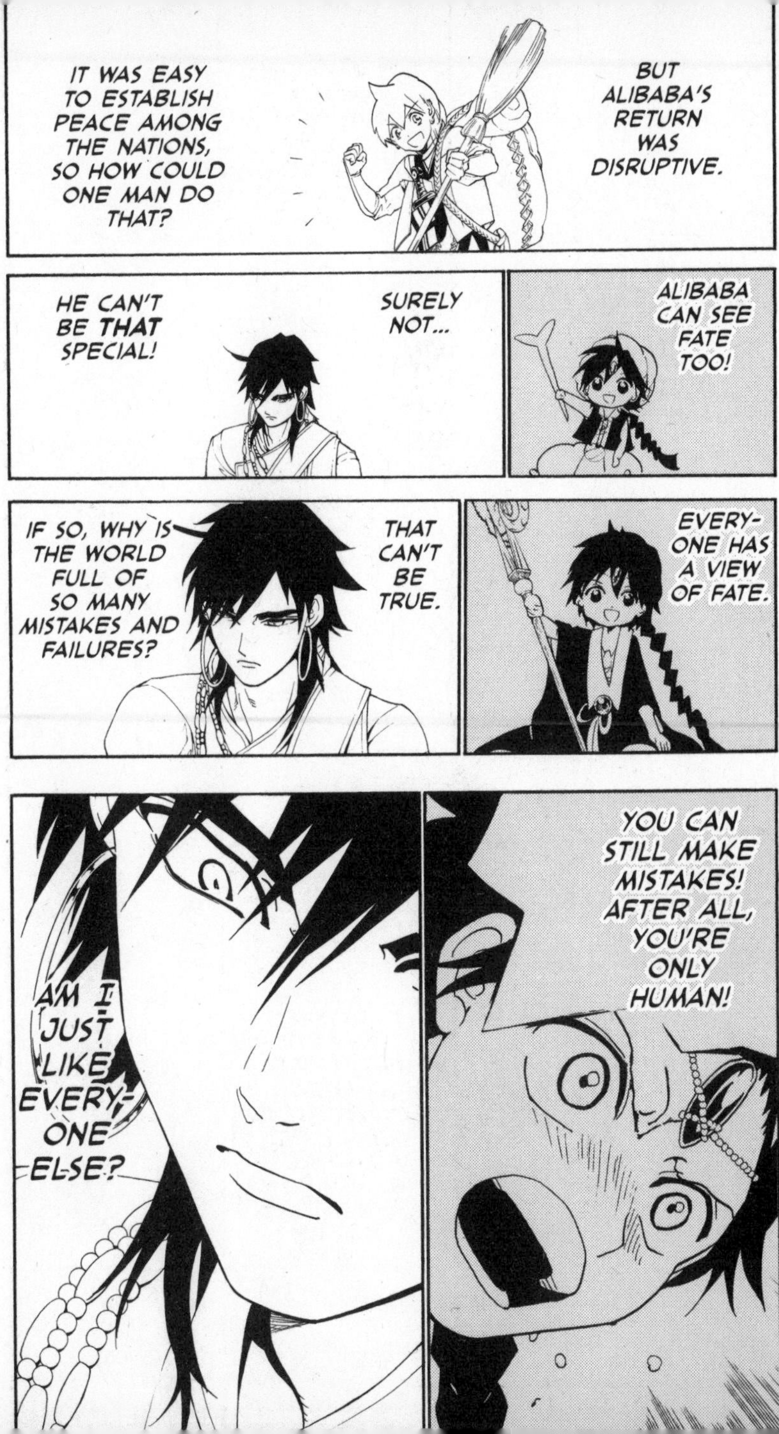
BUT ALIBABA'S RETURN WAS DISRUPTIVE.
IT WAS EASY TO ESTABLISH PEACE AMONG THE NATIONS, SO HOW COULD ONE MAN DO THAT?
ALIBABA CAN SEE FATE TOO!
SURELY NOT...
HE CAN'T BE **THAT** SPECIAL!
EVERY-ONE HAS A VIEW OF FATE.
THAT CAN'T BE TRUE.
IF SO, WHY IS THE WORLD FULL OF SO MANY MISTAKES AND FAILURES?
YOU CAN STILL MAKE MISTAKES! AFTER ALL, YOU'RE ONLY HUMAN!
AM I JUST LIKE EVERY-ONE ELSE?

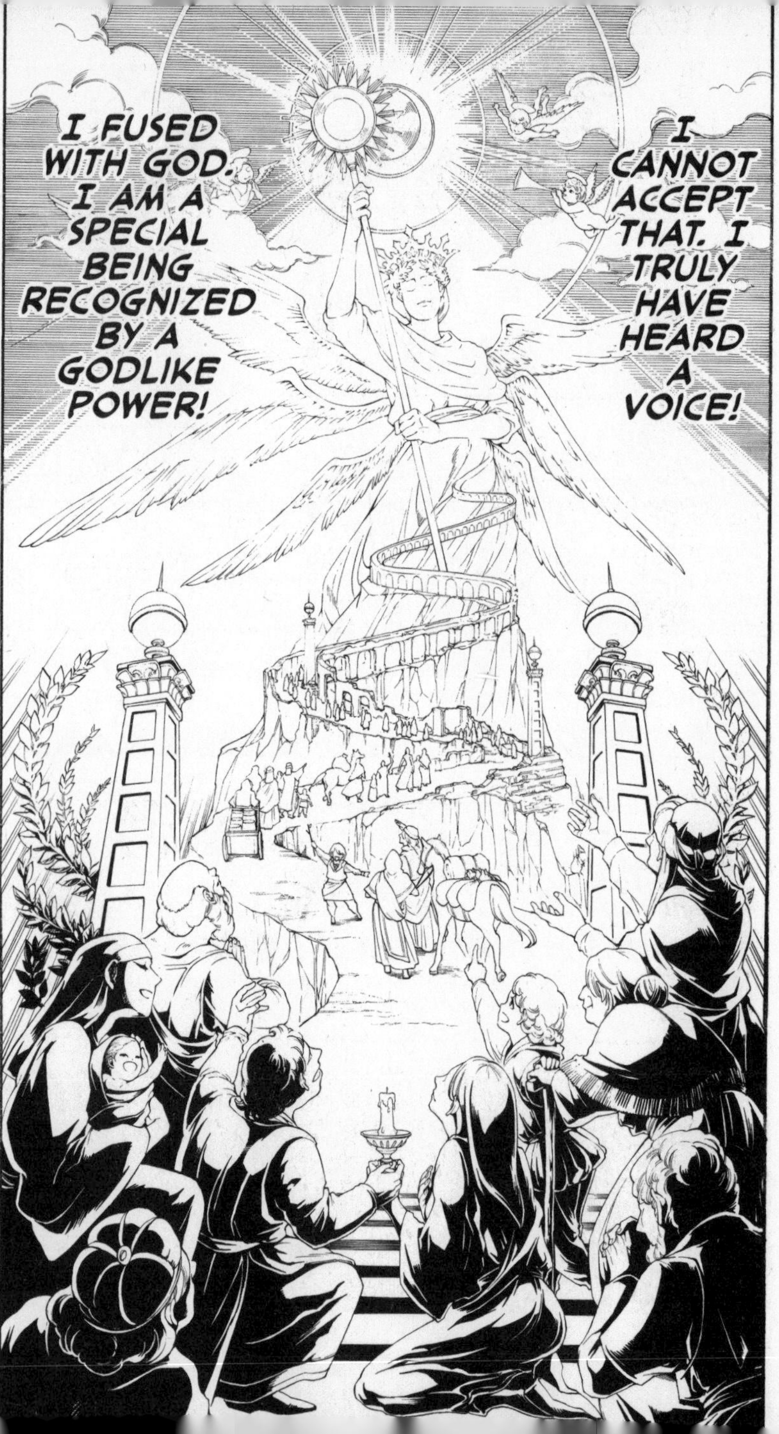
I CANNOT ACCEPT THAT. I TRULY HAVE HEARD A VOICE!
I FUSED WITH GOD. I AM A SPECIAL BEING RECOGNIZED BY A GODLIKE POWER!

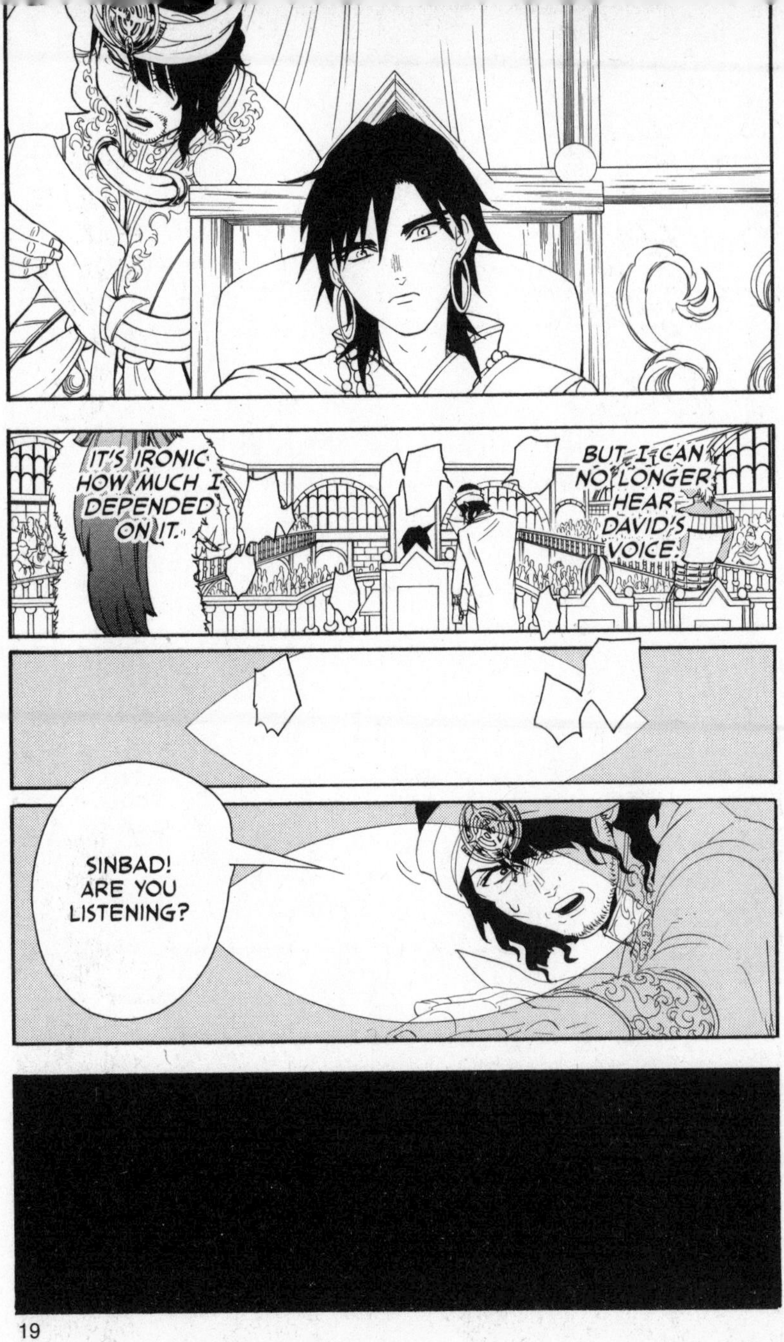
BUT I CAN NO LONGER HEAR DAVID'S VOICE.
IT'S IRONIC HOW MUCH I DEPENDED ON IT.
SINBAD! ARE YOU LISTENING?

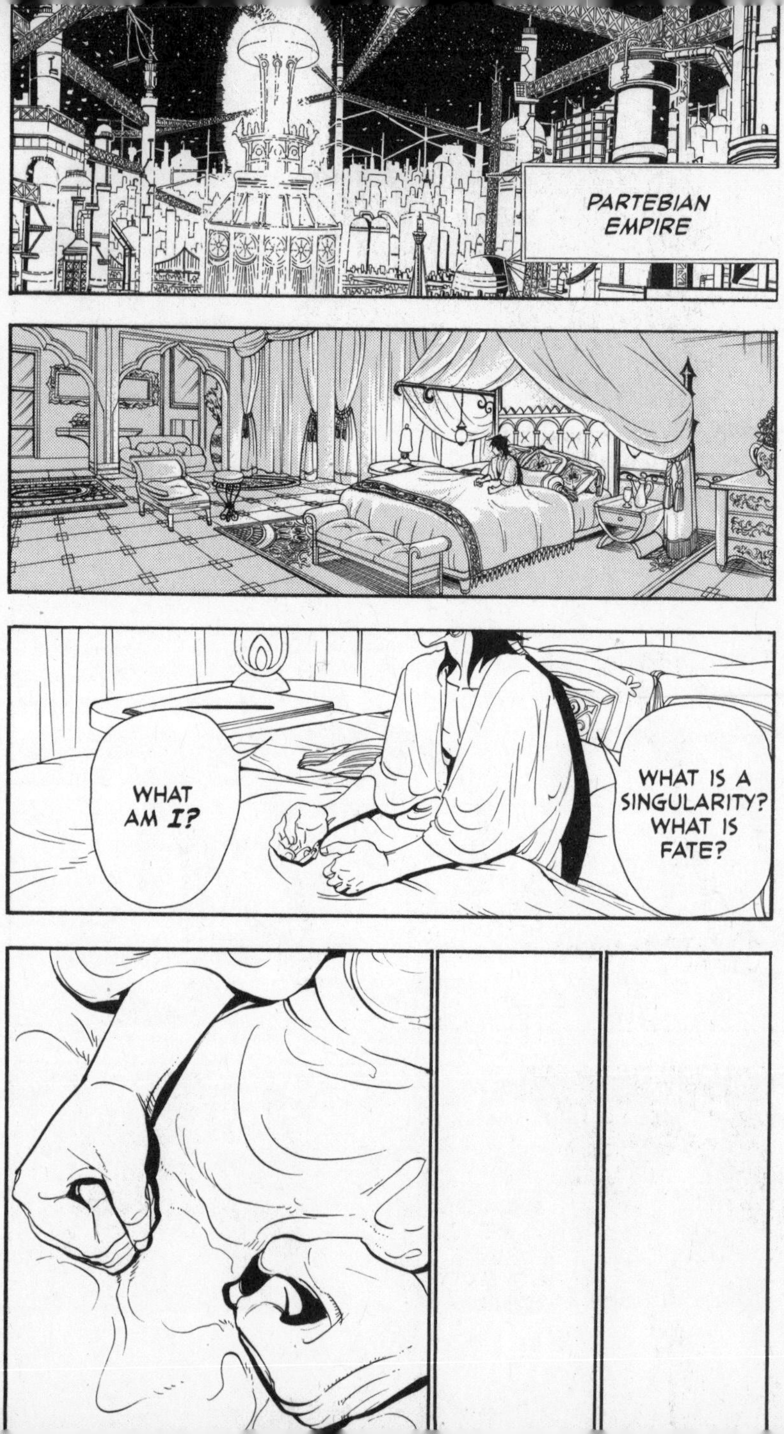
PARTEBIAN EMPIRE
WHAT IS A SINGULARITY? WHAT IS FATE?
WHAT AM *I*?

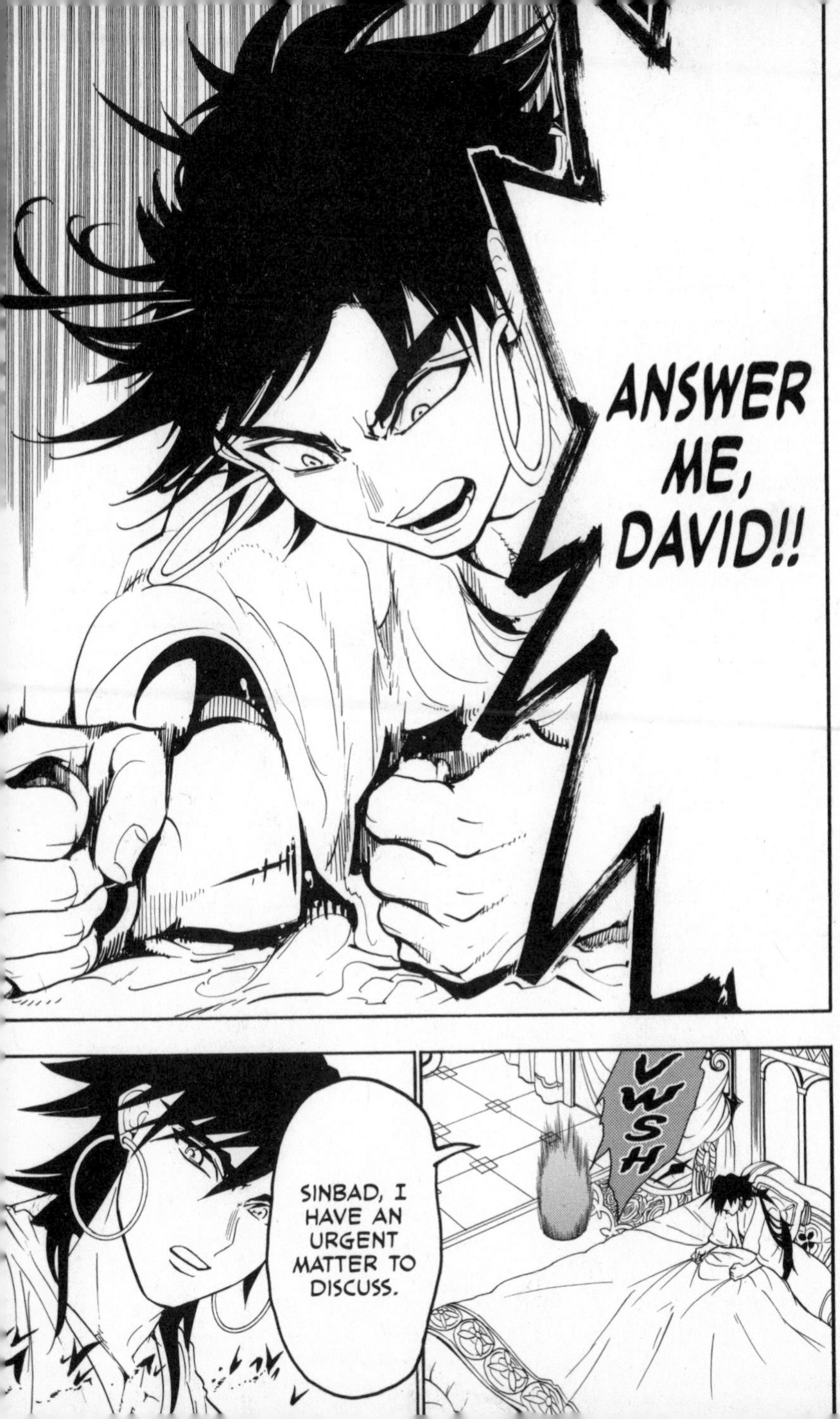
ANSWER ME, DAVID!!
VWSH
SINBAD, I HAVE AN URGENT MATTER TO DISCUSS.

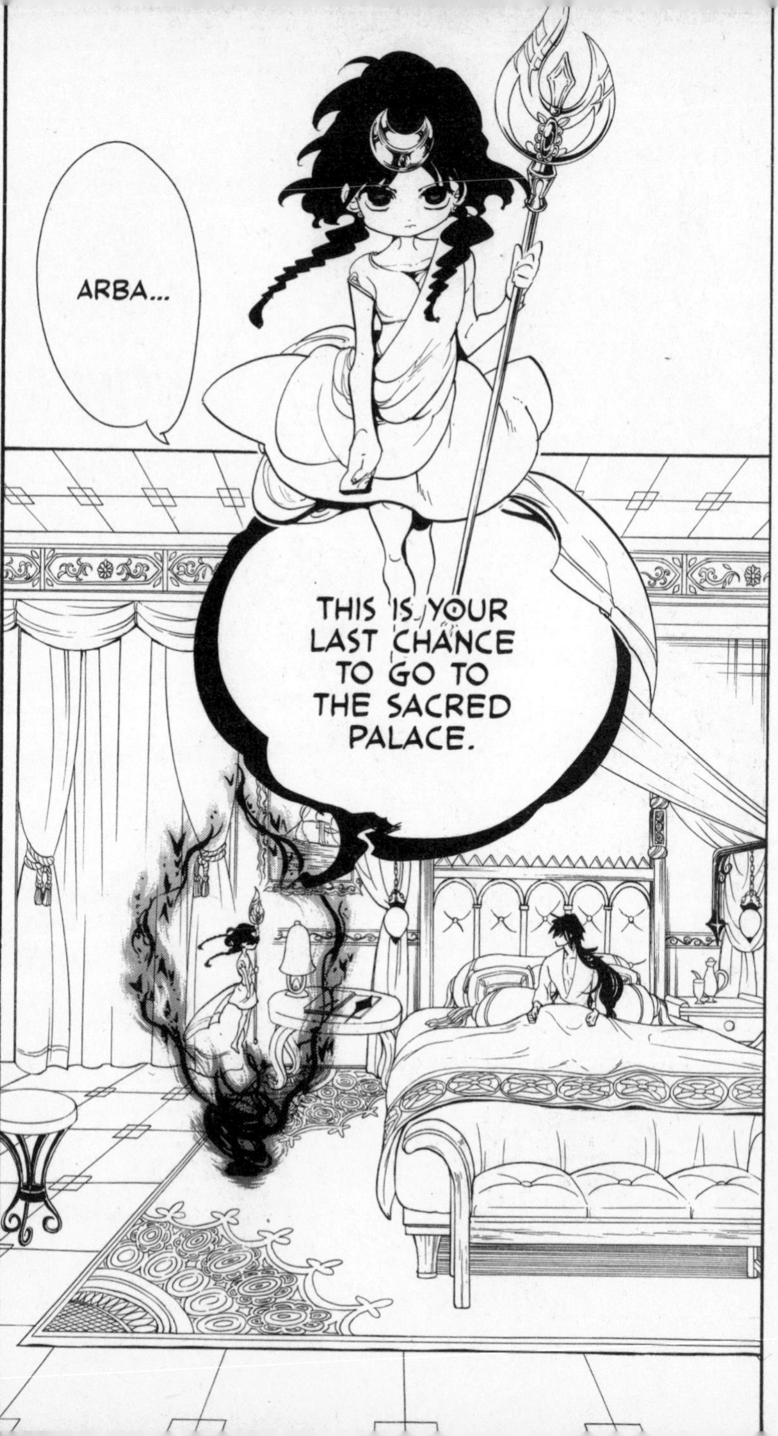
THIS IS YOUR LAST CHANCE TO GO TO THE SACRED PALACE.
ARBA...

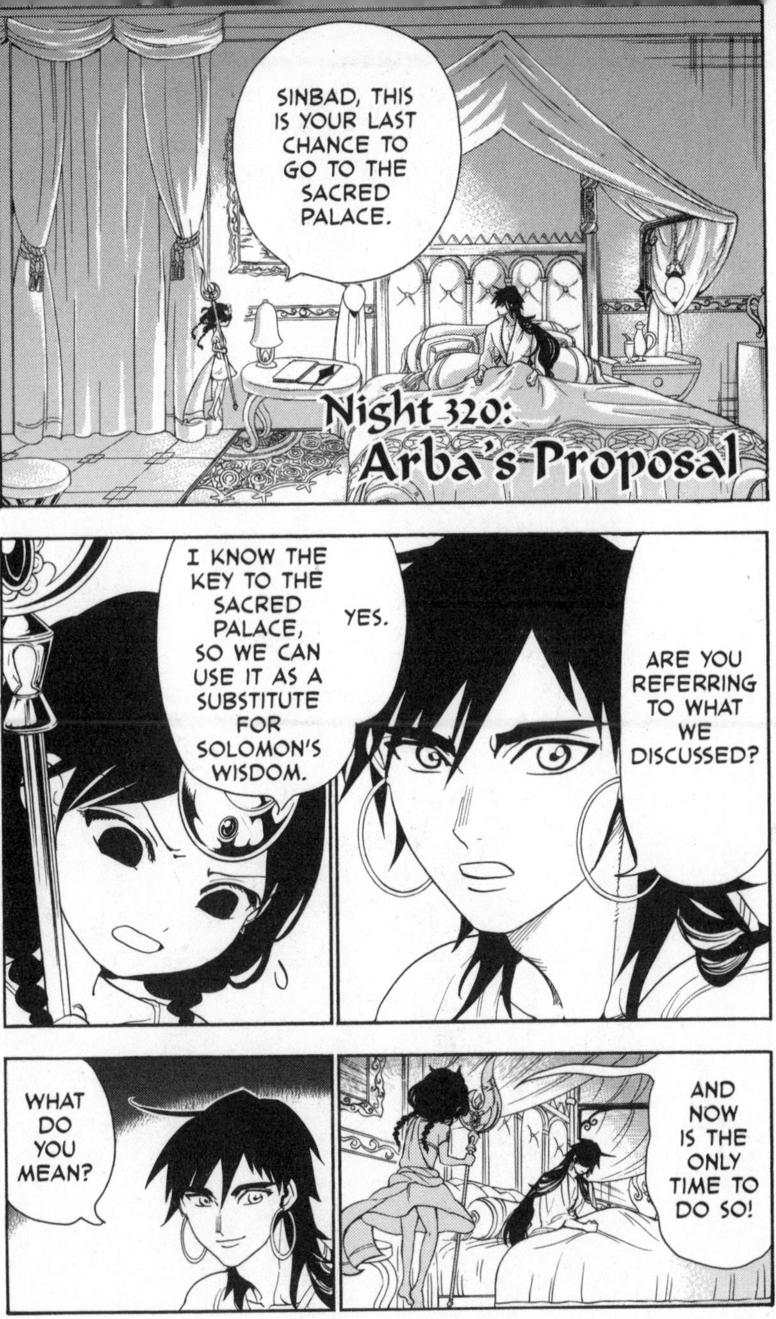
SINBAD, THIS IS YOUR LAST CHANCE TO GO TO THE SACRED PALACE.
Night 320: Arba's Proposal
ARE YOU REFERRING TO WHAT WE DISCUSSED?
YES.
I KNOW THE KEY TO THE SACRED PALACE, SO WE CAN USE IT AS A SUBSTITUTE FOR SOLOMON'S WISDOM.
AND NOW IS THE ONLY TIME TO DO SO!
WHAT DO YOU MEAN?

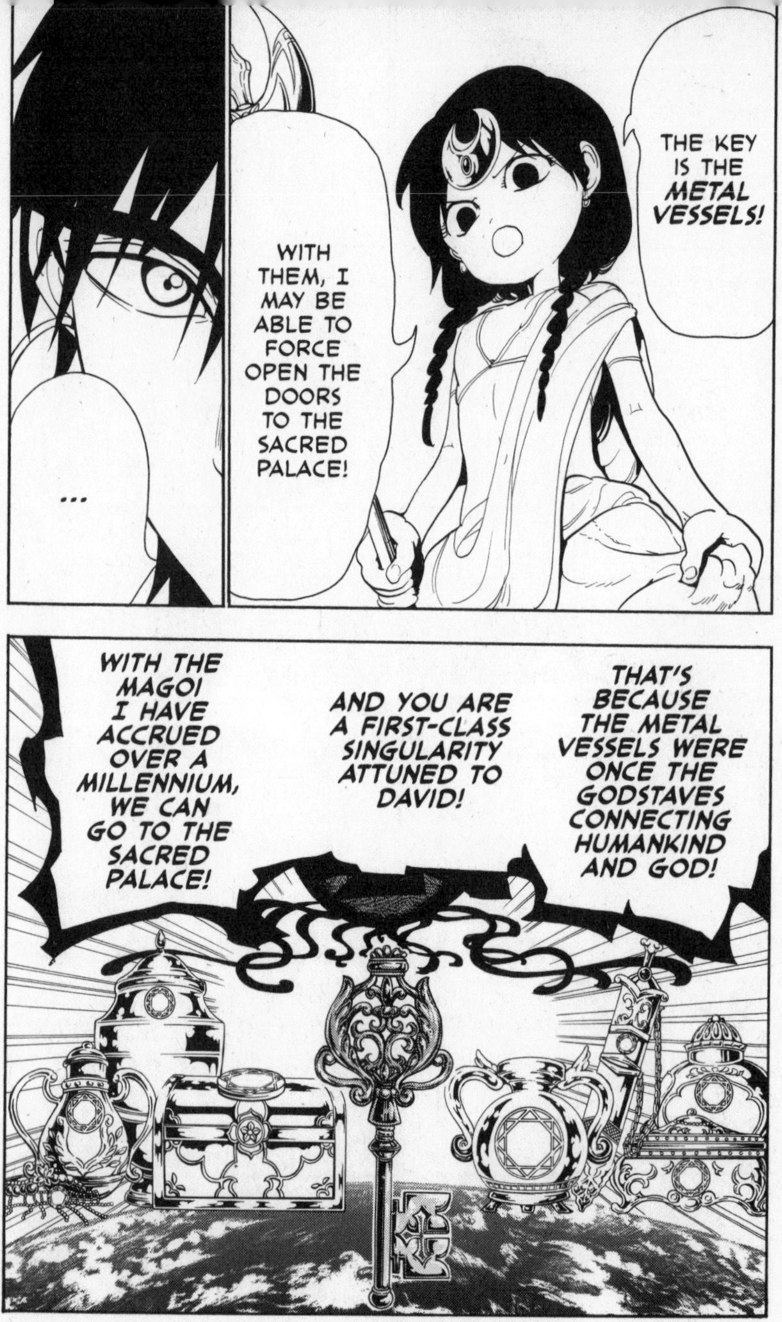
THE KEY IS THE METAL VESSELS!
WITH THEM, I MAY BE ABLE TO FORCE OPEN THE DOORS TO THE SACRED PALACE!
...
THAT'S BECAUSE THE METAL VESSELS WERE ONCE THE GODSTAVES CONNECTING HUMANKIND AND GOD!
AND YOU ARE A FIRST-CLASS SINGULARITY ATTUNED TO DAVID!
WITH THE MAGOI I HAVE ACCRUED OVER A MILLENNIUM, WE CAN GO TO THE SACRED PALACE!

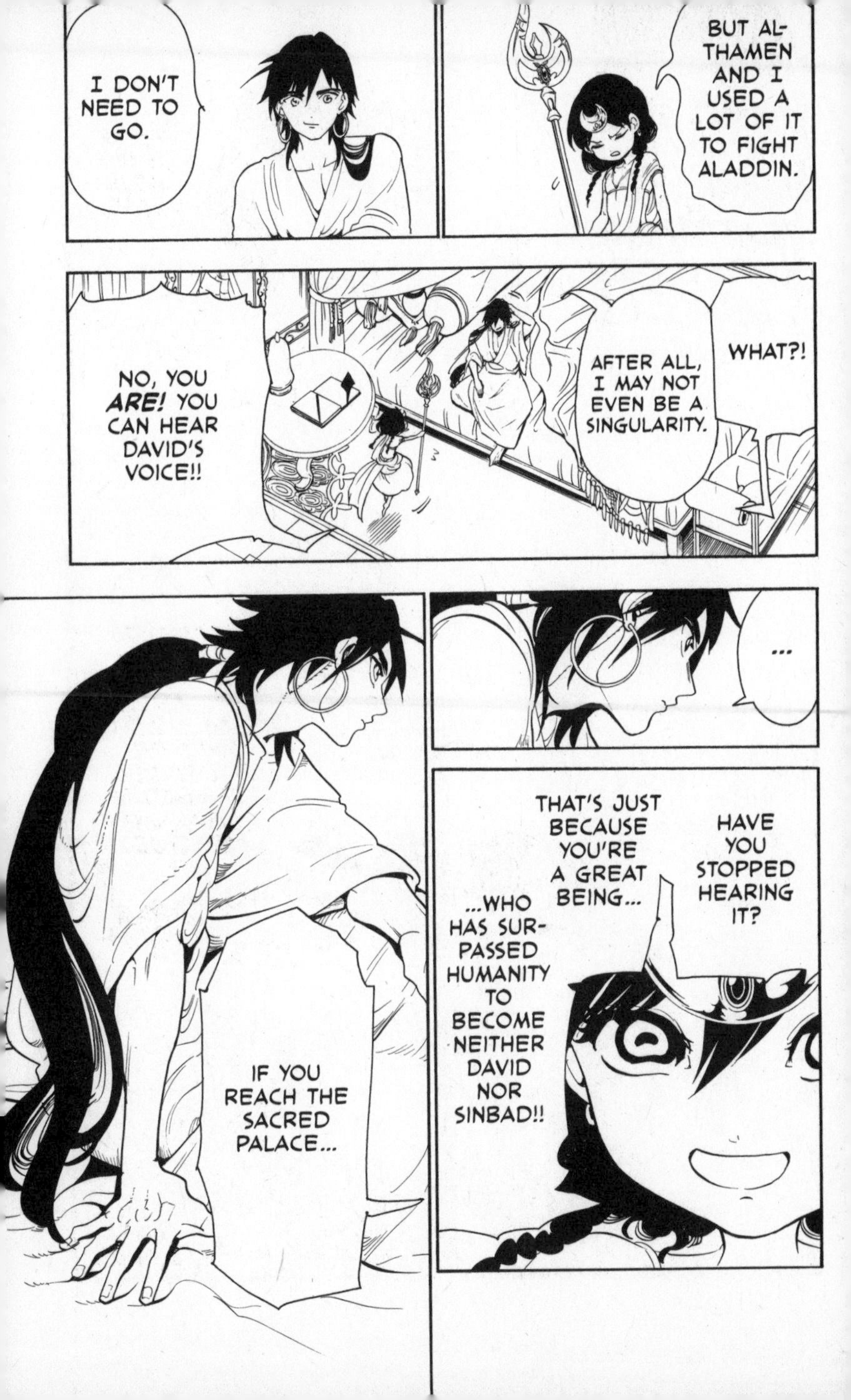
BUT AL-THAMEN AND I USED A LOT OF IT TO FIGHT ALADDIN.
I DON'T NEED TO GO.
WHAT?!
AFTER ALL, I MAY NOT EVEN BE A SINGULARITY.
NO, YOU *ARE!* YOU CAN HEAR DAVID'S VOICE!!
...
HAVE YOU STOPPED HEARING IT?
THAT'S JUST BECAUSE YOU'RE A GREAT BEING...
...WHO HAS SURPASSED HUMANITY TO BECOME NEITHER DAVID NOR SINBAD!!
IF YOU REACH THE SACRED PALACE...

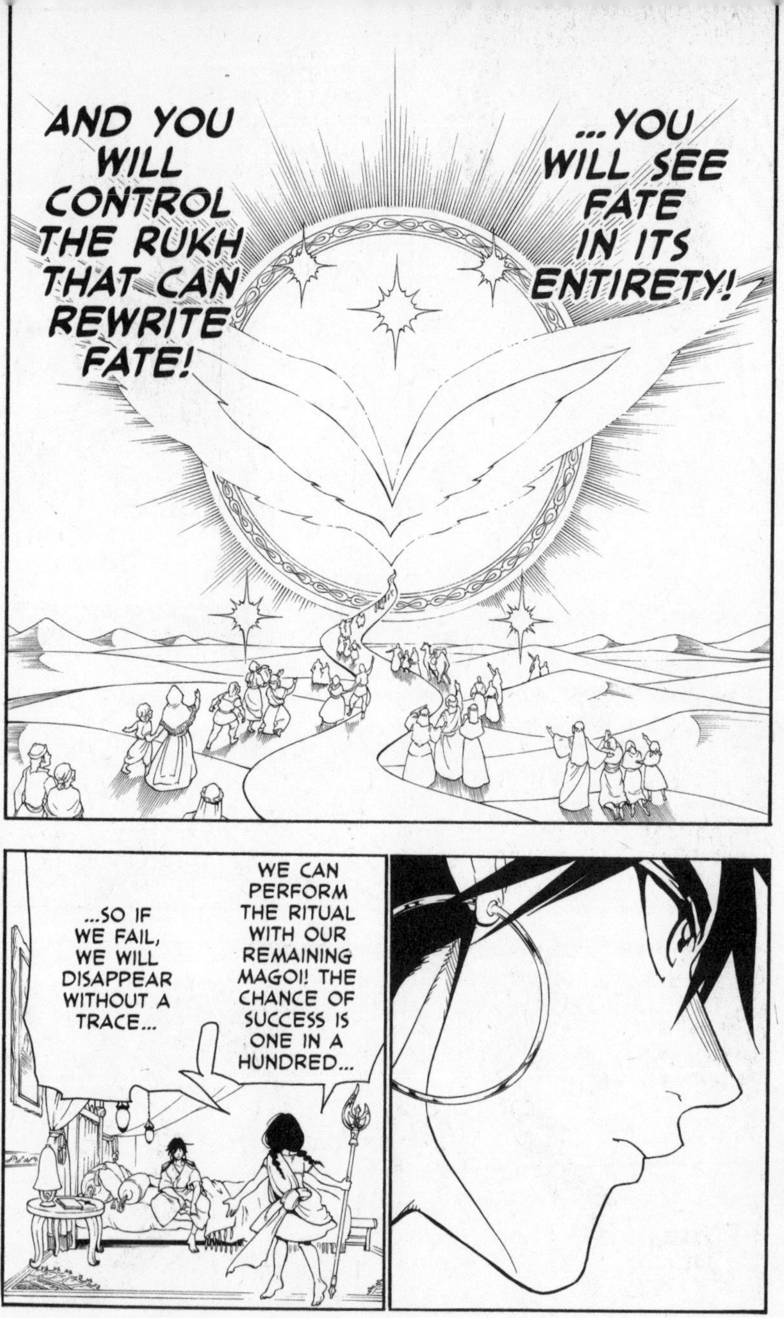
...YOU WILL SEE FATE IN ITS ENTIRETY!
AND YOU WILL CONTROL THE RUKH THAT CAN REWRITE FATE!
WE CAN PERFORM THE RITUAL WITH OUR REMAINING MAGOI! THE CHANCE OF SUCCESS IS ONE IN A HUNDRED...
...SO IF WE FAIL, WE WILL DISAPPEAR WITHOUT A TRACE...

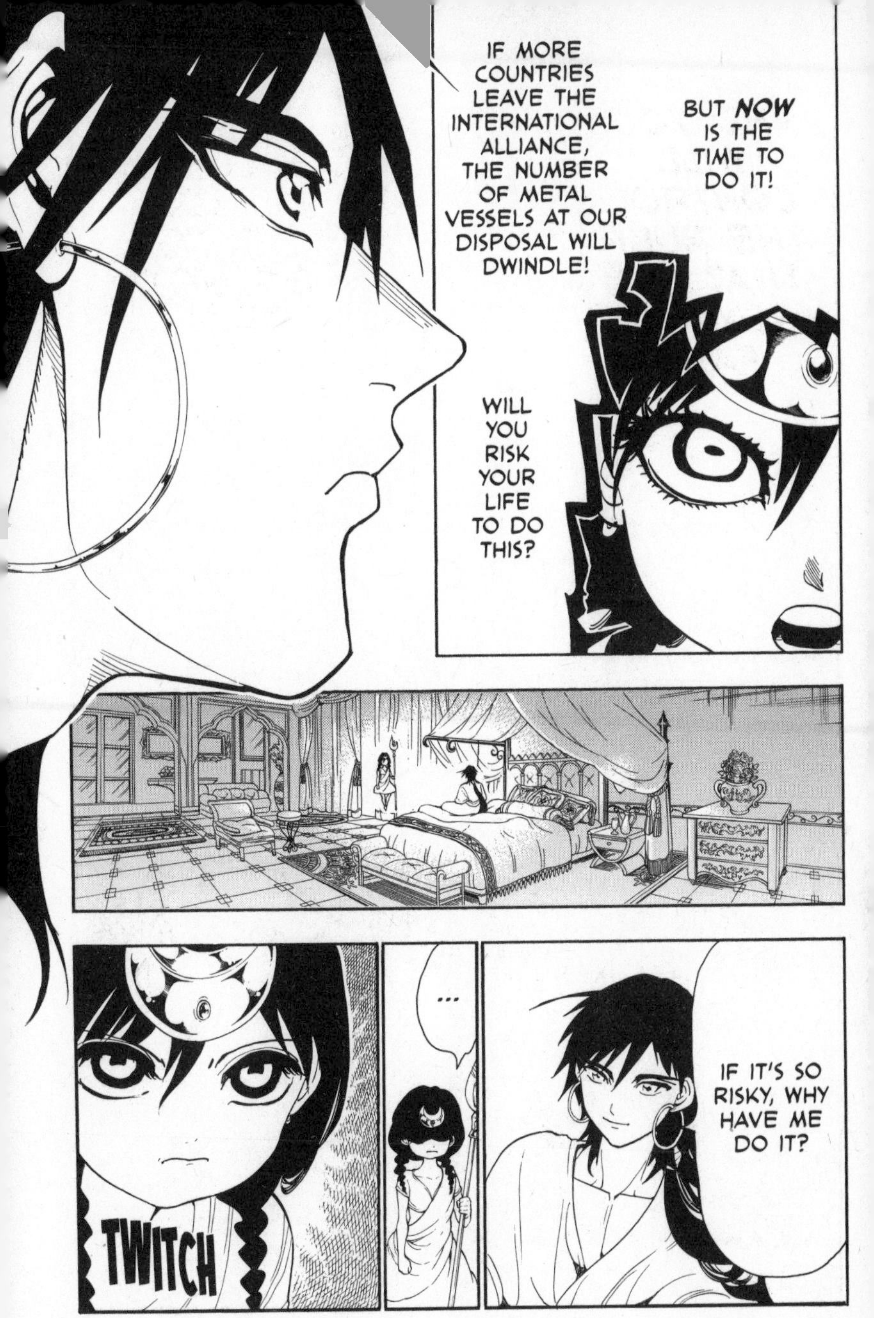
IF MORE COUNTRIES LEAVE THE INTERNATIONAL ALLIANCE, THE NUMBER OF METAL VESSELS AT OUR DISPOSAL WILL DWINDLE!
BUT **NOW** IS THE TIME TO DO IT!
WILL YOU RISK YOUR LIFE TO DO THIS?
IF IT'S SO RISKY, WHY HAVE ME DO IT?
...
TWITCH

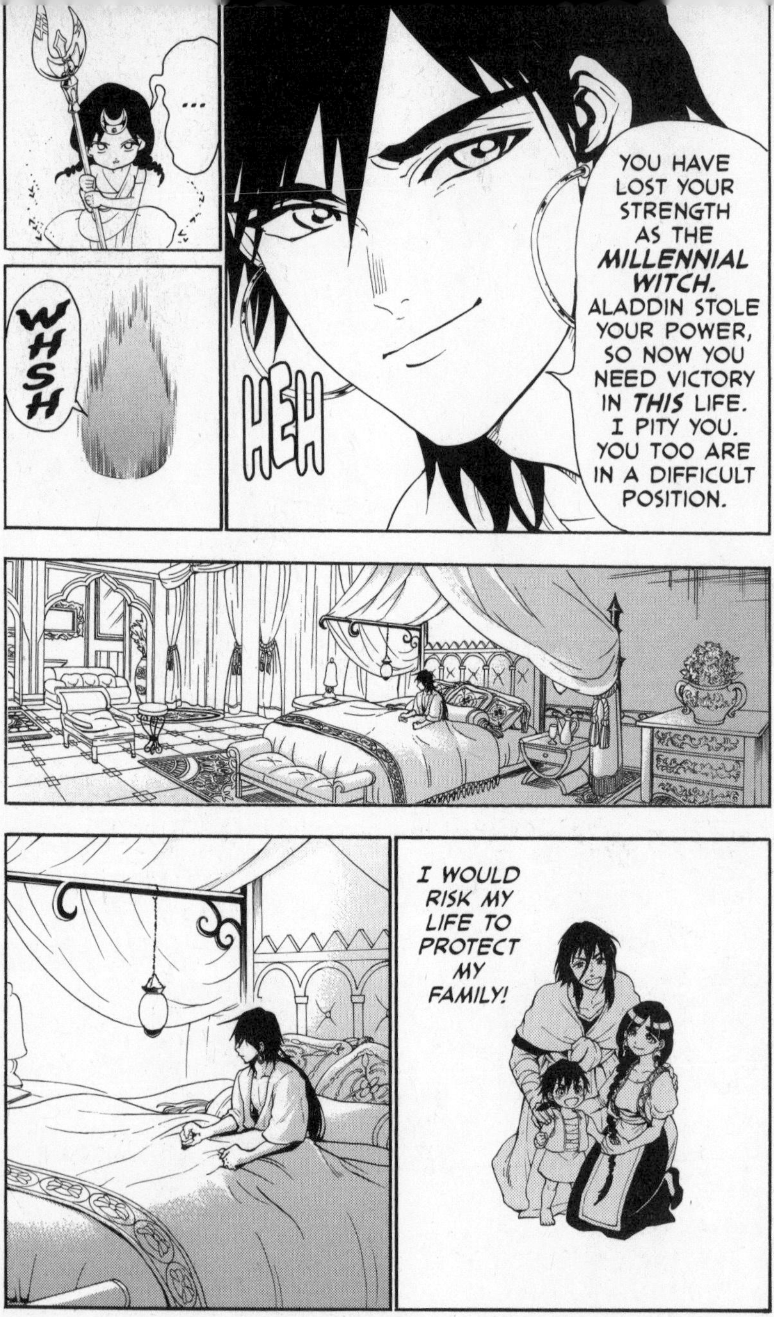
YOU HAVE LOST YOUR STRENGTH AS THE *MILLENNIAL WITCH.* ALADDIN STOLE YOUR POWER, SO NOW YOU NEED VICTORY IN *THIS* LIFE. I PITY YOU. YOU TOO ARE IN A DIFFICULT POSITION.
HEH
...
WHSH
I WOULD RISK MY LIFE TO PROTECT MY FAMILY!

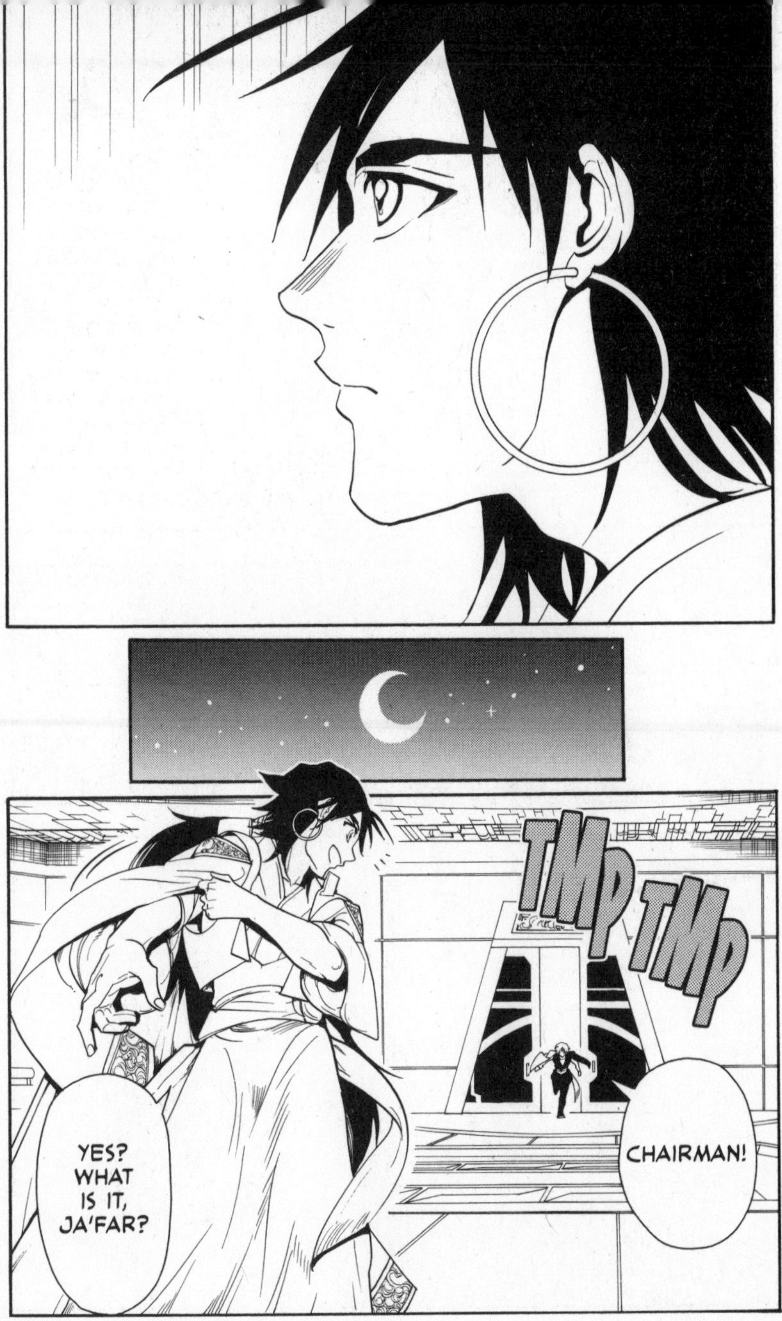
TMP TMP
CHAIRMAN!
YES? WHAT IS IT, JA'FAR?

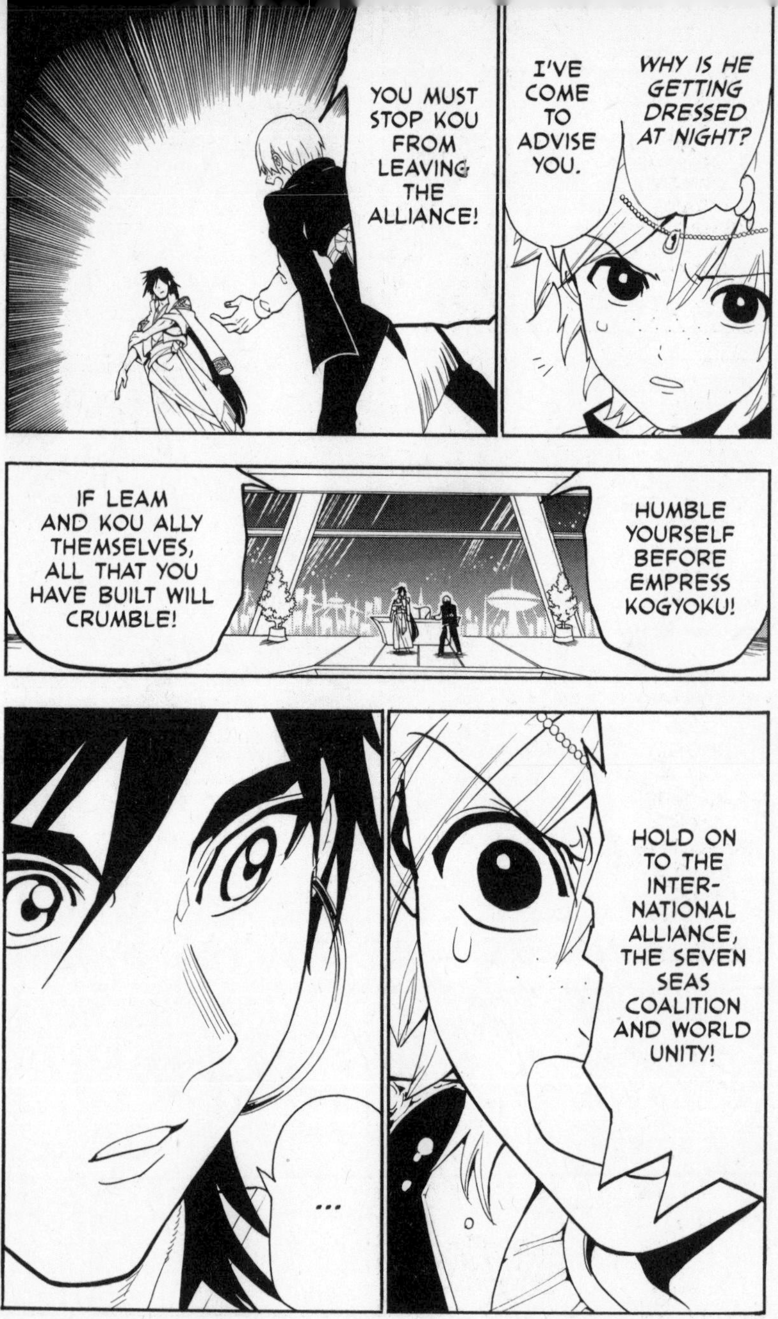
WHY IS HE GETTING DRESSED AT NIGHT?
I'VE COME TO ADVISE YOU.
YOU MUST STOP KOU FROM LEAVING THE ALLIANCE!
HUMBLE YOURSELF BEFORE EMPRESS KOGYOKU!
IF LEAM AND KOU ALLY THEMSELVES, ALL THAT YOU HAVE BUILT WILL CRUMBLE!
HOLD ON TO THE INTER-NATIONAL ALLIANCE, THE SEVEN SEAS COALITION AND WORLD UNITY!
...

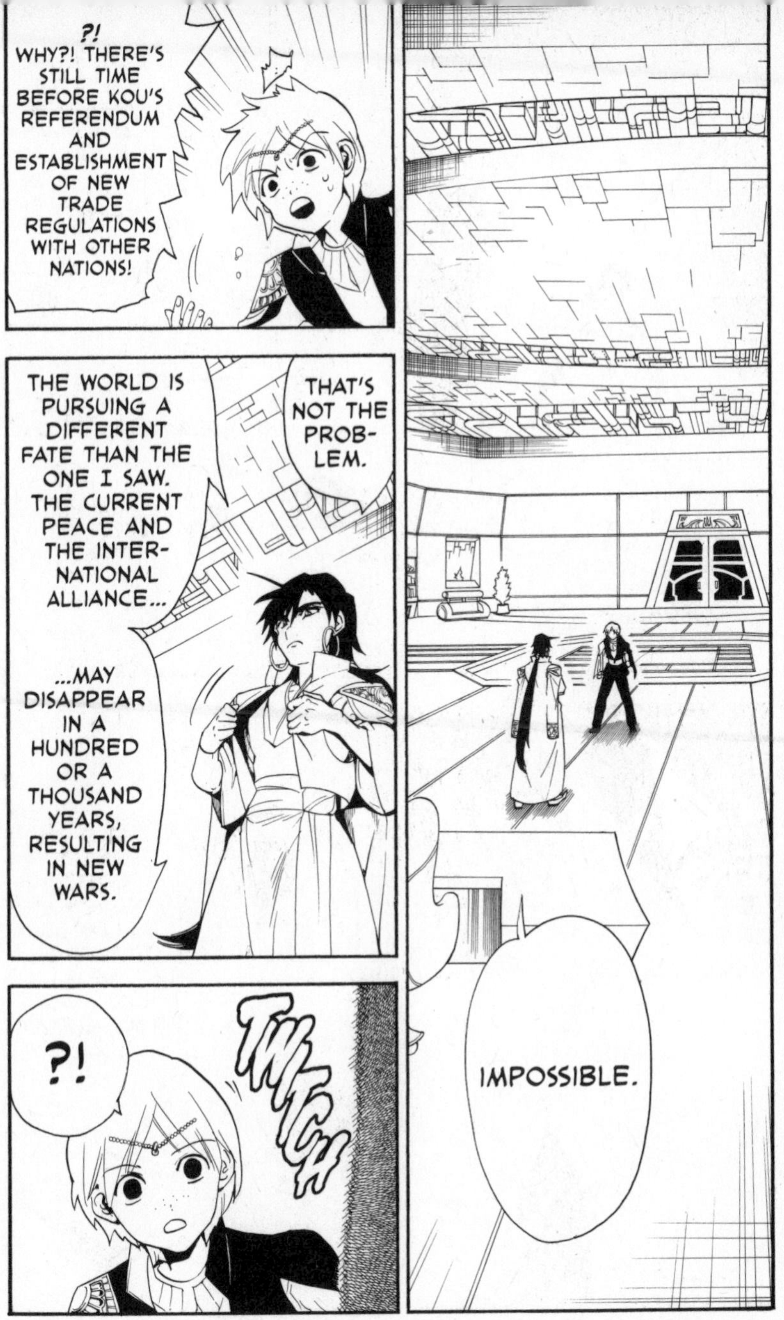
IMPOSSIBLE.
?! WHY?! THERE'S STILL TIME BEFORE KOU'S REFERENDUM AND ESTABLISHMENT OF NEW TRADE REGULATIONS WITH OTHER NATIONS!
THAT'S NOT THE PROB-LEM.
THE WORLD IS PURSUING A DIFFERENT FATE THAN THE ONE I SAW. THE CURRENT PEACE AND THE INTER-NATIONAL ALLIANCE...
...MAY DISAPPEAR IN A HUNDRED OR A THOUSAND YEARS, RESULTING IN NEW WARS.
TWITCH
?!

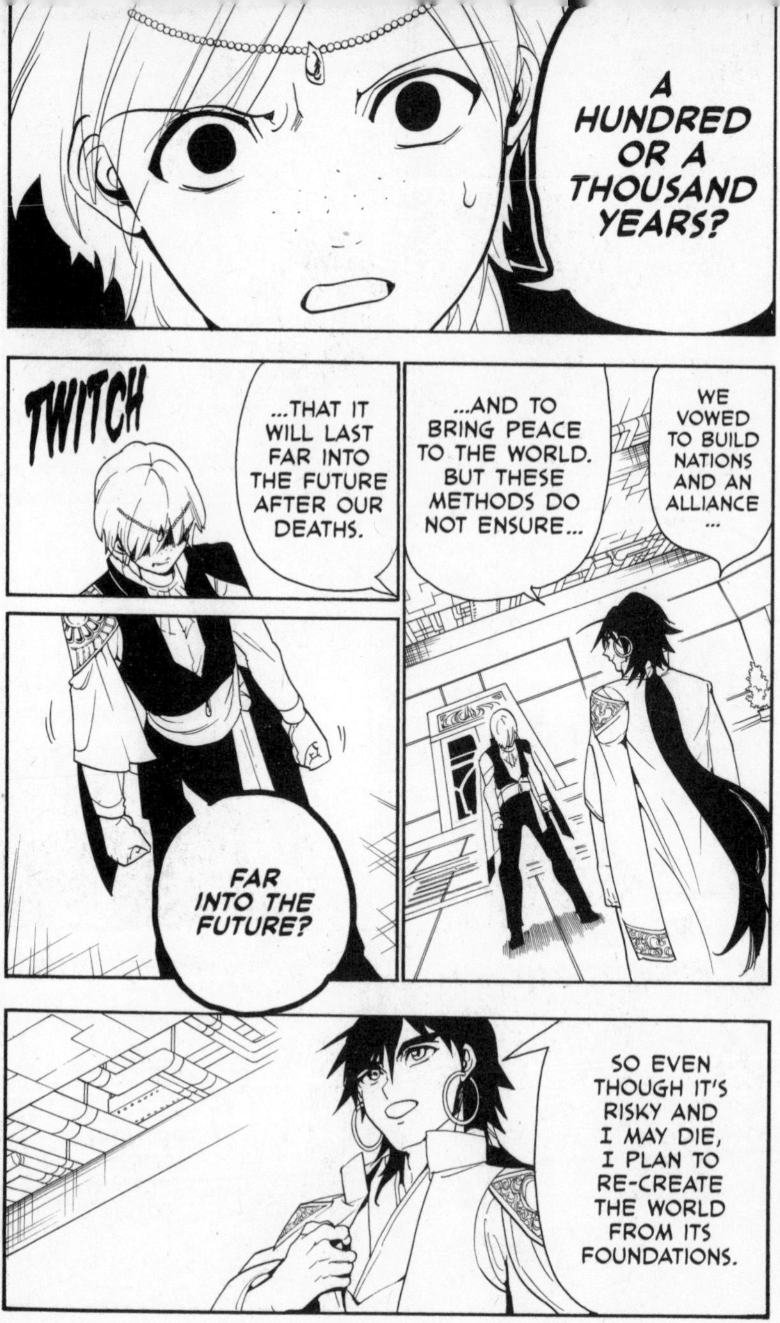
A HUNDRED OR A THOUSAND YEARS?
WE VOWED TO BUILD NATIONS AND AN ALLIANCE ...
...AND TO BRING PEACE TO THE WORLD. BUT THESE METHODS DO NOT ENSURE...
...THAT IT WILL LAST FAR INTO THE FUTURE AFTER OUR DEATHS.
TWITCH
FAR INTO THE FUTURE?
SO EVEN THOUGH IT'S RISKY AND I MAY DIE, I PLAN TO RE-CREATE THE WORLD FROM ITS FOUNDATIONS.

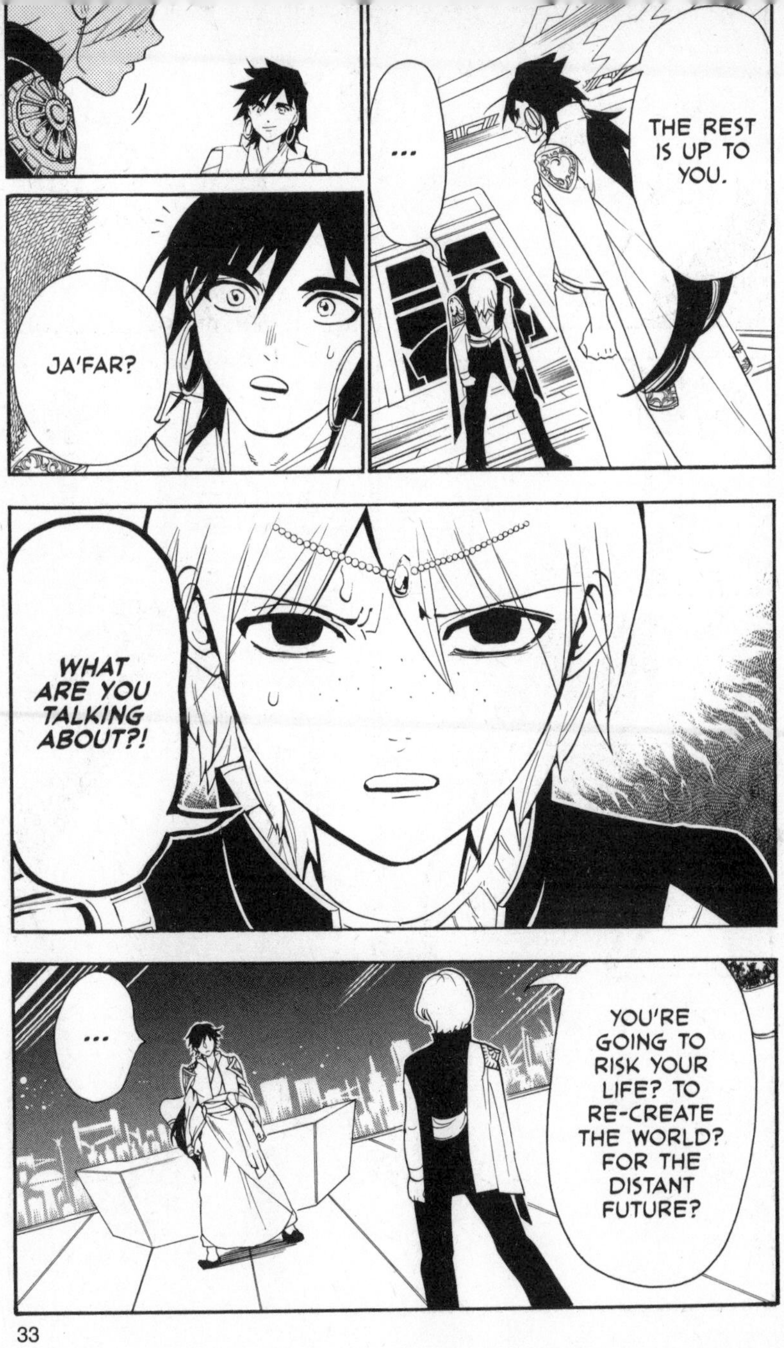
THE REST IS UP TO YOU.
...
JA'FAR?
WHAT ARE YOU TALKING ABOUT?!
YOU'RE GOING TO RISK YOUR LIFE? TO RE-CREATE THE WORLD? FOR THE DISTANT FUTURE?
...

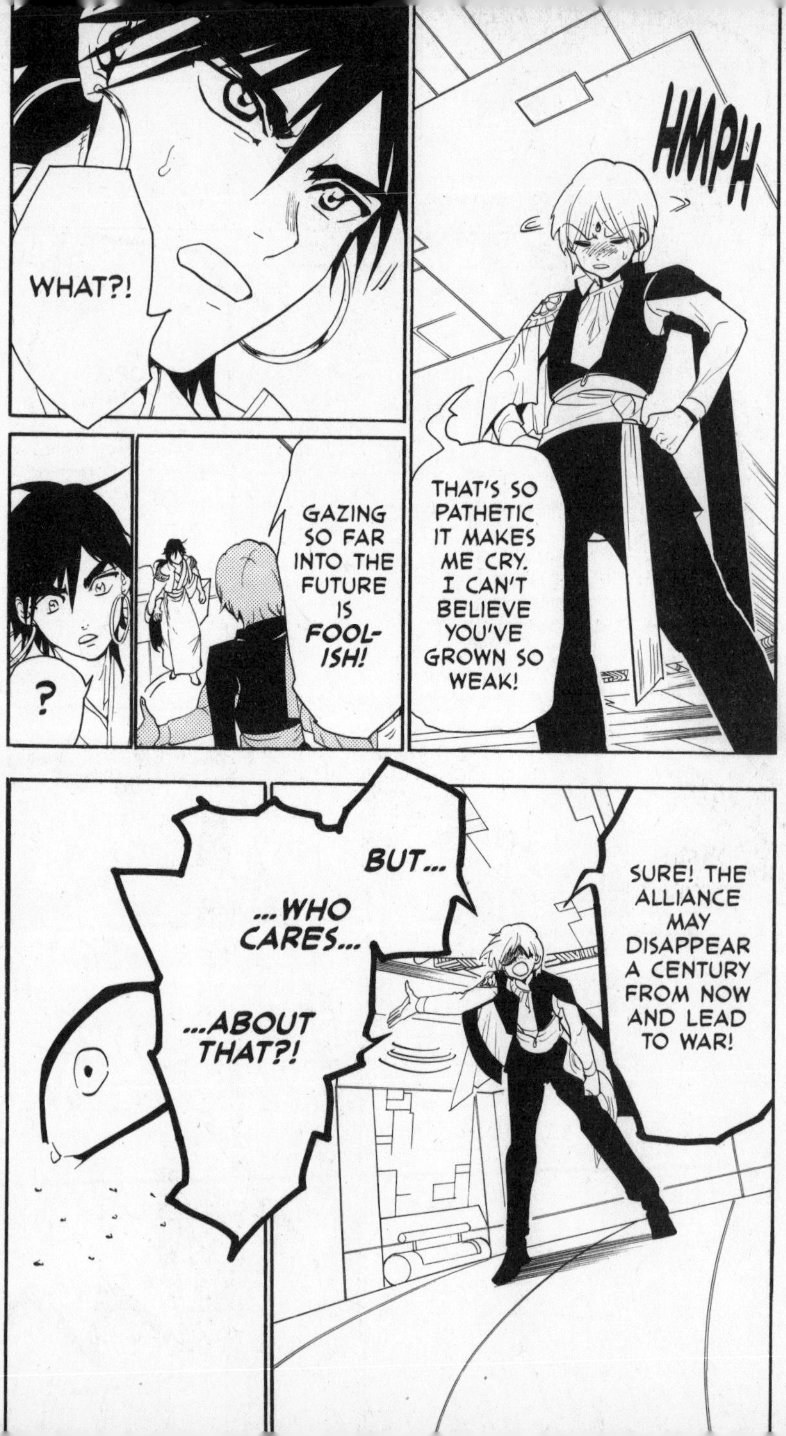
HMPH
THAT'S SO PATHETIC IT MAKES ME CRY. I CAN'T BELIEVE YOU'VE GROWN SO WEAK!
WHAT?!
GAZING SO FAR INTO THE FUTURE IS FOOL-ISH!
?
SURE! THE ALLIANCE MAY DISAPPEAR A CENTURY FROM NOW AND LEAD TO WAR!
BUT...
...WHO CARES...
...ABOUT THAT?!

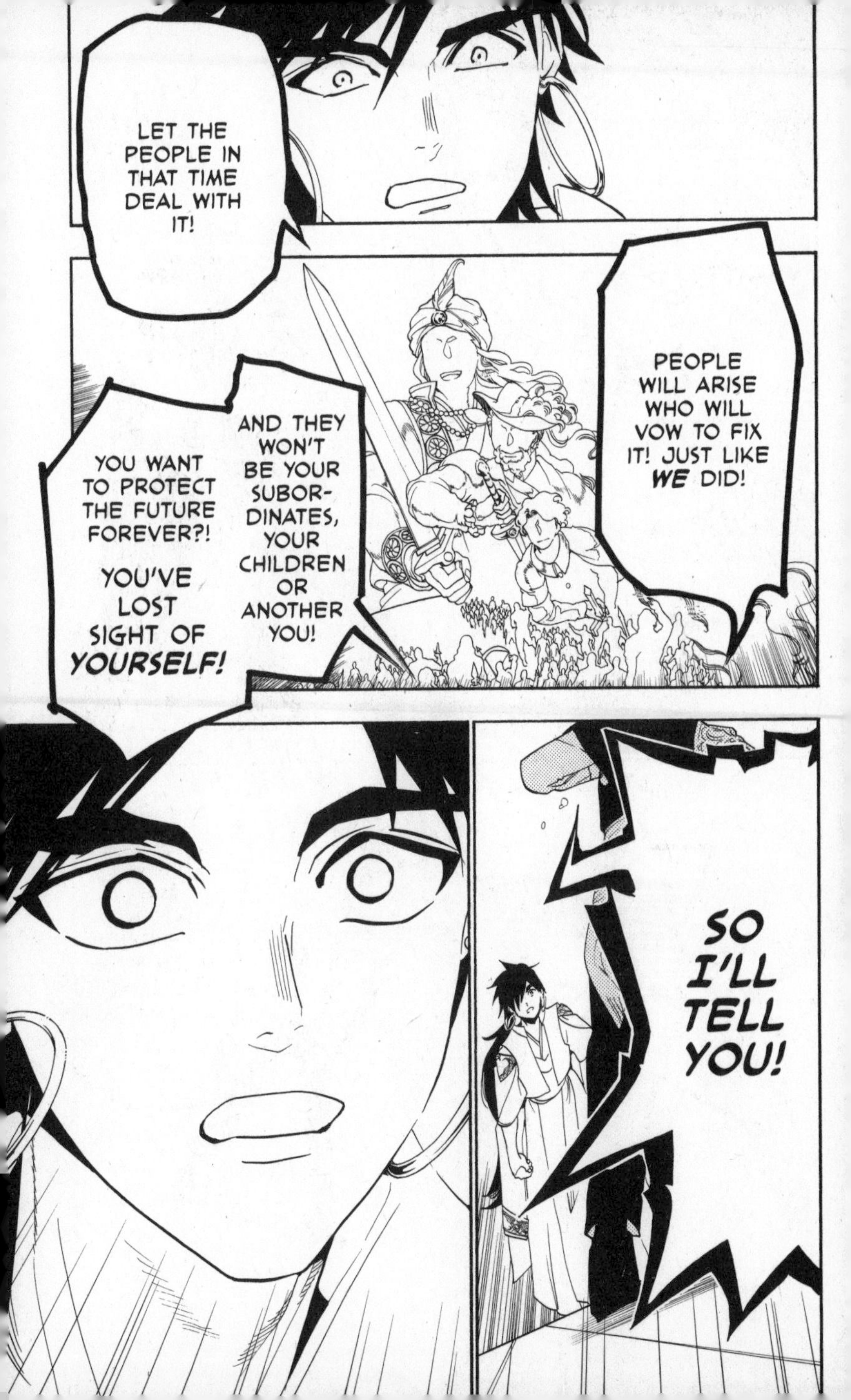
LET THE PEOPLE IN THAT TIME DEAL WITH IT!
PEOPLE WILL ARISE WHO WILL VOW TO FIX IT! JUST LIKE WE DID!
AND THEY WON'T BE YOUR SUBORDINATES, YOUR CHILDREN OR ANOTHER YOU!
YOU WANT TO PROTECT THE FUTURE FOREVER?!
YOU'VE LOST SIGHT OF YOURSELF!
SO I'LL TELL YOU!

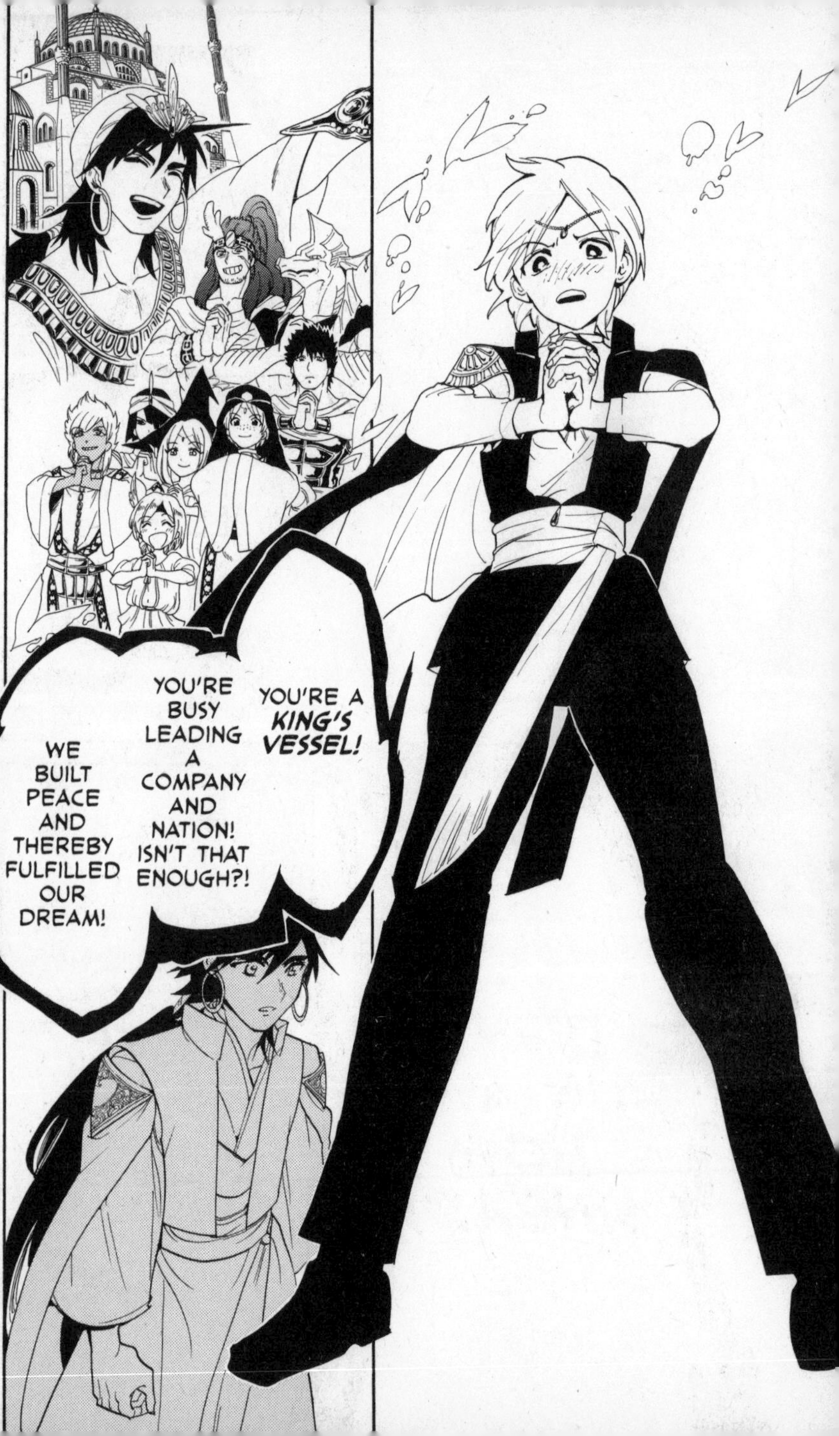
YOU'RE A KING'S VESSEL!
YOU'RE BUSY LEADING A COMPANY AND NATION! ISN'T THAT ENOUGH?!
WE BUILT PEACE AND THEREBY FULFILLED OUR DREAM!

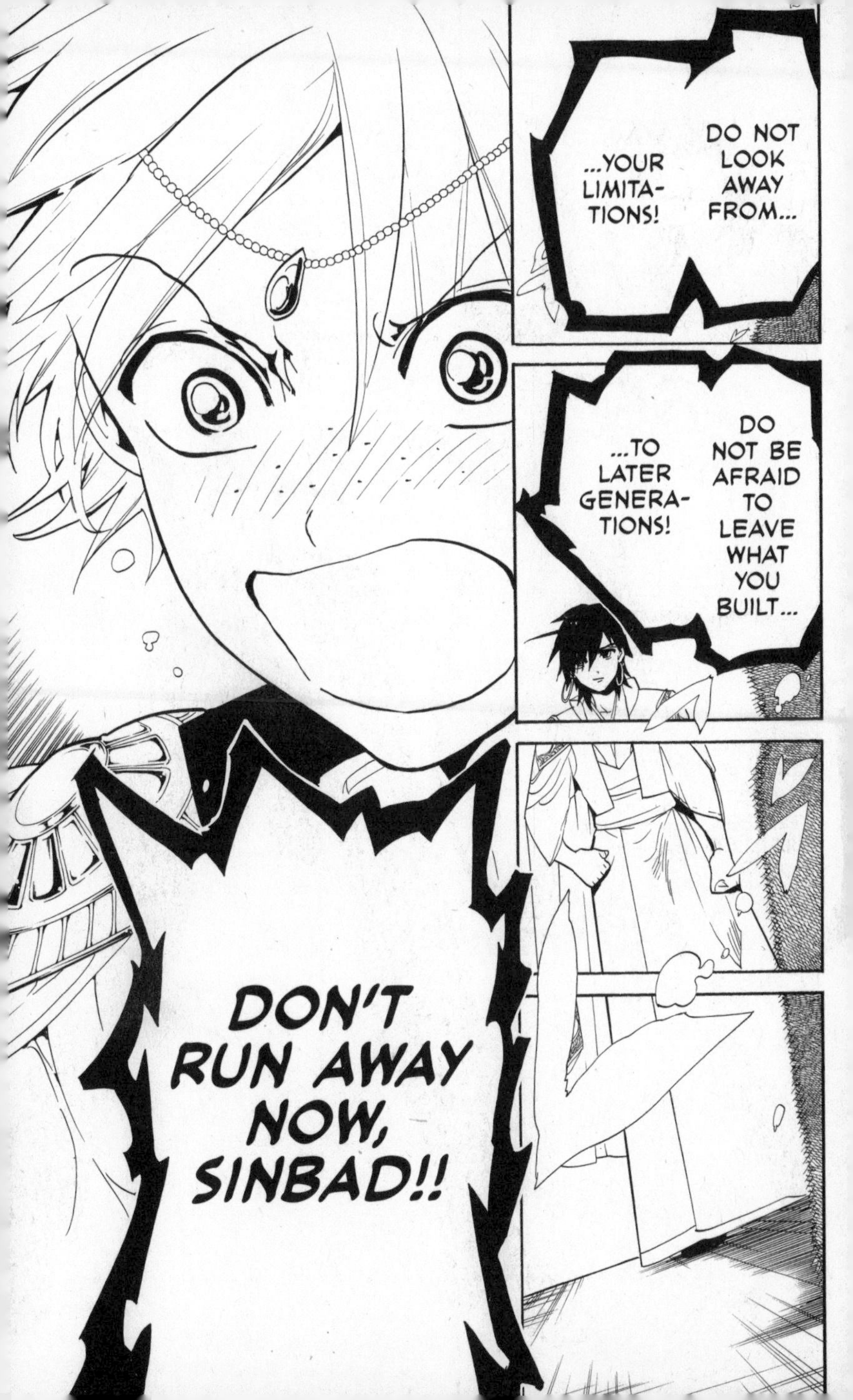
DO NOT LOOK AWAY FROM...
...YOUR LIMITA-TIONS!
DO NOT BE AFRAID TO LEAVE WHAT YOU BUILT...
...TO LATER GENERA-TIONS!
DON'T RUN AWAY NOW, SINBAD!!

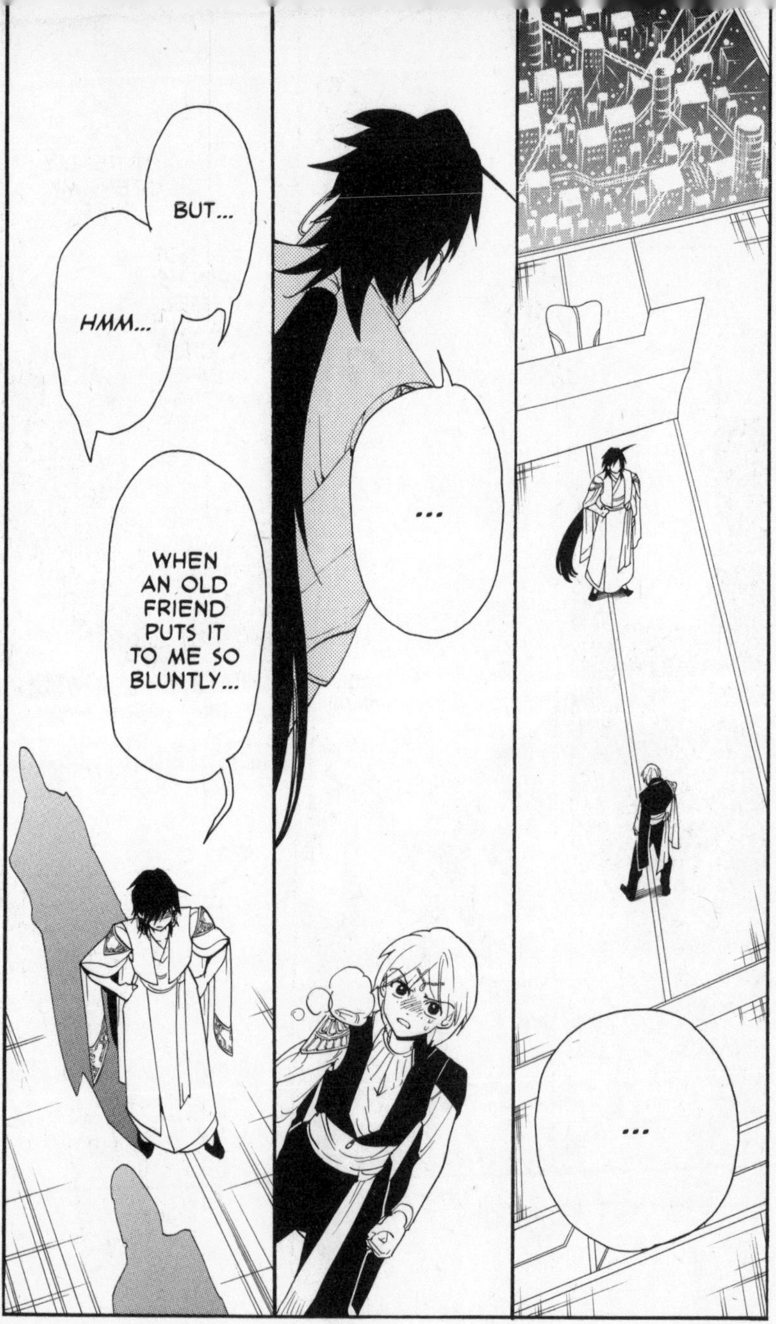
...
...
BUT...
HMM...
WHEN AN OLD FRIEND PUTS IT TO ME SO BLUNTLY...

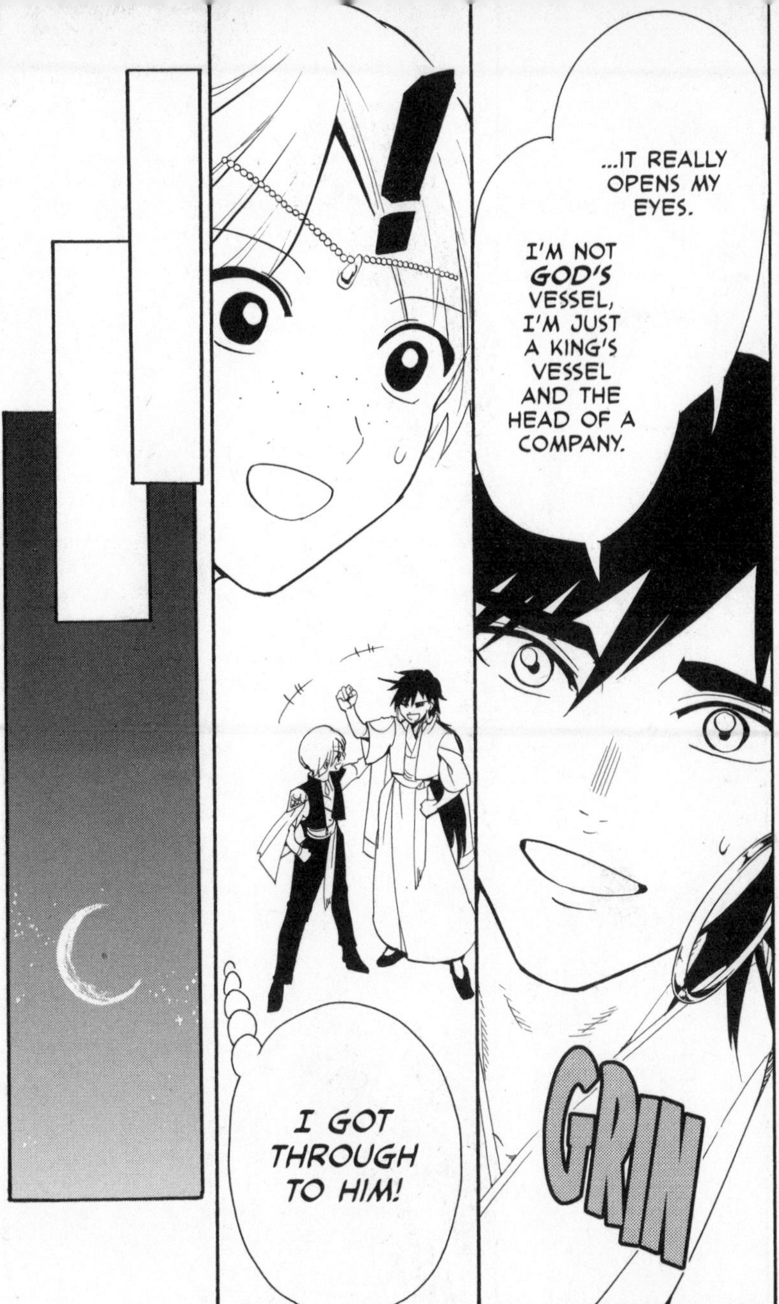
...IT REALLY OPENS MY EYES.
I'M NOT GOD'S VESSEL, I'M JUST A KING'S VESSEL AND THE HEAD OF A COMPANY.
GRIN
!
I GOT THROUGH TO HIM!

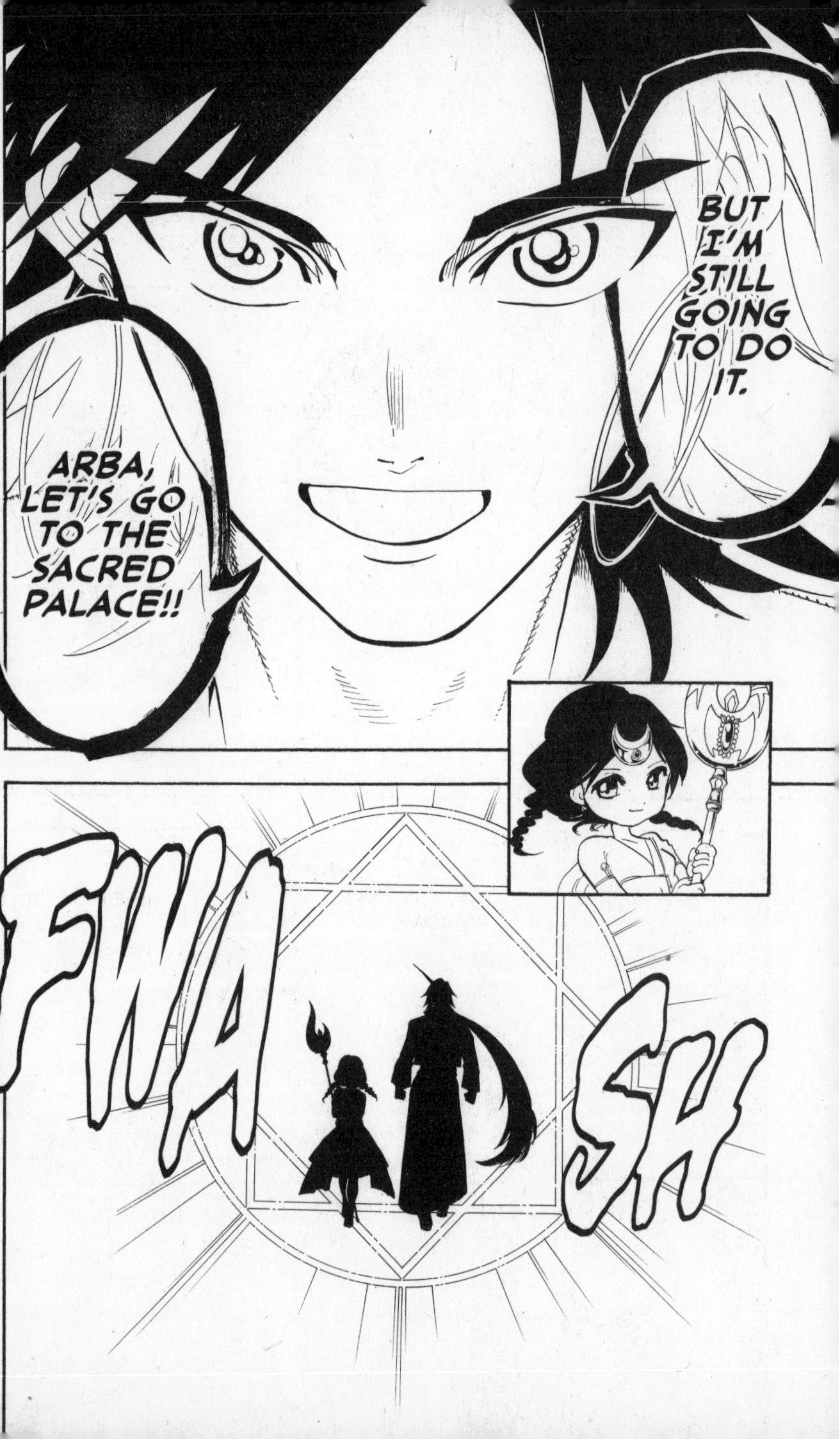
BUT I'M STILL GOING TO DO IT.
ARBA, LET'S GO TO THE SACRED PALACE!!
FWASH

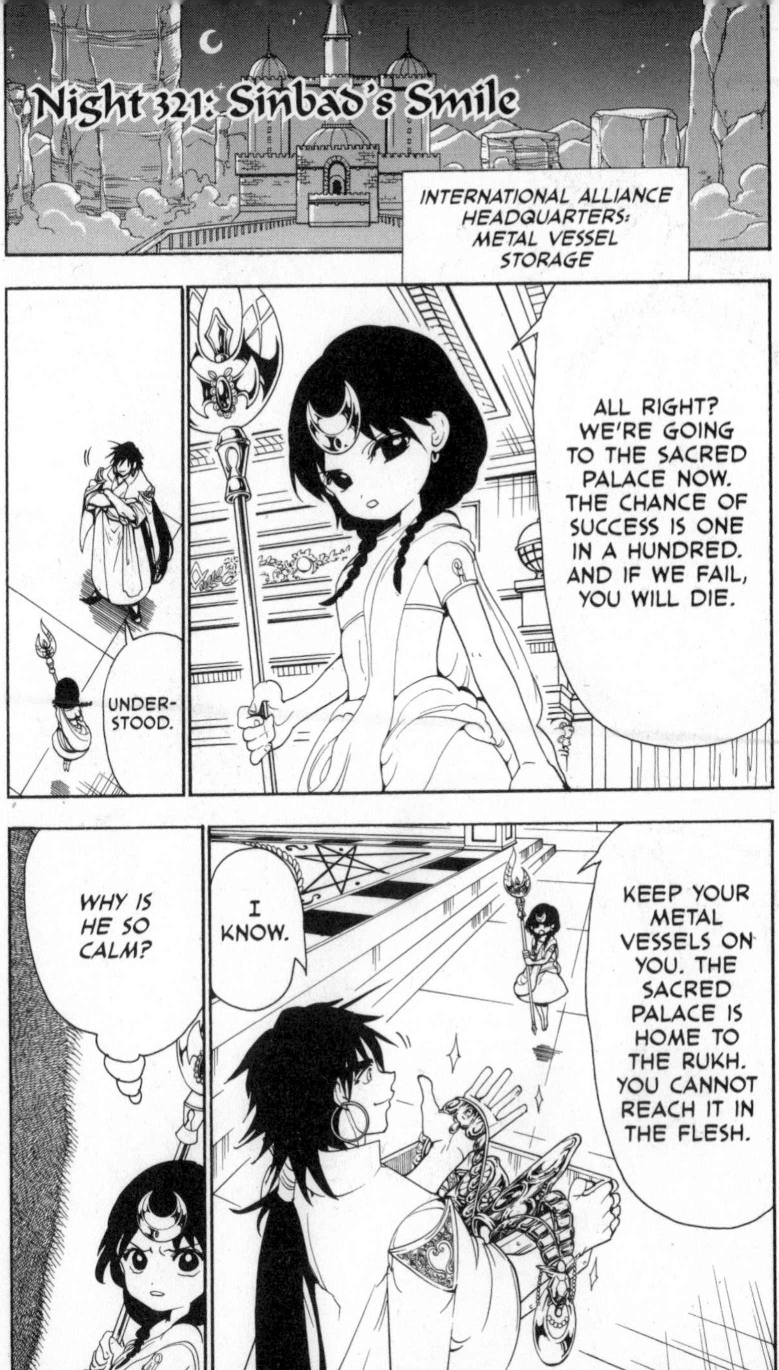
Night 321: Sinbad's Smile
INTERNATIONAL ALLIANCE HEADQUARTERS: METAL VESSEL STORAGE
ALL RIGHT? WE'RE GOING TO THE SACRED PALACE NOW. THE CHANCE OF SUCCESS IS ONE IN A HUNDRED. AND IF WE FAIL, YOU WILL DIE.
UNDER-STOOD.
KEEP YOUR METAL VESSELS ON YOU. THE SACRED PALACE IS HOME TO THE RUKH. YOU CANNOT REACH IT IN THE FLESH.
I KNOW.
WHY IS HE SO CALM?

IT'S STRANGE. I MAY DIE SOON, BUT MY MIND IS CLEAR. WHY IS THAT?

Night 321:
Sinbad's Smile

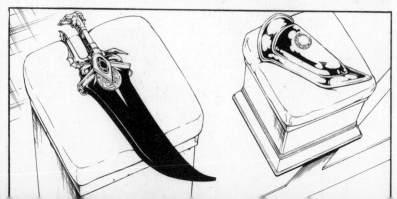

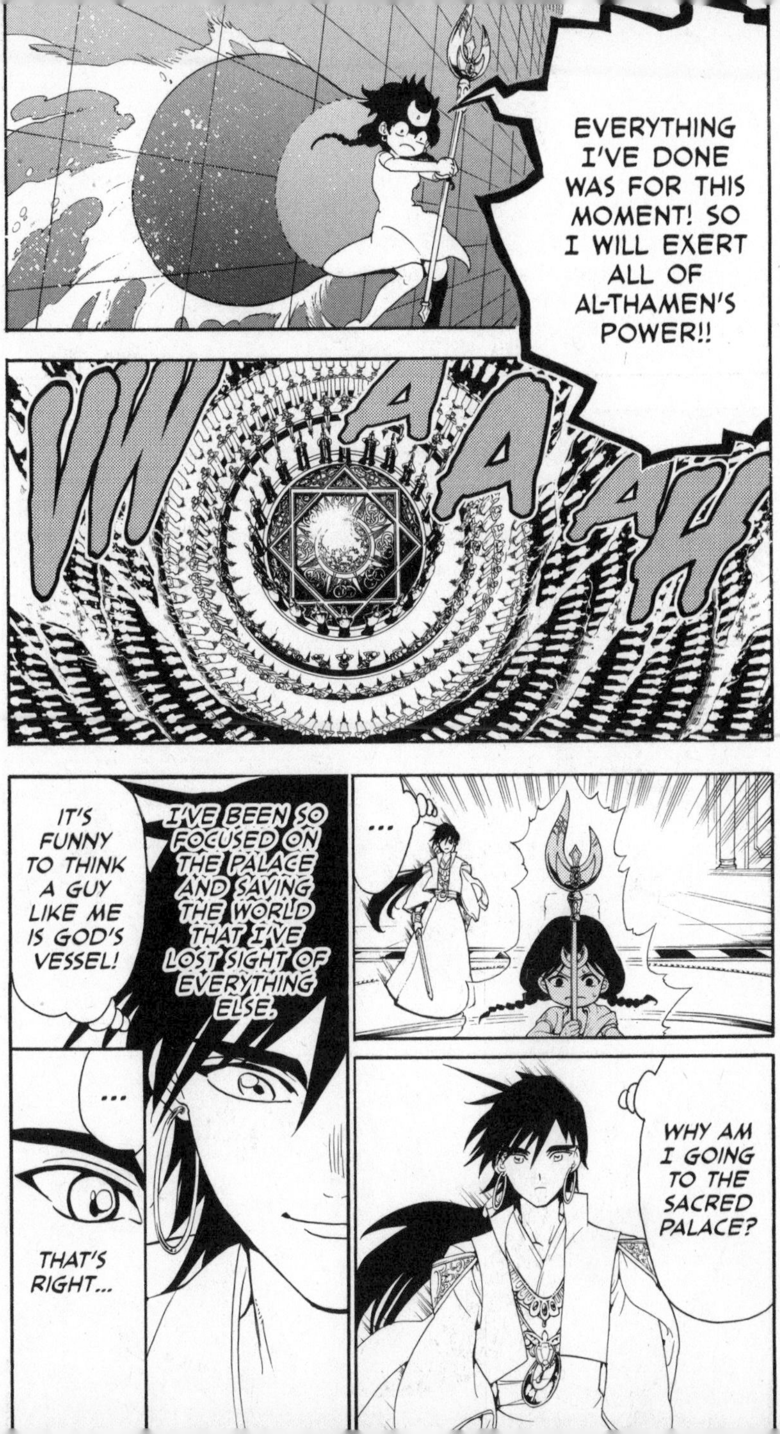
EVERYTHING I'VE DONE WAS FOR THIS MOMENT! SO I WILL EXERT ALL OF AL-THAMEN'S POWER!!
VWAAAH
...
I'VE BEEN SO FOCUSED ON THE PALACE AND SAVING THE WORLD THAT I'VE LOST SIGHT OF EVERYTHING ELSE.
IT'S FUNNY TO THINK A GUY LIKE ME IS GOD'S VESSEL!
WHY AM I GOING TO THE SACRED PALACE?
...
THAT'S RIGHT...

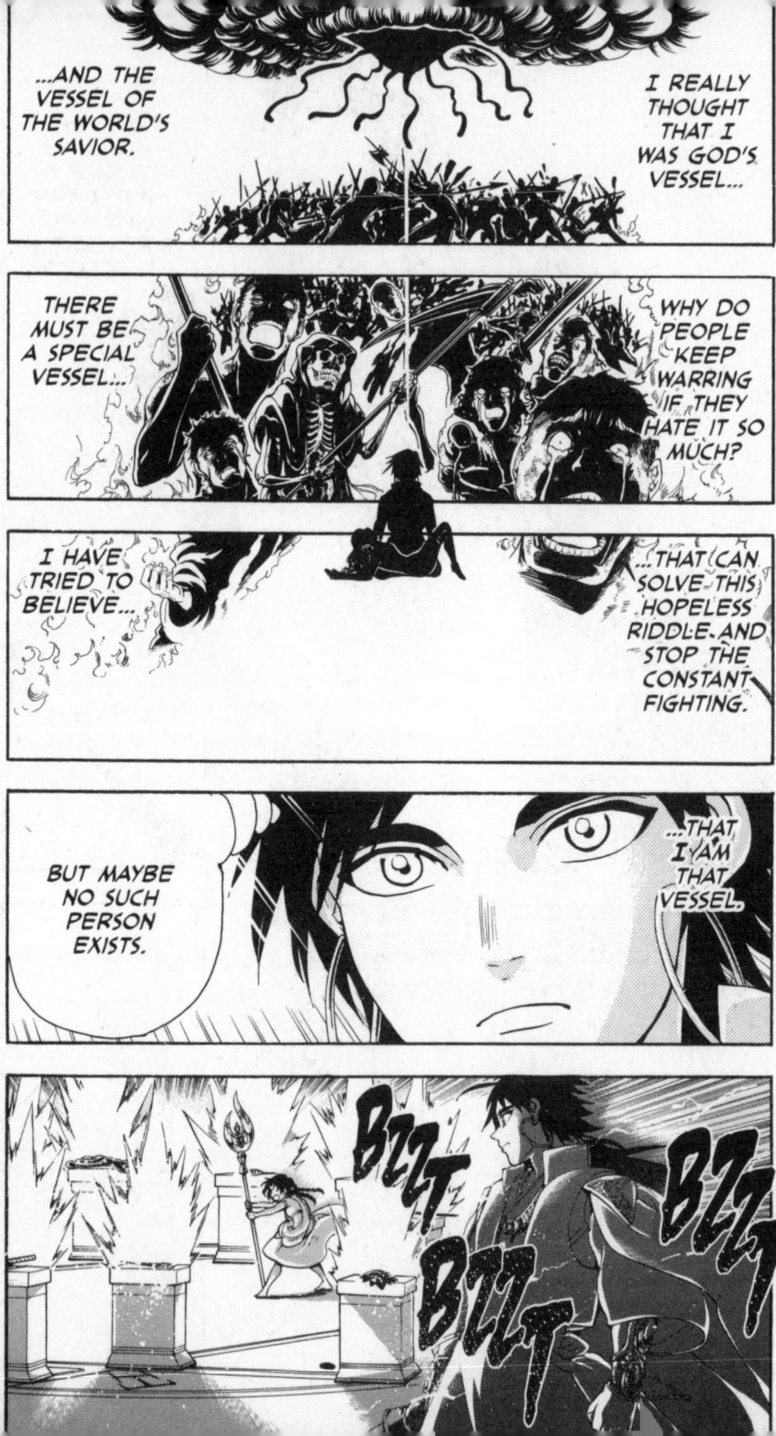
I REALLY THOUGHT THAT I WAS GOD'S VESSEL...
...AND THE VESSEL OF THE WORLD'S SAVIOR.
WHY DO PEOPLE KEEP WARRING IF THEY HATE IT SO MUCH?
THERE MUST BE A SPECIAL VESSEL...
...THAT CAN SOLVE THIS HOPELESS RIDDLE AND STOP THE CONSTANT FIGHTING.
I HAVE TRIED TO BELIEVE...
...THAT I AM THAT VESSEL.
BUT MAYBE NO SUCH PERSON EXISTS.
BZZT
BZZT
BZZT

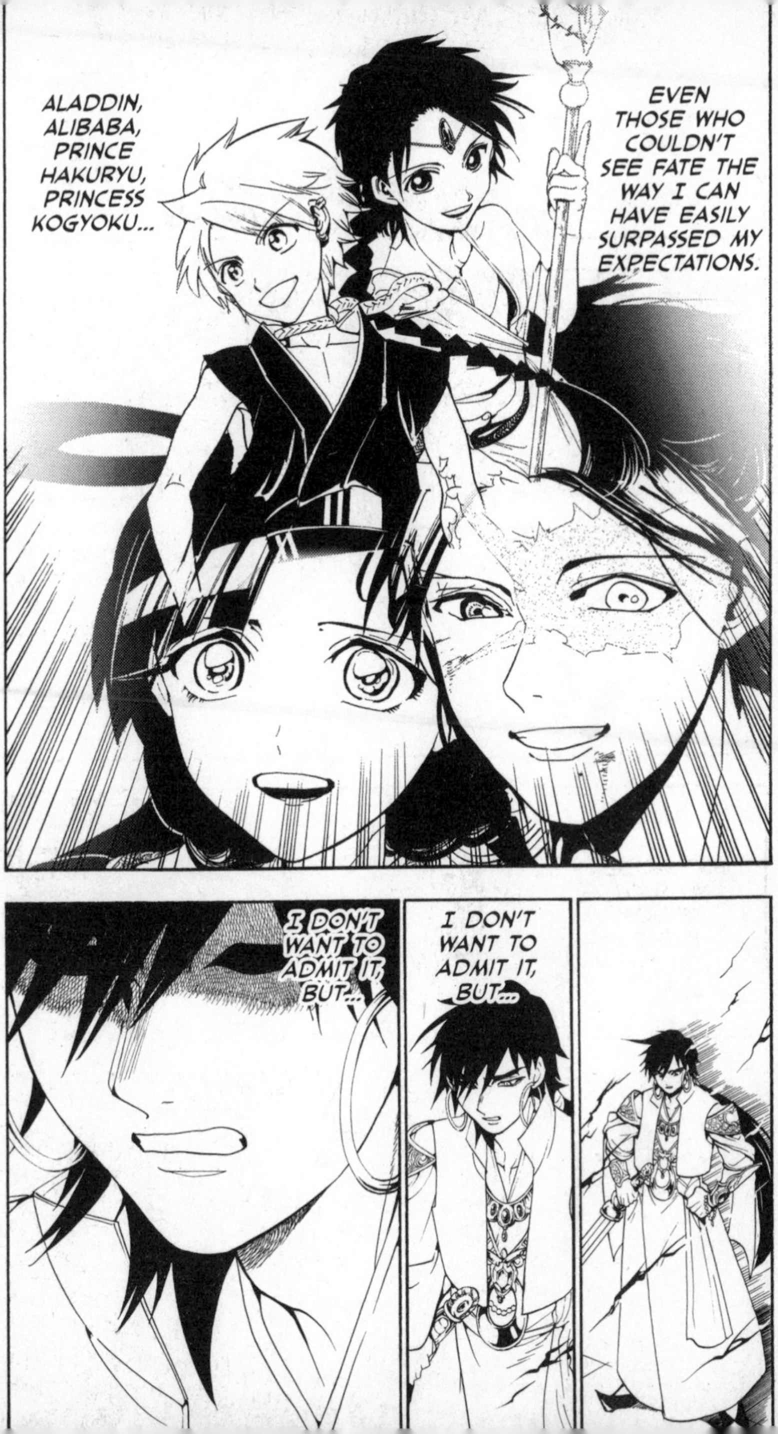
EVEN THOSE WHO COULDN'T SEE FATE THE WAY I CAN HAVE EASILY SURPASSED MY EXPECTATIONS.
ALADDIN, ALIBABA, PRINCE HAKURYU, PRINCESS KOGYOKU...
I DON'T WANT TO ADMIT IT, BUT...
I DON'T WANT TO ADMIT IT, BUT...

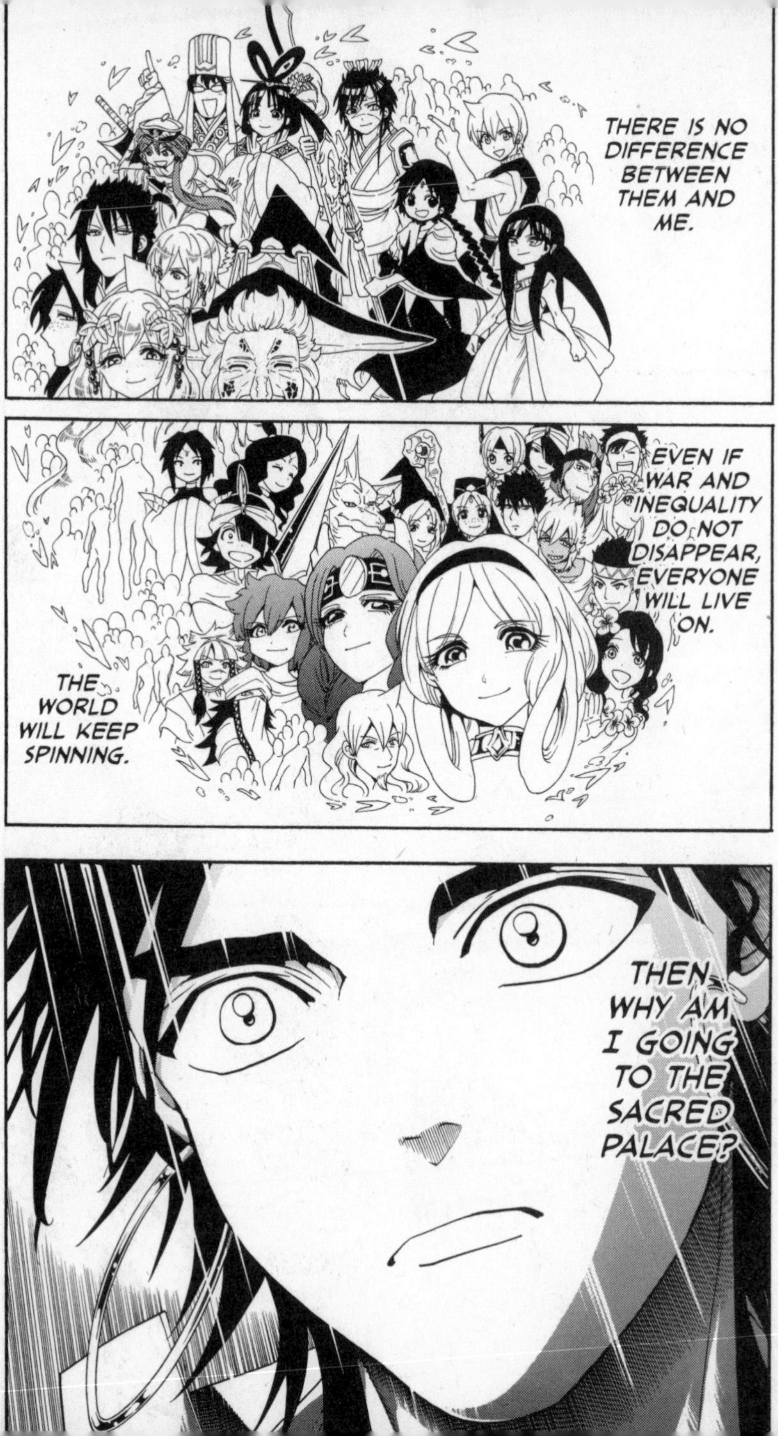
THERE IS NO DIFFERENCE BETWEEN THEM AND ME.
EVEN IF WAR AND INEQUALITY DO NOT DISAPPEAR, EVERYONE WILL LIVE ON.
THE WORLD WILL KEEP SPINNING.
THEN WHY AM I GOING TO THE SACRED PALACE?

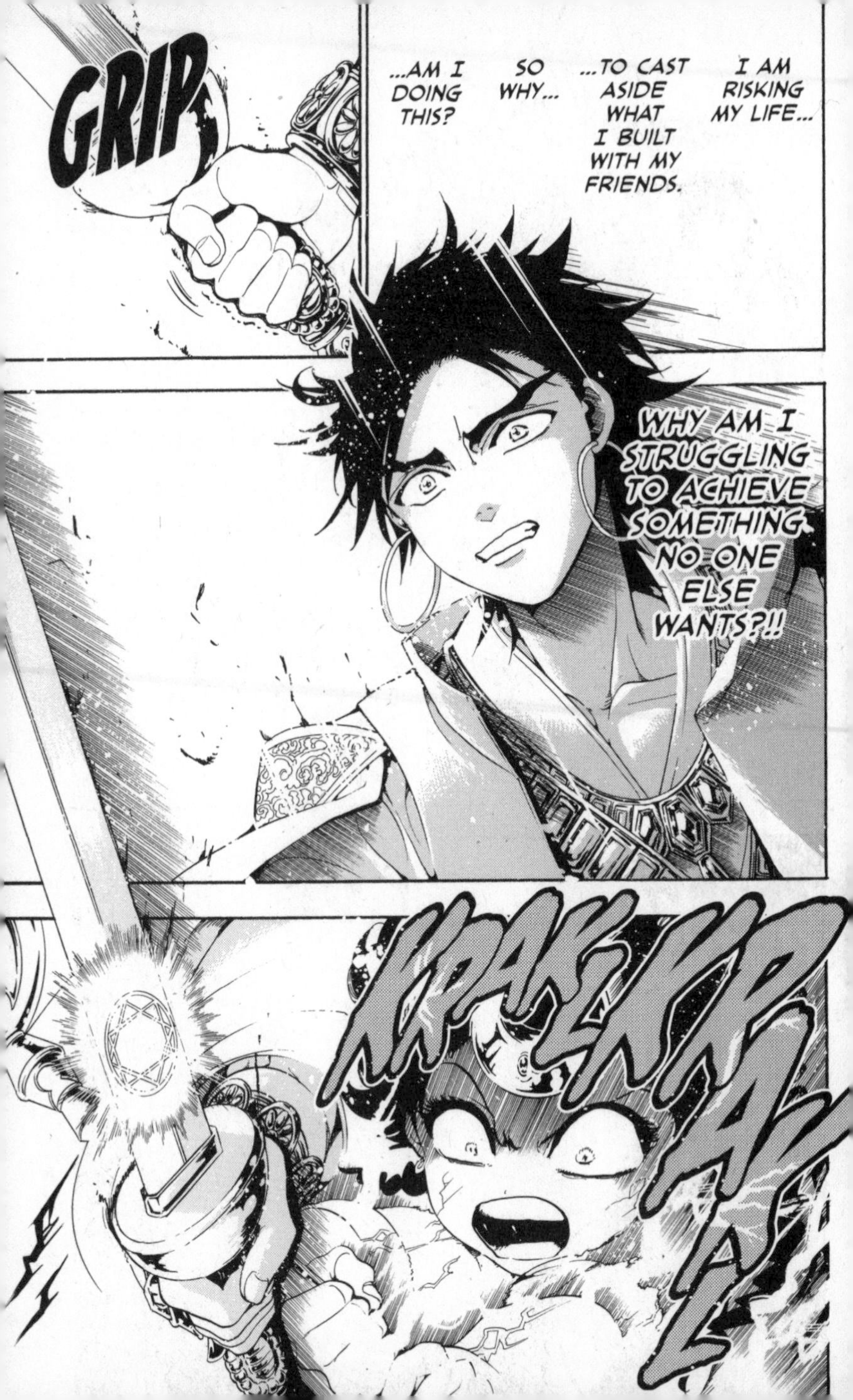
I AM RISKING MY LIFE...
...TO CAST ASIDE WHAT I BUILT WITH MY FRIENDS.
SO WHY...
...AM I DOING THIS?
GRIP
WHY AM I STRUGGLING TO ACHIEVE SOMETHING NO ONE ELSE WANTS?!!

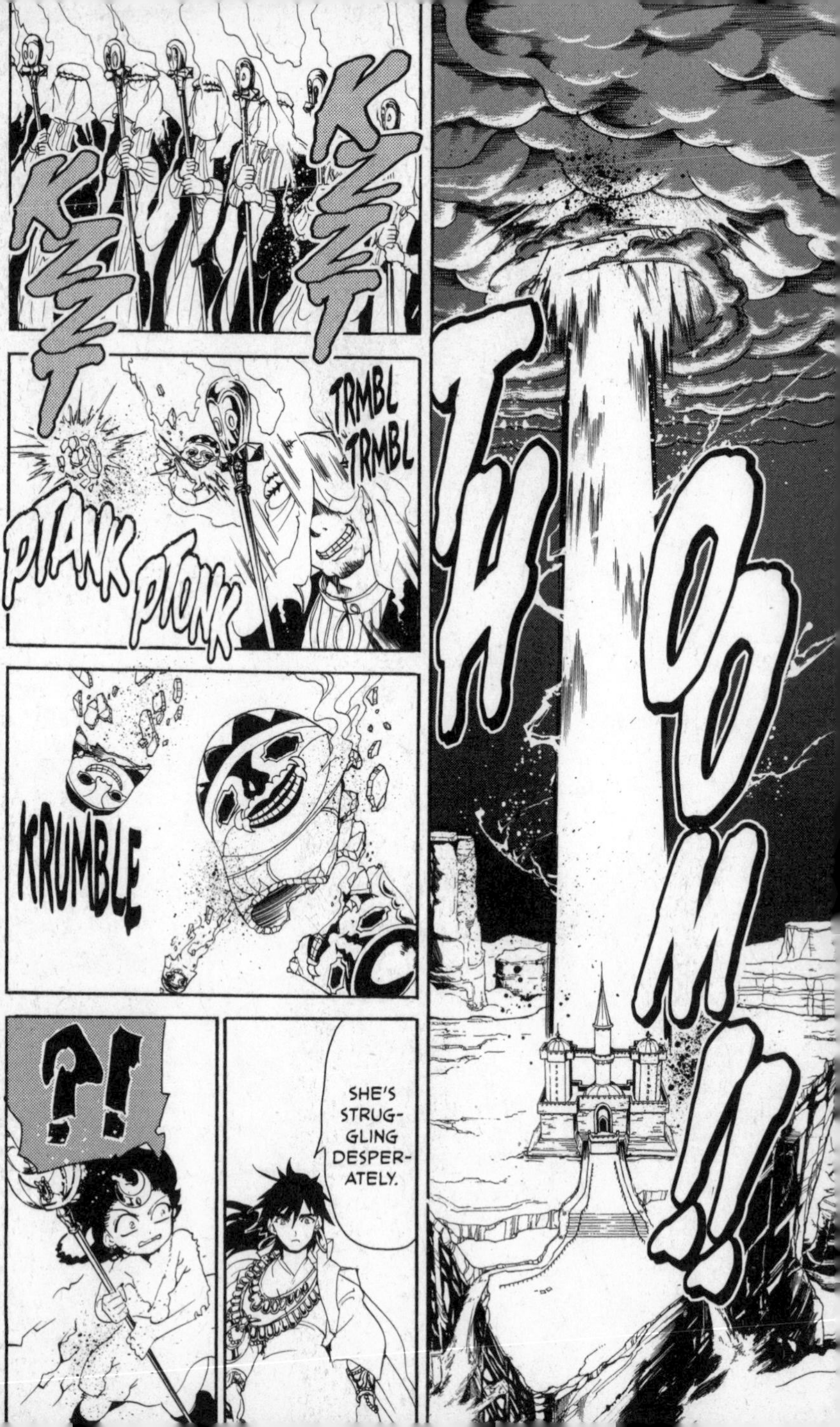
WHOOM!!
KZZT
KZZT
TRMBL
TRMBL
PTANK
PTONK
KRUMBLE
SHE'S STRUG-GLING DESPER-ATELY.
?!

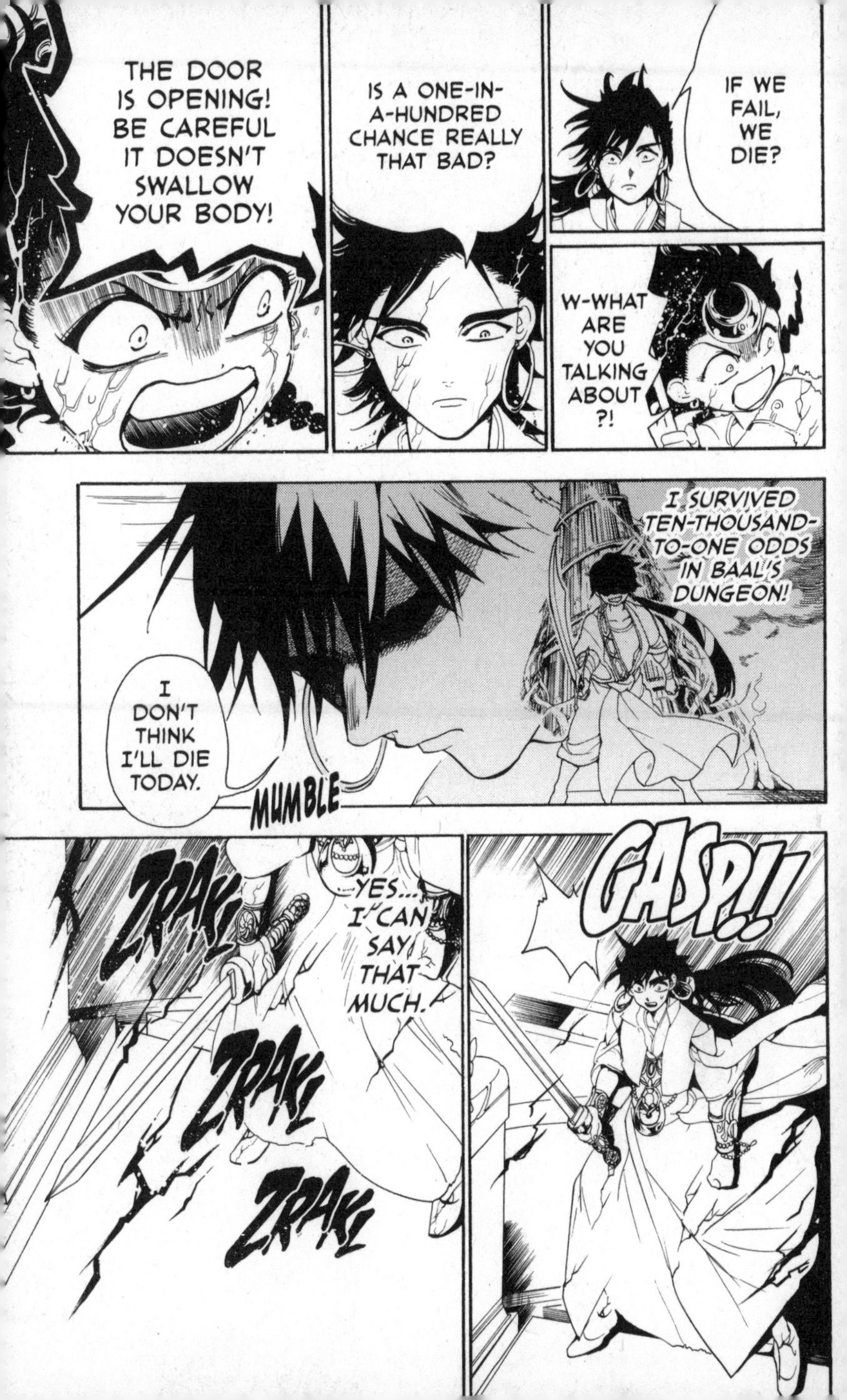
IF WE FAIL, WE DIE?
W-WHAT ARE YOU TALKING ABOUT?!
IS A ONE-IN-A-HUNDRED CHANCE REALLY THAT BAD?
THE DOOR IS OPENING! BE CAREFUL IT DOESN'T SWALLOW YOUR BODY!
I SURVIVED TEN-THOUSAND-TO-ONE ODDS IN BAAL'S DUNGEON!
I DON'T THINK I'LL DIE TODAY.
MUMBLE
GASP!!
YES... I CAN SAY THAT MUCH.
ZRAK!
ZRAK!
ZRAK!

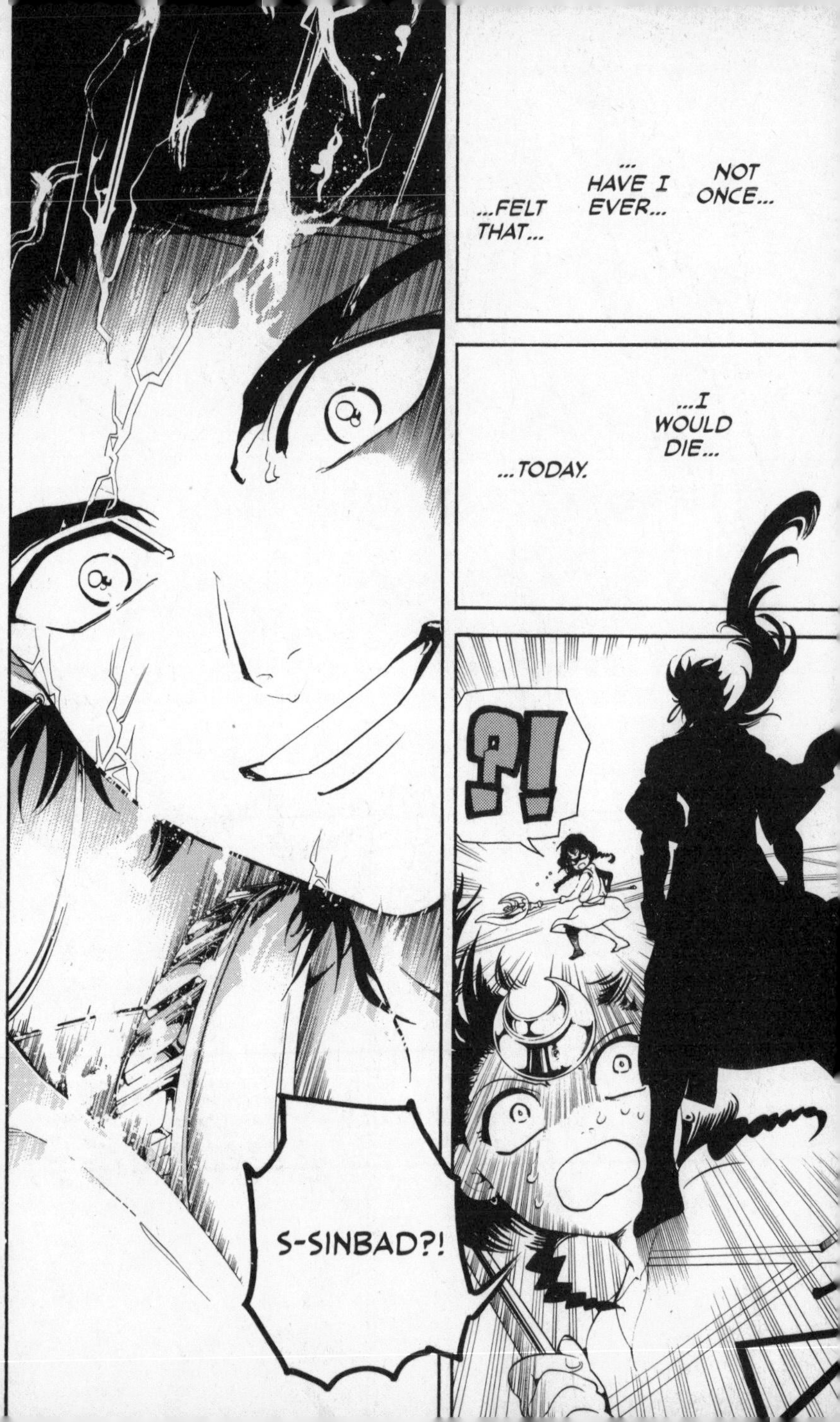
NOT ONCE...
... HAVE I EVER...
...FELT THAT...
...I WOULD DIE...
...TODAY.
?!
S-SINBAD?!

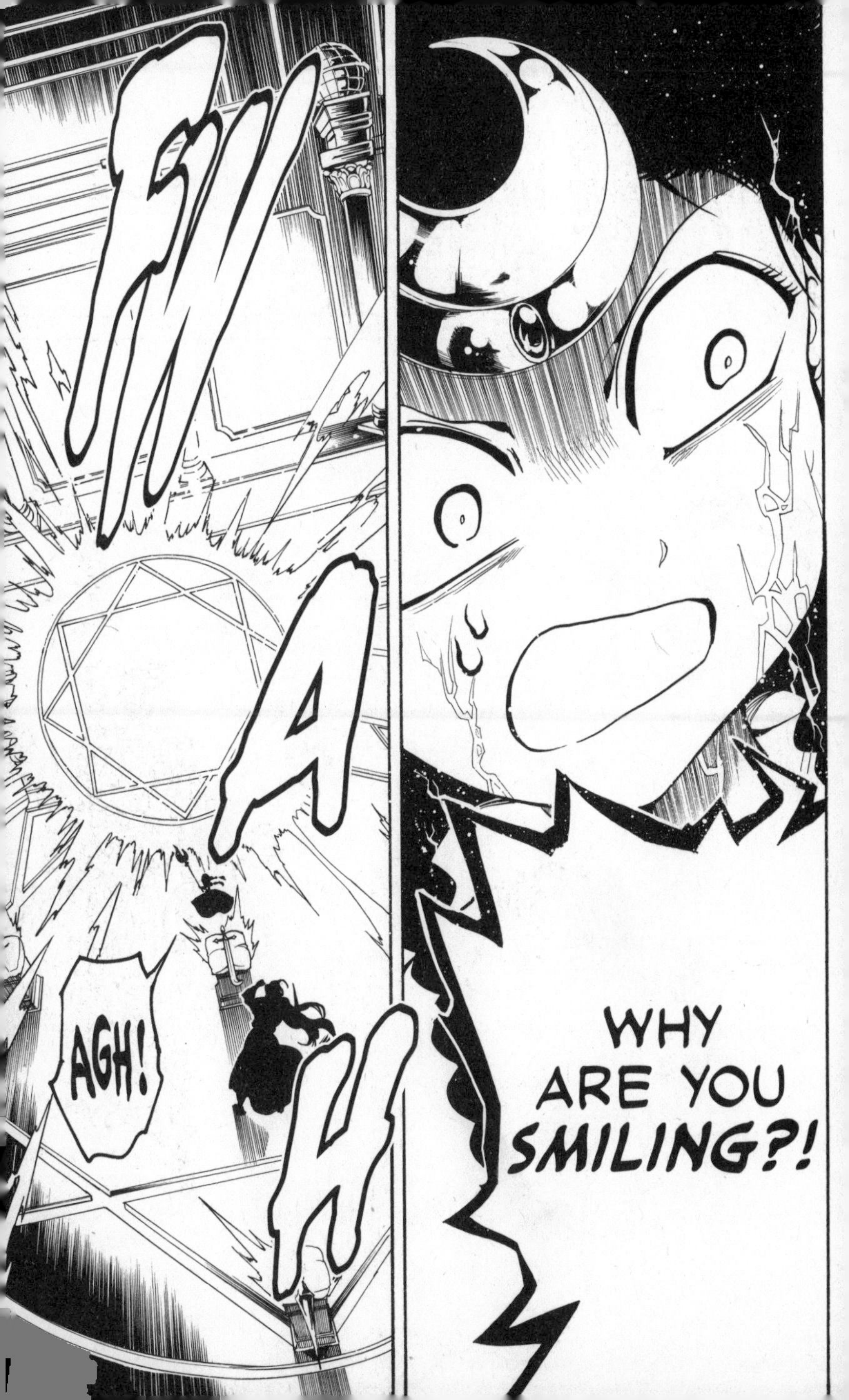
WHY ARE YOU SMILING?!
AGH!

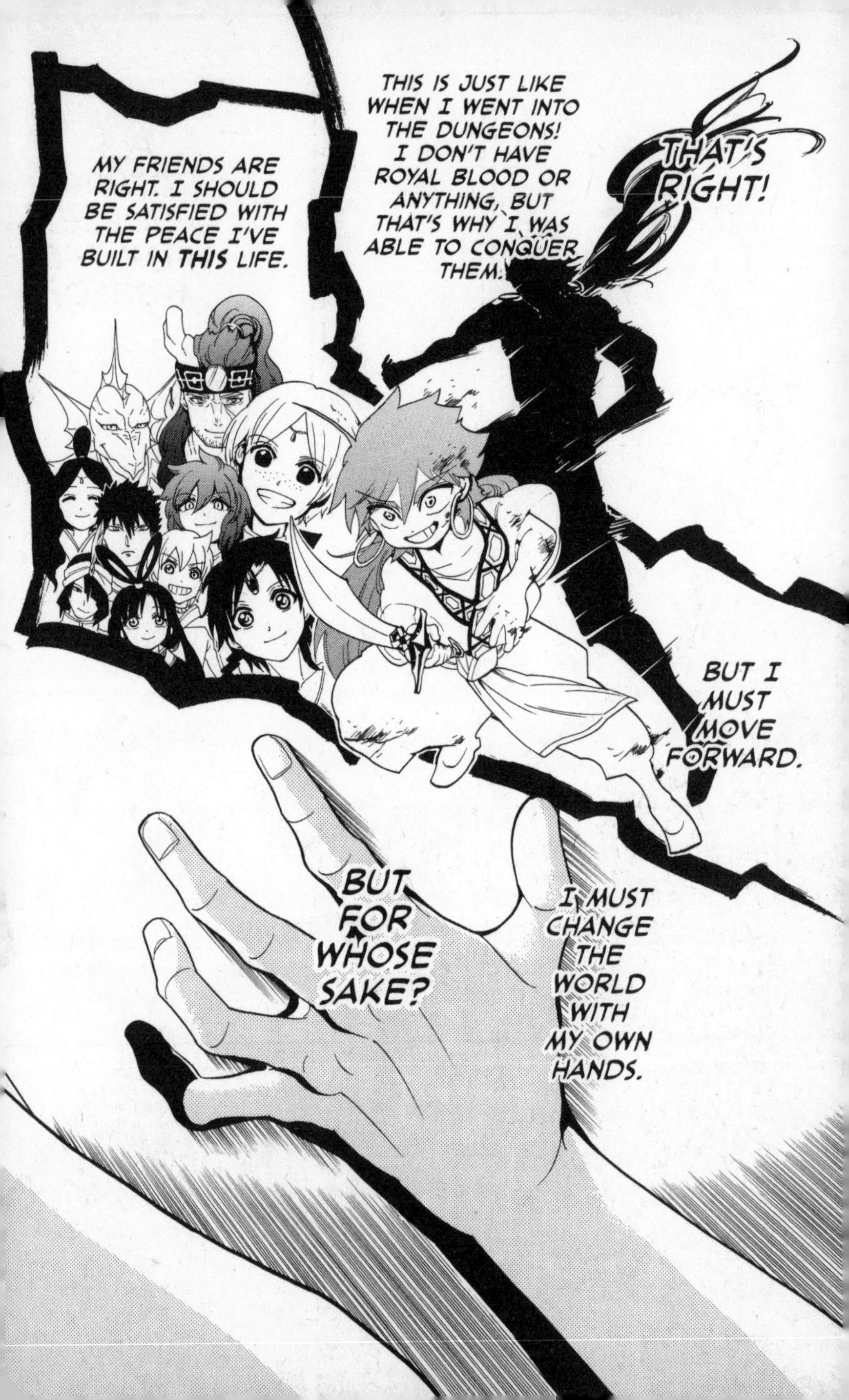
THAT'S RIGHT!
THIS IS JUST LIKE WHEN I WENT INTO THE DUNGEONS! I DON'T HAVE ROYAL BLOOD OR ANYTHING, BUT THAT'S WHY I WAS ABLE TO CONQUER THEM.
MY FRIENDS ARE RIGHT. I SHOULD BE SATISFIED WITH THE PEACE I'VE BUILT IN THIS LIFE.
BUT I MUST MOVE FORWARD.
I MUST CHANGE THE WORLD WITH MY OWN HANDS.
BUT FOR WHOSE SAKE?

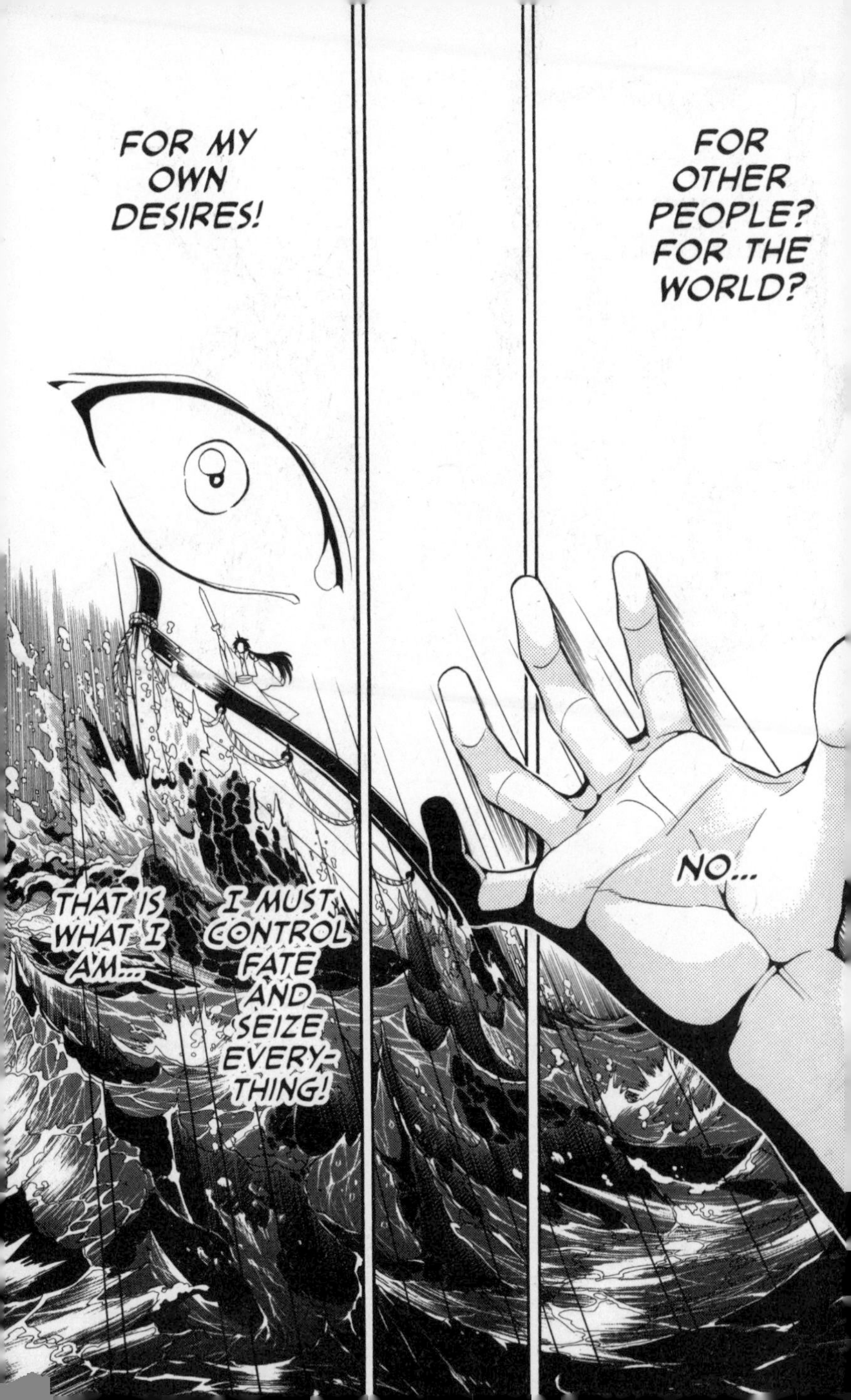
FOR OTHER PEOPLE? FOR THE WORLD?
NO...
FOR MY OWN DESIRES!
I MUST CONTROL FATE AND SEIZE EVERY-THING!
THAT IS WHAT I AM...

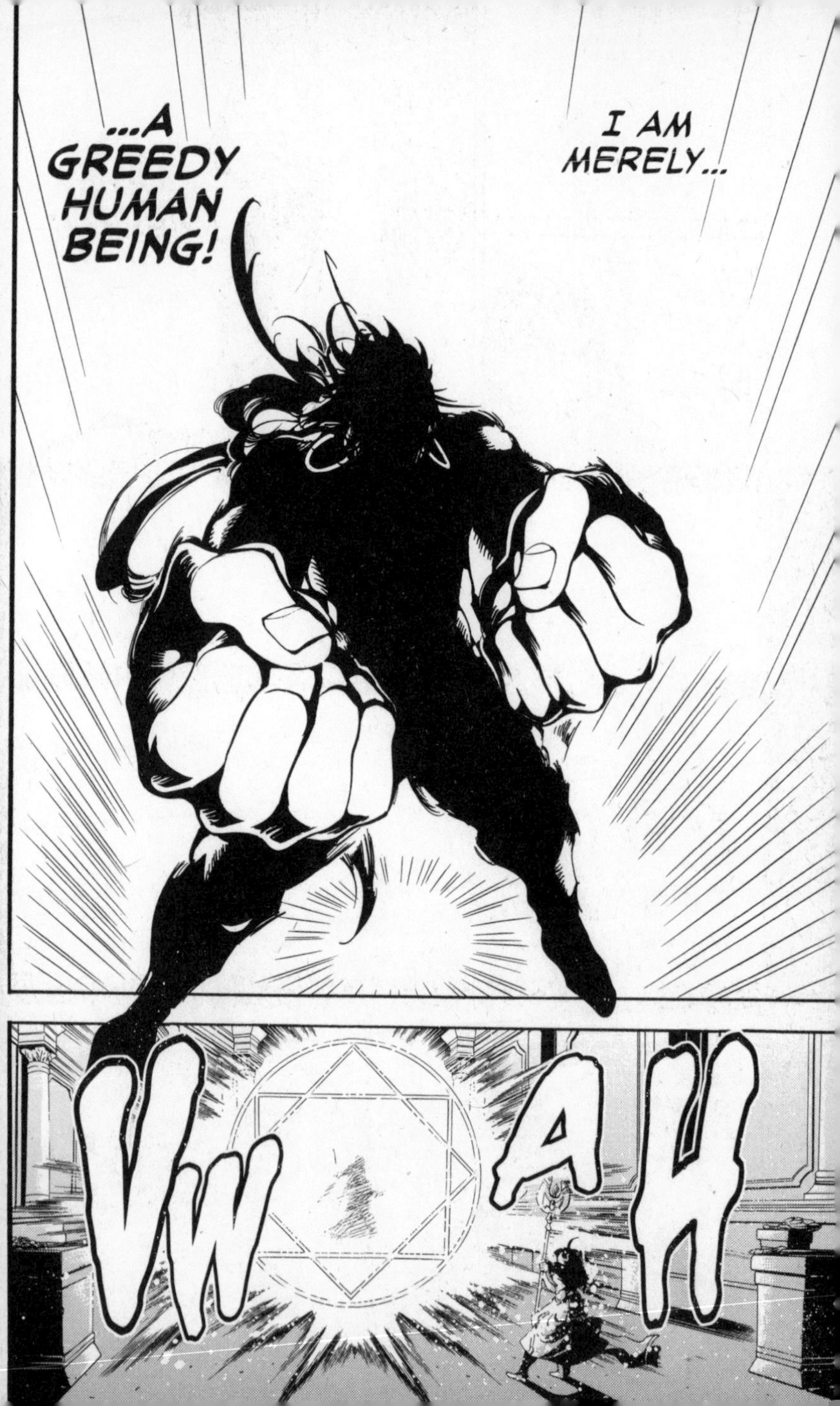
I AM MERELY...
...A GREEDY HUMAN BEING!
VWAH

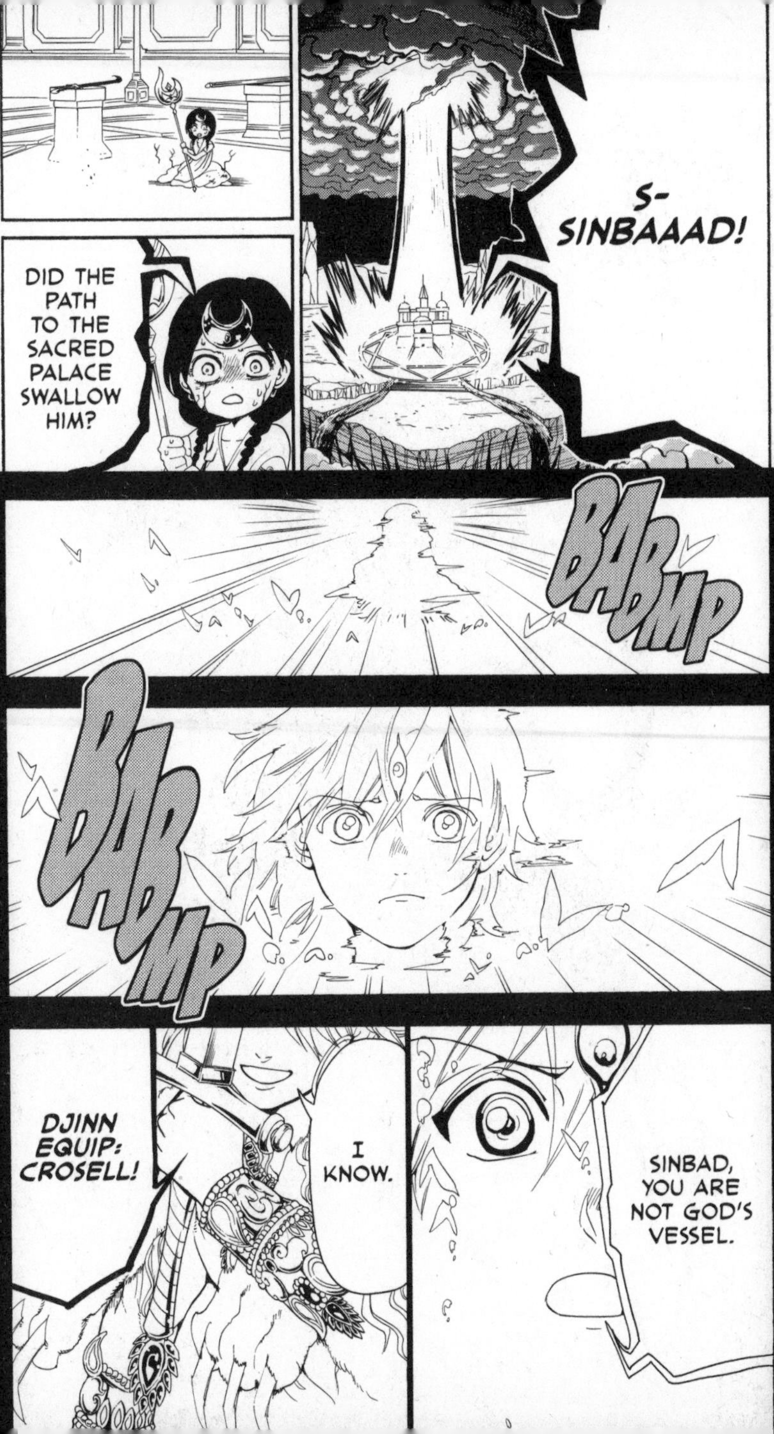
S-SINBAAAD!
DID THE PATH TO THE SACRED PALACE SWALLOW HIM?
BABMP
BABMP
SINBAD, YOU ARE NOT GOD'S VESSEL.
I KNOW.
DJINN EQUIP: CROSELL!

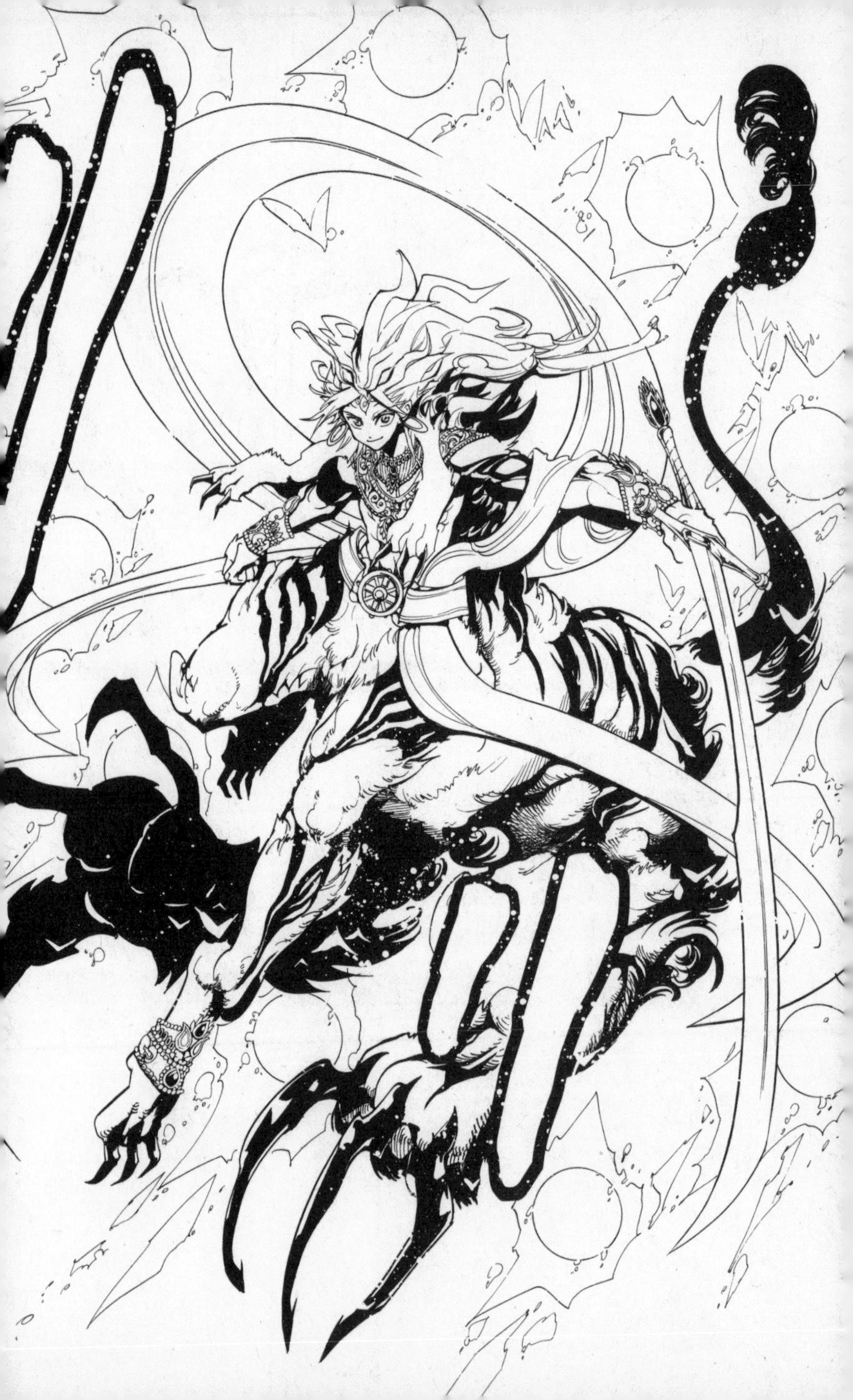

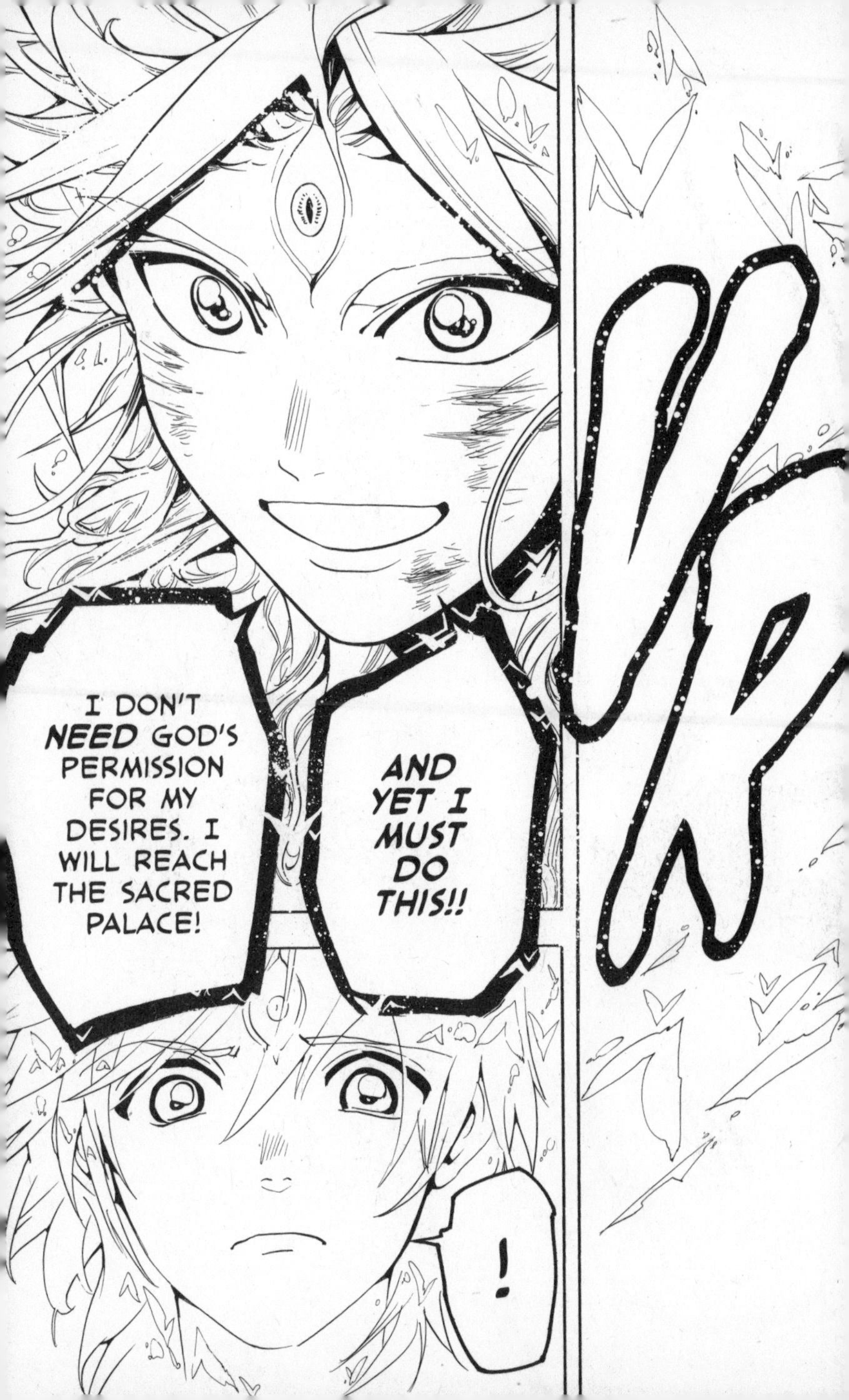
I DON'T *NEED* GOD'S PERMISSION FOR MY DESIRES. I WILL REACH THE SACRED PALACE!
AND YET I MUST DO THIS!!
!

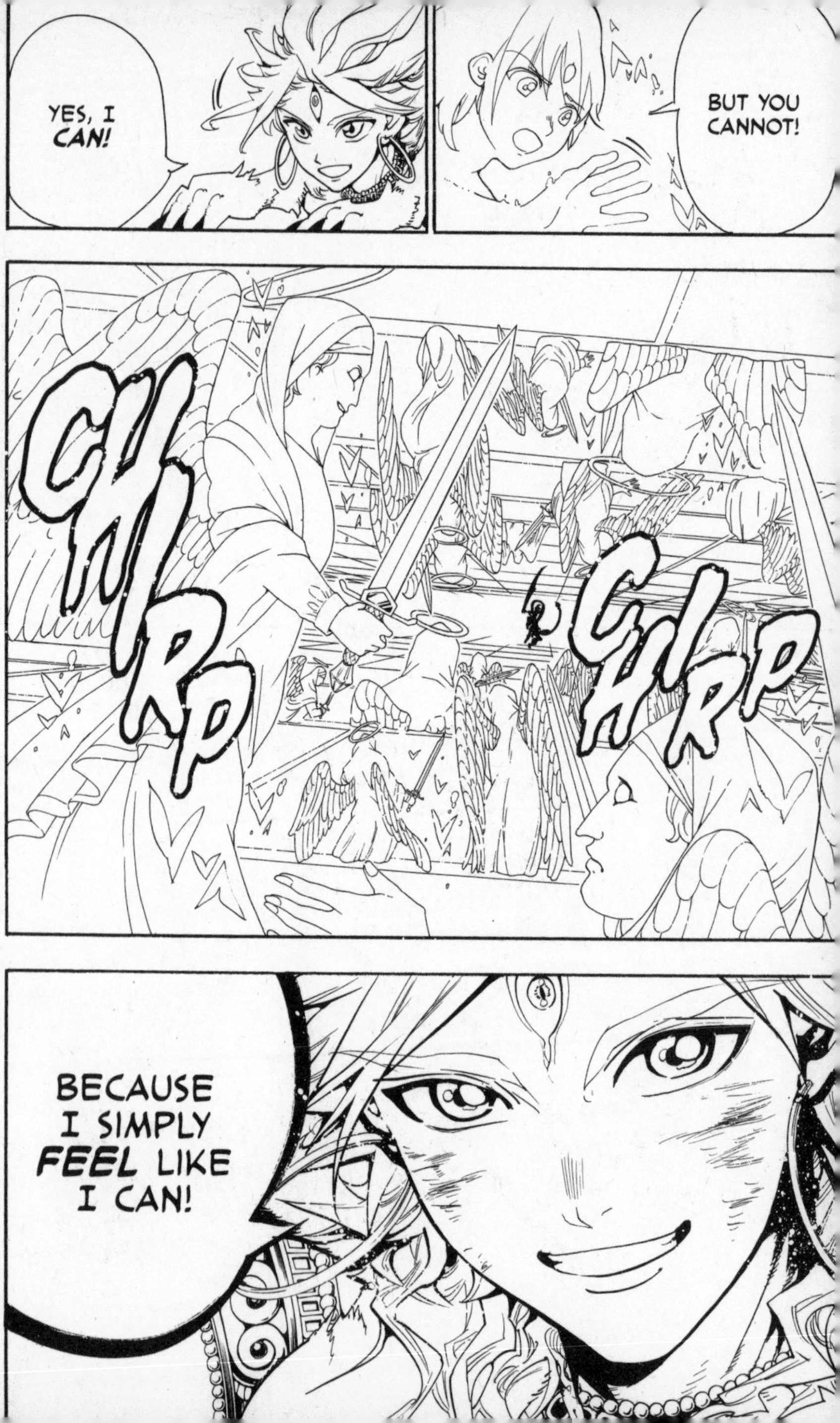
BUT YOU CANNOT!
YES, I CAN!
CHIRP
CHIRP
CHIRP
BECAUSE I SIMPLY FEEL LIKE I CAN!

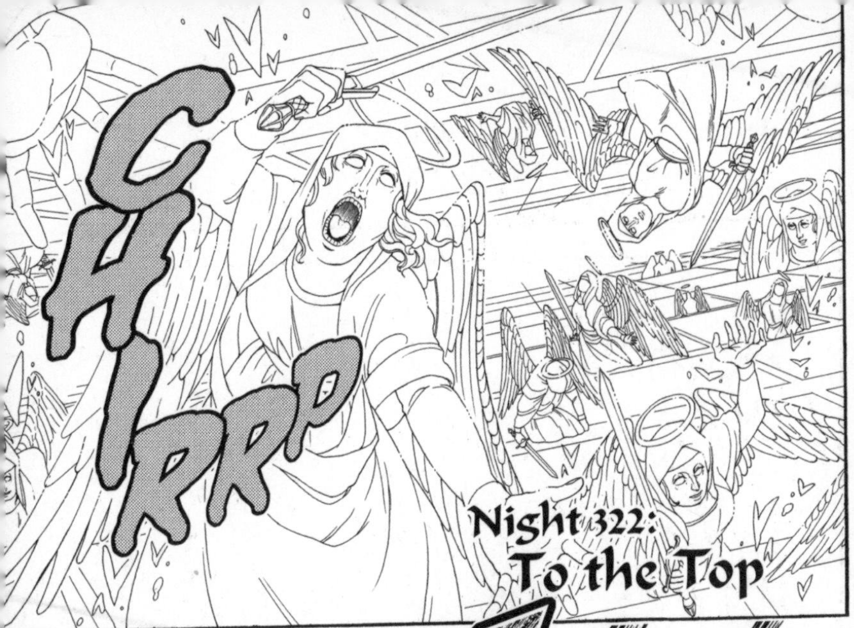
CHIRRP
Night 322:
To the Top
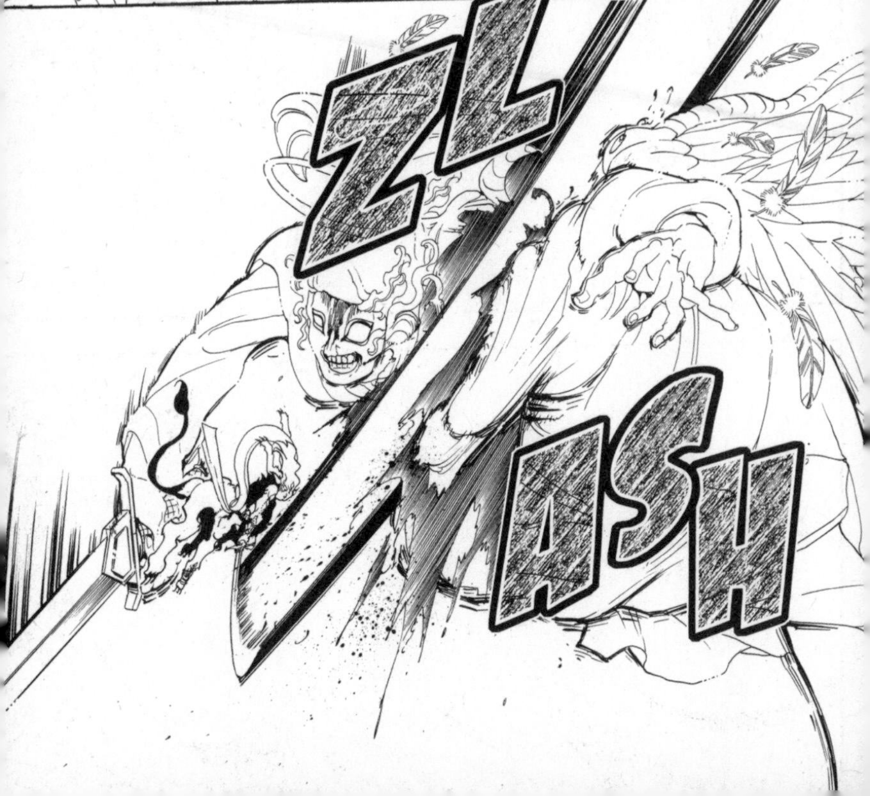
ZLASH

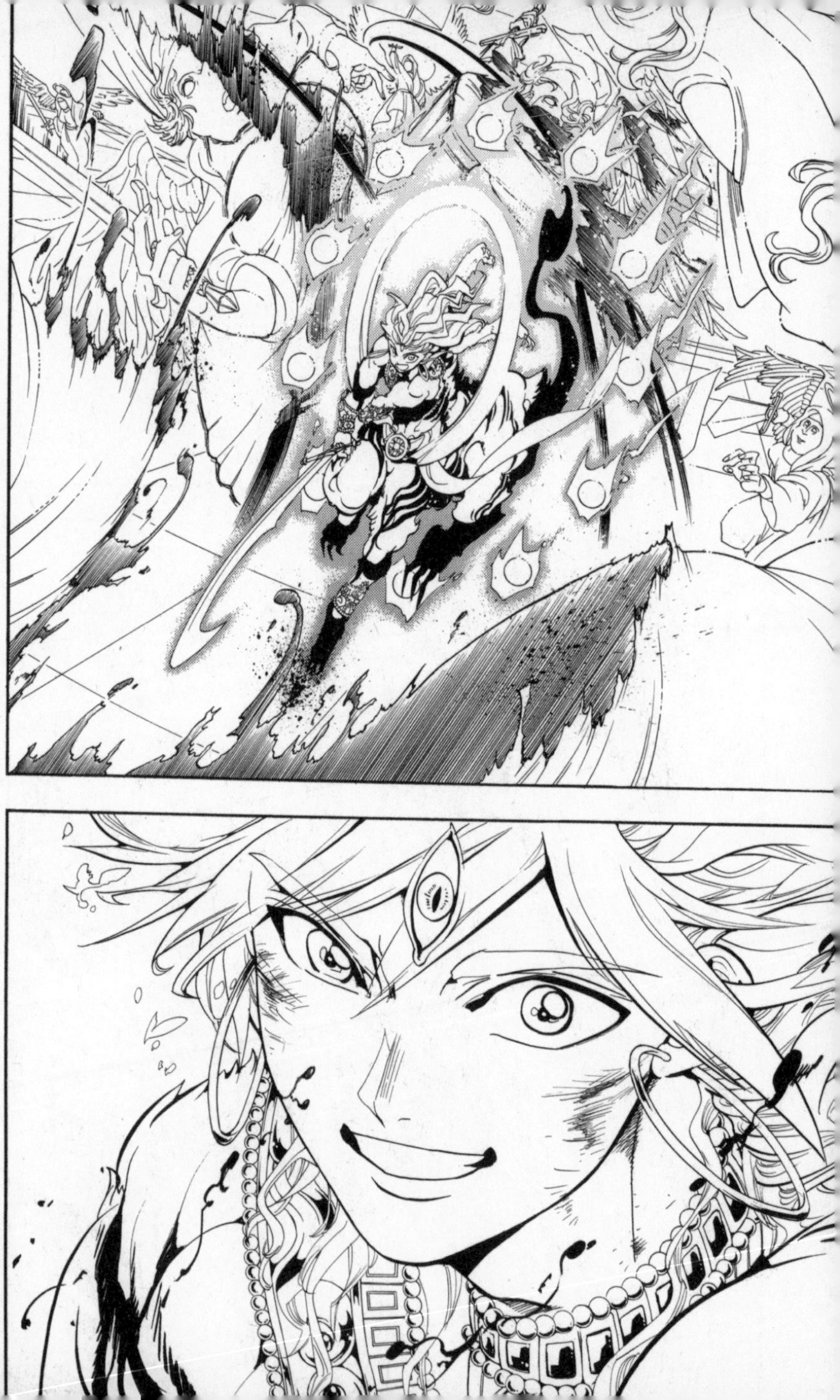

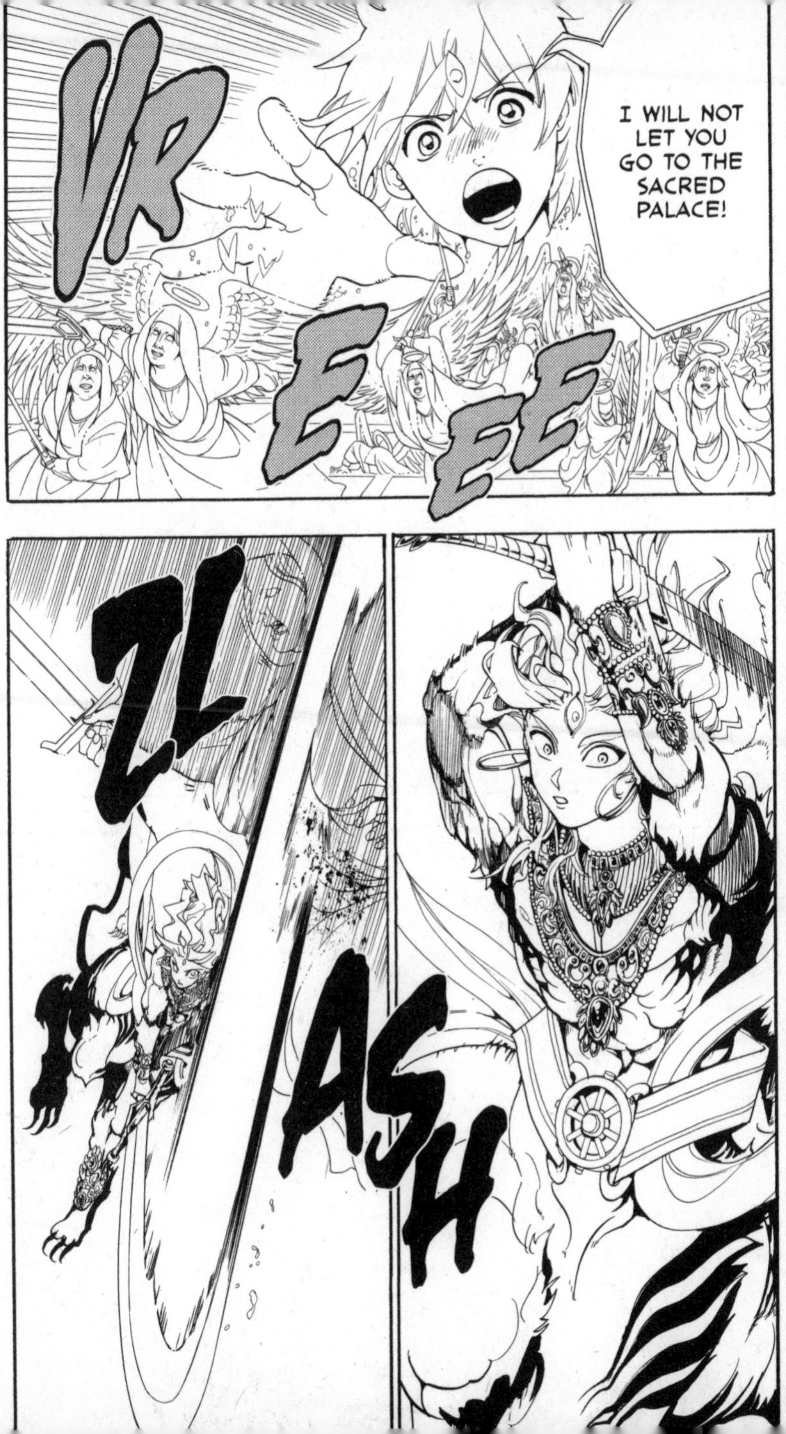
VR
E
EE
I WILL NOT LET YOU GO TO THE SACRED PALACE!
ZL
ASH

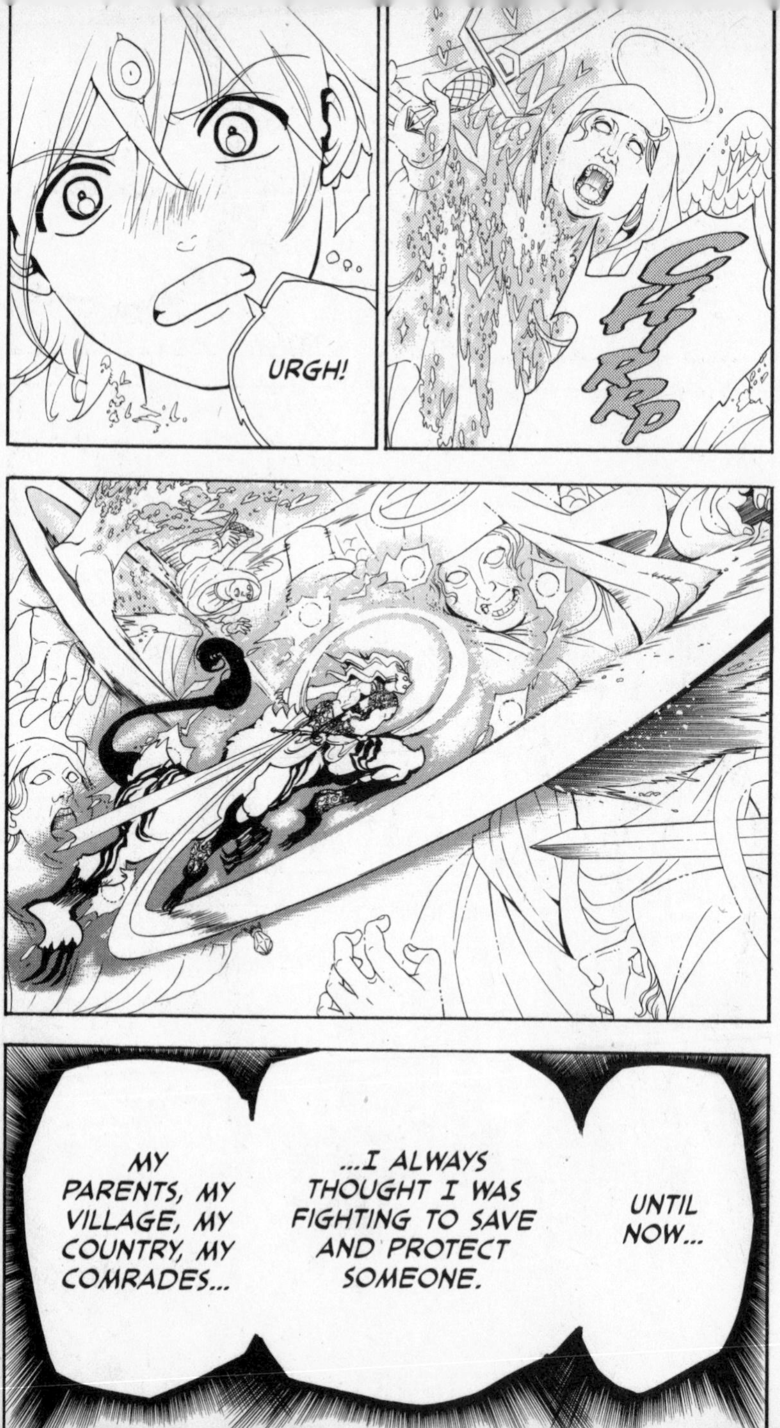
CHIRRP
URGH!
UNTIL NOW...
...I ALWAYS THOUGHT I WAS FIGHTING TO SAVE AND PROTECT SOMEONE.
MY PARENTS, MY VILLAGE, MY COUNTRY, MY COMRADES...

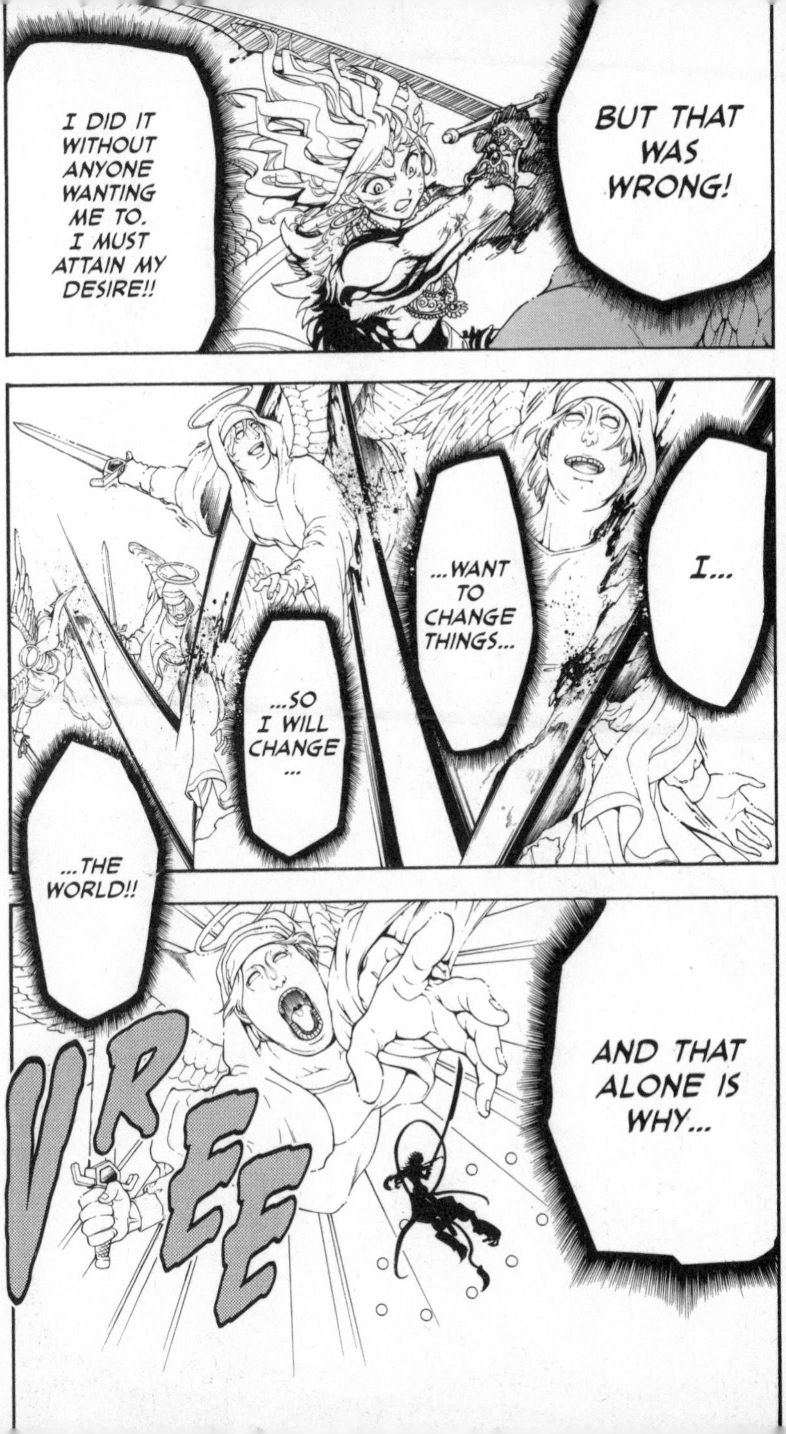
BUT THAT WAS WRONG!
I DID IT WITHOUT ANYONE WANTING ME TO. I MUST ATTAIN MY DESIRE!!
I...
...WANT TO CHANGE THINGS...
...SO I WILL CHANGE ...
...THE WORLD!!
AND THAT ALONE IS WHY...
VREE

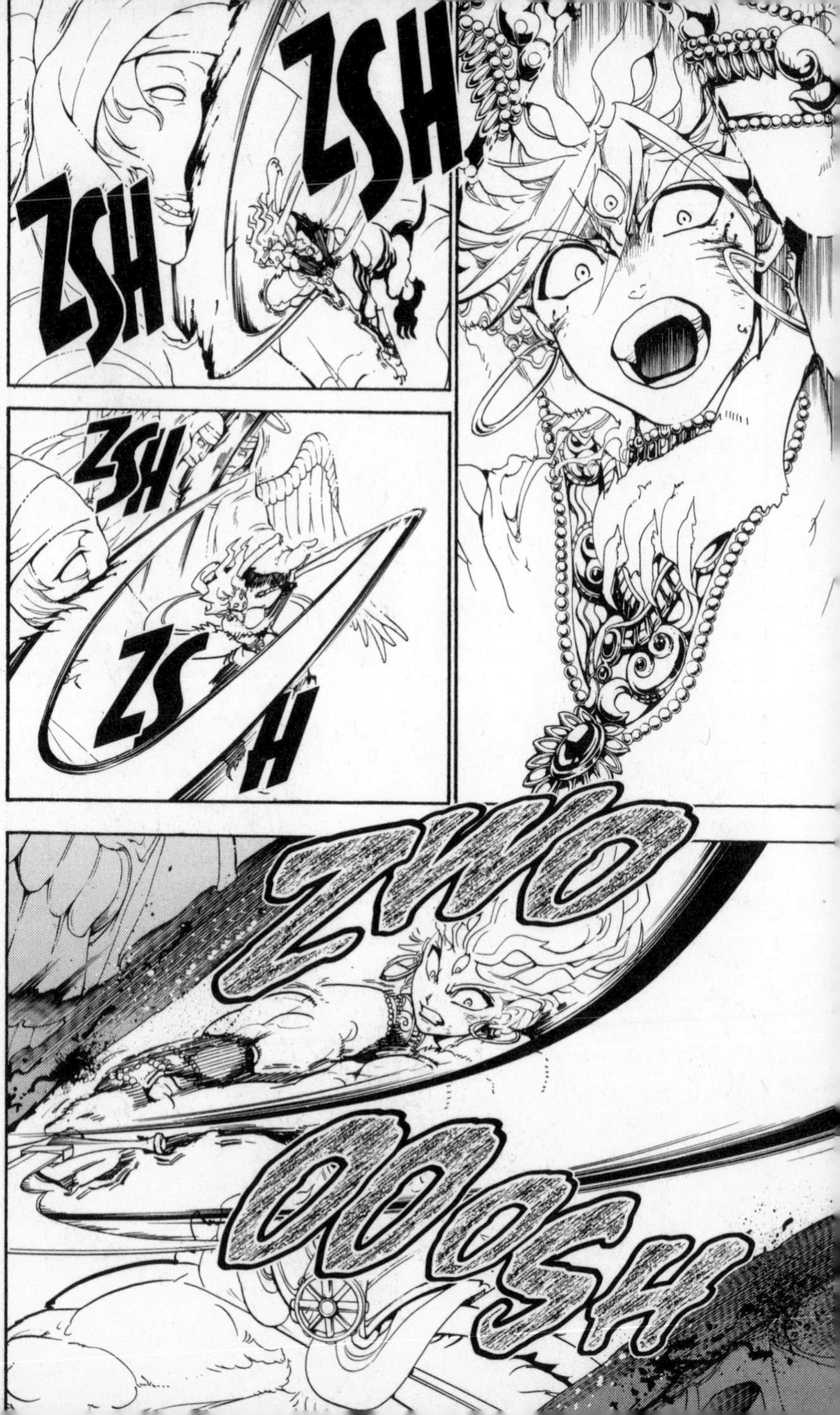
ZSH
ZSH
ZSH
ZSH
ZWOOOSH

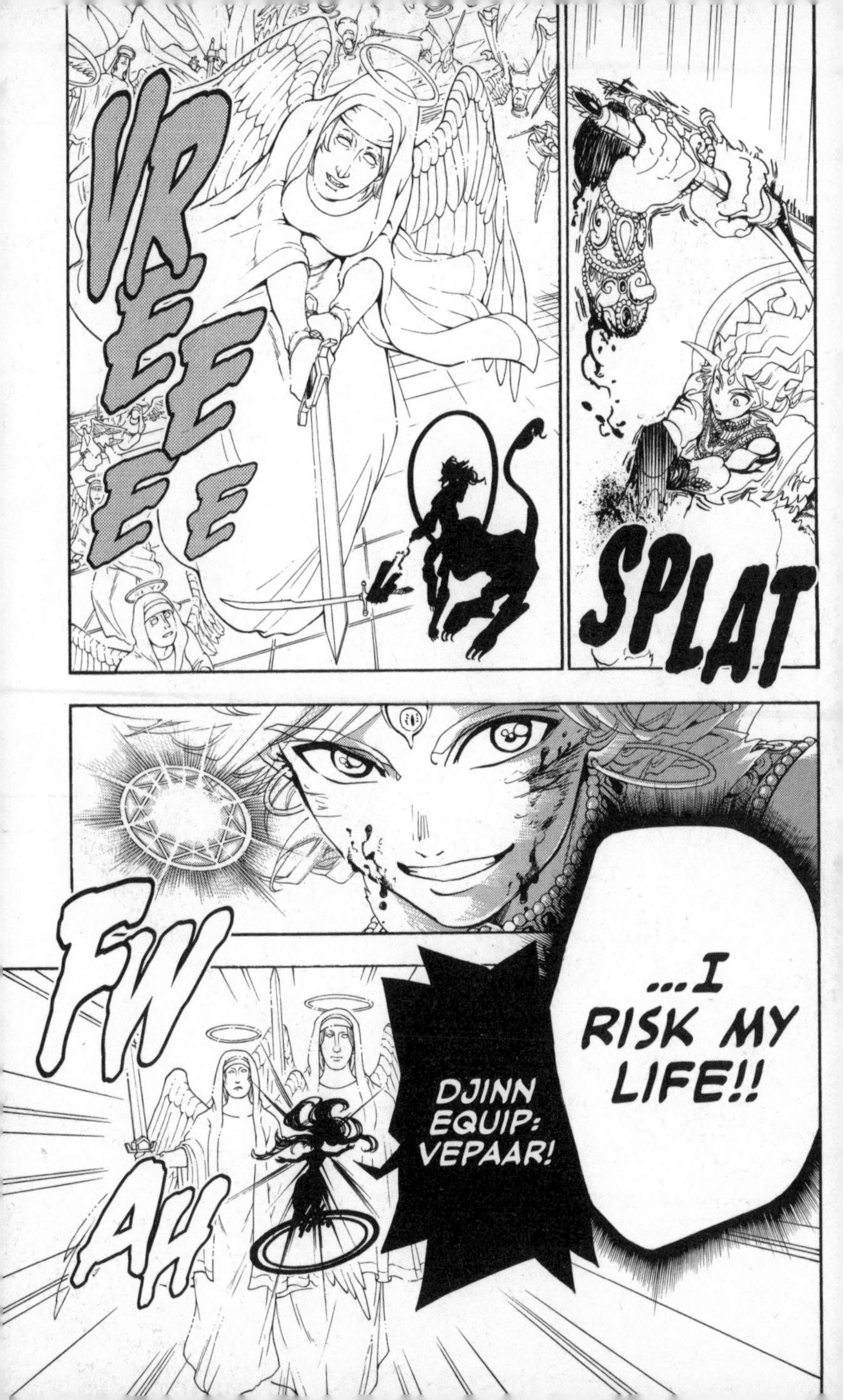
SPLAT
VREEEEE
...I RISK MY LIFE!!
DJINN EQUIP: VEPAAR!
FWAH

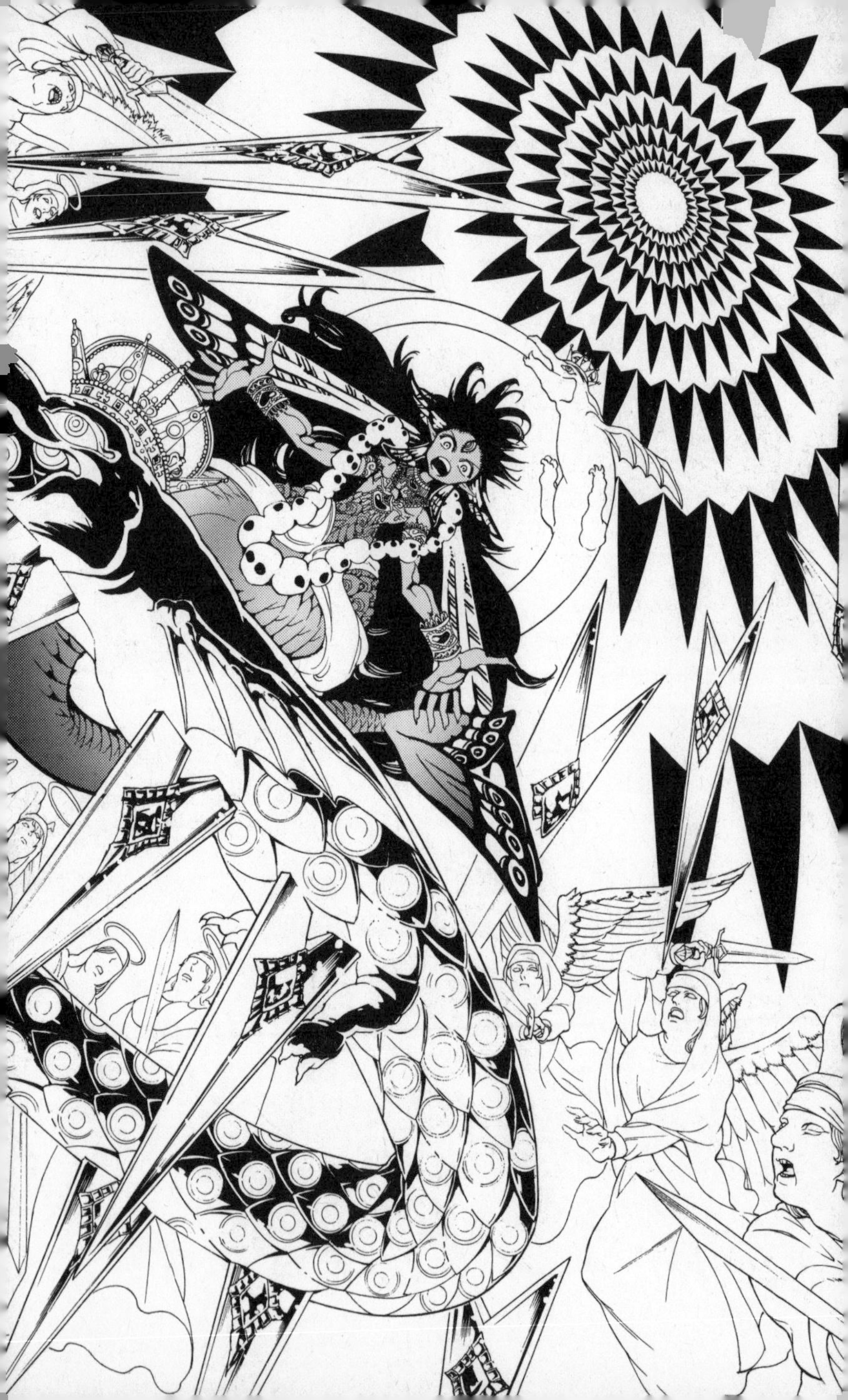

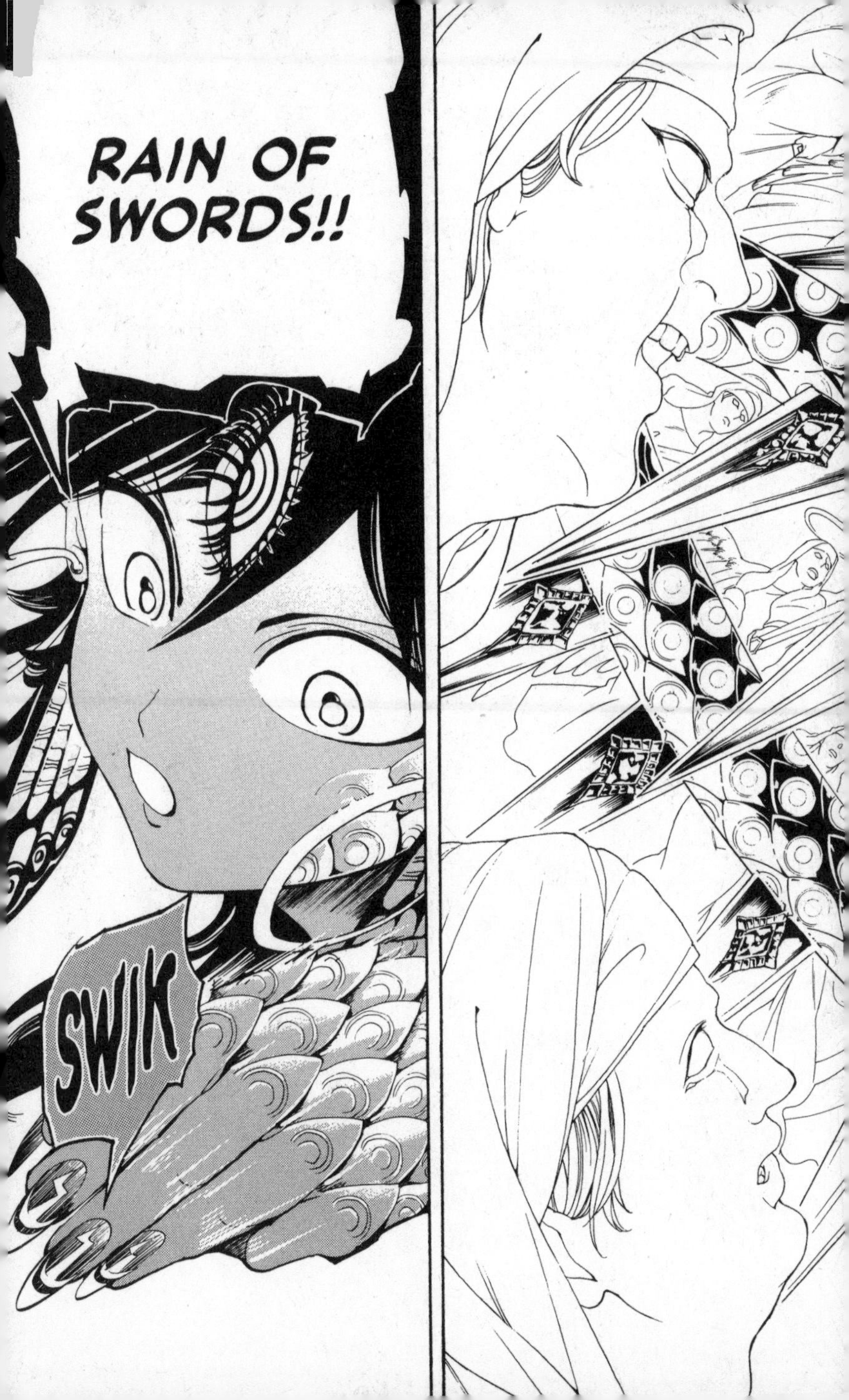
RAIN OF SWORDS!!
SWIK

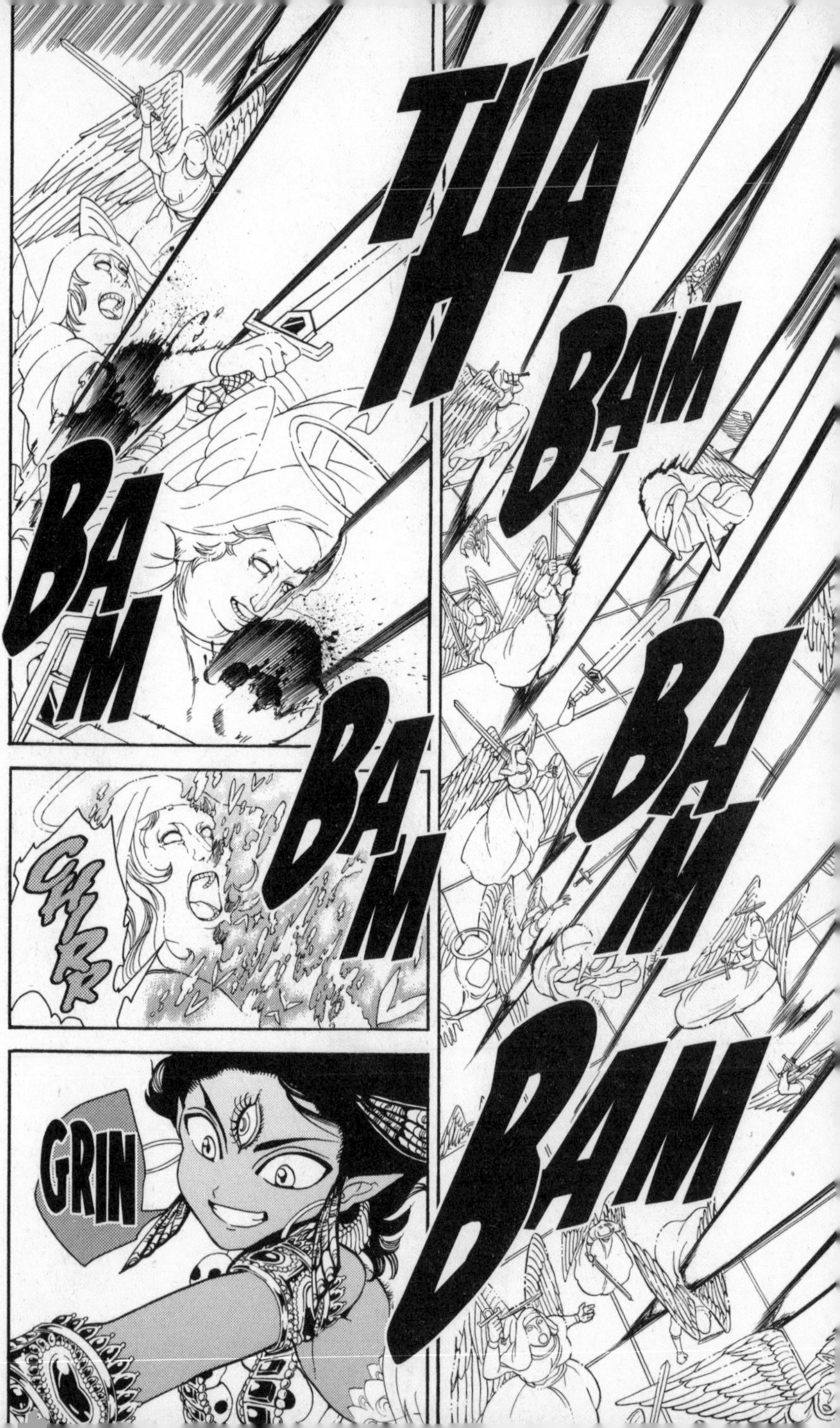
THA
BAM
BABAM
BAM
BAM
BAM
GHKK
GRIN

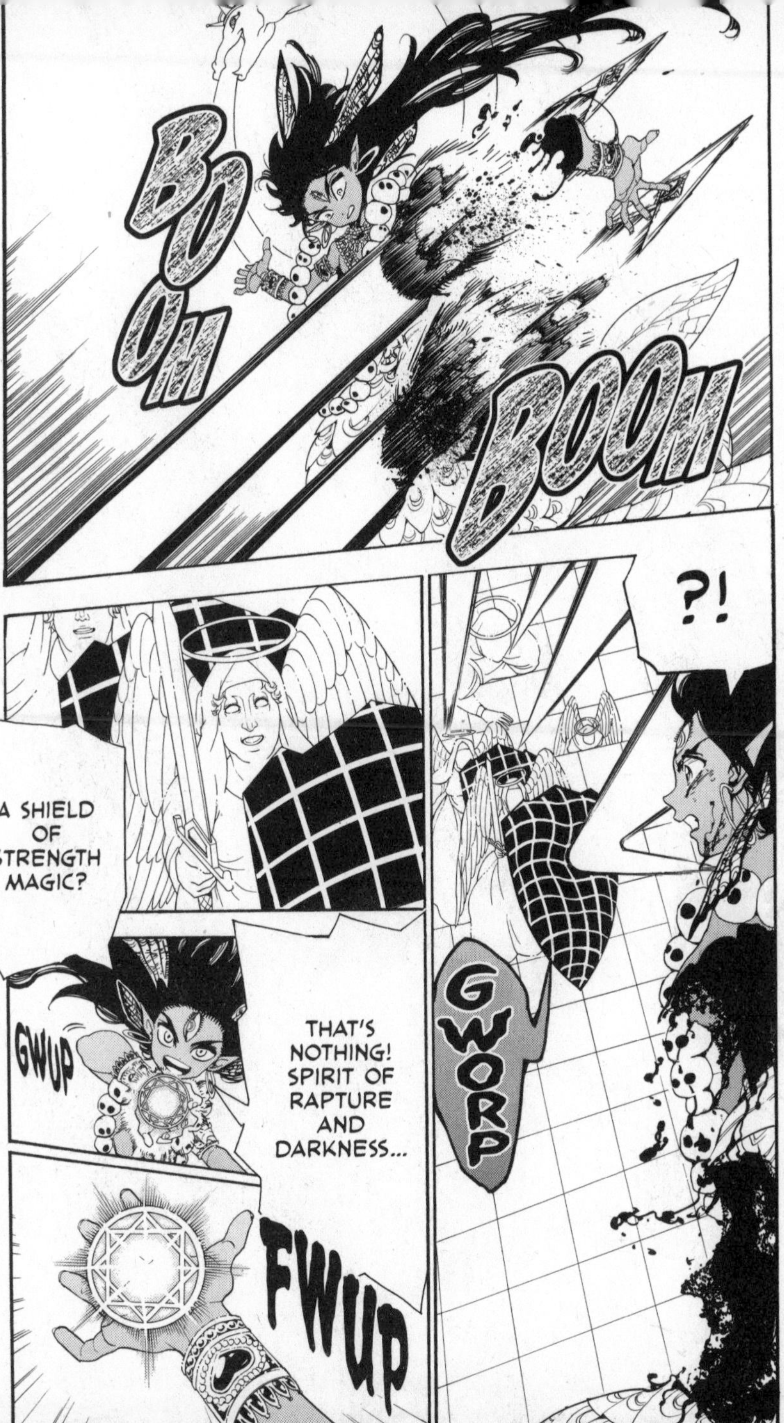
BOOM
BOOM
?!
GWORP
A SHIELD OF STRENGTH MAGIC?
THAT'S NOTHING! SPIRIT OF RAPTURE AND DARKNESS...
GWUP
FWUP

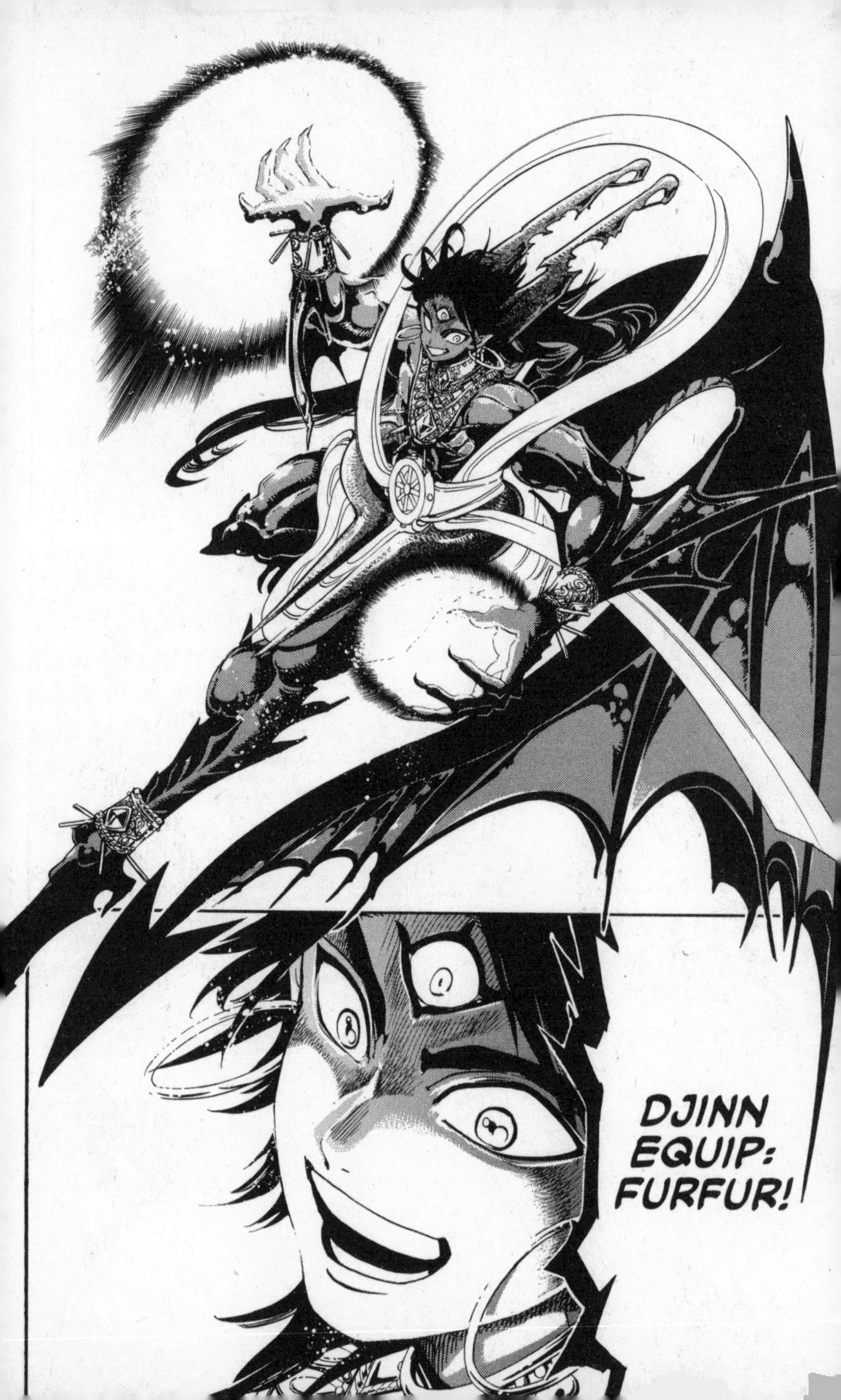
DJINN EQUIP: FURFUR!

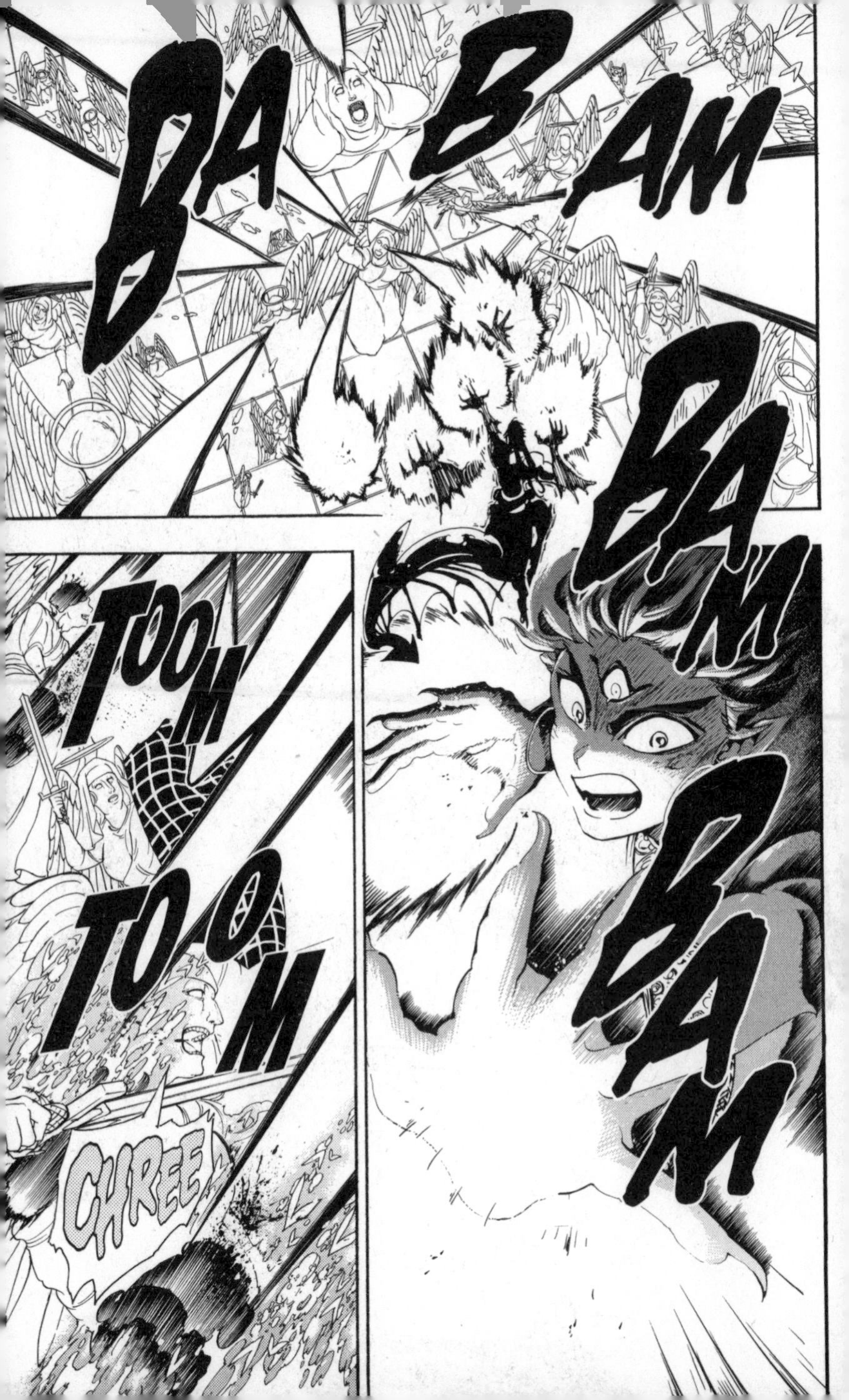

BA BAM
BA BAM
BA BAM
TOOM
TOOM
CHREE

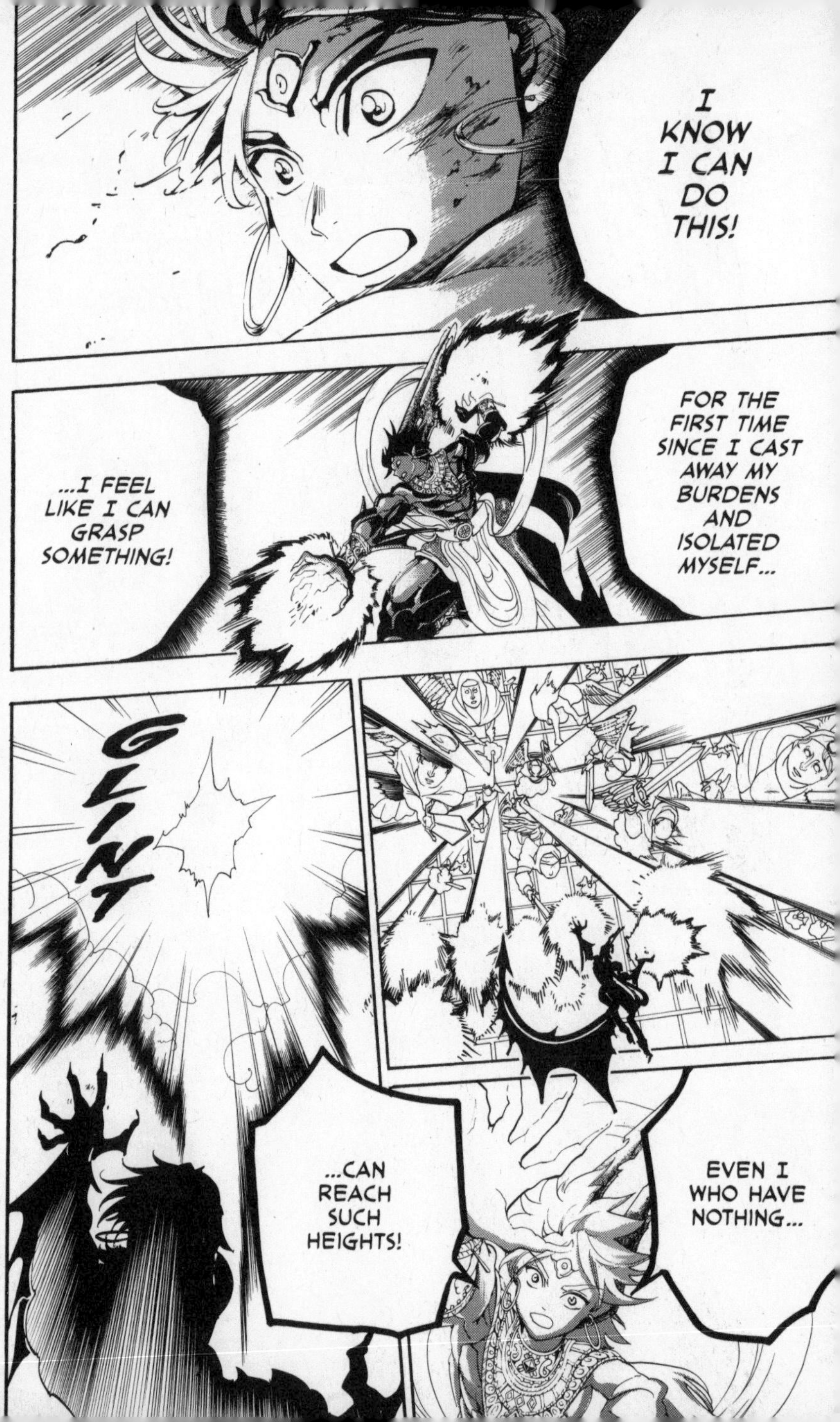
I KNOW I CAN DO THIS!
FOR THE FIRST TIME SINCE I CAST AWAY MY BURDENS AND ISOLATED MYSELF...
...I FEEL LIKE I CAN GRASP SOMETHING!
GLINT
EVEN I WHO HAVE NOTHING...
...CAN REACH SUCH HEIGHTS!

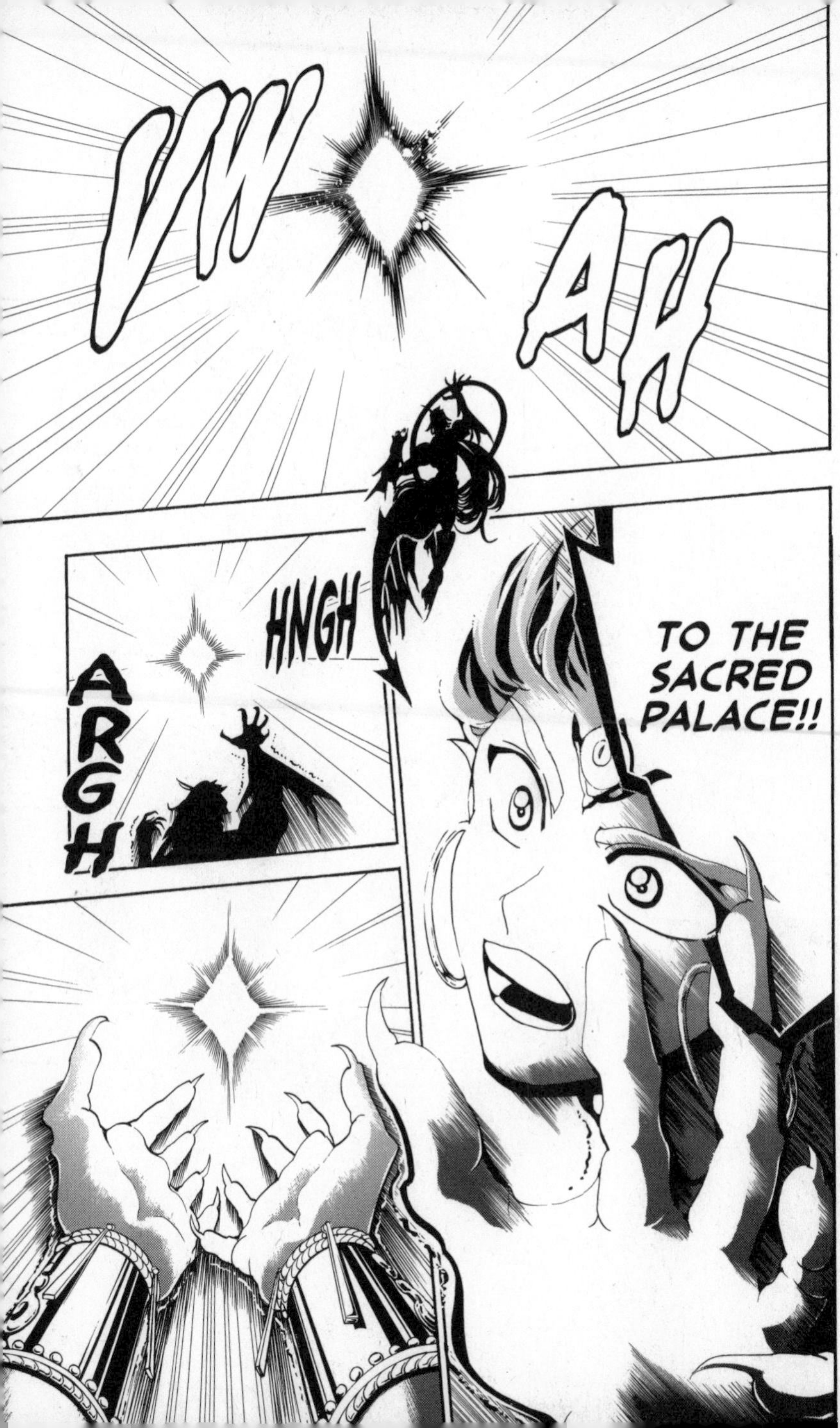
UW
AH
TO THE SACRED PALACE!!
HNGH
ARGH

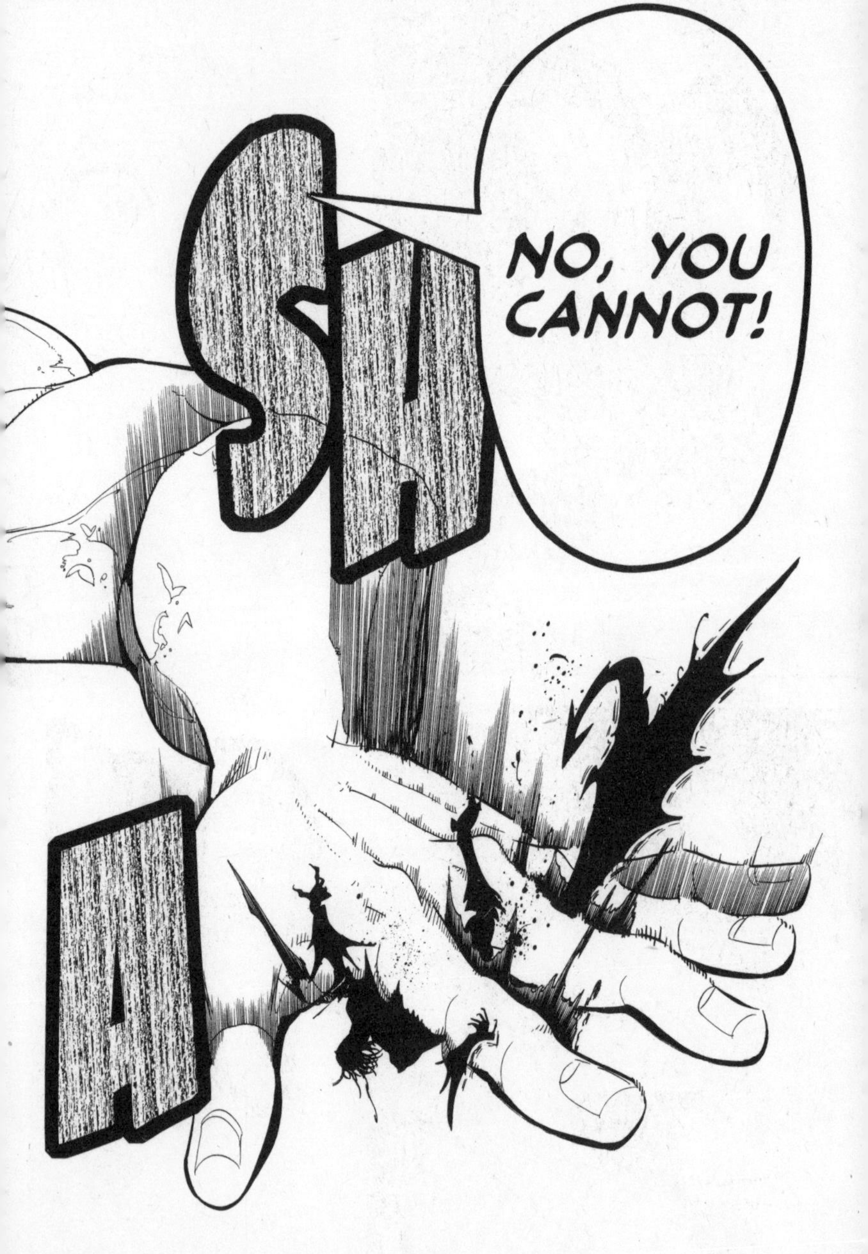
NO, YOU CANNOT!
SHA

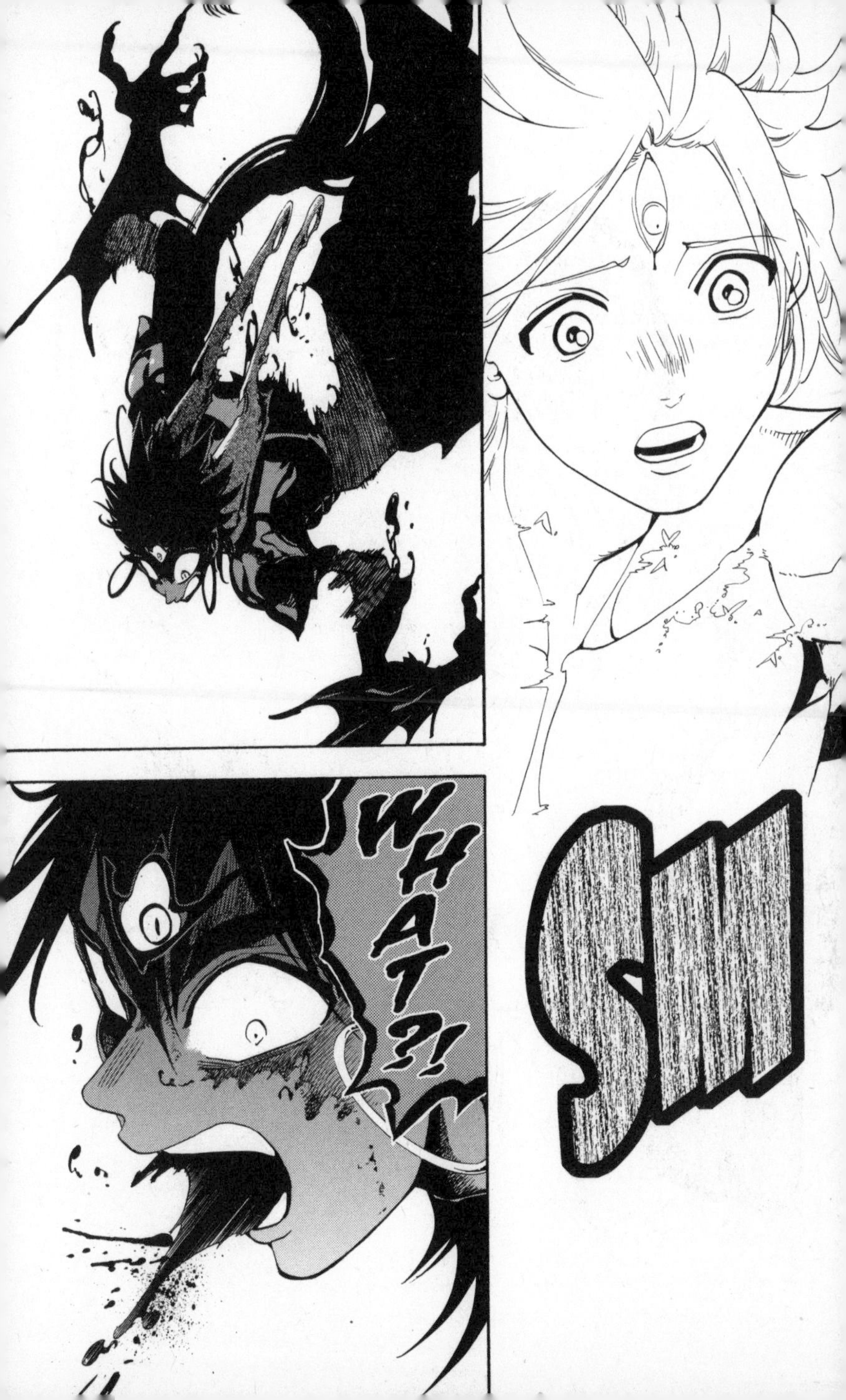
SHN
WHAT?!

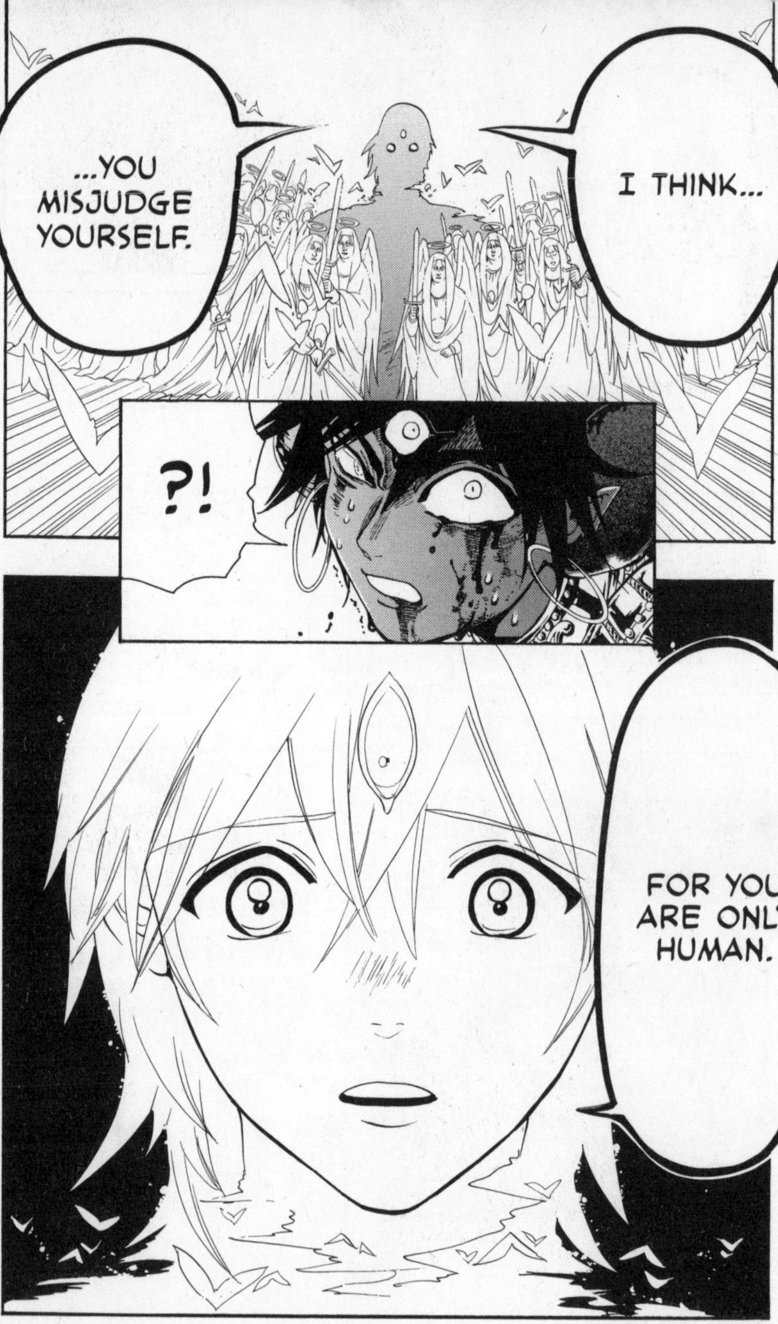
I THINK...
...YOU MISJUDGE YOURSELF.
?!
FOR YOU ARE ONLY HUMAN.

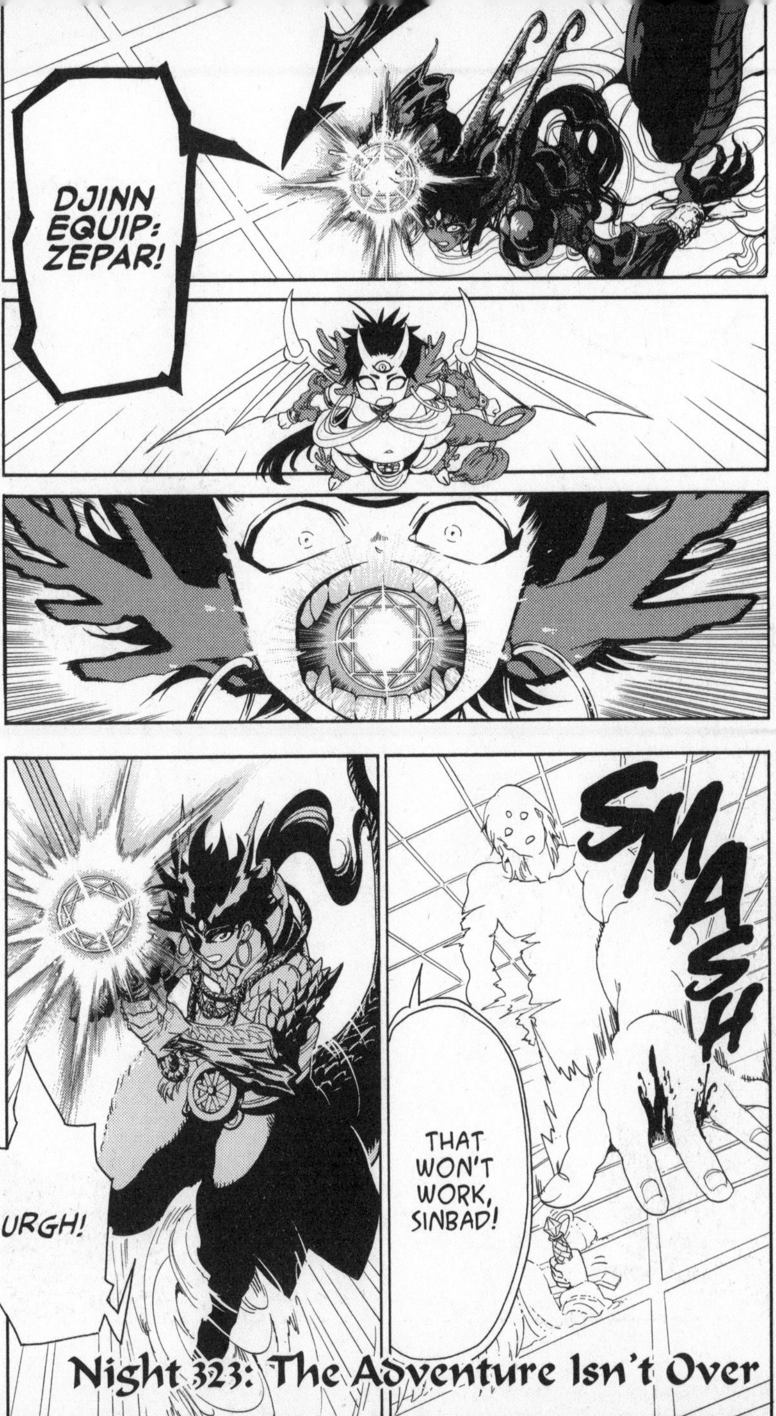
DJINN EQUIP: ZEPAR!
SMASH
THAT WON'T WORK, SINBAD!
URGH!

Night 323: The Adventure Isn't Over

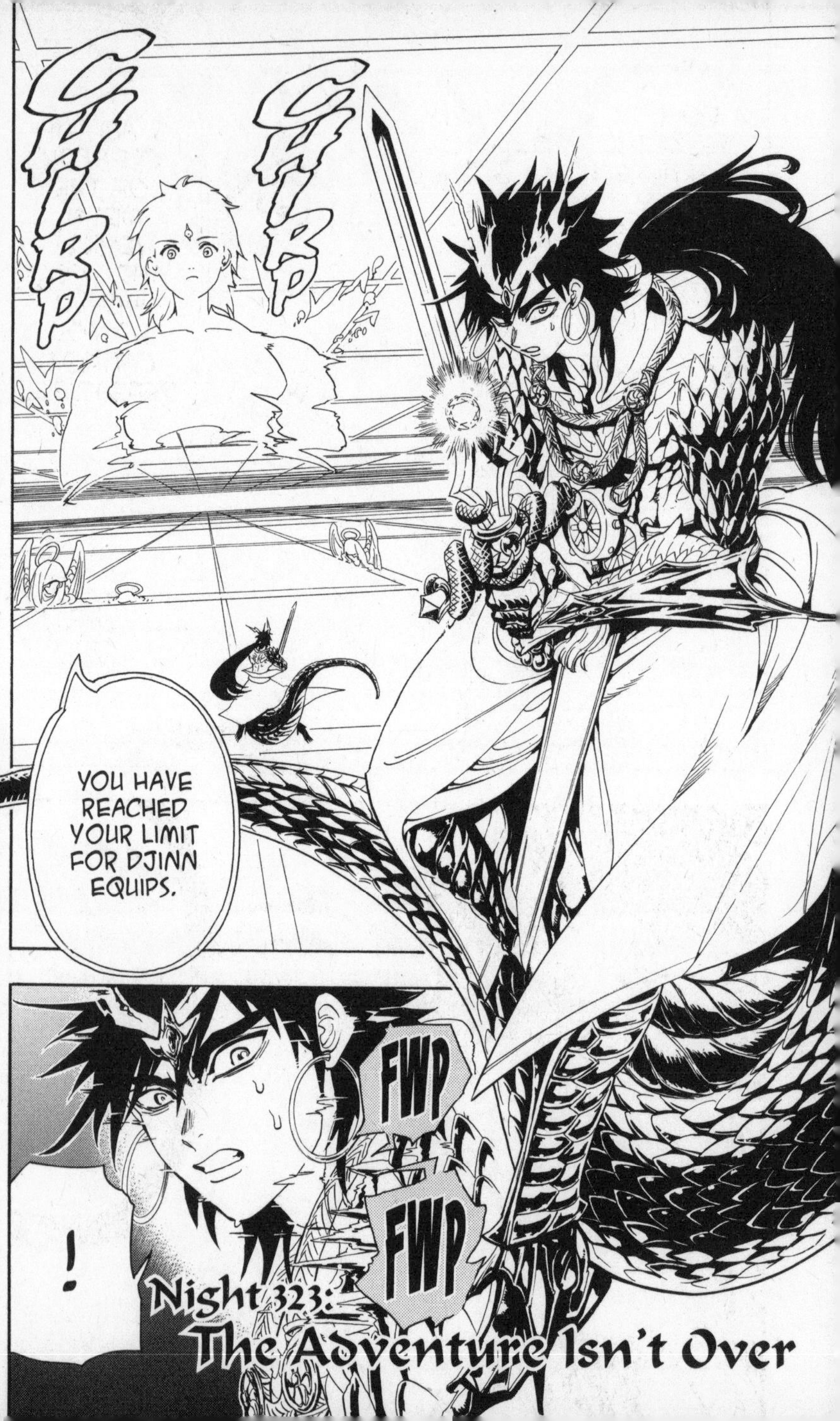
GHBP
GHBP
YOU HAVE REACHED YOUR LIMIT FOR DJINN EQUIPS.
FWP
FWP
!
Night 323:
The Adventure Isn't Over

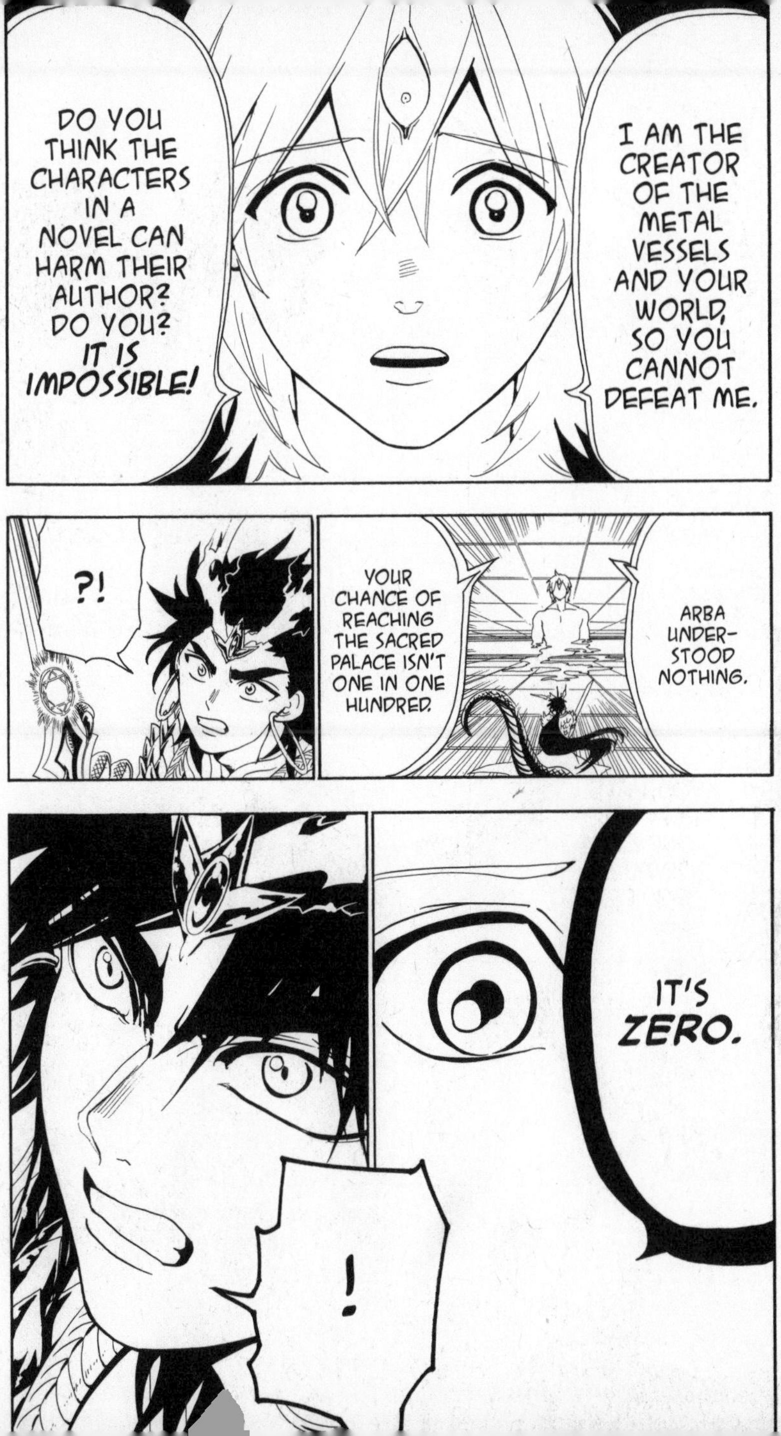

I AM THE CREATOR OF THE METAL VESSELS AND YOUR WORLD, SO YOU CANNOT DEFEAT ME.
DO YOU THINK THE CHARACTERS IN A NOVEL CAN HARM THEIR AUTHOR? DO YOU? IT IS IMPOSSIBLE!
ARBA UNDER-STOOD NOTHING.
YOUR CHANCE OF REACHING THE SACRED PALACE ISN'T ONE IN ONE HUNDRED.
?!
IT'S ZERO.
!

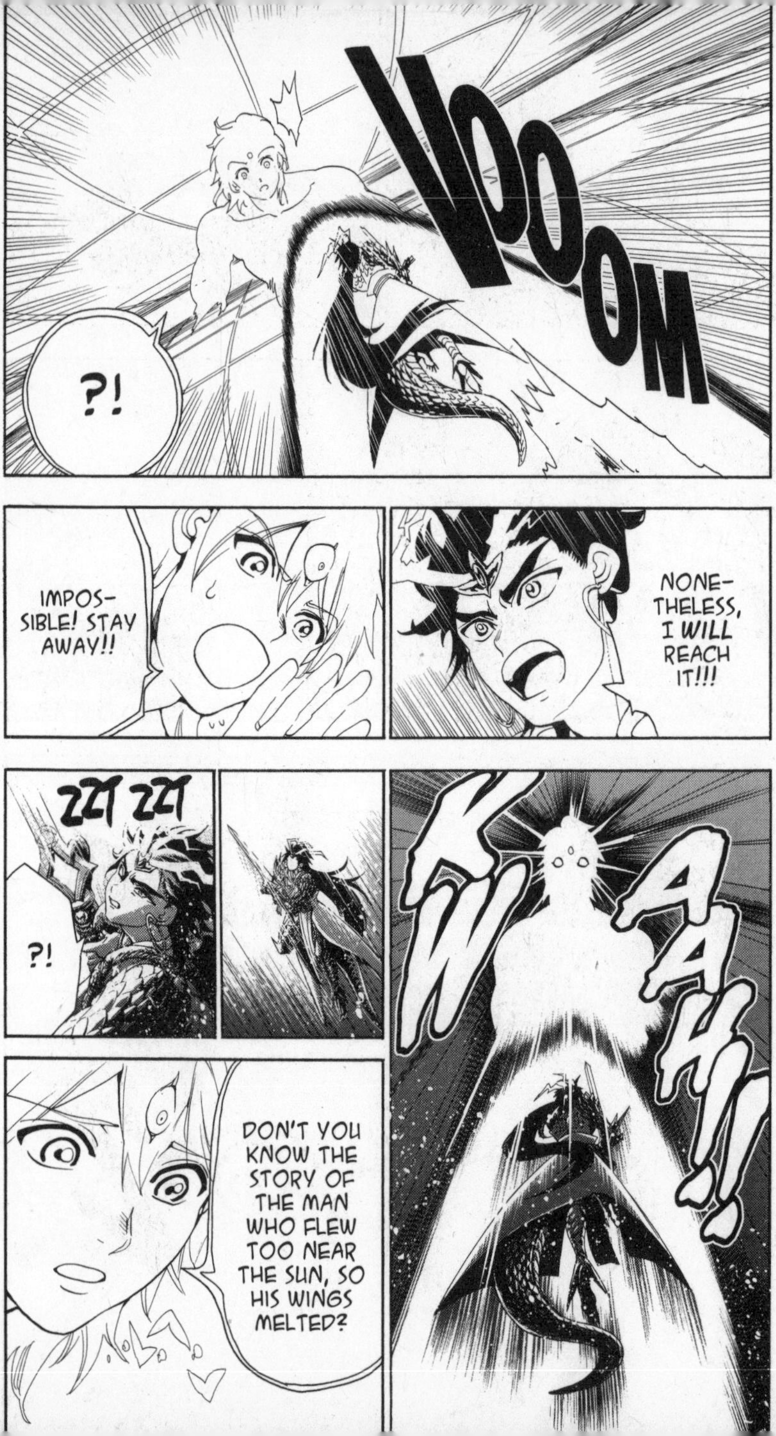
VOOOM
?!
NONE-THELESS, I WILL REACH IT!!!
IMPOS-SIBLE! STAY AWAY!!
WAAH!!
ZZT ZZT
?!
DON'T YOU KNOW THE STORY OF THE MAN WHO FLEW TOO NEAR THE SUN, SO HIS WINGS MELTED?

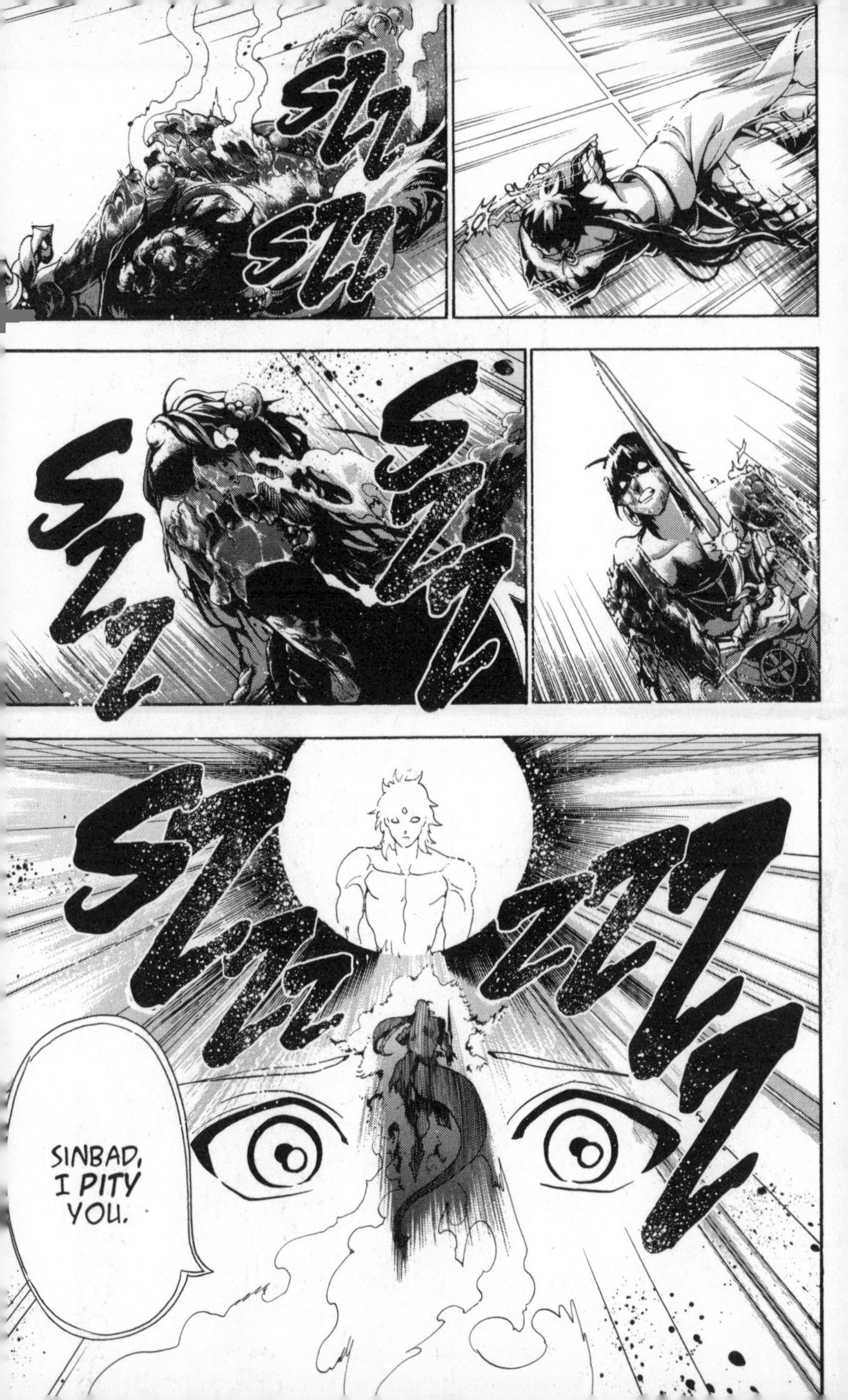
SINBAD, I PITY YOU.

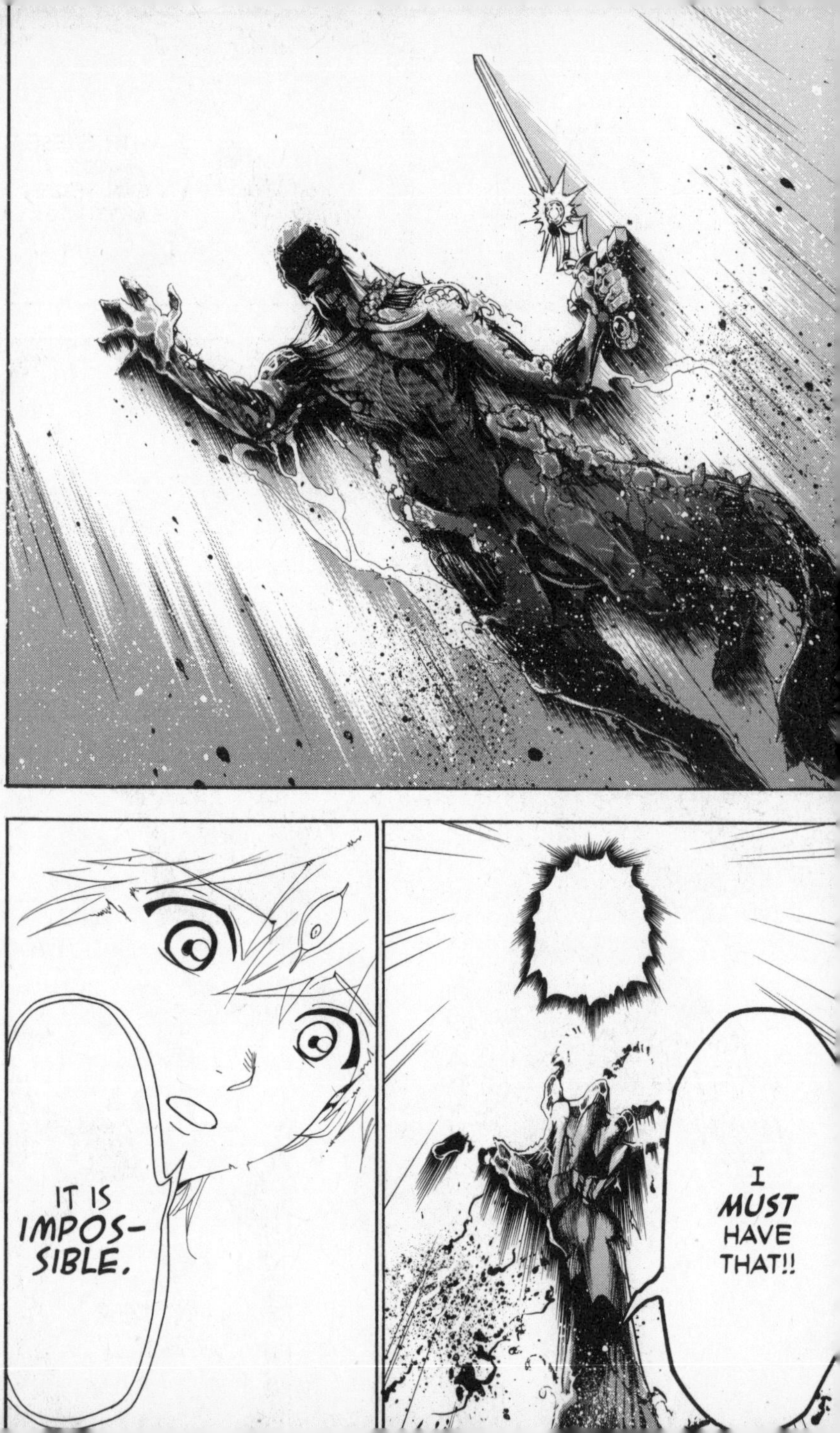
I MUST HAVE THAT!!
IT IS IMPOSSIBLE.

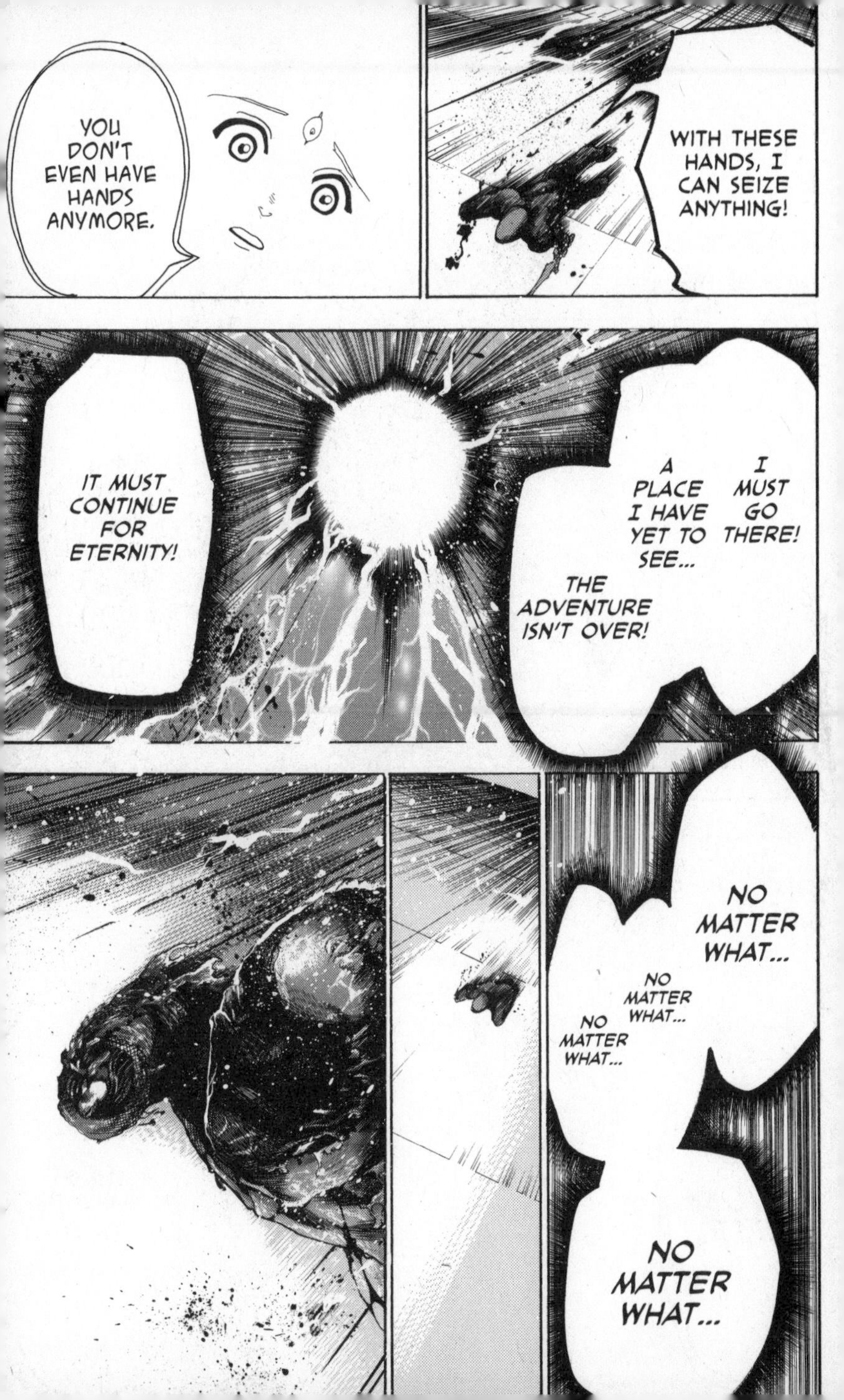
WITH THESE HANDS, I CAN SEIZE ANYTHING!
YOU DON'T EVEN HAVE HANDS ANYMORE.
I MUST GO THERE!
A PLACE I HAVE YET TO SEE...
THE ADVENTURE ISN'T OVER!
IT MUST CONTINUE FOR ETERNITY!
NO MATTER WHAT...
NO MATTER WHAT...
NO MATTER WHAT...
NO MATTER WHAT...

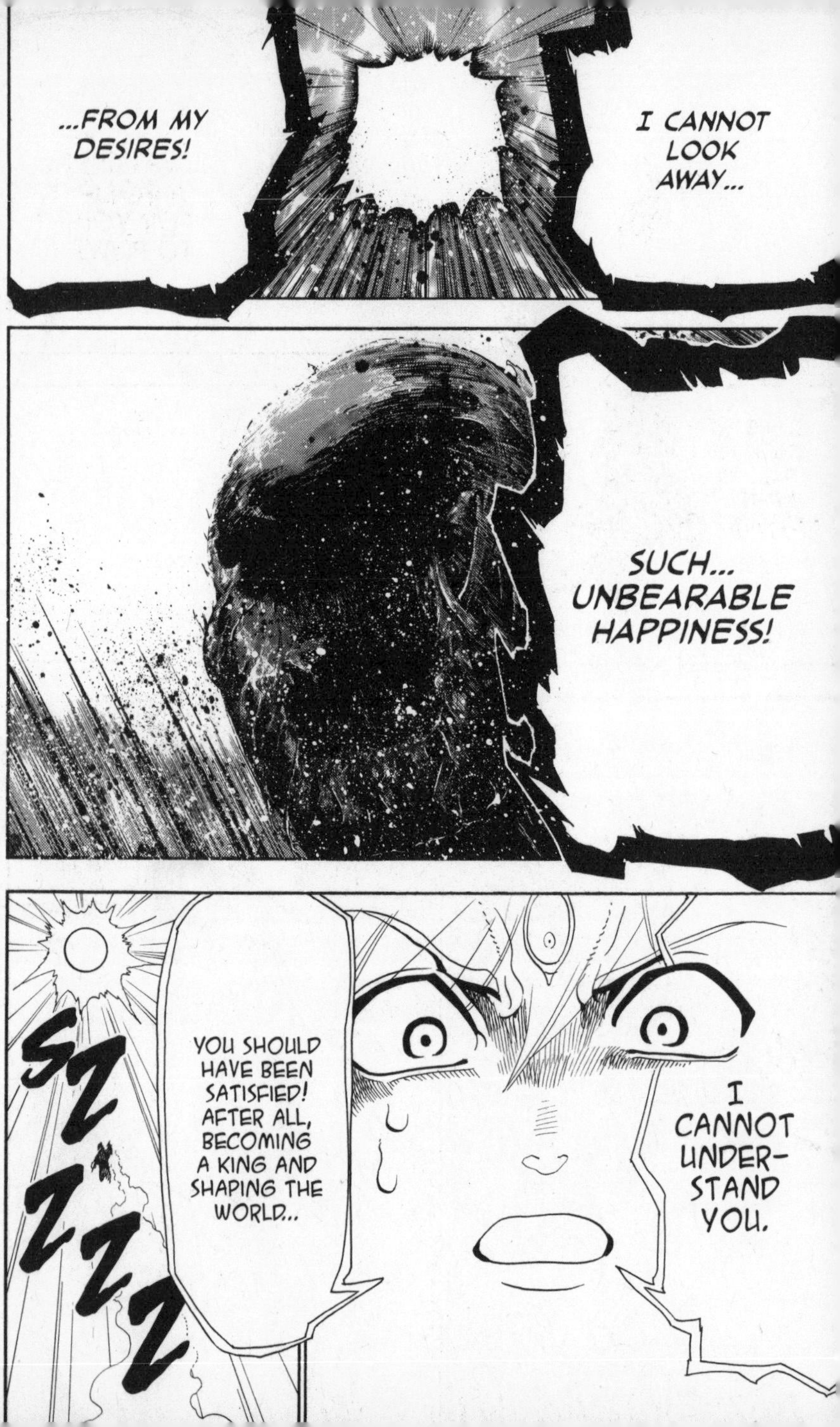
I CANNOT LOOK AWAY...
...FROM MY DESIRES!
SUCH... UNBEARABLE HAPPINESS!
I CANNOT UNDER-STAND YOU.
YOU SHOULD HAVE BEEN SATISFIED! AFTER ALL, BECOMING A KING AND SHAPING THE WORLD...
SZZZZ

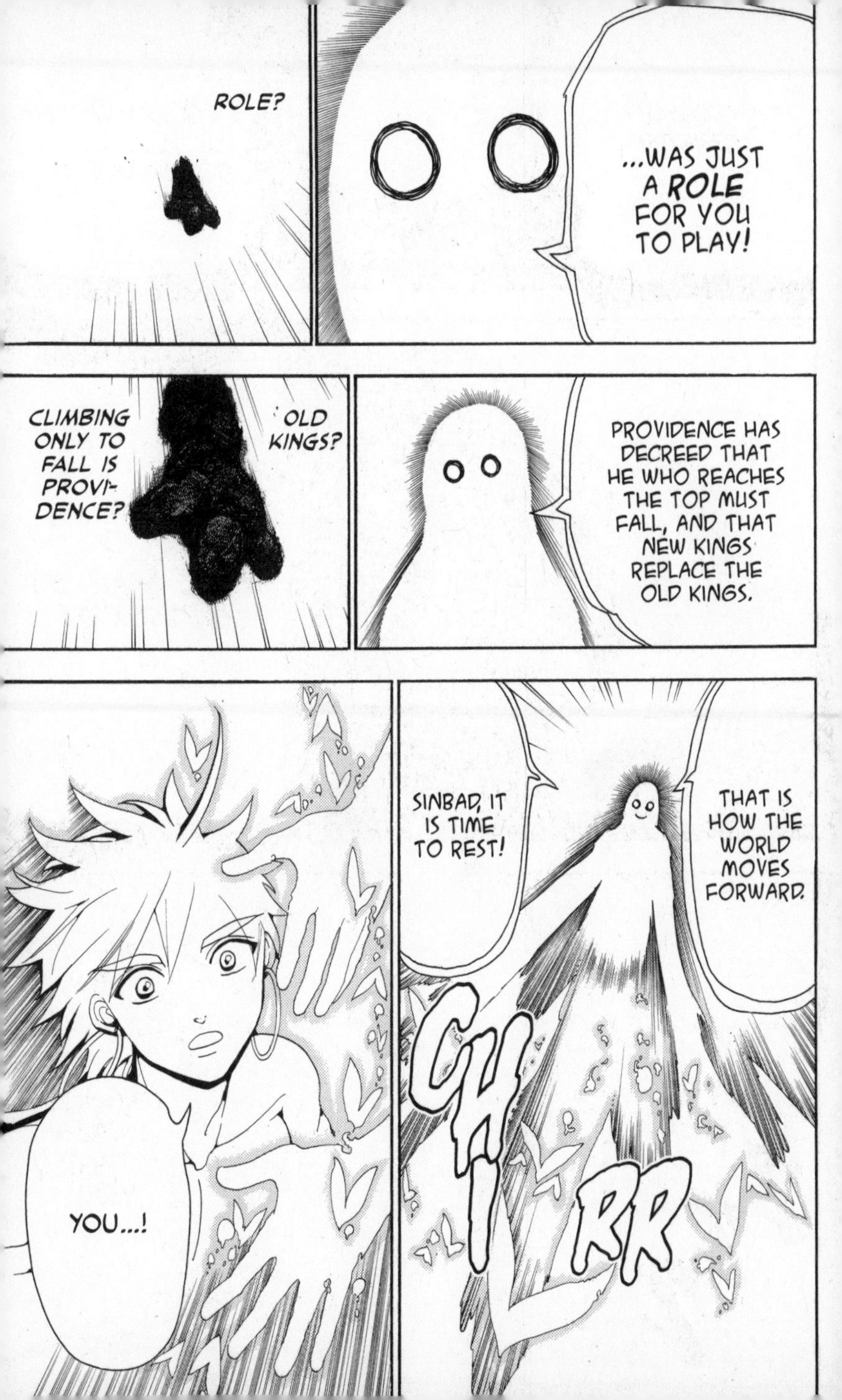
...WAS JUST A ROLE FOR YOU TO PLAY!
ROLE?
PROVIDENCE HAS DECREED THAT HE WHO REACHES THE TOP MUST FALL, AND THAT NEW KINGS REPLACE THE OLD KINGS.
OLD KINGS?
CLIMBING ONLY TO FALL IS PROVI-DENCE?
THAT IS HOW THE WORLD MOVES FORWARD.
SINBAD, IT IS TIME TO REST!
CHIRR
YOU...!

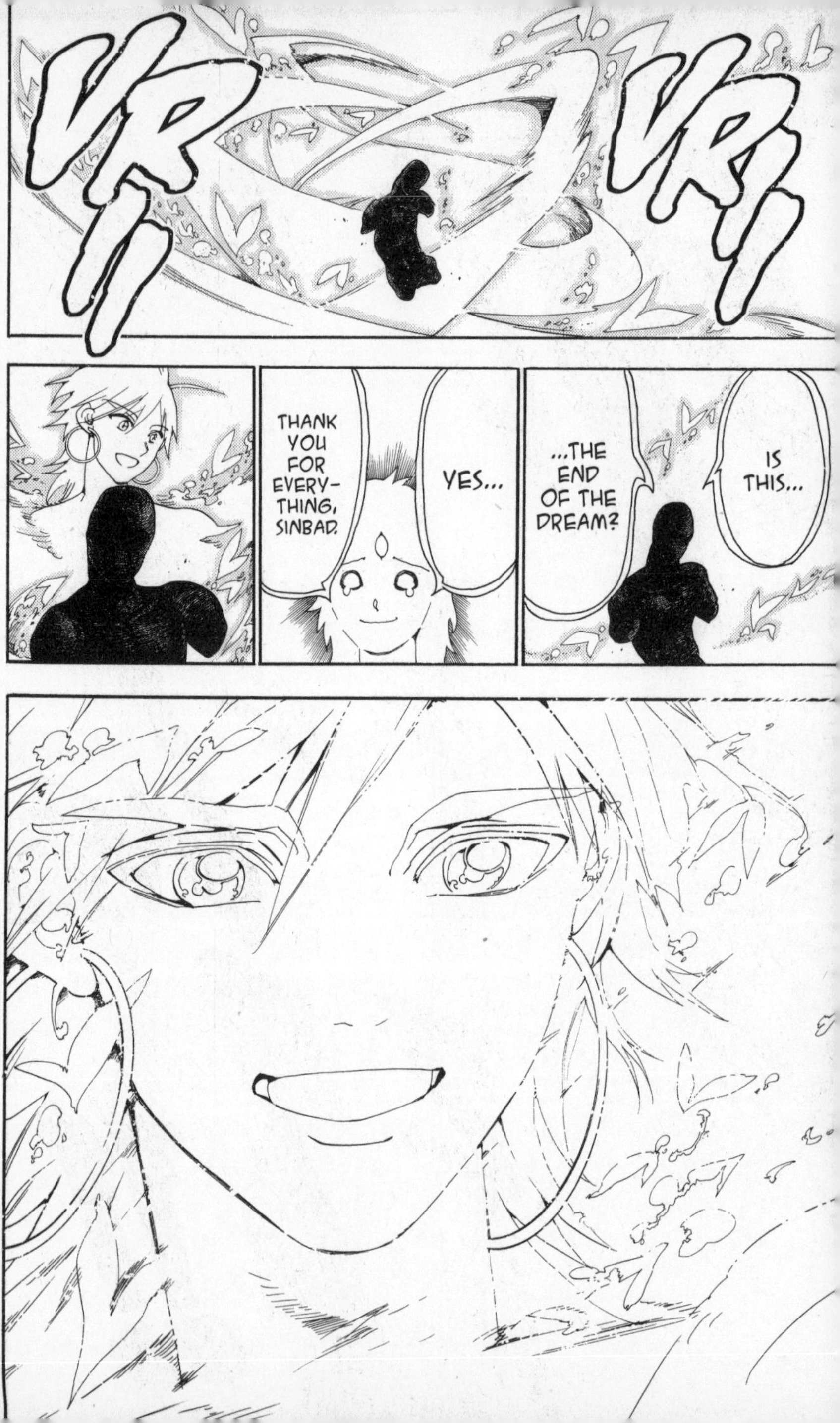
IS THIS...
...THE END OF THE DREAM?
YES...
THANK YOU FOR EVERYTHING, SINBAD.

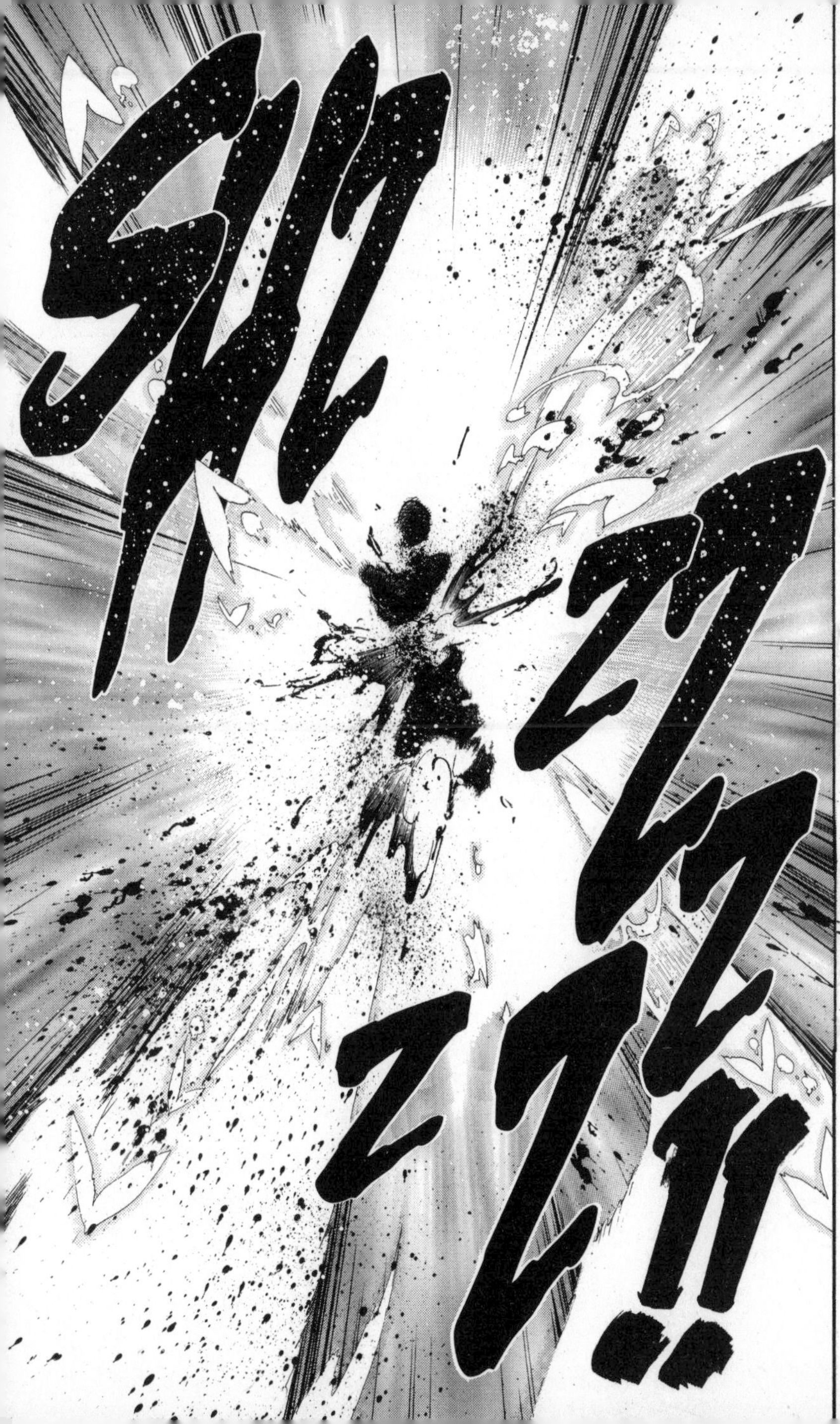

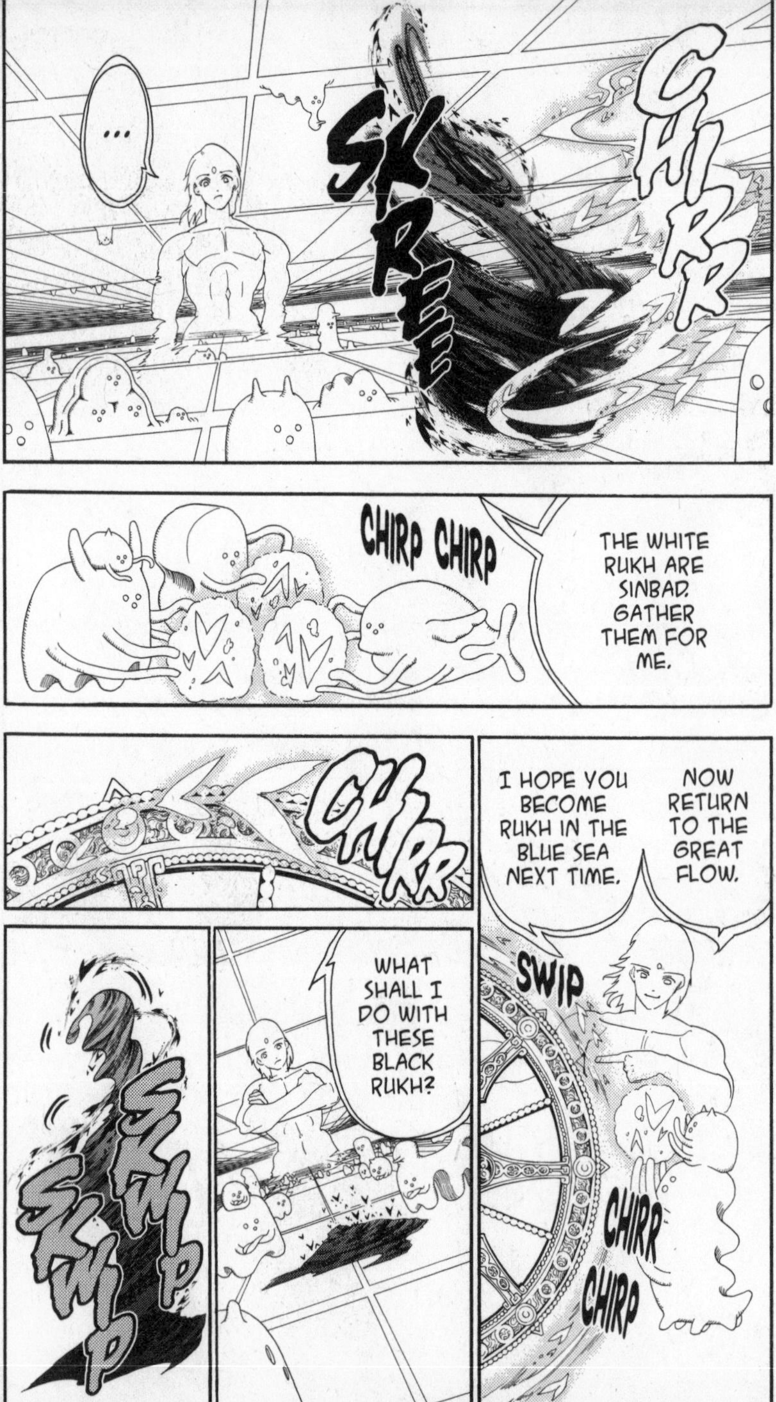
CHIRR
SKREE
...
THE WHITE RUKH ARE SINBAD. GATHER THEM FOR ME.
CHIRP CHIRP
NOW RETURN TO THE GREAT FLOW.
I HOPE YOU BECOME RUKH IN THE BLUE SEA NEXT TIME.
SWIP
CHIRR
CHIRP
CHIRR
WHAT SHALL I DO WITH THESE BLACK RUKH?
SKWIP
SKWIP

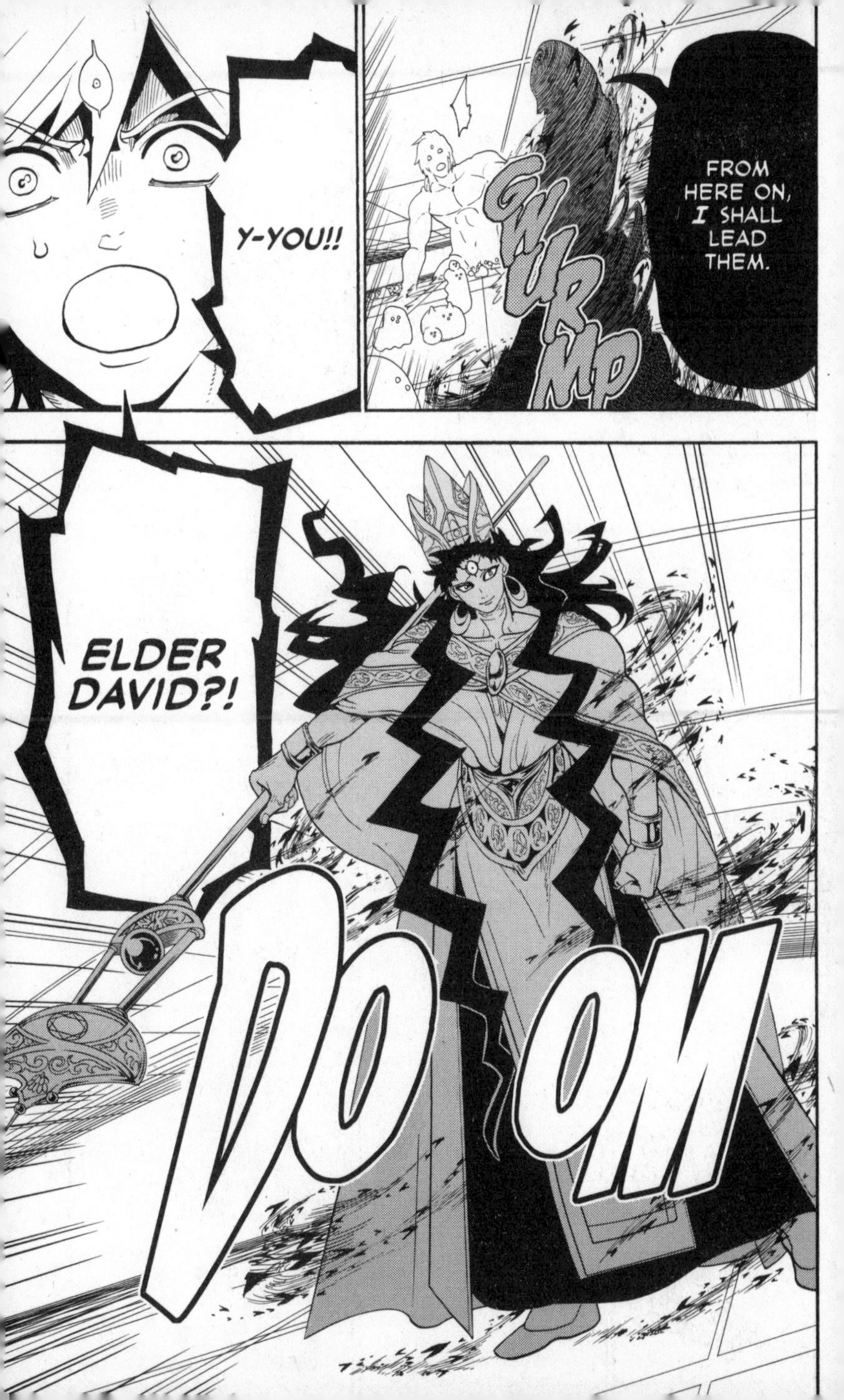
FROM HERE ON, I SHALL LEAD THEM.
GWURMP
Y-YOU!!
ELDER DAVID?!
DOOM

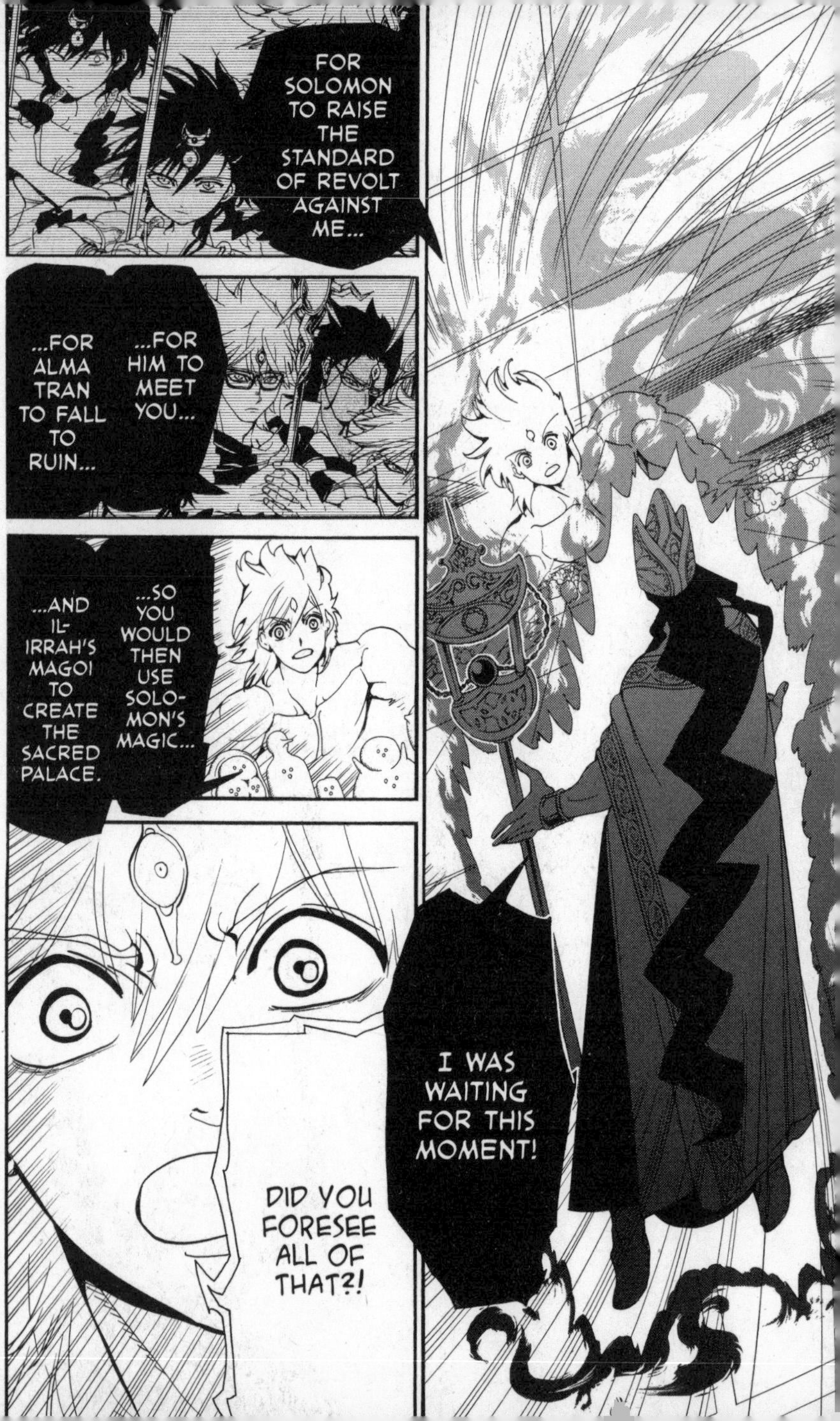
FOR SOLOMON TO RAISE THE STANDARD OF REVOLT AGAINST ME...
...FOR HIM TO MEET YOU...
...FOR ALMA TRAN TO FALL TO RUIN...
...SO YOU WOULD THEN USE SOLO-MON'S MAGIC...
...AND IL-IRRAH'S MAGOI TO CREATE THE SACRED PALACE.
I WAS WAITING FOR THIS MOMENT!
DID YOU FORESEE ALL OF THAT?!

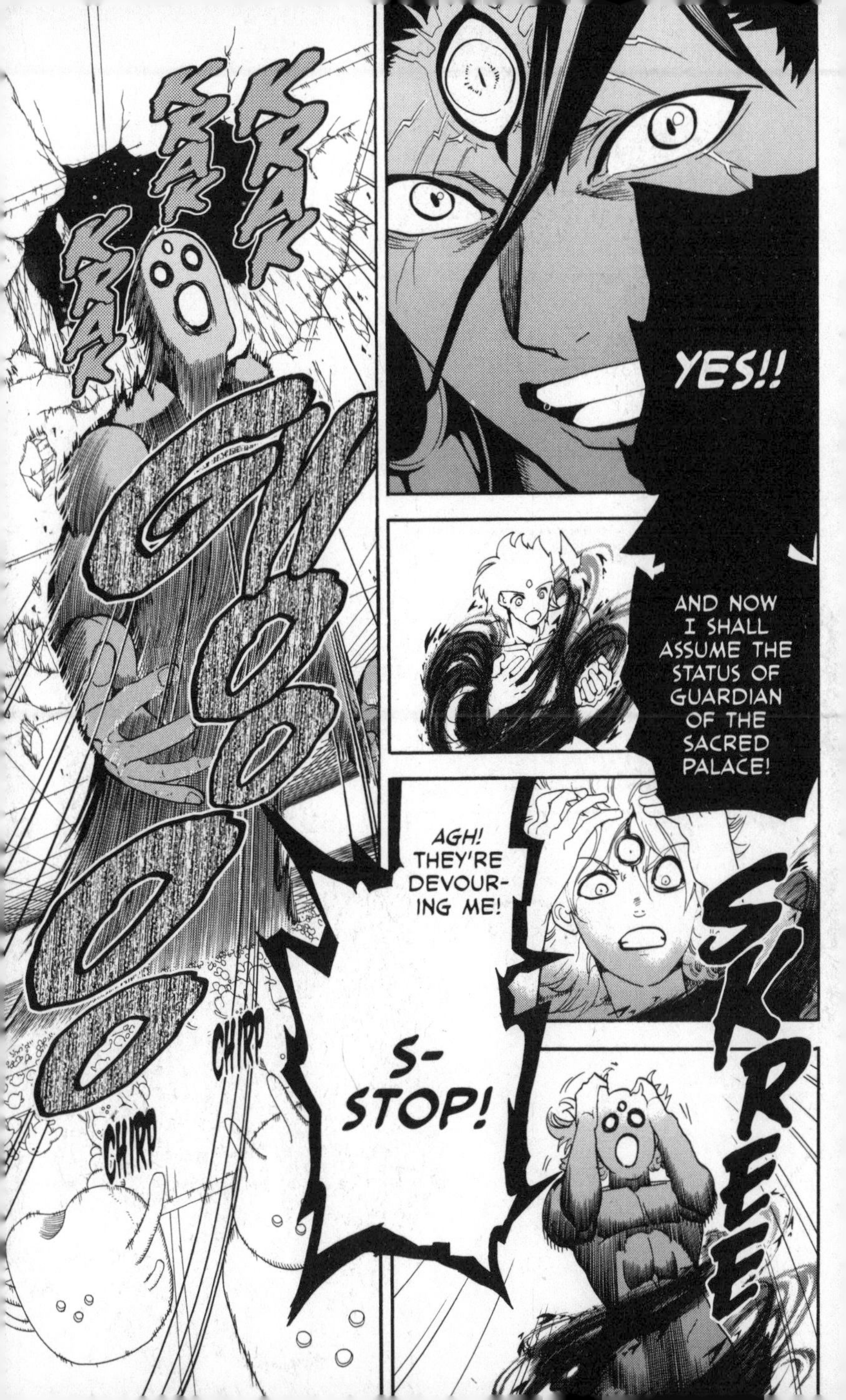
YES!!
AND NOW I SHALL ASSUME THE STATUS OF GUARDIAN OF THE SACRED PALACE!
AGH! THEY'RE DEVOUR-ING ME!
SKREEE
S-STOP!
KRAK KRAK KRAK
CHIRP
CHIRP

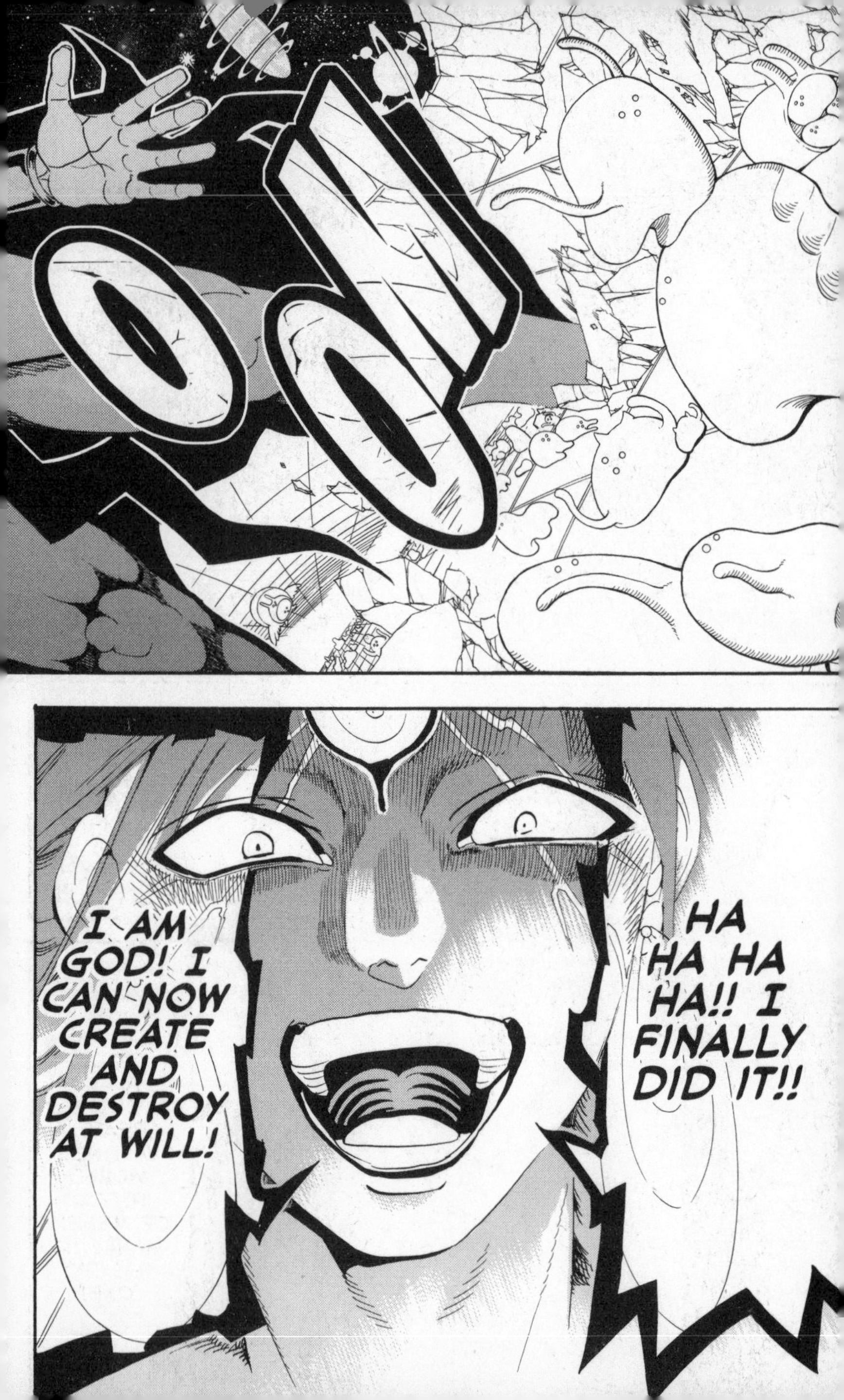
HA HA HA HA!! I FINALLY DID IT!!
I AM GOD! I CAN NOW CREATE AND DESTROY AT WILL!

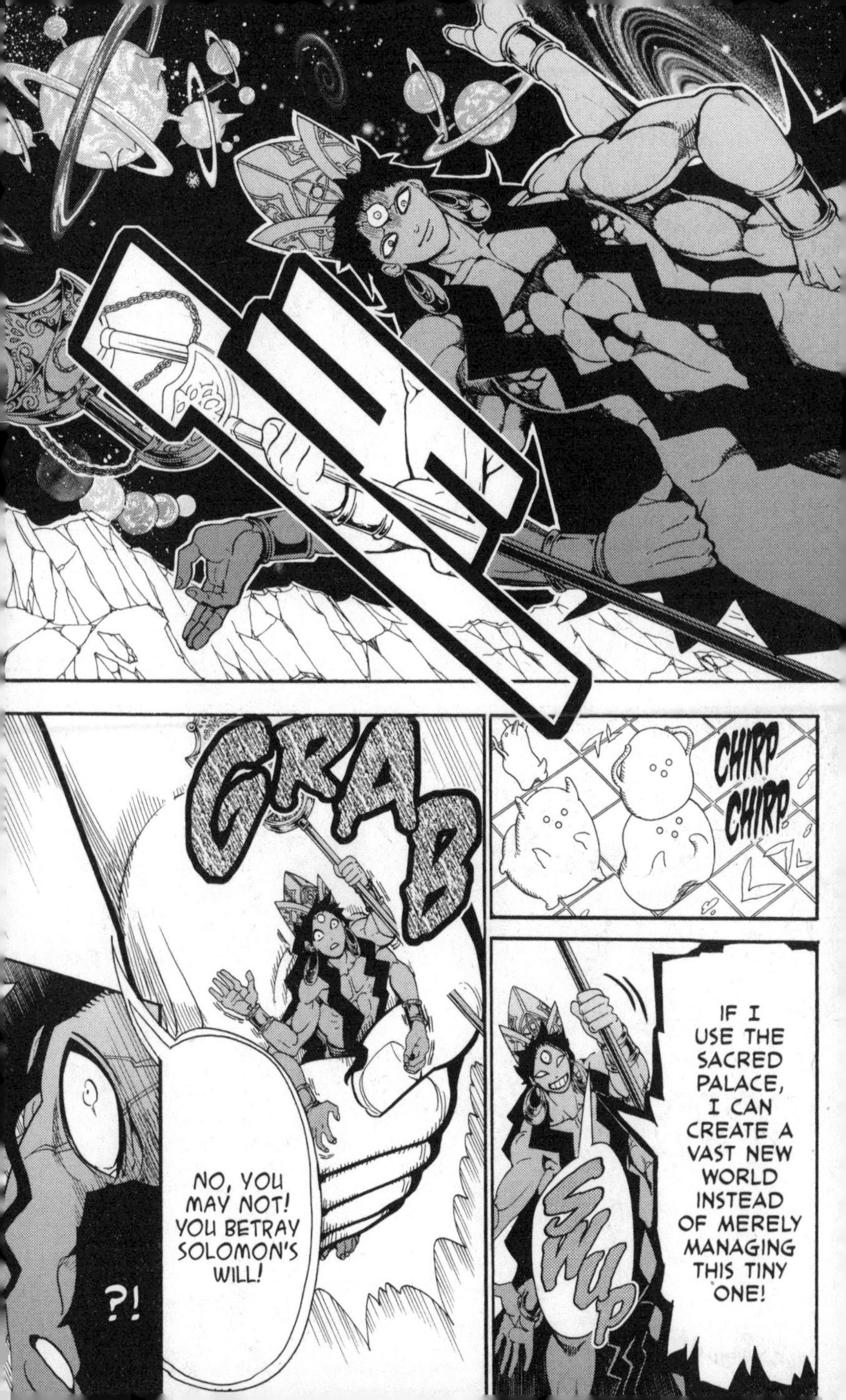
CHIRP CHIRP
IF I USE THE SACRED PALACE, I CAN CREATE A VAST NEW WORLD INSTEAD OF MERELY MANAGING THIS TINY ONE!
SWUP
GRAB
NO, YOU MAY NOT! YOU BETRAY SOLOMON'S WILL!
?!

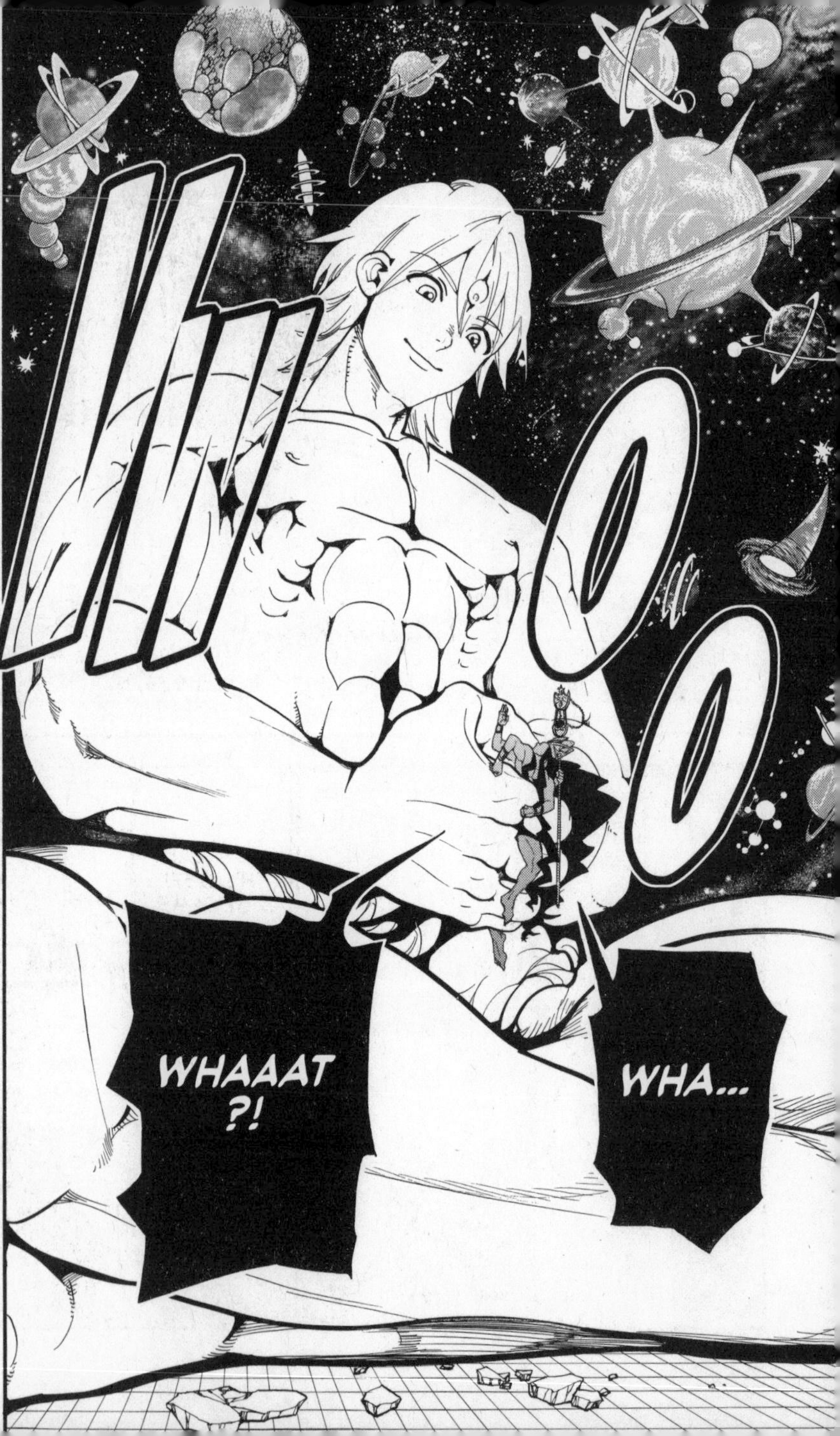
WHA...
WHAAAT ?!

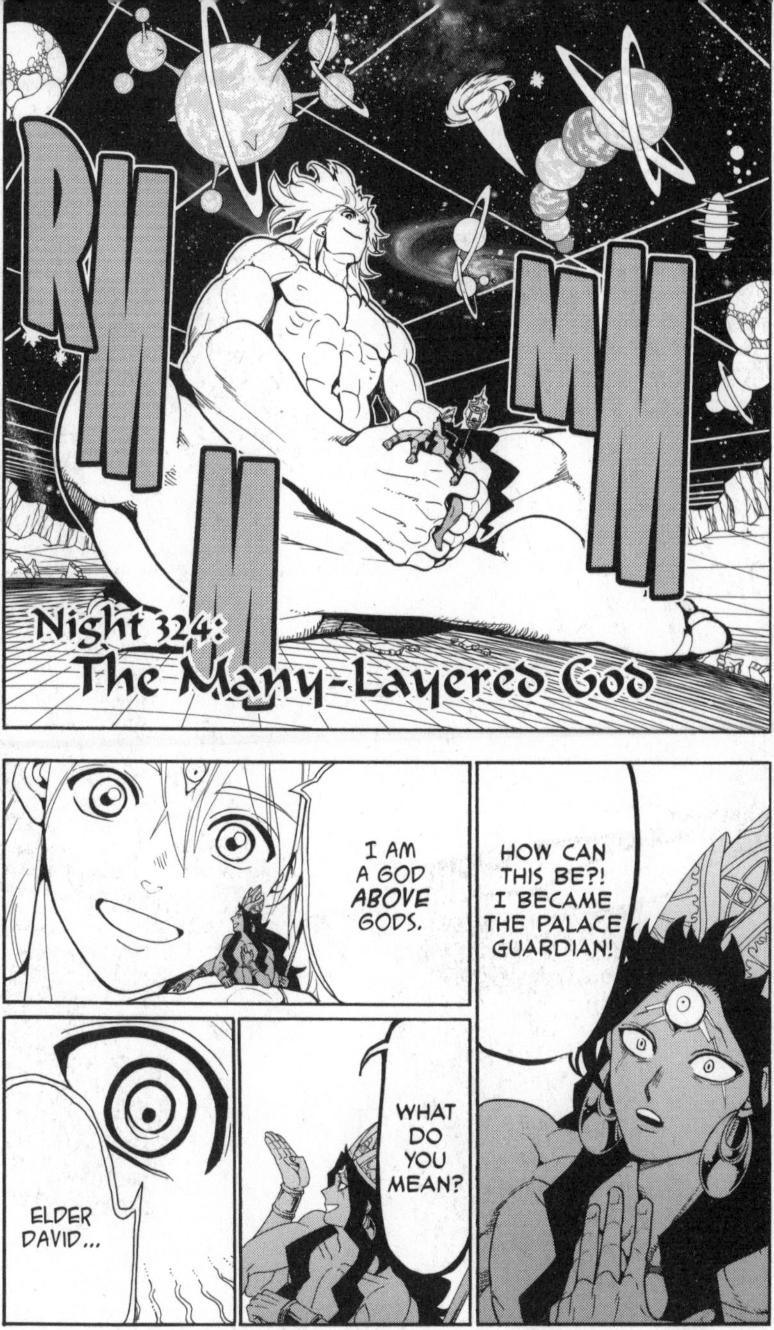

Night 324:
The Many-Layered God
HOW CAN THIS BE?! I BECAME THE PALACE GUARDIAN!
I AM A GOD *ABOVE* GODS.
WHAT DO YOU MEAN?
ELDER DAVID...

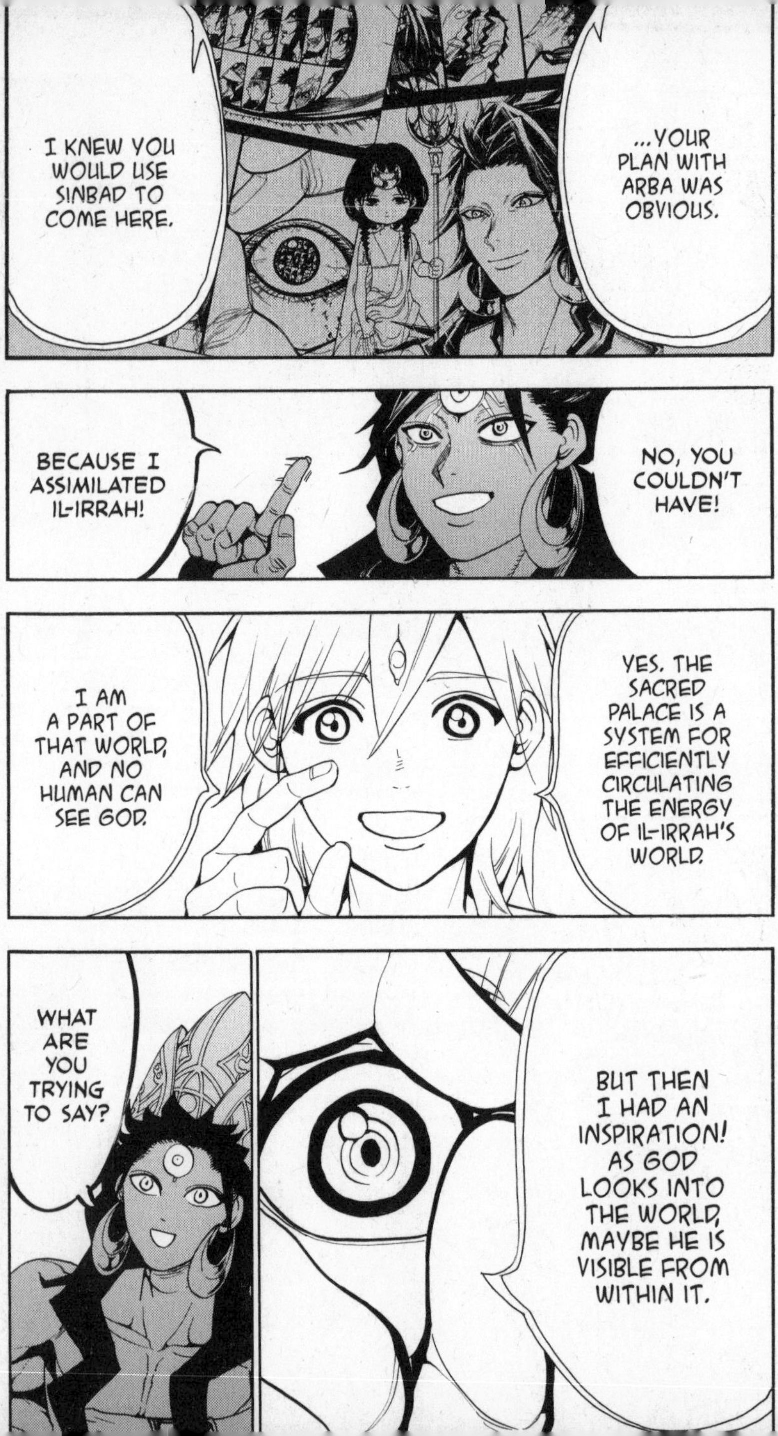
...YOUR PLAN WITH ARBA WAS OBVIOUS.
I KNEW YOU WOULD USE SINBAD TO COME HERE.
NO, YOU COULDN'T HAVE!
BECAUSE I ASSIMILATED IL-IRRAH!
YES. THE SACRED PALACE IS A SYSTEM FOR EFFICIENTLY CIRCULATING THE ENERGY OF IL-IRRAH'S WORLD.
I AM A PART OF THAT WORLD, AND NO HUMAN CAN SEE GOD.
BUT THEN I HAD AN INSPIRATION! AS GOD LOOKS INTO THE WORLD, MAYBE HE IS VISIBLE FROM WITHIN IT.
WHAT ARE YOU TRYING TO SAY?

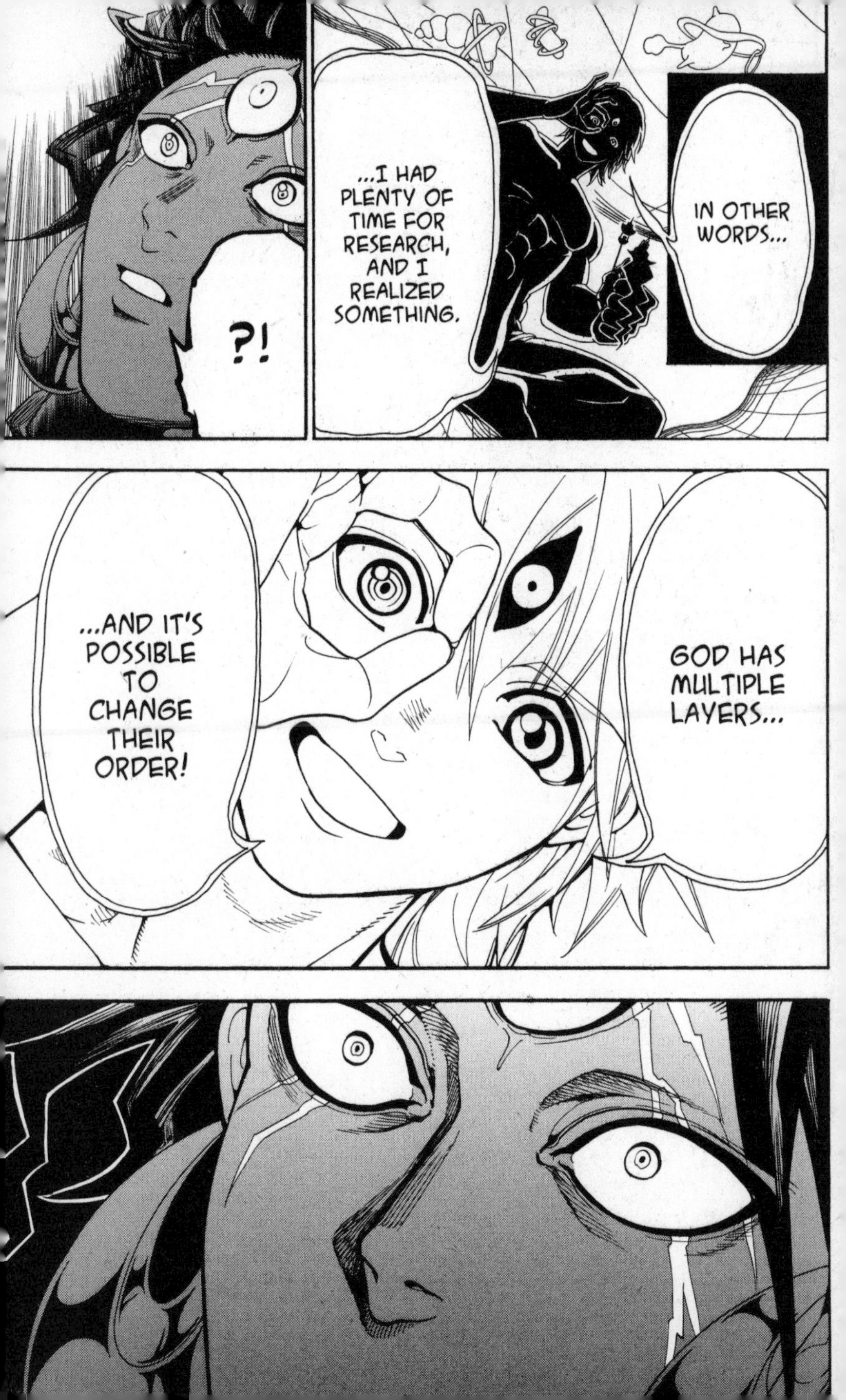
IN OTHER WORDS...
...I HAD PLENTY OF TIME FOR RESEARCH, AND I REALIZED SOMETHING.
?!
GOD HAS MULTIPLE LAYERS...
...AND IT'S POSSIBLE TO CHANGE THEIR ORDER!

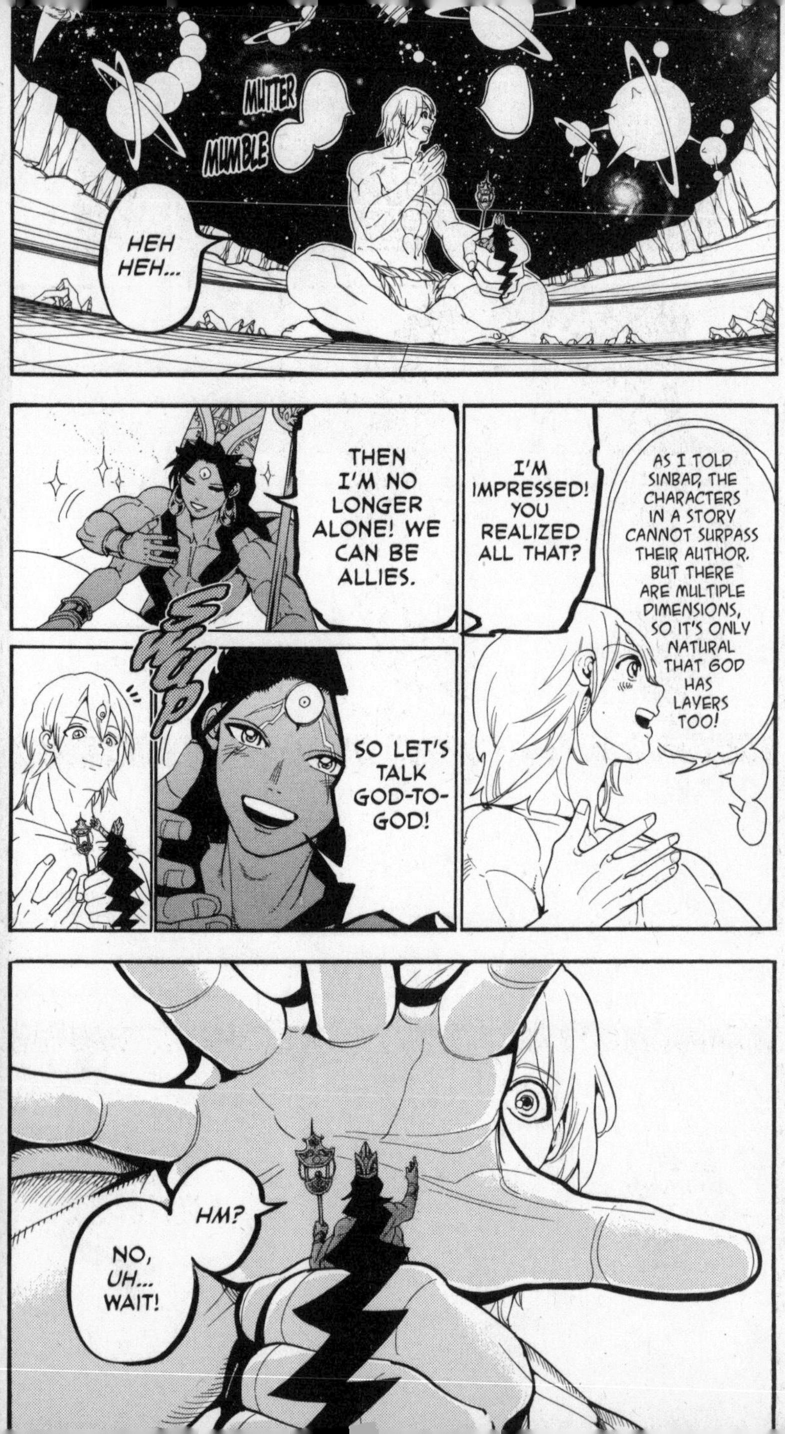
MUTTER
MUMBLE
HEH HEH...
AS I TOLD SINBAD, THE CHARACTERS IN A STORY CANNOT SURPASS THEIR AUTHOR. BUT THERE ARE MULTIPLE DIMENSIONS, SO IT'S ONLY NATURAL THAT GOD HAS LAYERS TOO!
I'M IMPRESSED! YOU REALIZED ALL THAT?
THEN I'M NO LONGER ALONE! WE CAN BE ALLIES.
SHUP
SO LET'S TALK GOD-TO-GOD!
HM?
NO, UH... WAIT!

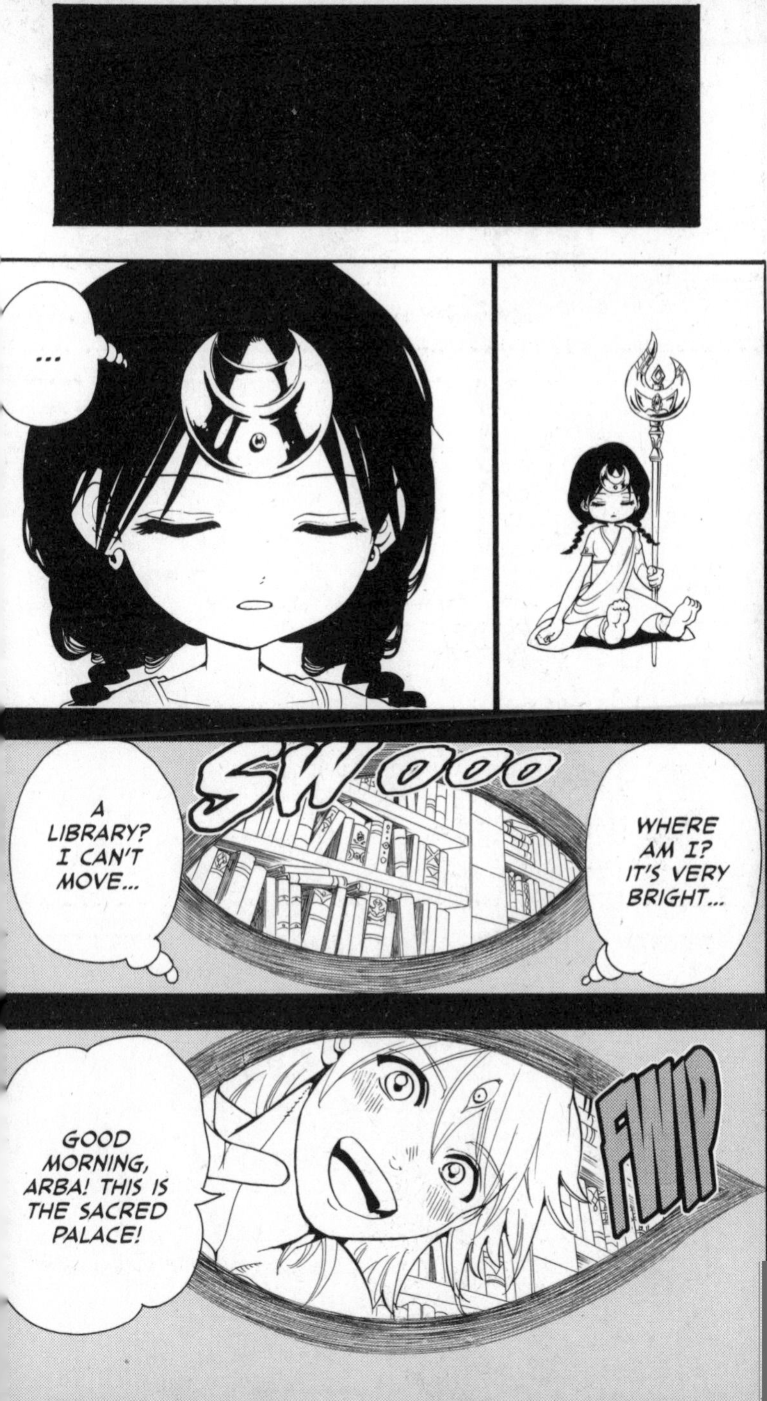
...
WHERE AM I? IT'S VERY BRIGHT...
SWOOO
A LIBRARY? I CAN'T MOVE...
FWIP
GOOD MORNING, ARBA! THIS IS THE SACRED PALACE!

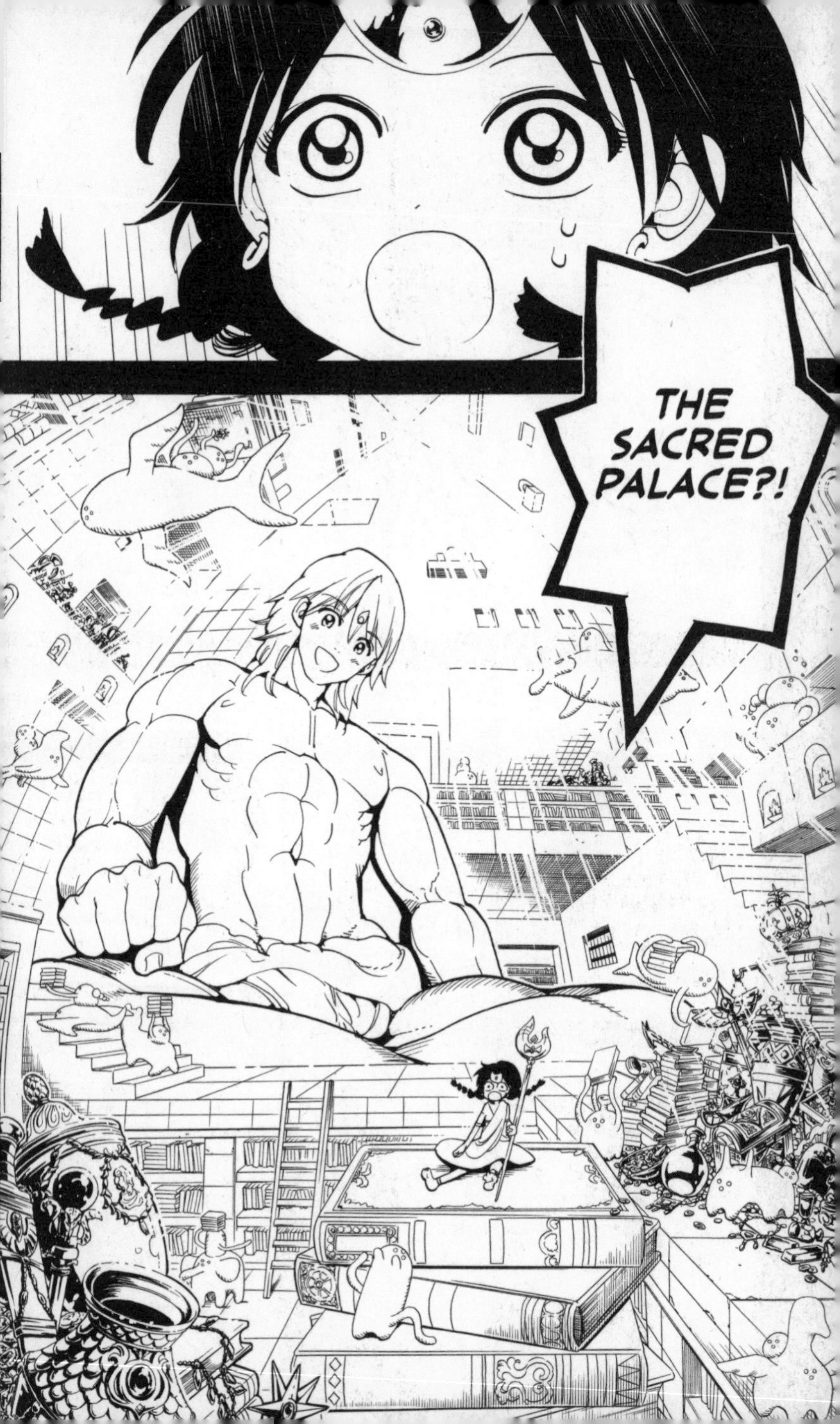
THE SACRED PALACE?!

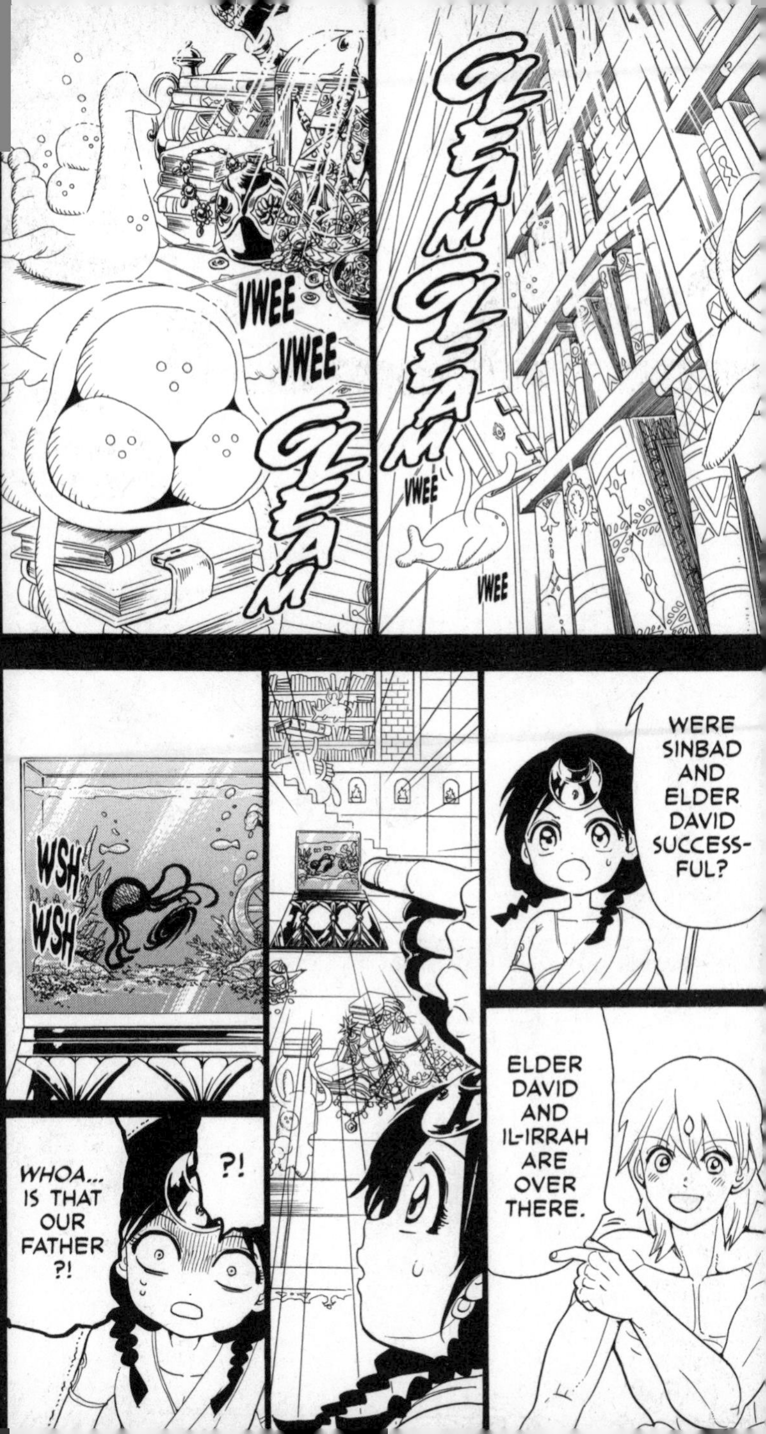
GLEAM
GLEAM
VWEE
VWEE
VWEE
VWEE
GLEAM
WERE SINBAD AND ELDER DAVID SUCCESS-FUL?
ELDER DAVID AND IL-IRRAH ARE OVER THERE.
WSH WSH
?!
WHOA... IS THAT OUR FATHER ?!

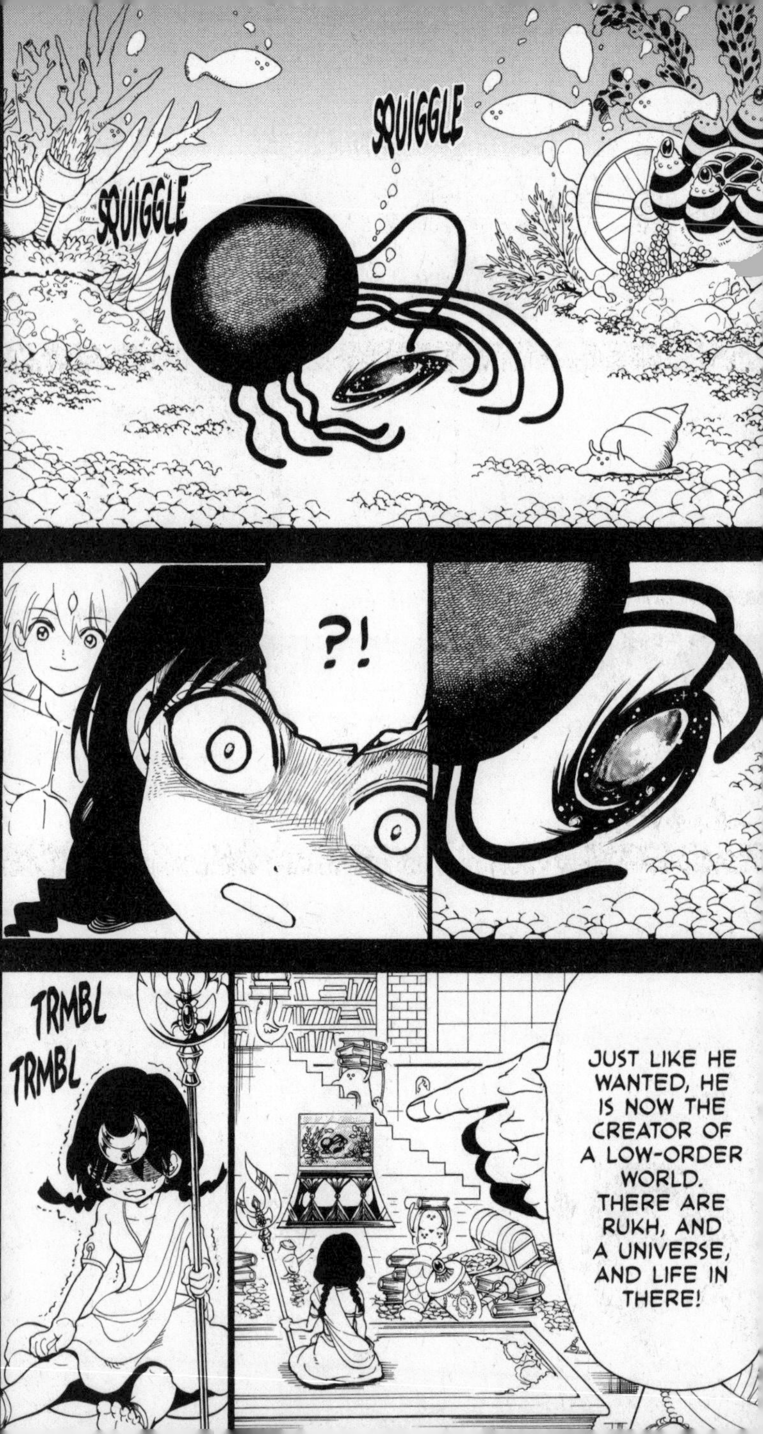
SQUIGGLE
SQUIGGLE
?!
JUST LIKE HE WANTED, HE IS NOW THE CREATOR OF A LOW-ORDER WORLD. THERE ARE RUKH, AND A UNIVERSE, AND LIFE IN THERE!
TRMBL
TRMBL

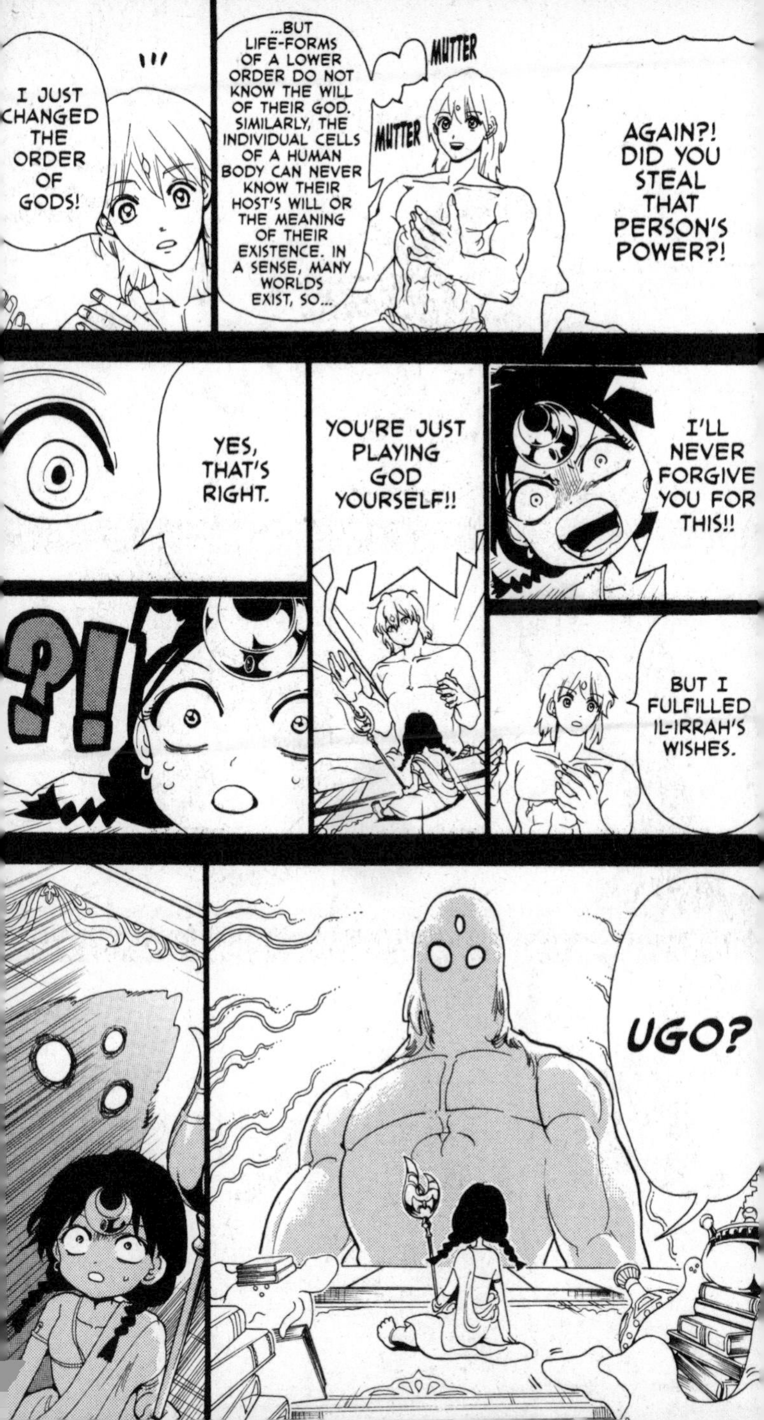
AGAIN?! DID YOU STEAL THAT PERSON'S POWER?!
MUTTER
MUTTER
...BUT LIFE-FORMS OF A LOWER ORDER DO NOT KNOW THE WILL OF THEIR GOD. SIMILARLY, THE INDIVIDUAL CELLS OF A HUMAN BODY CAN NEVER KNOW THEIR HOST'S WILL OR THE MEANING OF THEIR EXISTENCE. IN A SENSE, MANY WORLDS EXIST, SO...
I JUST CHANGED THE ORDER OF GODS!
I'LL NEVER FORGIVE YOU FOR THIS!!
YOU'RE JUST PLAYING GOD YOURSELF!!
YES, THAT'S RIGHT.
BUT I FULFILLED IL-IRRAH'S WISHES.
?!
UGO?

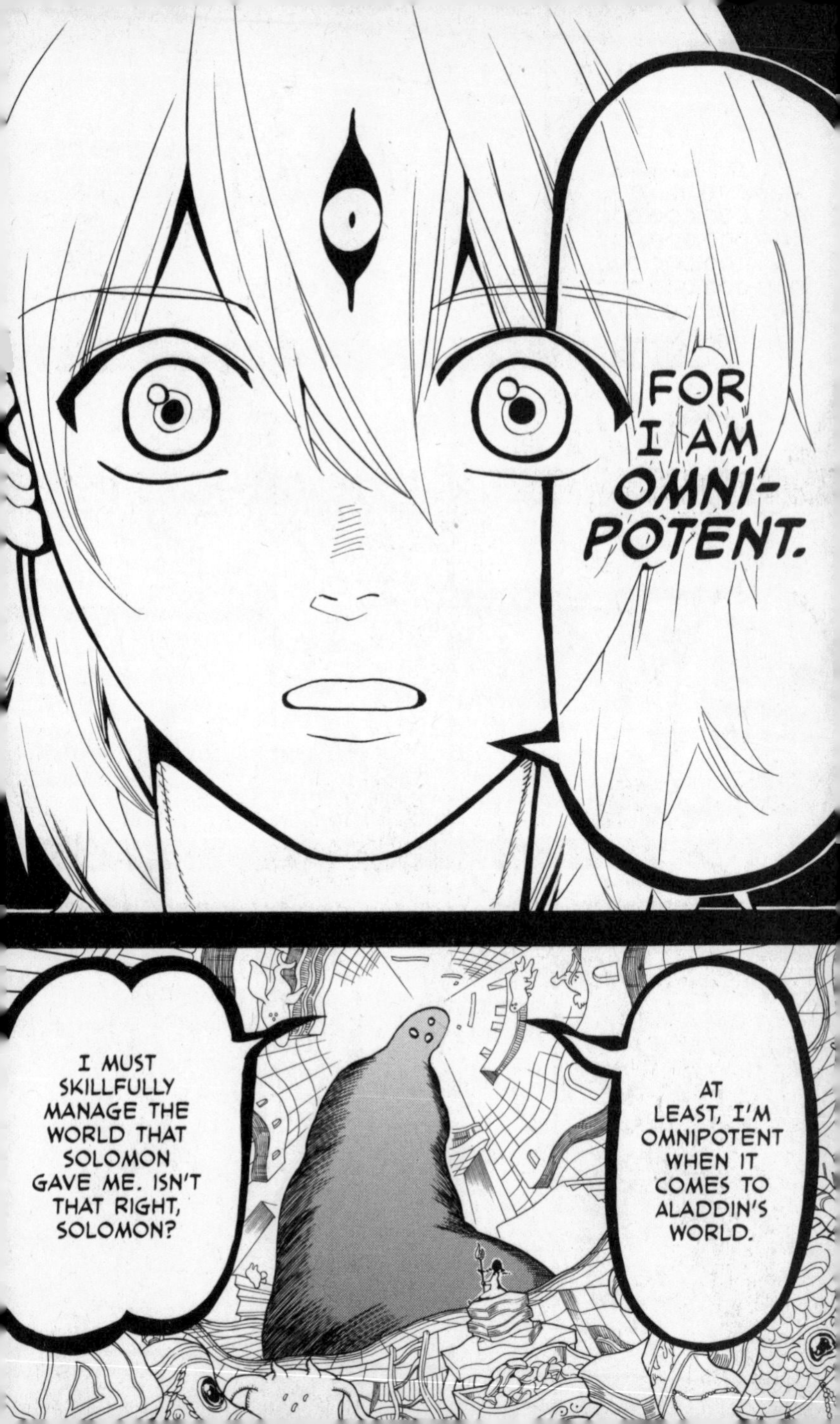
FOR I AM OMNI-POTENT.
AT LEAST, I'M OMNIPOTENT WHEN IT COMES TO ALADDIN'S WORLD.
I MUST SKILLFULLY MANAGE THE WORLD THAT SOLOMON GAVE ME. ISN'T THAT RIGHT, SOLOMON?

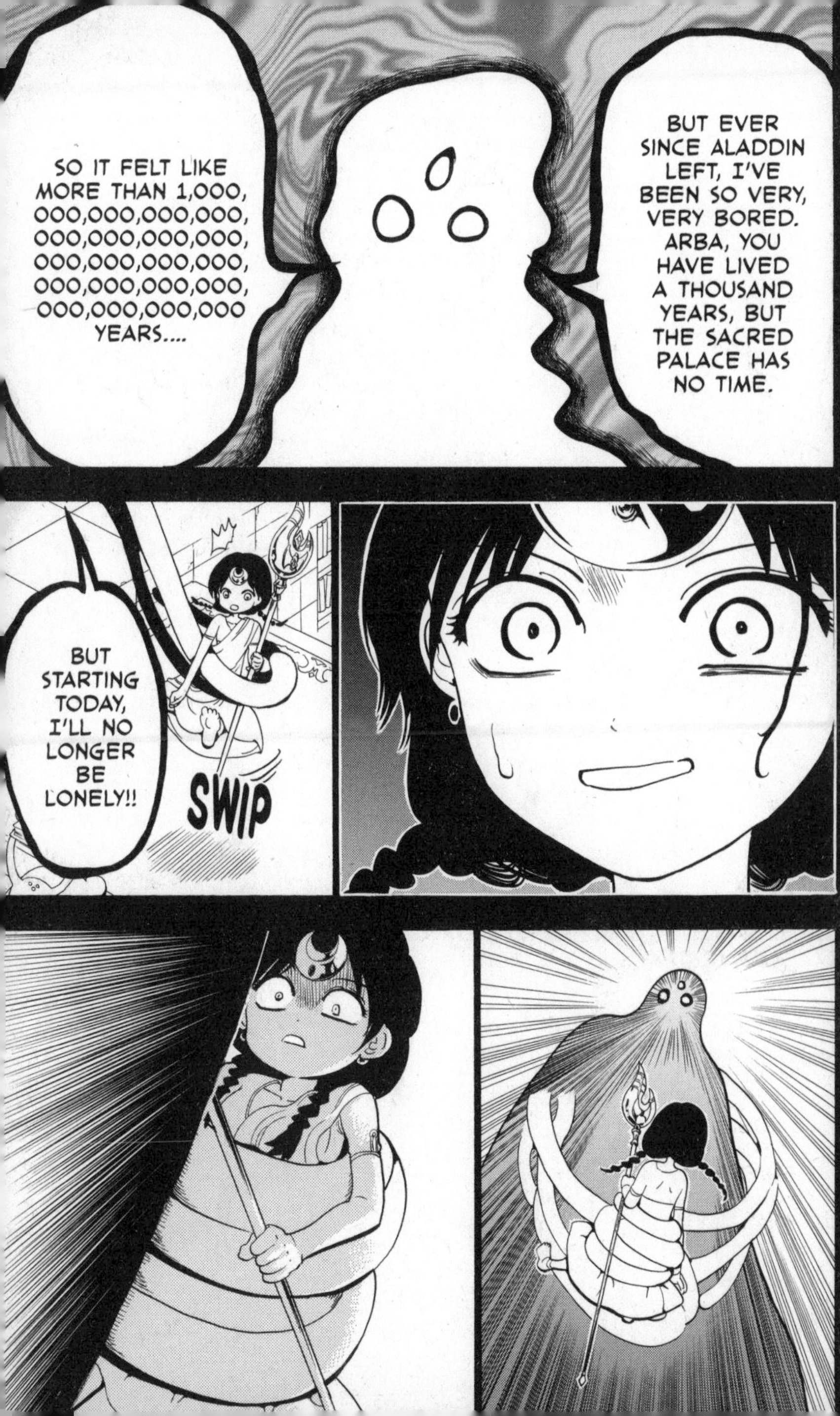
BUT EVER SINCE ALADDIN LEFT, I'VE BEEN SO VERY, VERY BORED. ARBA, YOU HAVE LIVED A THOUSAND YEARS, BUT THE SACRED PALACE HAS NO TIME.
SO IT FELT LIKE MORE THAN 1,000, 000,000,000,000, 000,000,000,000, 000,000,000,000, 000,000,000,000, 000,000,000,000 YEARS....
BUT STARTING TODAY, I'LL NO LONGER BE LONELY!!
SWIP

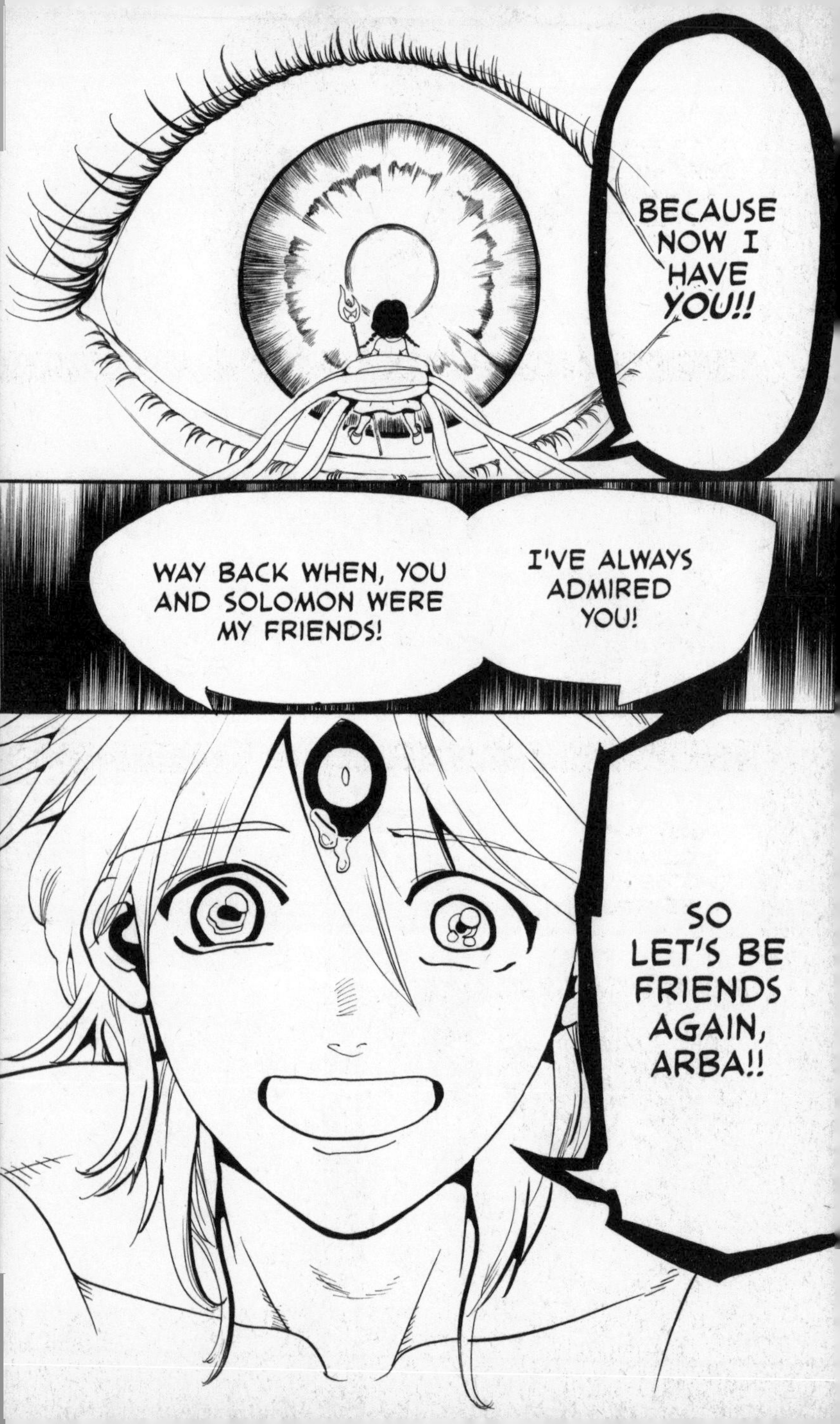
BECAUSE NOW I HAVE YOU!!
I'VE ALWAYS ADMIRED YOU!
WAY BACK WHEN, YOU AND SOLOMON WERE MY FRIENDS!
SO LET'S BE FRIENDS AGAIN, ARBA!!

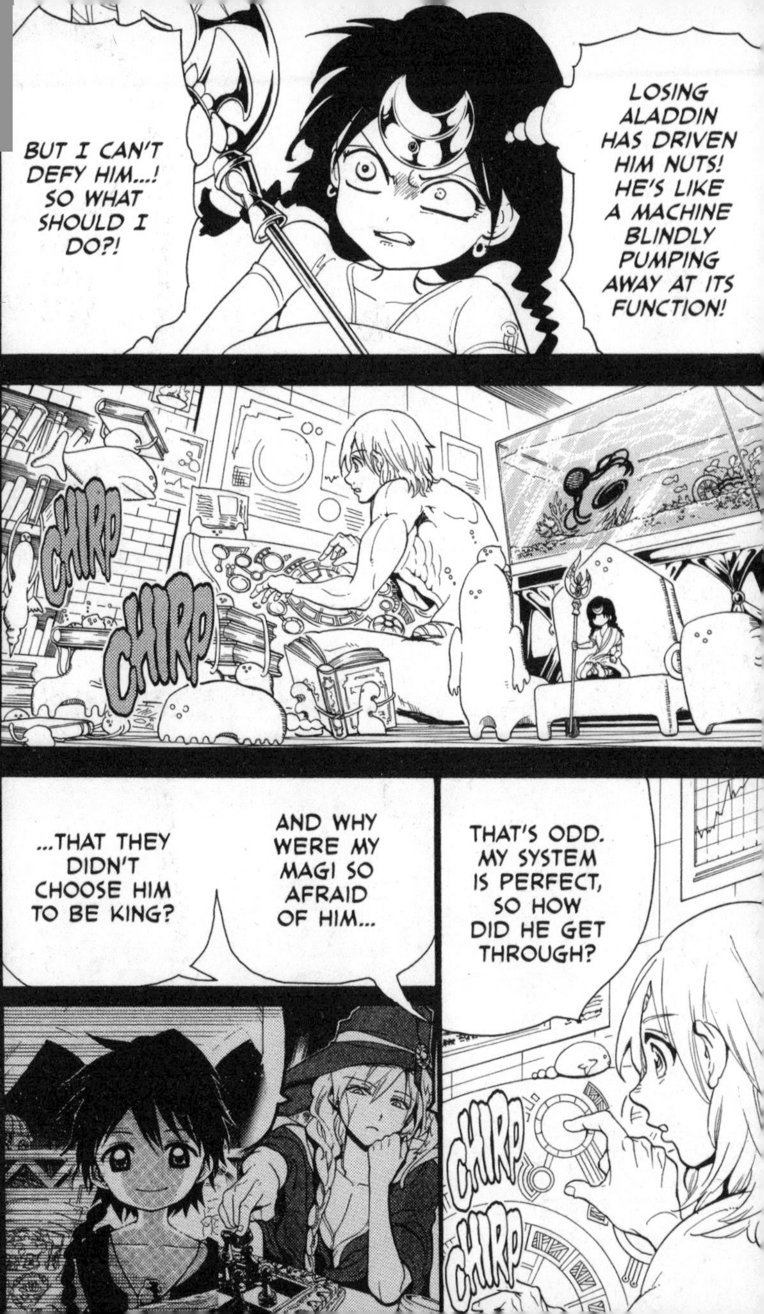
LOSING ALADDIN HAS DRIVEN HIM NUTS! HE'S LIKE A MACHINE BLINDLY PUMPING AWAY AT ITS FUNCTION!
BUT I CAN'T DEFY HIM...! SO WHAT SHOULD I DO?!
CHIRP
CHIRP
THAT'S ODD. MY SYSTEM IS PERFECT, SO HOW DID HE GET THROUGH?
CHIRP
CHIRP
AND WHY WERE MY MAGI SO AFRAID OF HIM...
...THAT THEY DIDN'T CHOOSE HIM TO BE KING?

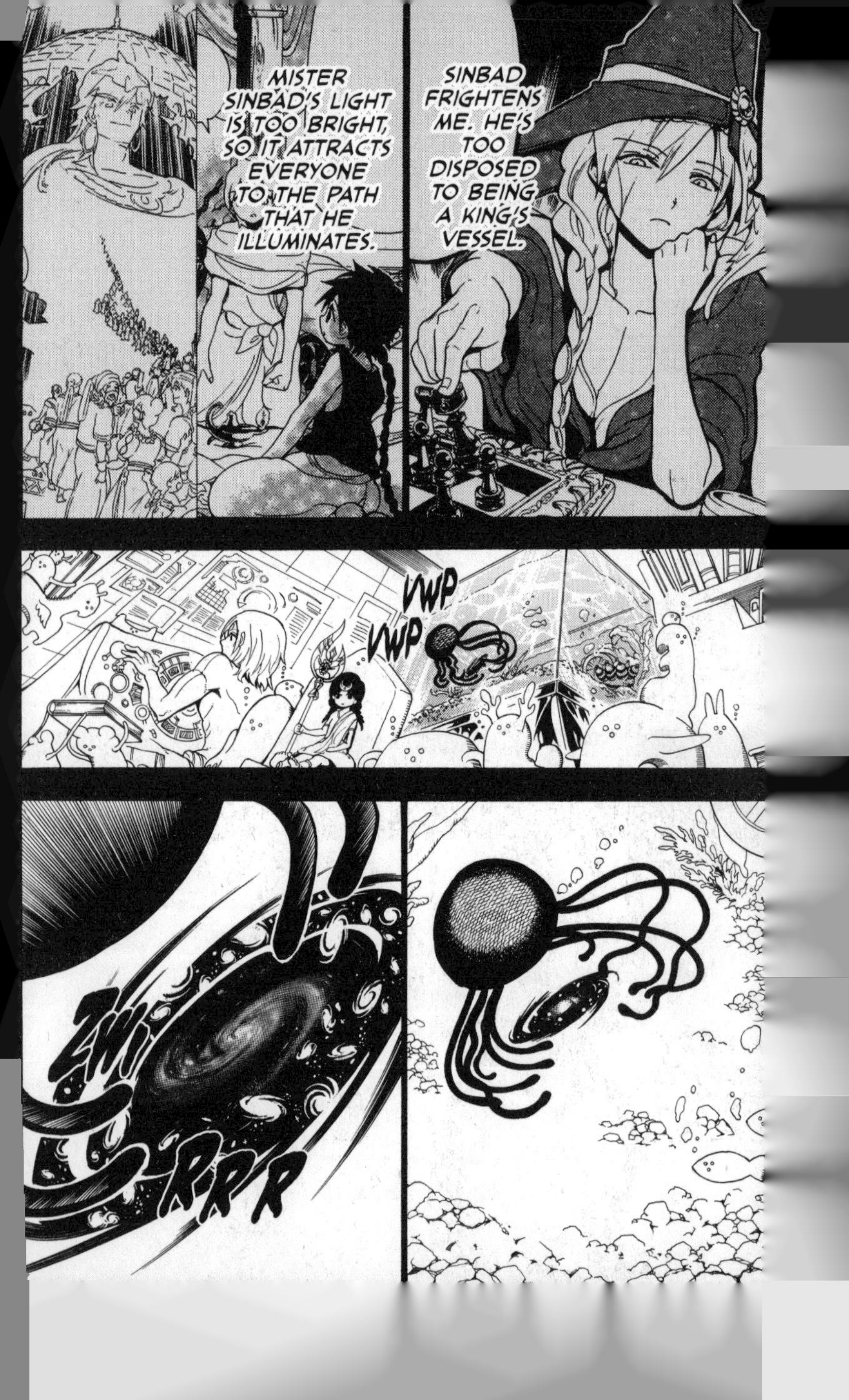
SINBAD FRIGHTENS ME. HE'S TOO DISPOSED TO BEING A KING'S VESSEL.
MISTER SINBAD'S LIGHT IS TOO BRIGHT, SO IT ATTRACTS EVERYONE TO THE PATH THAT HE ILLUMINATES.
VWP
VWP
ZWIRRRR

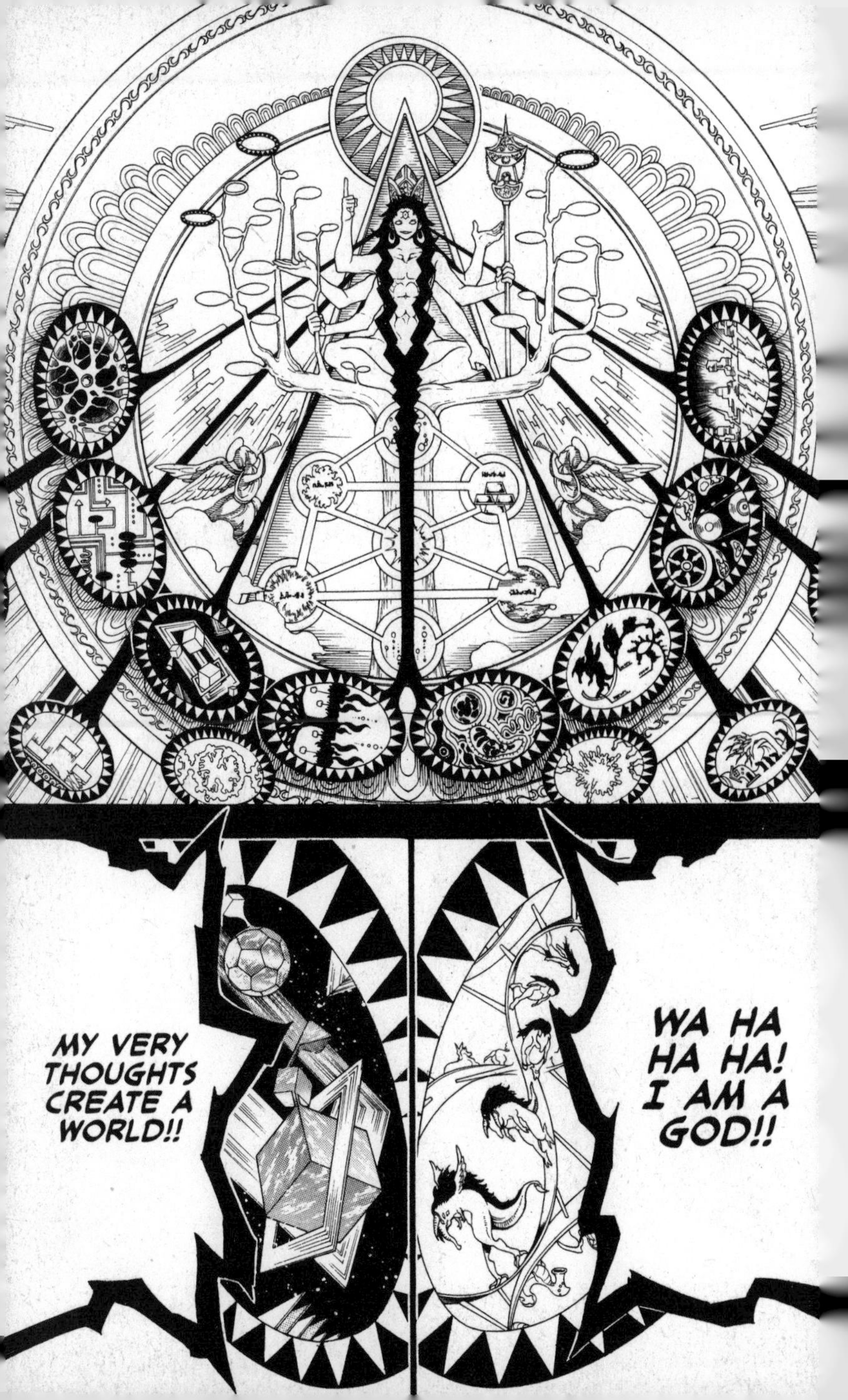
WA HA HA HA! I AM A GOD!!
MY VERY THOUGHTS CREATE A WORLD!!

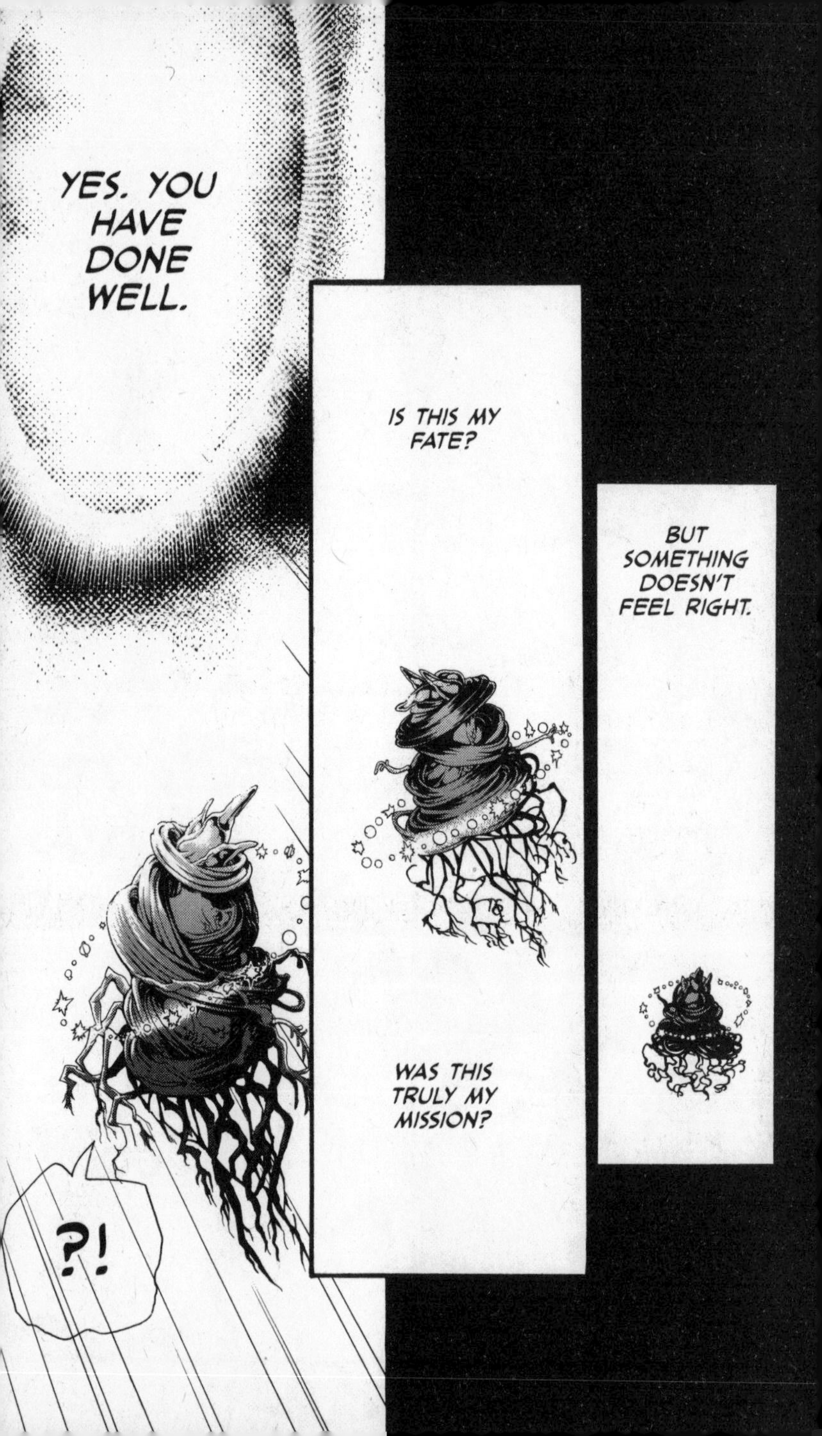
YES. YOU HAVE DONE WELL.
IS THIS MY FATE?
WAS THIS TRULY MY MISSION?
BUT SOMETHING DOESN'T FEEL RIGHT.
?!

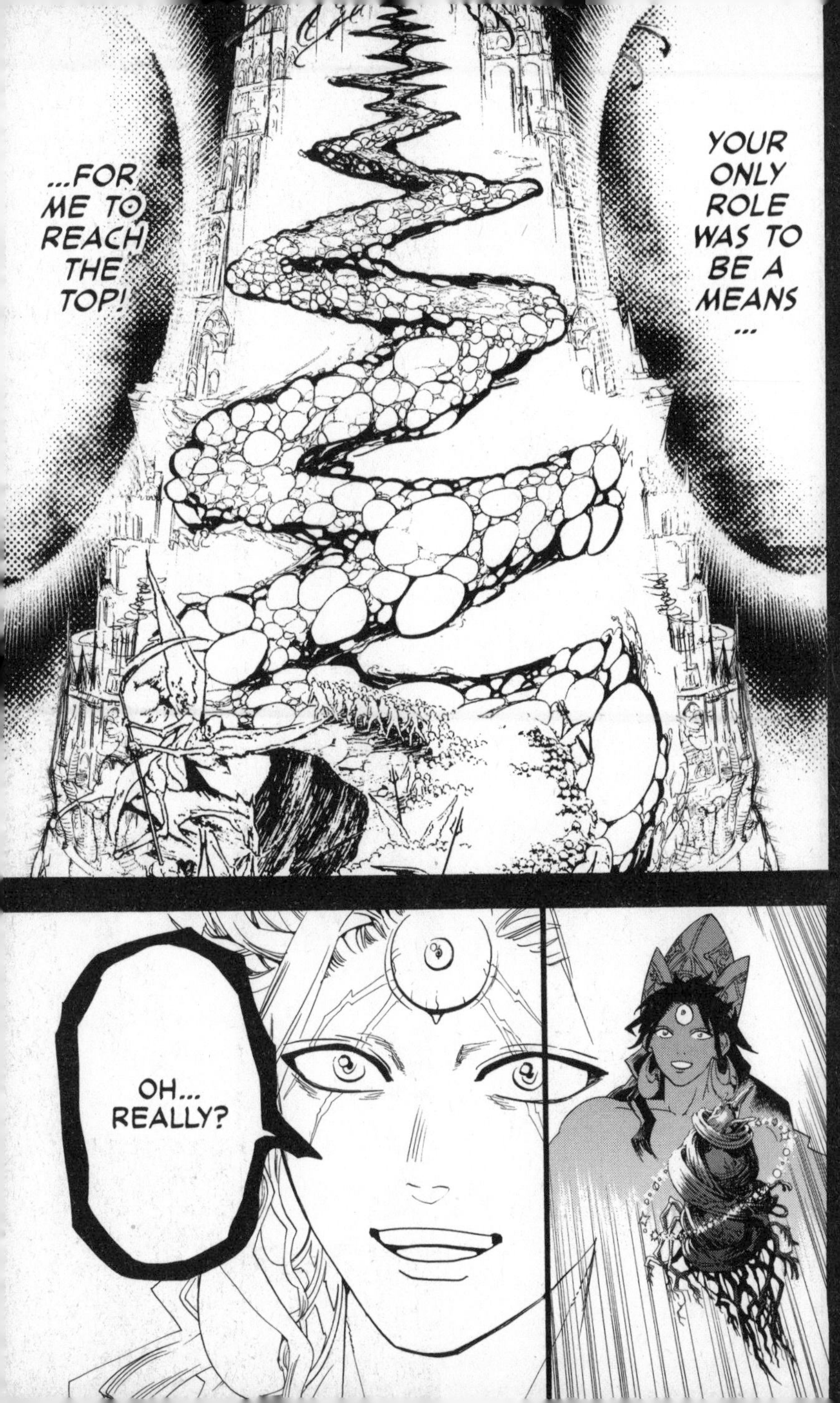
YOUR ONLY ROLE WAS TO BE A MEANS ...
...FOR ME TO REACH THE TOP!
OH... REALLY?

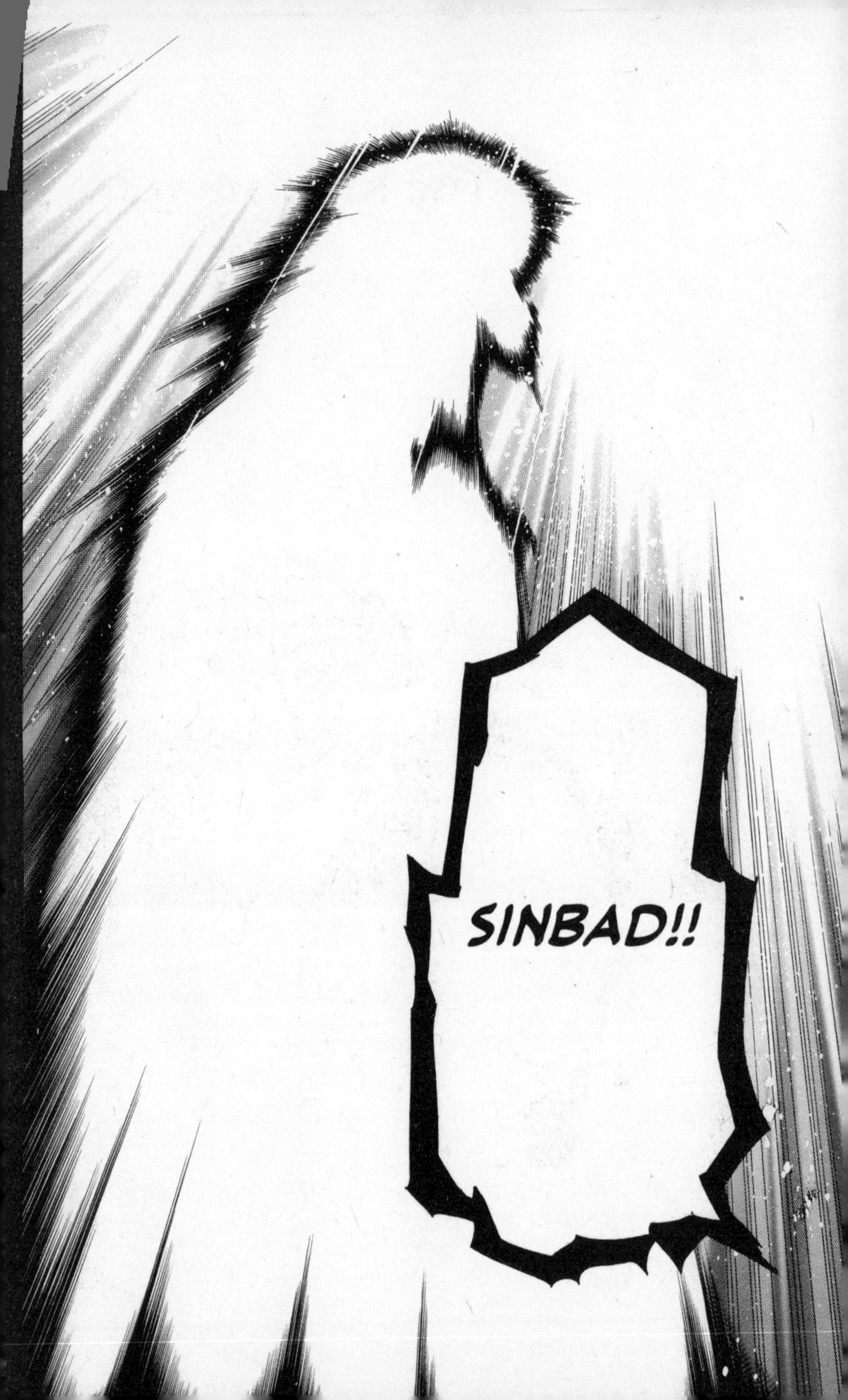
SINBAD!!

Night 325: The King's Sage

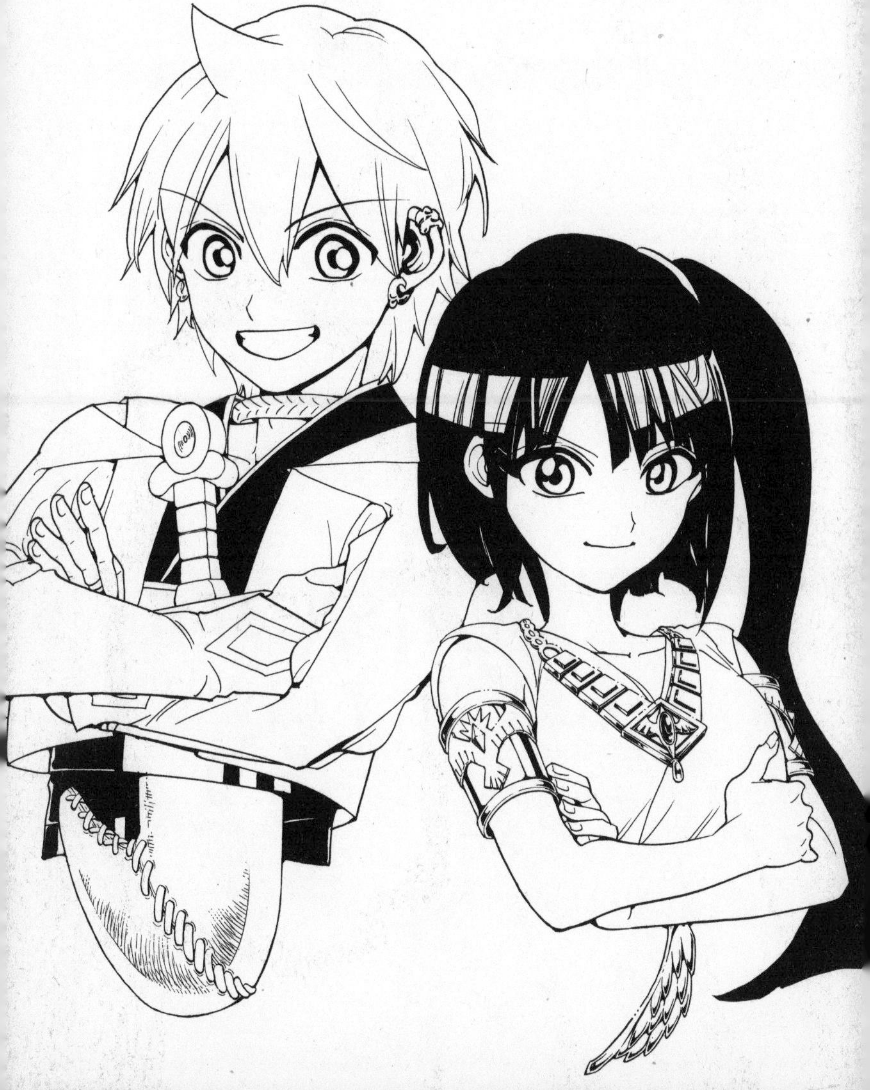

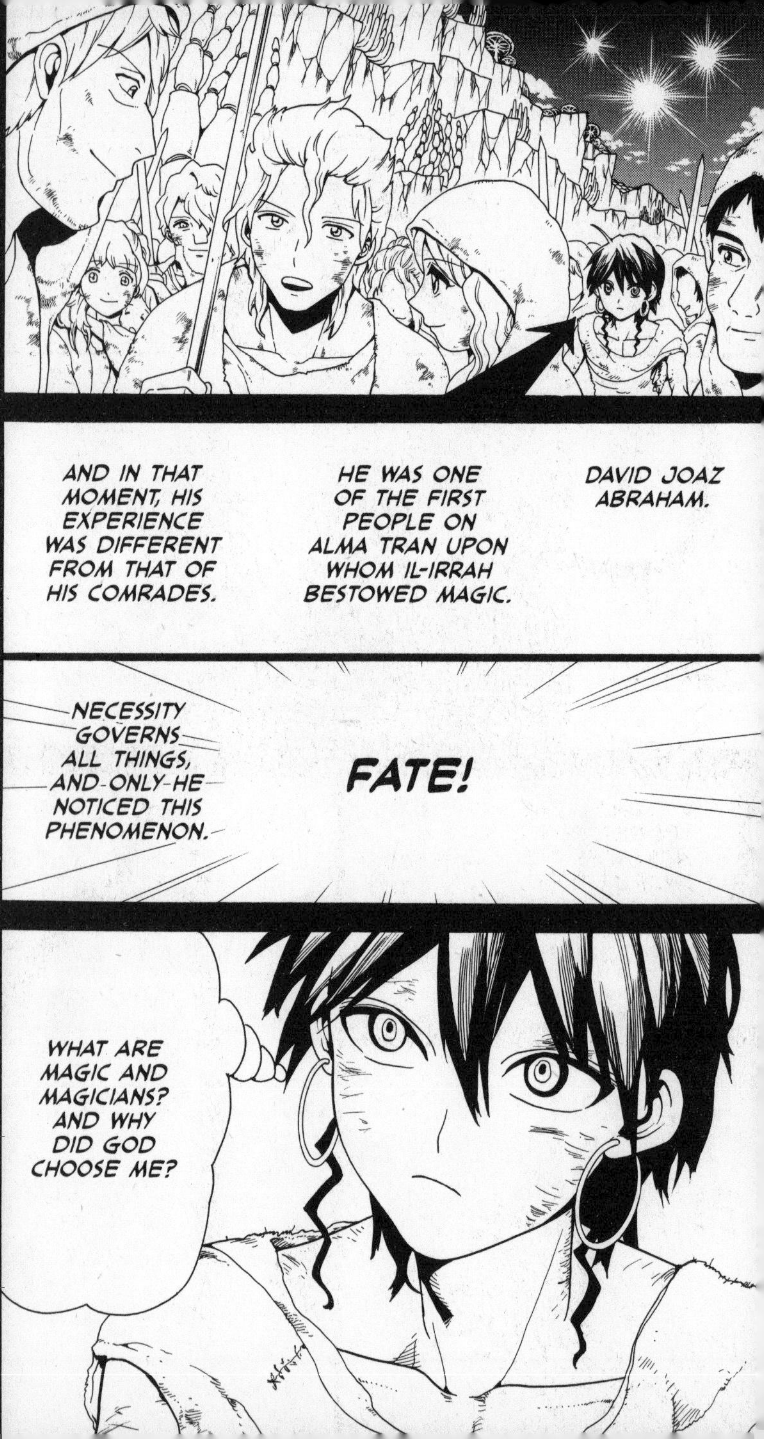
DAVID JOAZ ABRAHAM.
HE WAS ONE OF THE FIRST PEOPLE ON ALMA TRAN UPON WHOM IL-IRRAH BESTOWED MAGIC.
AND IN THAT MOMENT, HIS EXPERIENCE WAS DIFFERENT FROM THAT OF HIS COMRADES.
FATE!
NECESSITY GOVERNS ALL THINGS, AND ONLY HE NOTICED THIS PHENOMENON.
WHAT ARE MAGIC AND MAGICIANS? AND WHY DID GOD CHOOSE ME?

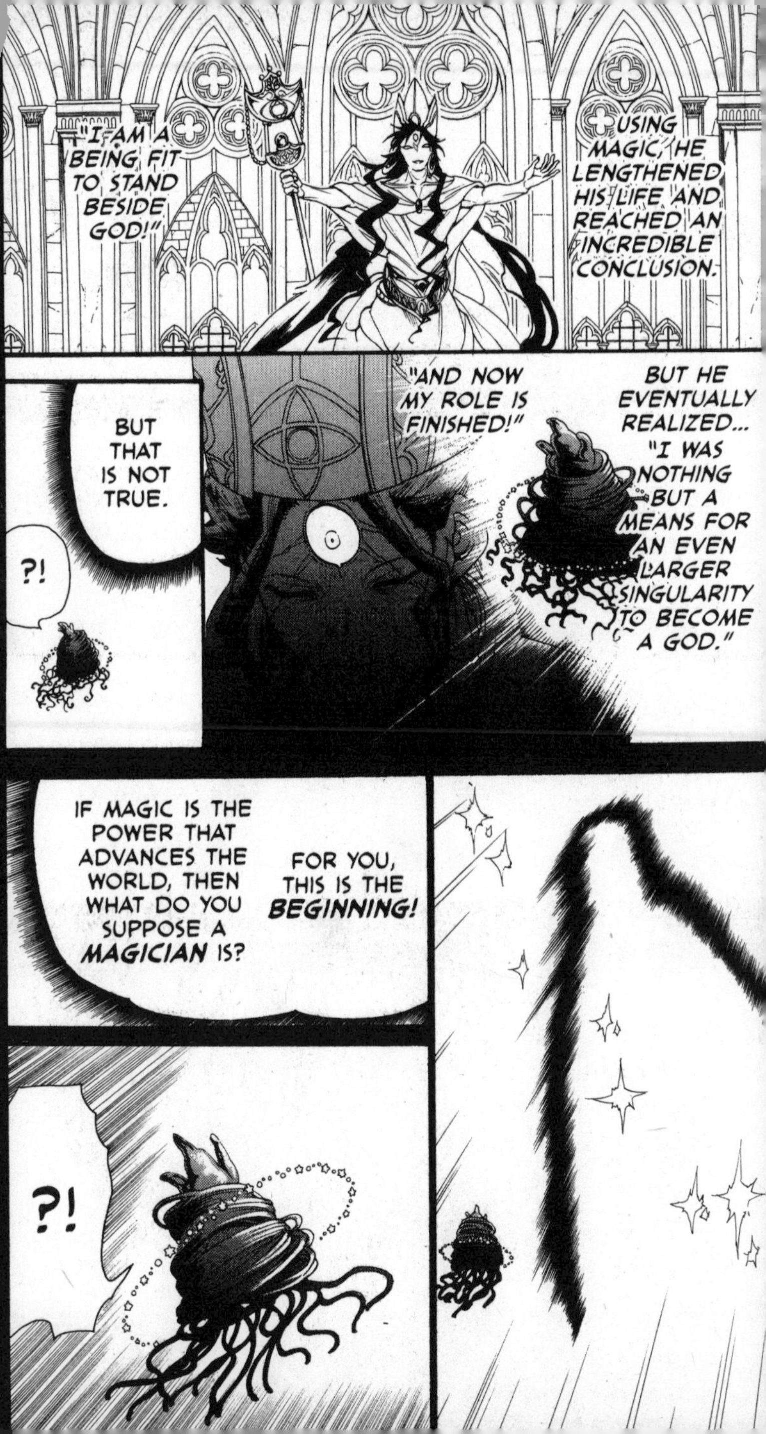
USING MAGIC, HE LENGTHENED HIS LIFE AND REACHED AN INCREDIBLE CONCLUSION.
"I AM A BEING FIT TO STAND BESIDE GOD!"
BUT HE EVENTUALLY REALIZED... "I WAS NOTHING BUT A MEANS FOR AN EVEN LARGER SINGULARITY TO BECOME A GOD."
"AND NOW MY ROLE IS FINISHED!"
BUT THAT IS NOT TRUE.
?!
FOR YOU, THIS IS THE BEGINNING!
IF MAGIC IS THE POWER THAT ADVANCES THE WORLD, THEN WHAT DO YOU SUPPOSE A MAGICIAN IS?
?!

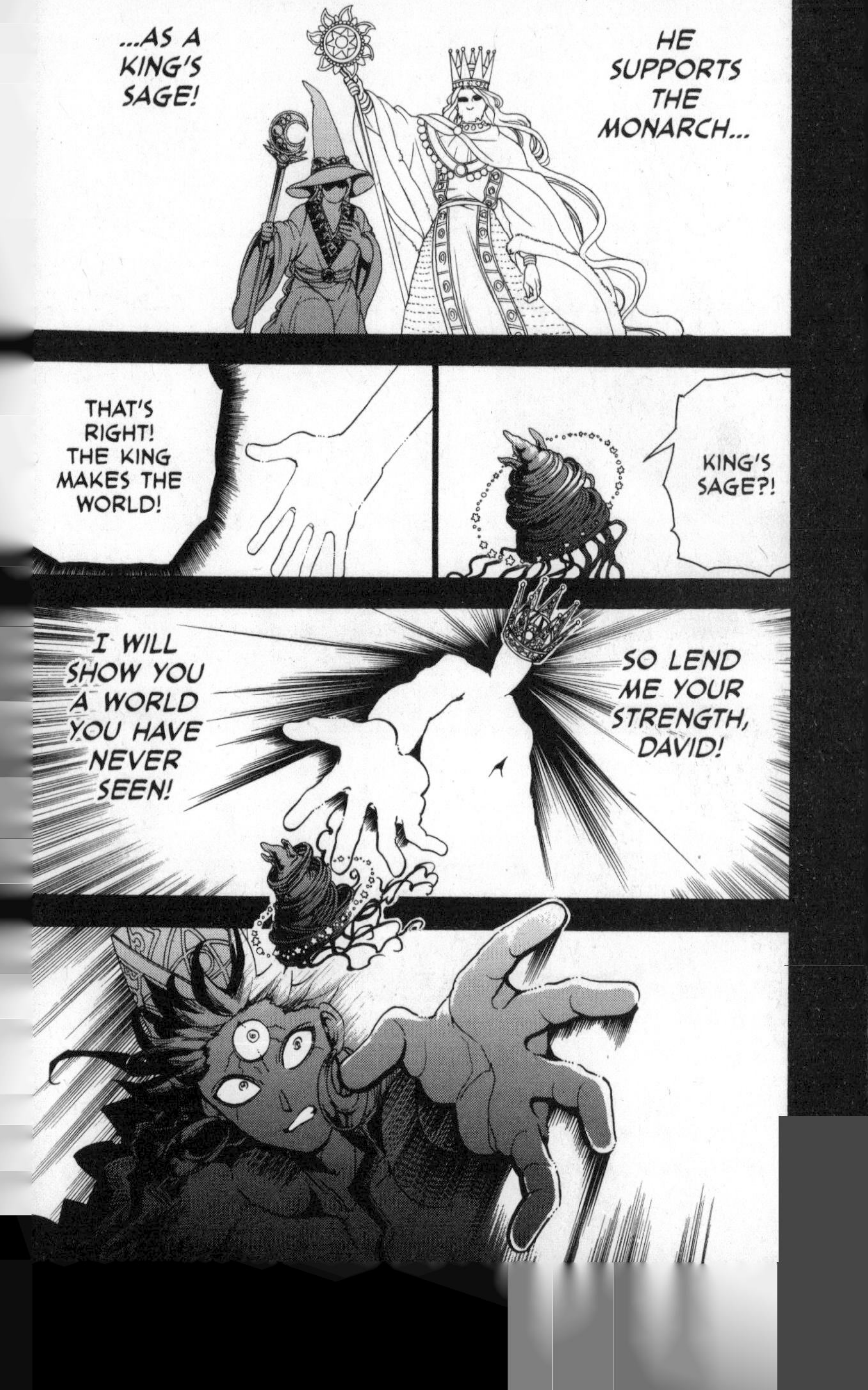
HE SUPPORTS THE MONARCH...
...AS A KING'S SAGE!
KING'S SAGE?!
THAT'S RIGHT! THE KING MAKES THE WORLD!
SO LEND ME YOUR STRENGTH, DAVID!
I WILL SHOW YOU A WORLD YOU HAVE NEVER SEEN!

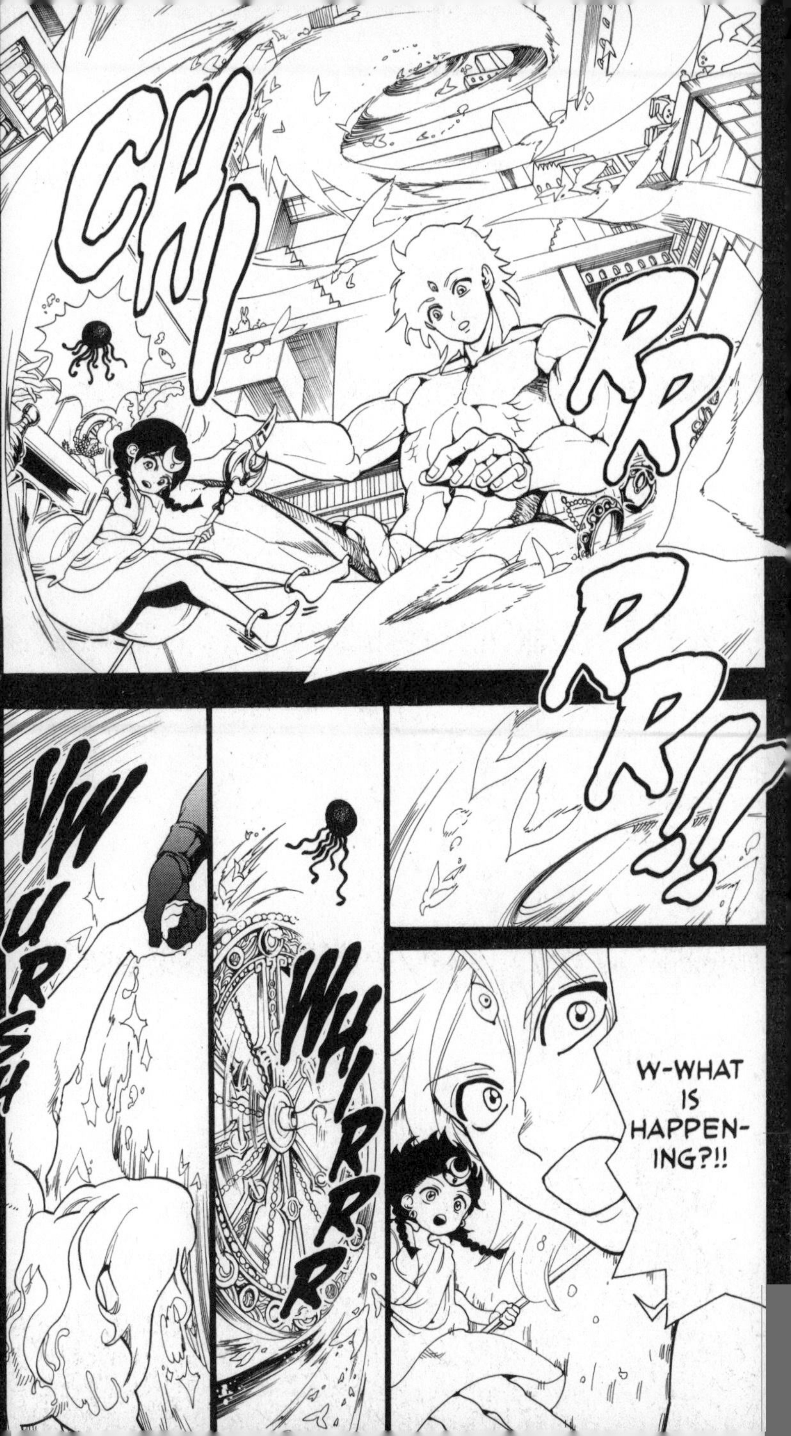
CHRRRR!!
W-WHAT IS HAPPEN-ING?!!
WHIRRRR
VWURSH

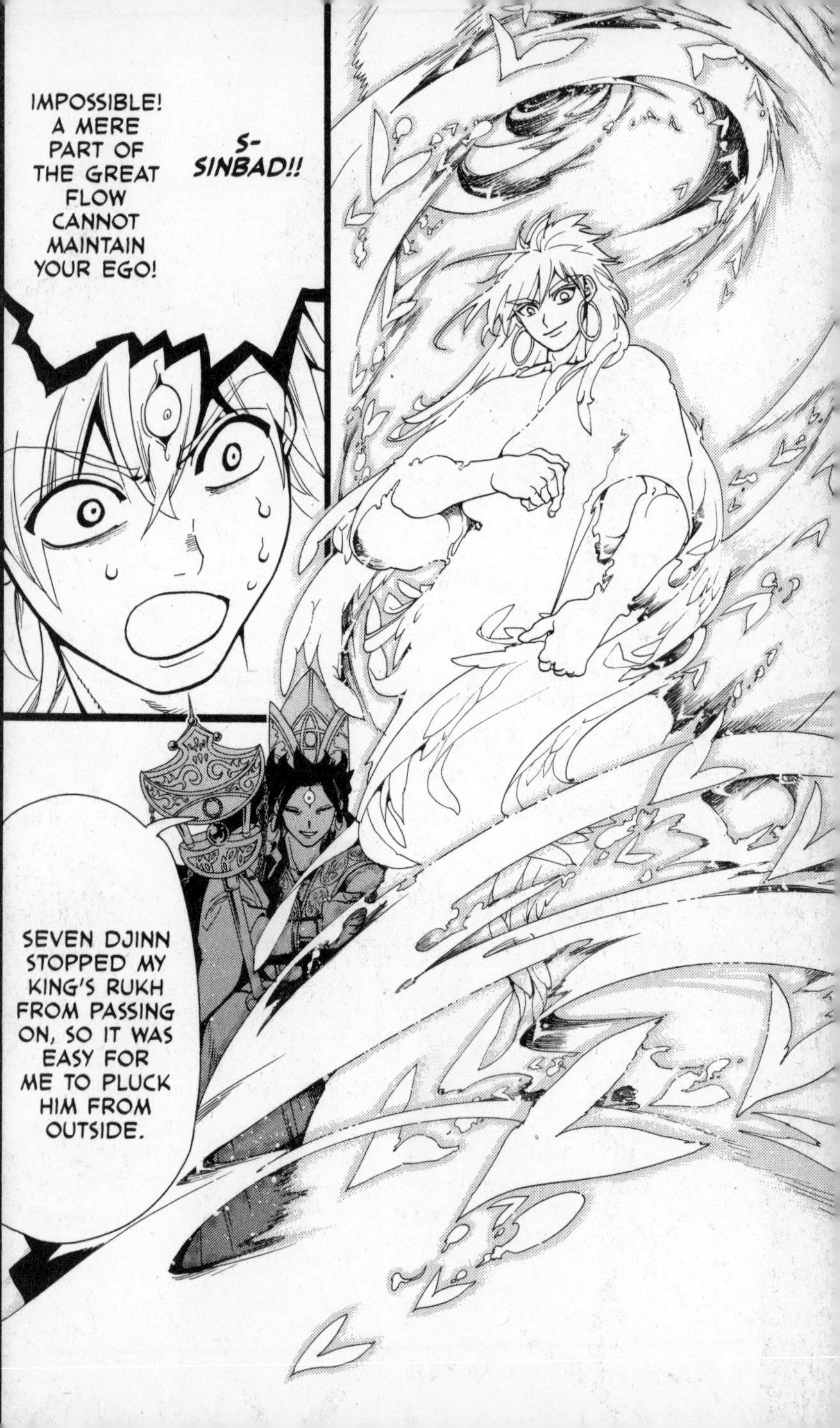

S-SINBAD!!
IMPOSSIBLE! A MERE PART OF THE GREAT FLOW CANNOT MAINTAIN YOUR EGO!
SEVEN DJINN STOPPED MY KING'S RUKH FROM PASSING ON, SO IT WAS EASY FOR ME TO PLUCK HIM FROM OUTSIDE.

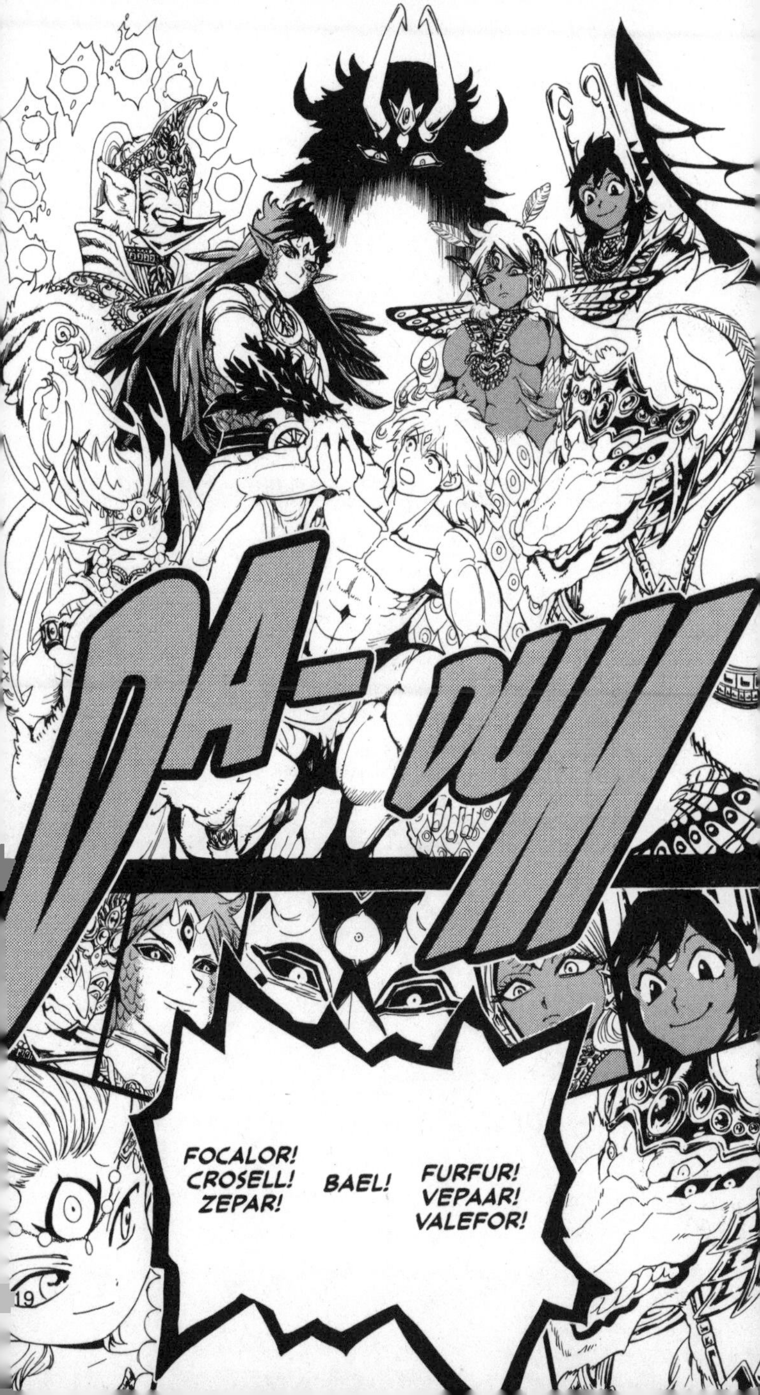
FOCALOR! CROSELL! ZEPAR!
BAEL!
FURFUR! VEPAAR! VALEFOR!

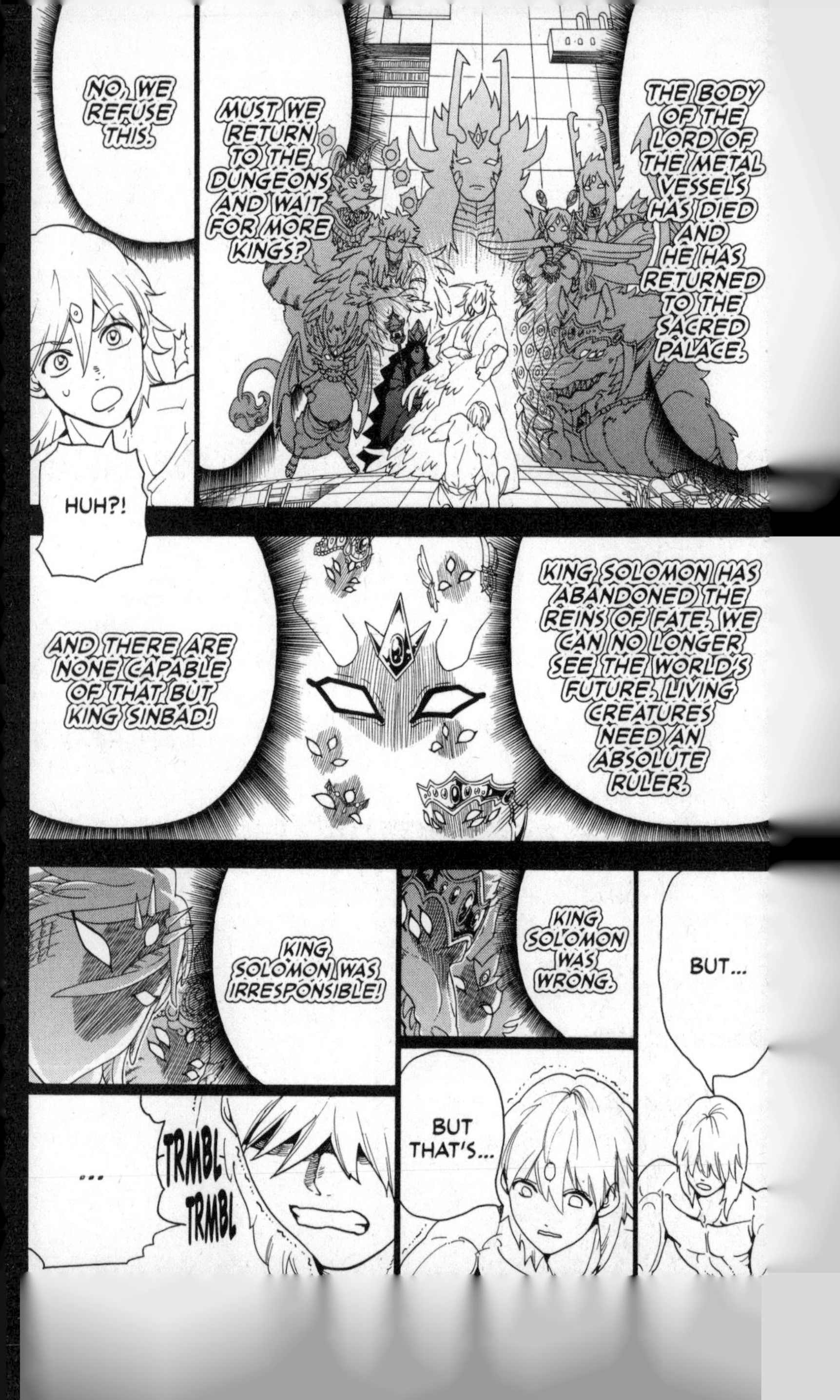
THE BODY OF THE LORD OF THE METAL VESSELS HAS DIED AND HE HAS RETURNED TO THE SACRED PALACE.
MUST WE RETURN TO THE DUNGEONS AND WAIT FOR MORE KINGS?
NO, WE REFUSE THIS.
HUH?!
KING SOLOMON HAS ABANDONED THE REINS OF FATE. WE CAN NO LONGER SEE THE WORLD'S FUTURE. LIVING CREATURES NEED AN ABSOLUTE RULER.
AND THERE ARE NONE CAPABLE OF THAT BUT KING SINBAD!
BUT...
KING SOLOMON WAS WRONG.
KING SOLOMON WAS IRRESPONSIBLE!
BUT THAT'S...
...
TRMBL TRMBL

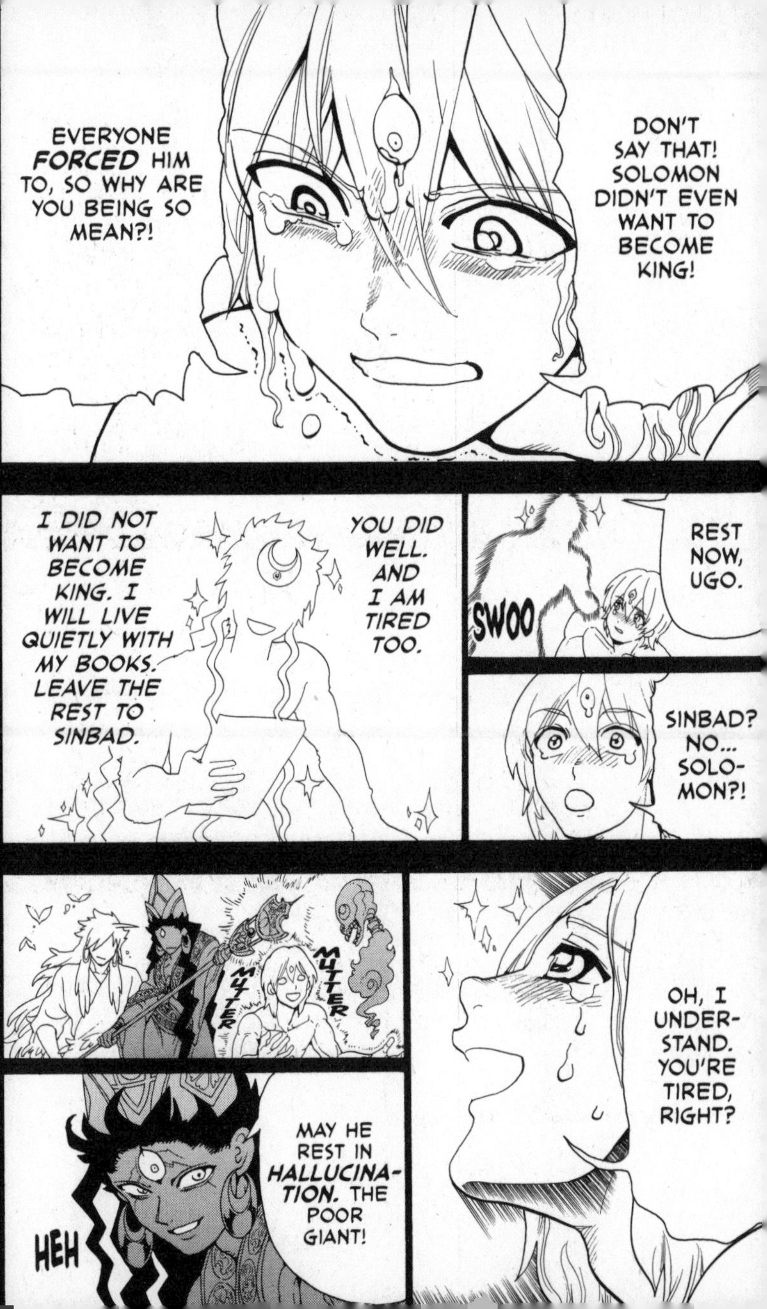
DON'T SAY THAT! SOLOMON DIDN'T EVEN WANT TO BECOME KING!
EVERYONE FORCED HIM TO, SO WHY ARE YOU BEING SO MEAN?!
SWOO
REST NOW, UGO.
SINBAD? NO... SOLOMON?!
YOU DID WELL. AND I AM TIRED TOO.
I DID NOT WANT TO BECOME KING. I WILL LIVE QUIETLY WITH MY BOOKS. LEAVE THE REST TO SINBAD.
OH, I UNDERSTAND. YOU'RE TIRED, RIGHT?
MUTTER
MUTTER
MAY HE REST IN HALLUCINATION. THE POOR GIANT!
HEH

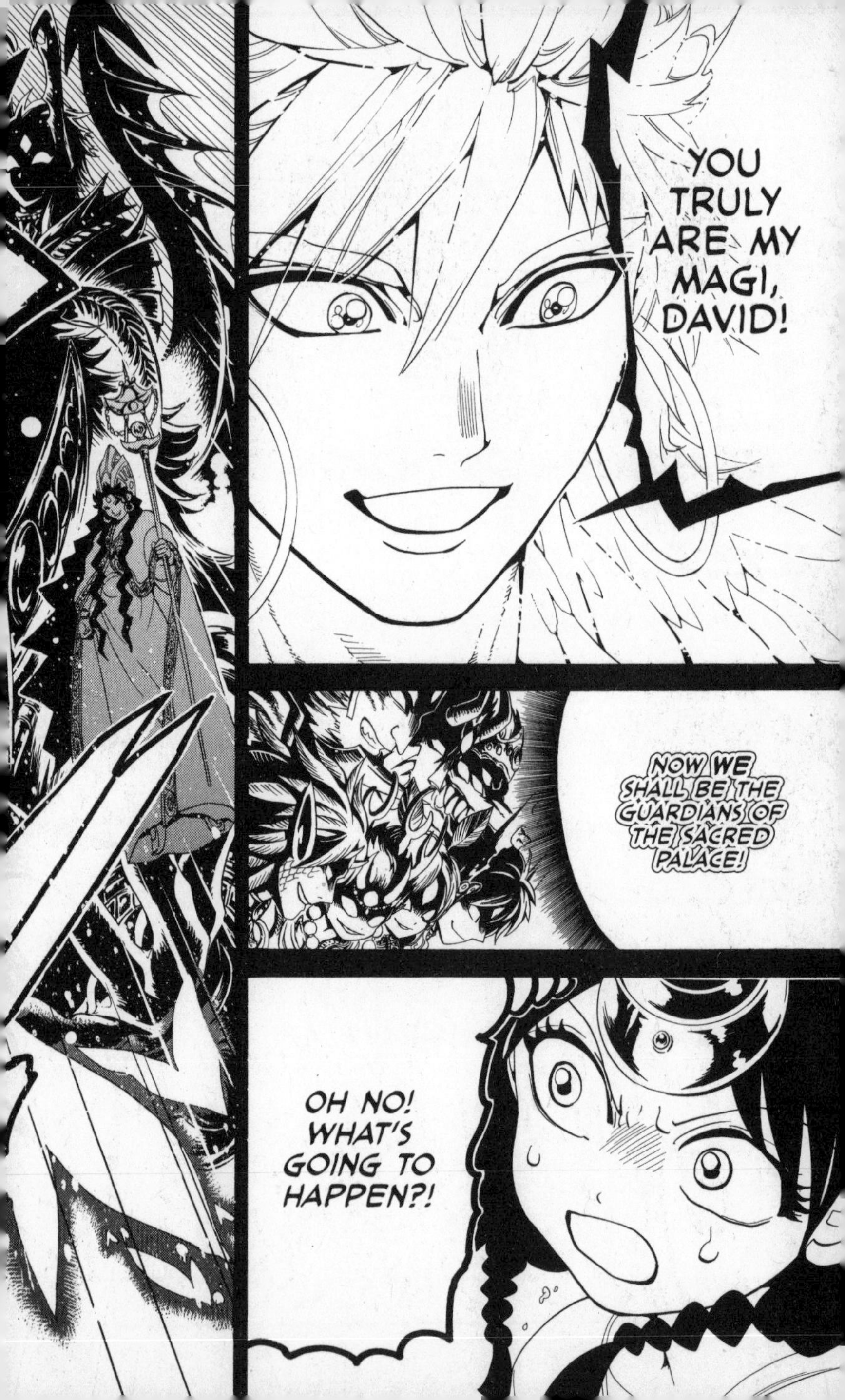
YOU TRULY ARE MY MAGI, DAVID!
NOW WE SHALL BE THE GUARDIANS OF THE SACRED PALACE!
OH NO! WHAT'S GOING TO HAPPEN?!

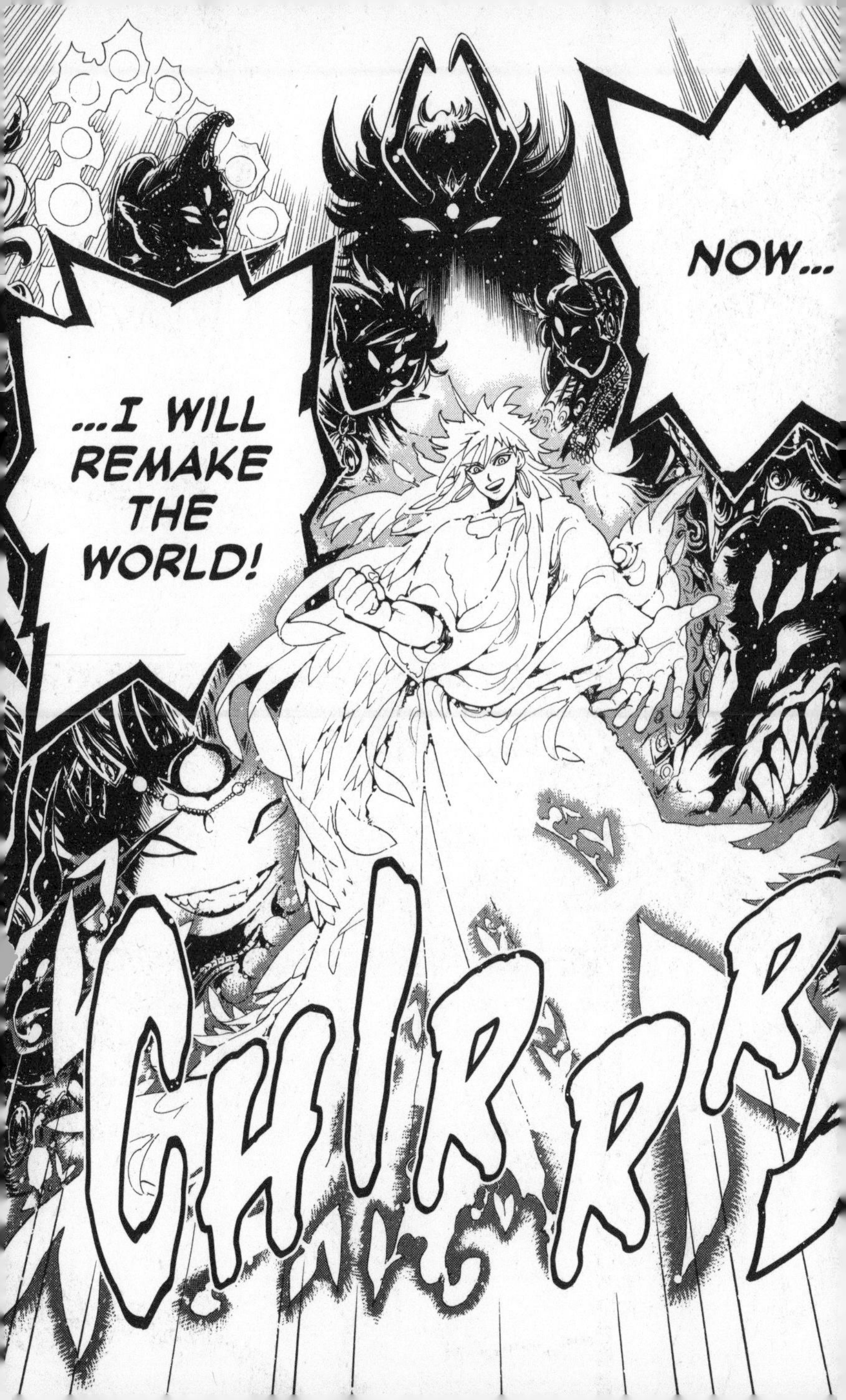
NOW...
...I WILL REMAKE THE WORLD!
CHIRRP

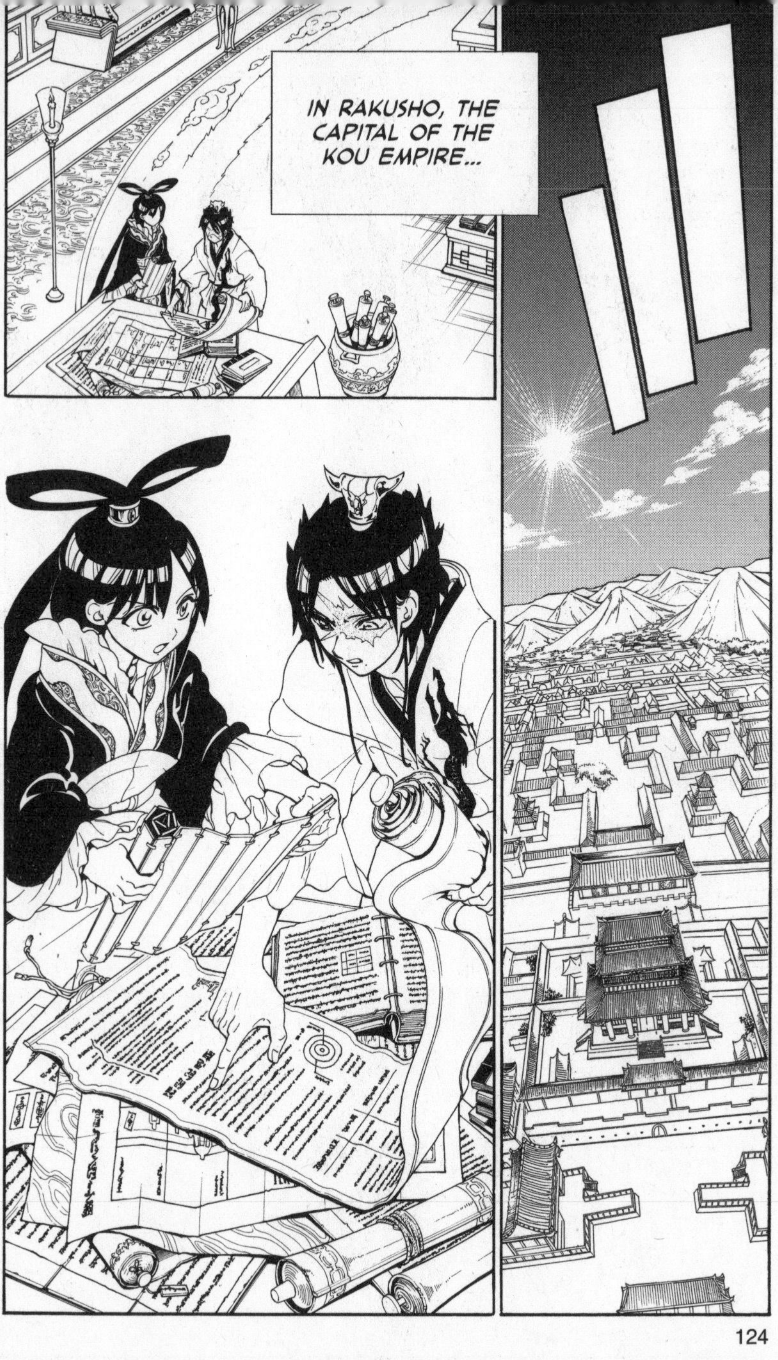
IN RAKUSHO, THE CAPITAL OF THE KOU EMPIRE...

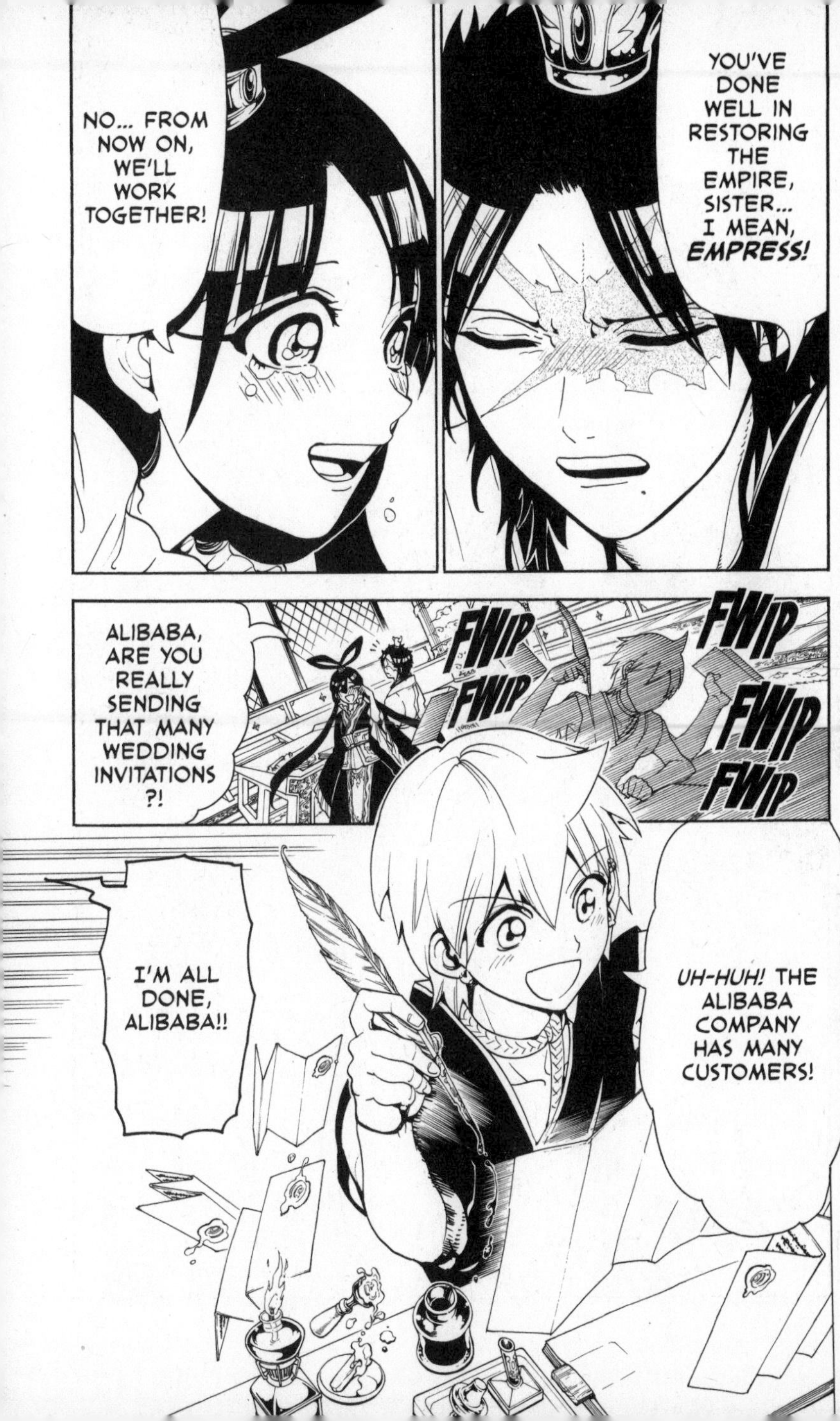

YOU'VE DONE WELL IN RESTORING THE EMPIRE, SISTER... I MEAN, *EMPRESS!*
NO... FROM NOW ON, WE'LL WORK TOGETHER!
FWIP
FWIP
FWIP
FWIP
FWIP
ALIBABA, ARE YOU REALLY SENDING THAT MANY WEDDING INVITATIONS ?!
UH-HUH! THE ALIBABA COMPANY HAS MANY CUSTOMERS!
I'M ALL DONE, ALIBABA!!

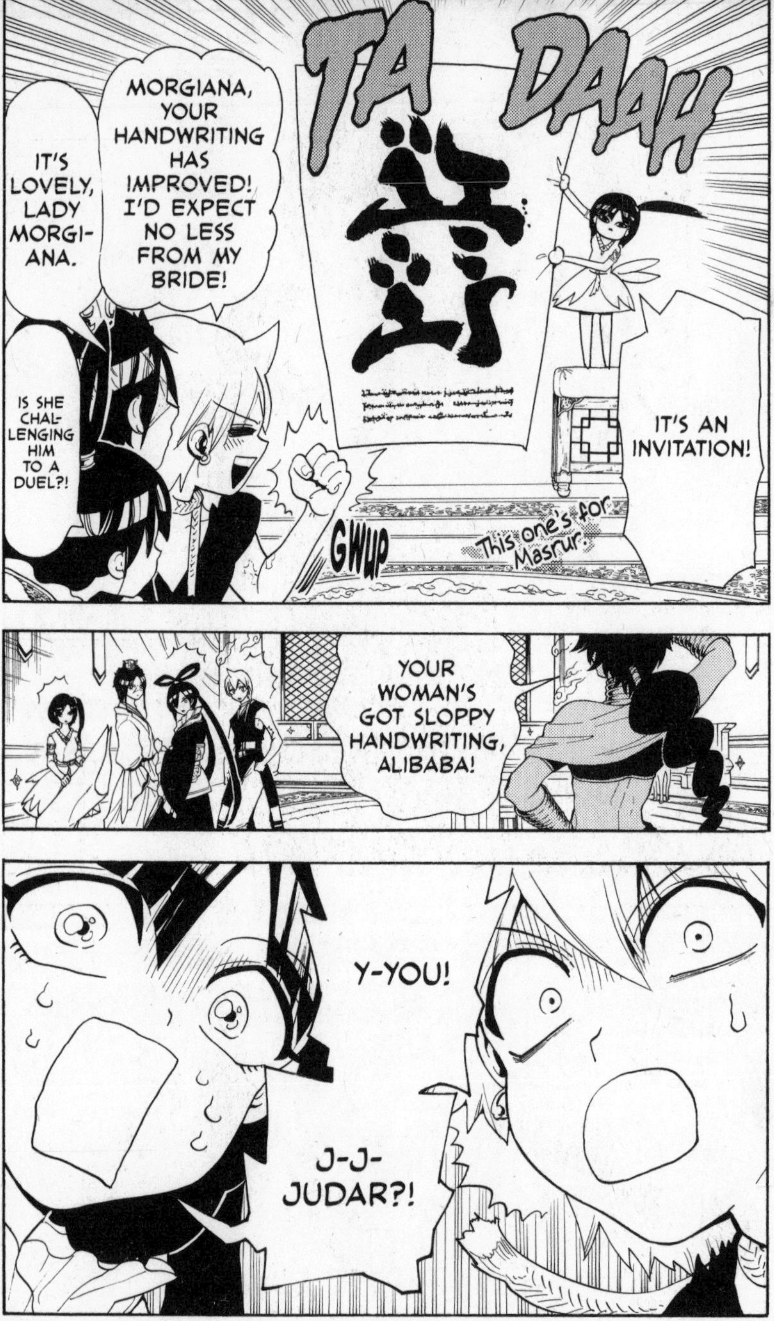
TA DAAH
IT'S AN INVITATION!
MORGIANA, YOUR HANDWRITING HAS IMPROVED! I'D EXPECT NO LESS FROM MY BRIDE!
IT'S LOVELY, LADY MORGIANA.
This one's for Masrur.
GWUP
IS SHE CHALLENGING HIM TO A DUEL?!
YOUR WOMAN'S GOT SLOPPY HANDWRITING, ALIBABA!
Y-YOU!
J-J-JUDAR?!

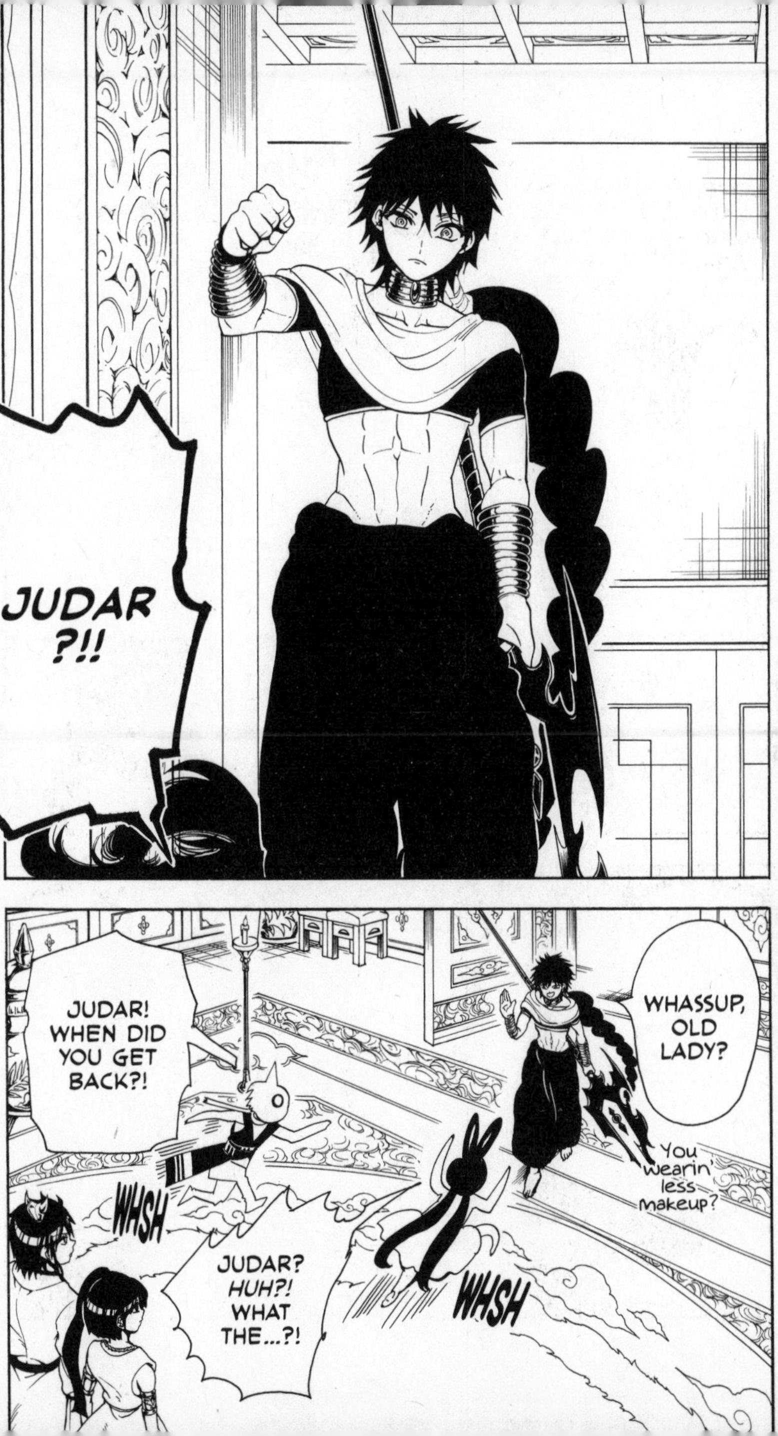
JUDAR ?!!
WHASSUP, OLD LADY?
You wearin' less makeup?
JUDAR! WHEN DID YOU GET BACK?!
WHSH
WHSH
JUDAR? HUH?! WHAT THE...?!

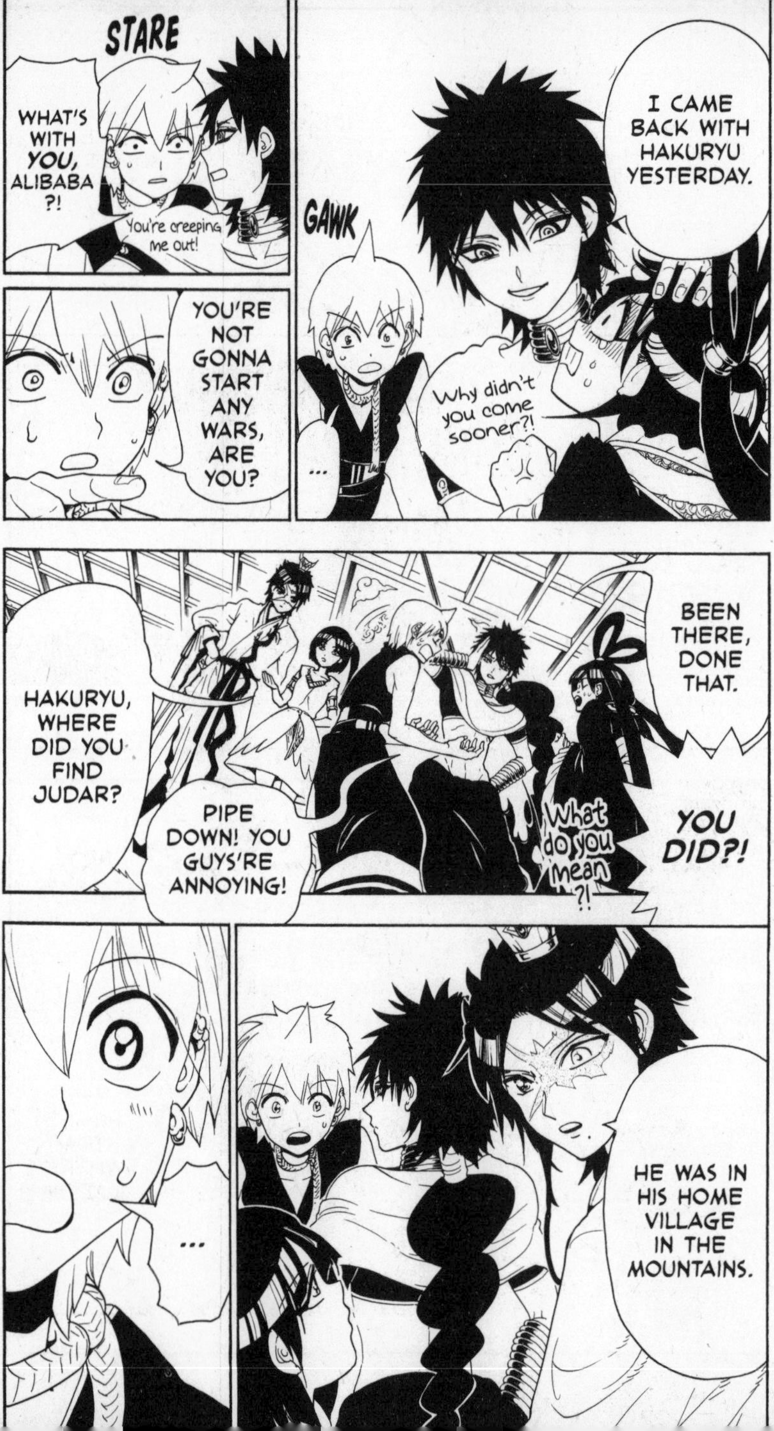
I CAME BACK WITH HAKURYU YESTERDAY.
GAWK
Why didn't you come sooner?!
...
STARE
WHAT'S WITH YOU, ALIBABA?!
You're creeping me out!
YOU'RE NOT GONNA START ANY WARS, ARE YOU?
BEEN THERE, DONE THAT.
YOU DID?!
What do you mean?!
PIPE DOWN! YOU GUYS'RE ANNOYING!
HAKURYU, WHERE DID YOU FIND JUDAR?
HE WAS IN HIS HOME VILLAGE IN THE MOUNTAINS.
...

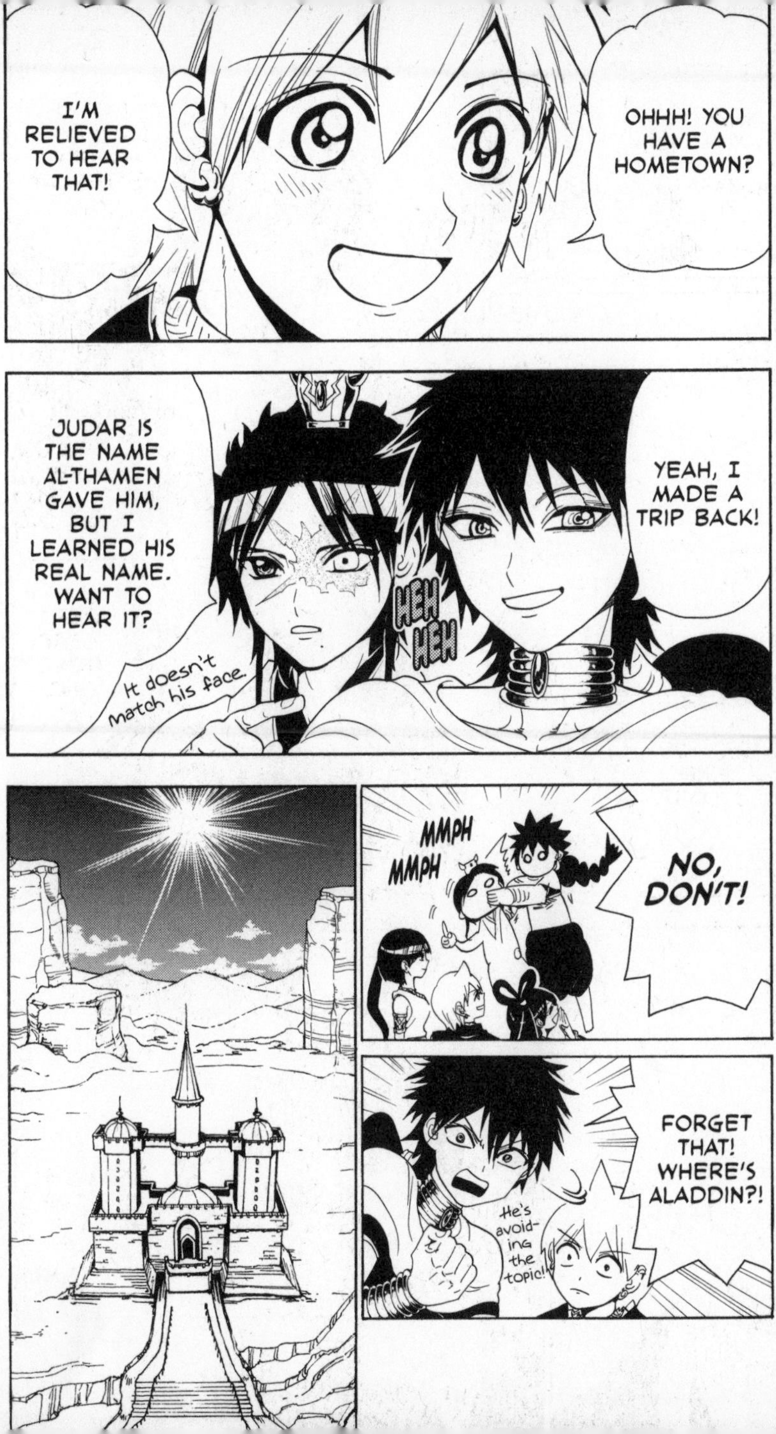
OHHH! YOU HAVE A HOMETOWN?
I'M RELIEVED TO HEAR THAT!
YEAH, I MADE A TRIP BACK!
HEH HEH
JUDAR IS THE NAME AL-THAMEN GAVE HIM, BUT I LEARNED HIS REAL NAME. WANT TO HEAR IT?
It doesn't match his face.
NO, DON'T!
MMPH MMPH
FORGET THAT! WHERE'S ALADDIN?!
He's avoiding the topic!

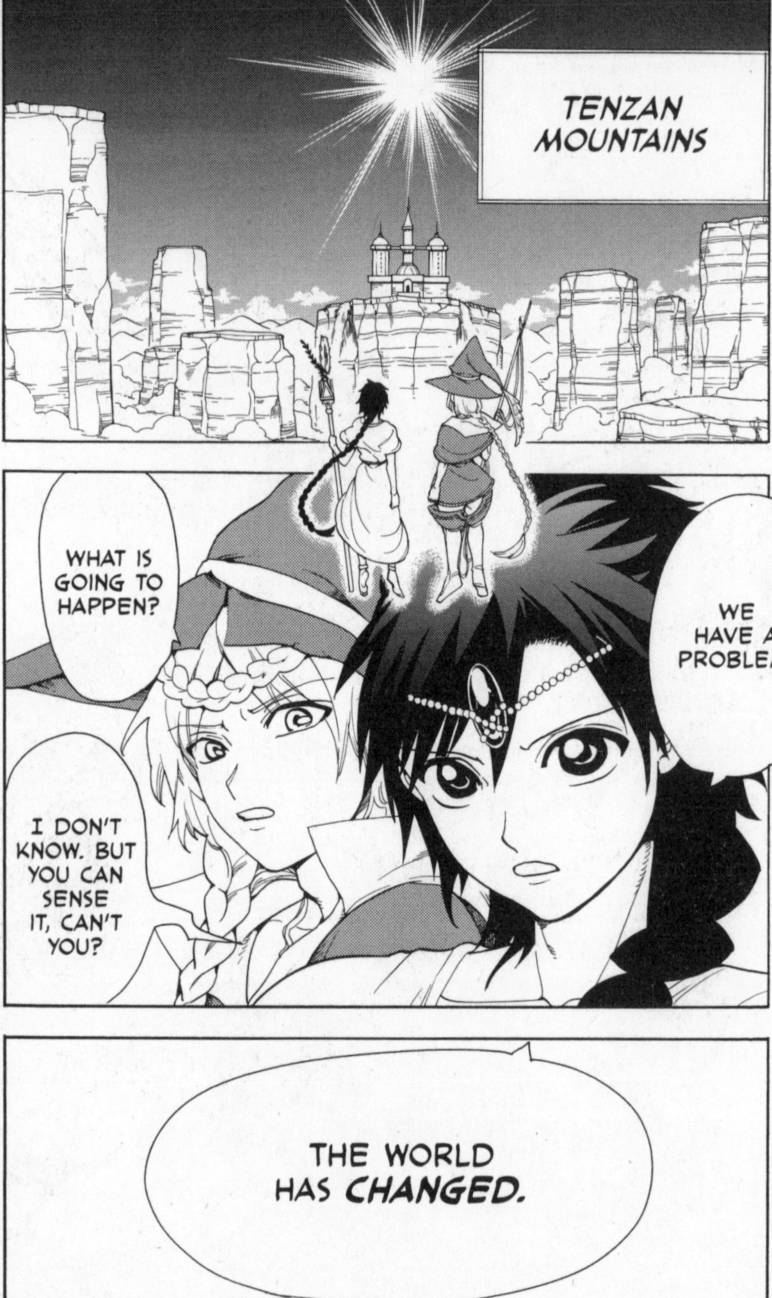
TENZAN MOUNTAINS
WE HAVE A PROBLEM.
WHAT IS GOING TO HAPPEN?
I DON'T KNOW. BUT YOU CAN SENSE IT, CAN'T YOU?
THE WORLD HAS CHANGED.

Night 326: An Awful Feeling

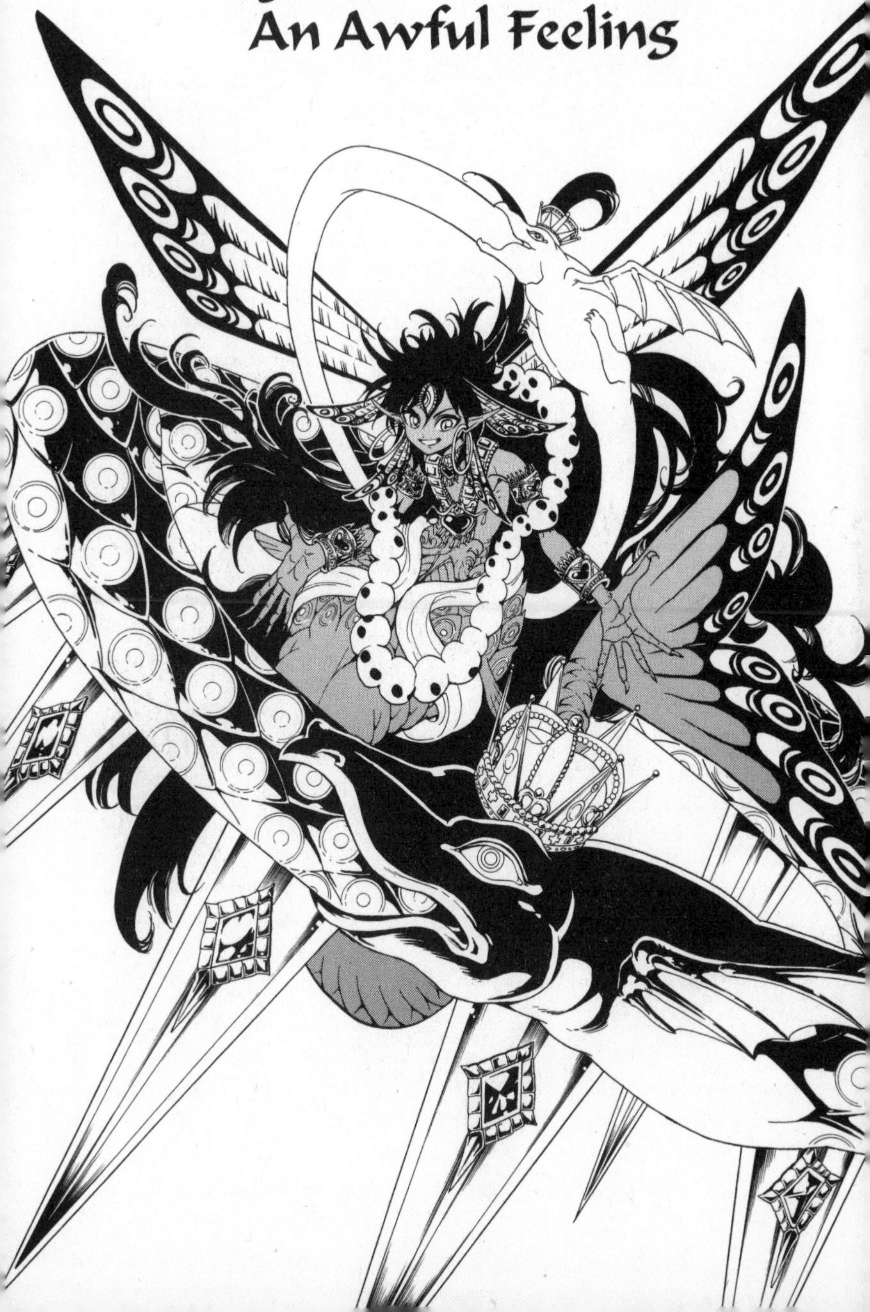

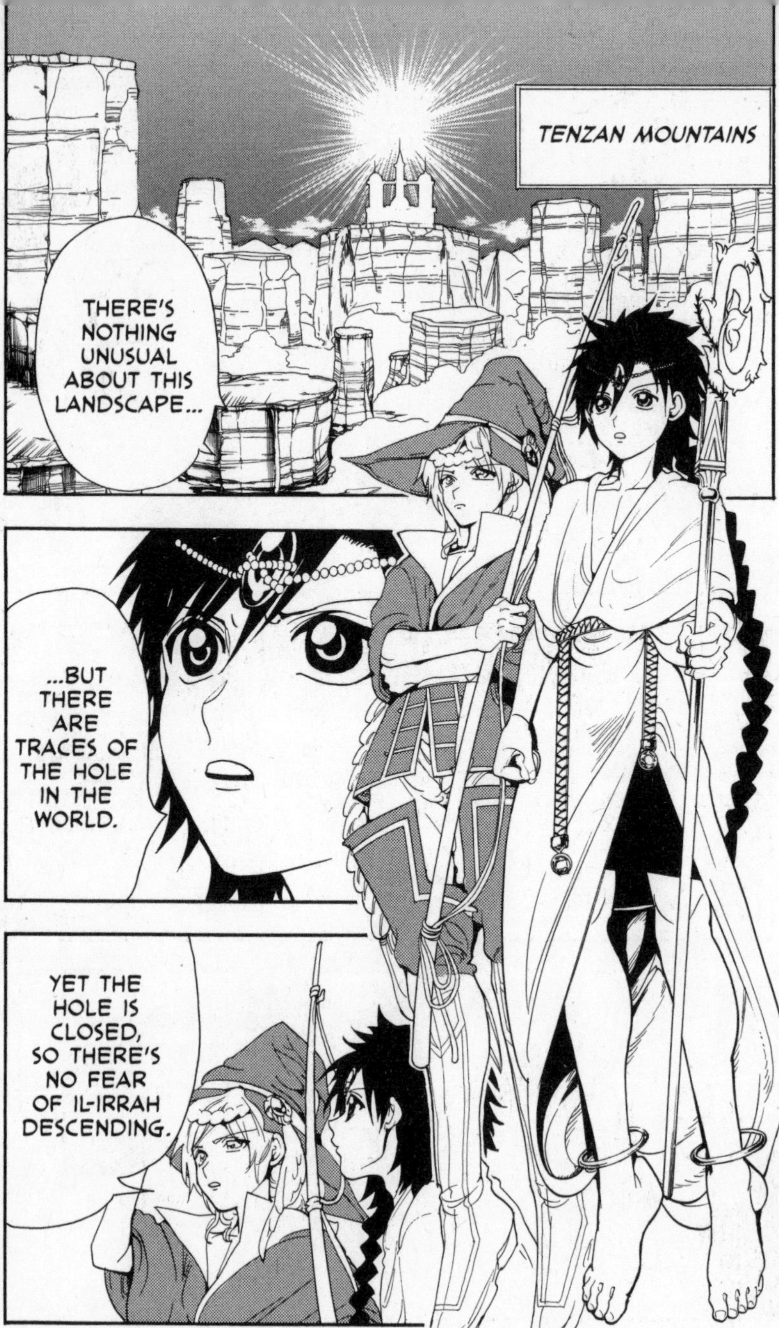
TENZAN MOUNTAINS
THERE'S NOTHING UNUSUAL ABOUT THIS LANDSCAPE...
...BUT THERE ARE TRACES OF THE HOLE IN THE WORLD.
YET THE HOLE IS CLOSED, SO THERE'S NO FEAR OF IL-IRRAH DESCENDING.

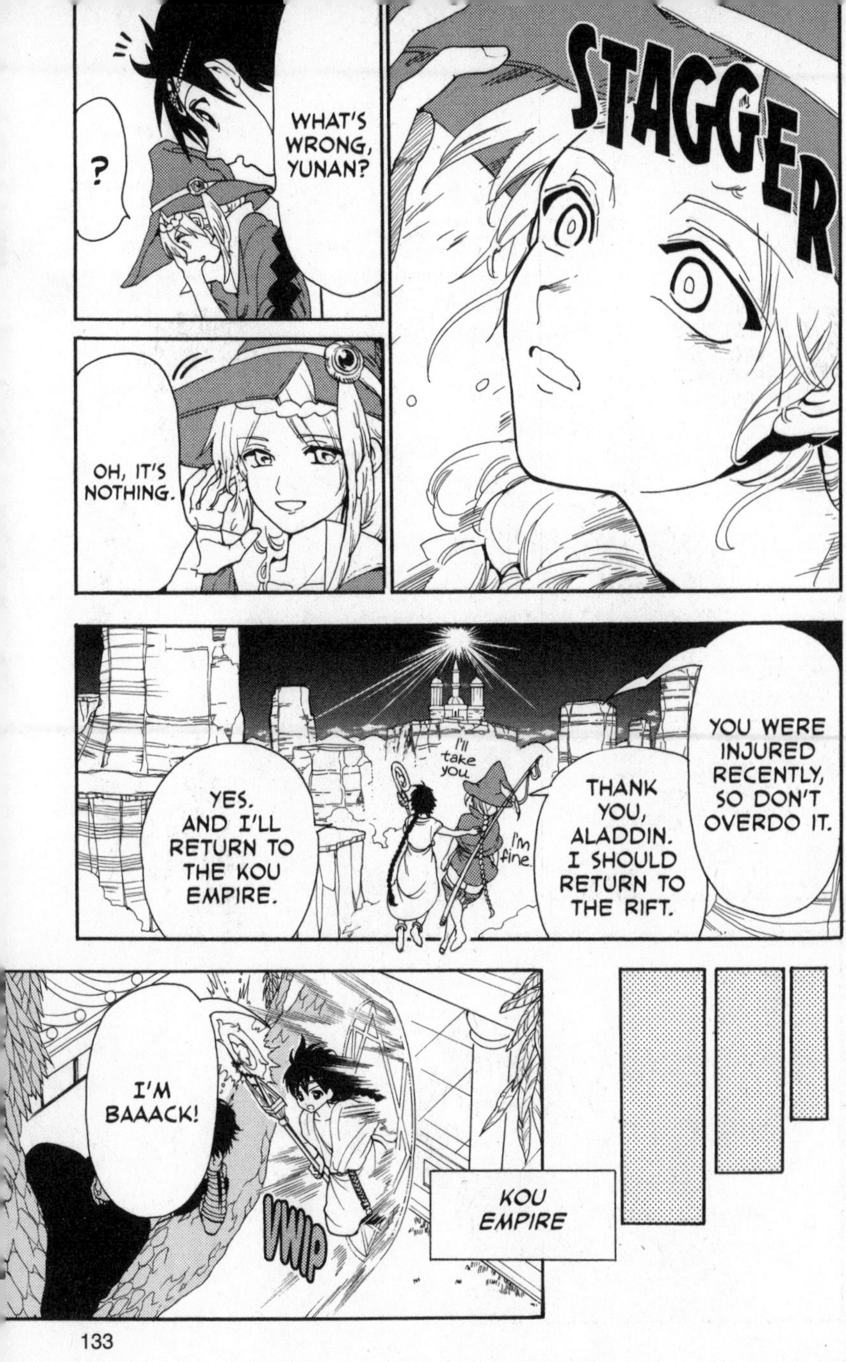
STAGGER
WHAT'S WRONG, YUNAN?
?
OH, IT'S NOTHING.
YOU WERE INJURED RECENTLY, SO DON'T OVERDO IT.
THANK YOU, ALADDIN. I SHOULD RETURN TO THE RIFT.
I'll take you.
I'm fine.
YES. AND I'LL RETURN TO THE KOU EMPIRE.
KOU EMPIRE
I'M BAAACK!
VWIP

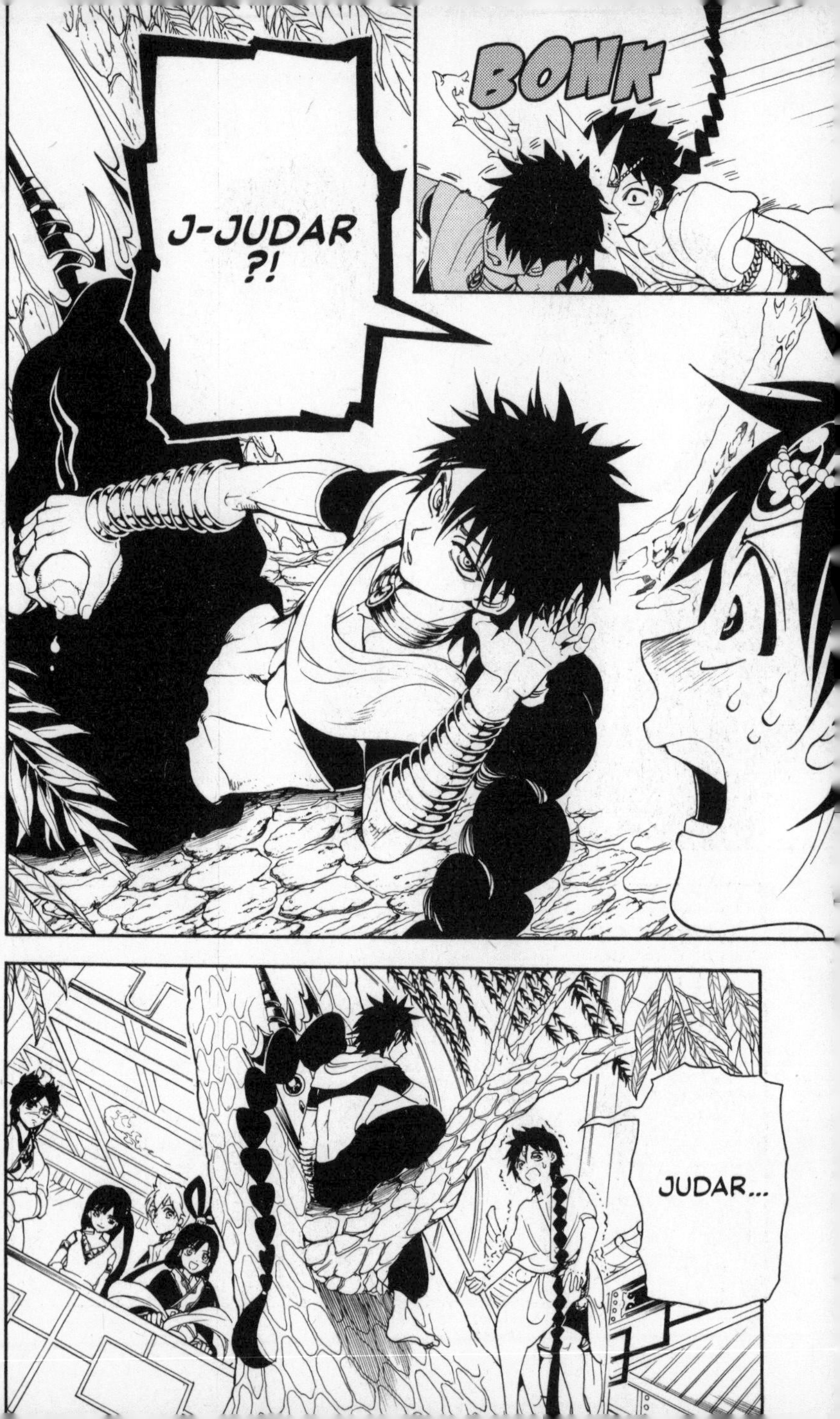
BONK
J-JUDAR ?!
JUDAR...

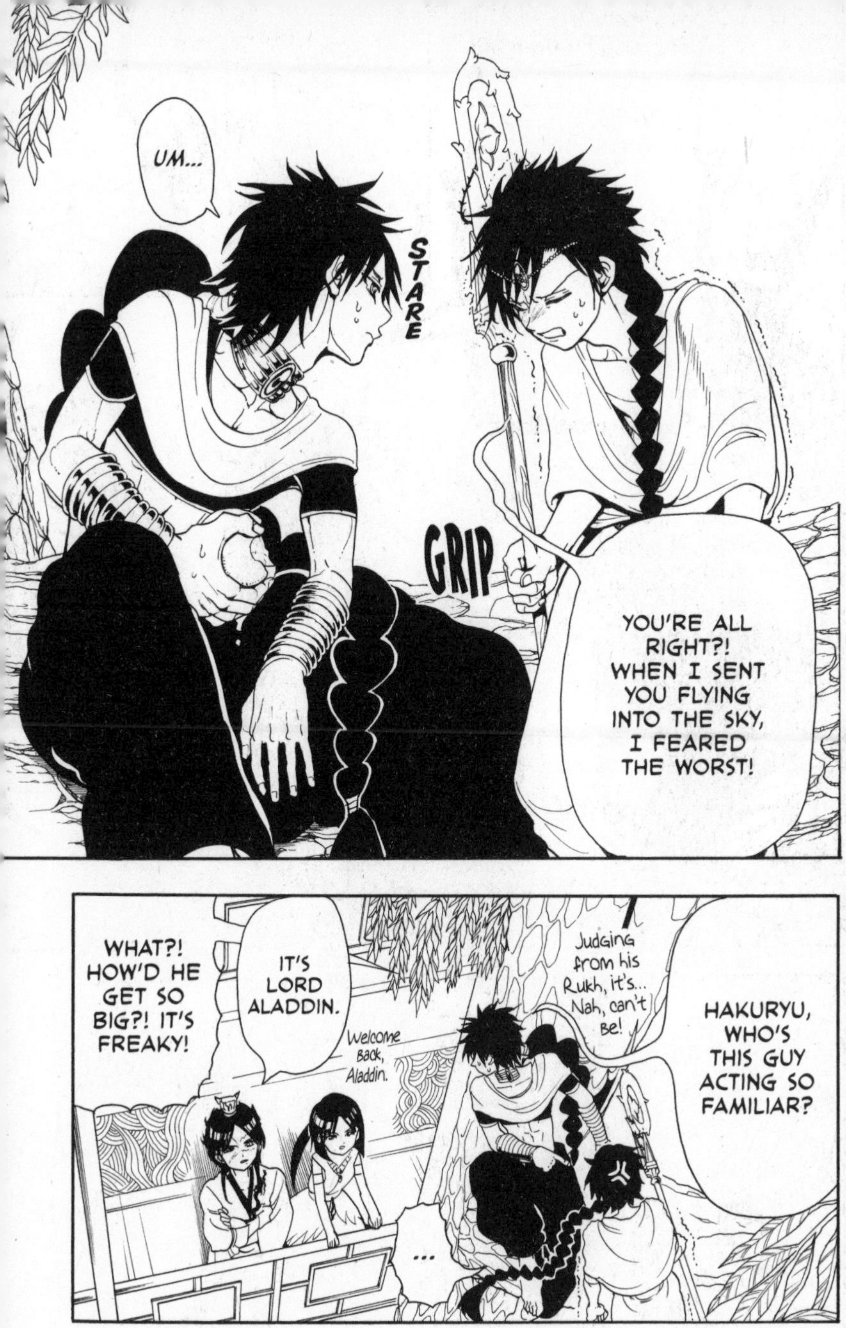
YOU'RE ALL RIGHT?! WHEN I SENT YOU FLYING INTO THE SKY, I FEARED THE WORST!
GRIP
STARE
UM...
HAKURYU, WHO'S THIS GUY ACTING SO FAMILIAR?
Judging from his Rukh, it's... Nah, can't be!
IT'S LORD ALADDIN.
Welcome back, Aladdin.
WHAT?! HOW'D HE GET SO BIG?! IT'S FREAKY!
...

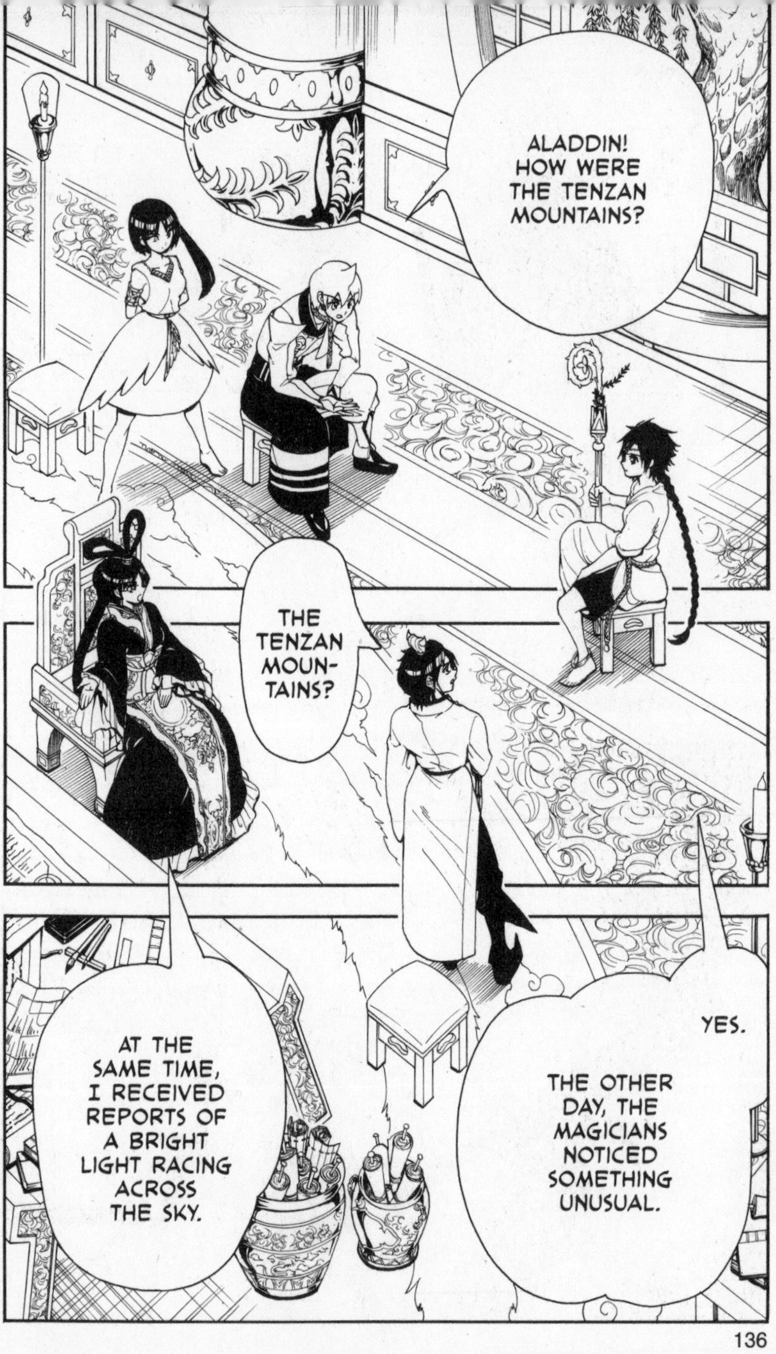
ALADDIN! HOW WERE THE TENZAN MOUNTAINS?
THE TENZAN MOUN-TAINS?
YES.
THE OTHER DAY, THE MAGICIANS NOTICED SOMETHING UNUSUAL.
AT THE SAME TIME, I RECEIVED REPORTS OF A BRIGHT LIGHT RACING ACROSS THE SKY.

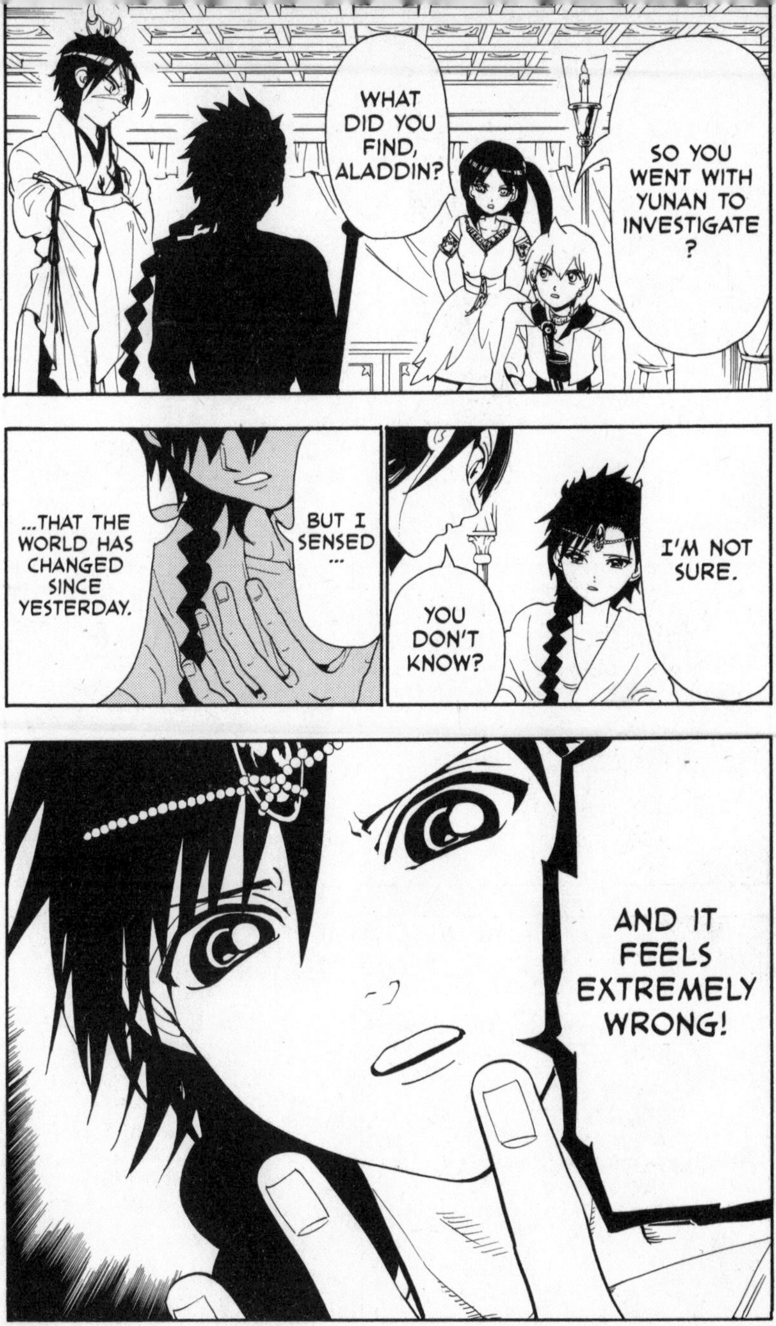
SO YOU WENT WITH YUNAN TO INVESTIGATE?
WHAT DID YOU FIND, ALADDIN?
I'M NOT SURE.
YOU DON'T KNOW?
BUT I SENSED...
...THAT THE WORLD HAS CHANGED SINCE YESTERDAY.
AND IT FEELS EXTREMELY WRONG!

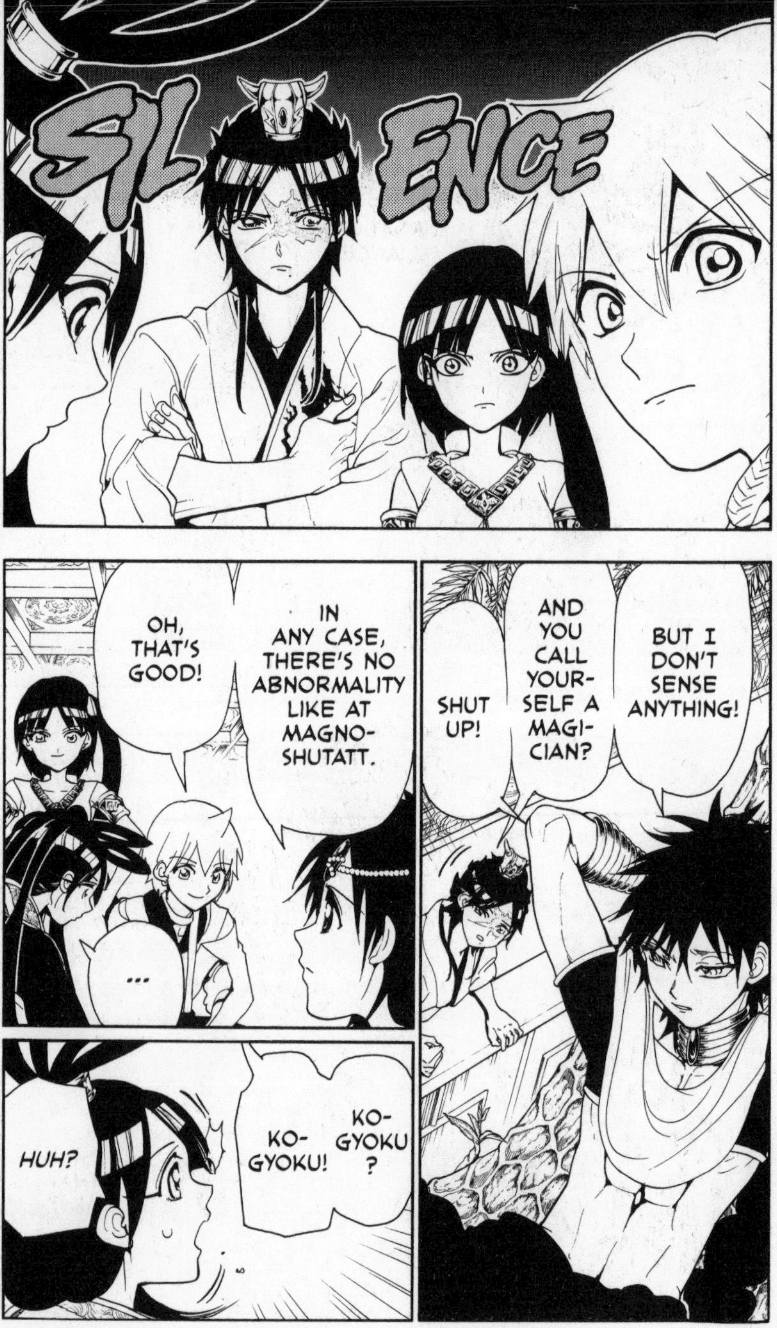
SILENCE
BUT I DON'T SENSE ANYTHING!
AND YOU CALL YOURSELF A MAGICIAN?
SHUT UP!
IN ANY CASE, THERE'S NO ABNORMALITY LIKE AT MAGNOSHUTATT.
OH, THAT'S GOOD!
...
KOGYOKU?
KOGYOKU!
HUH?

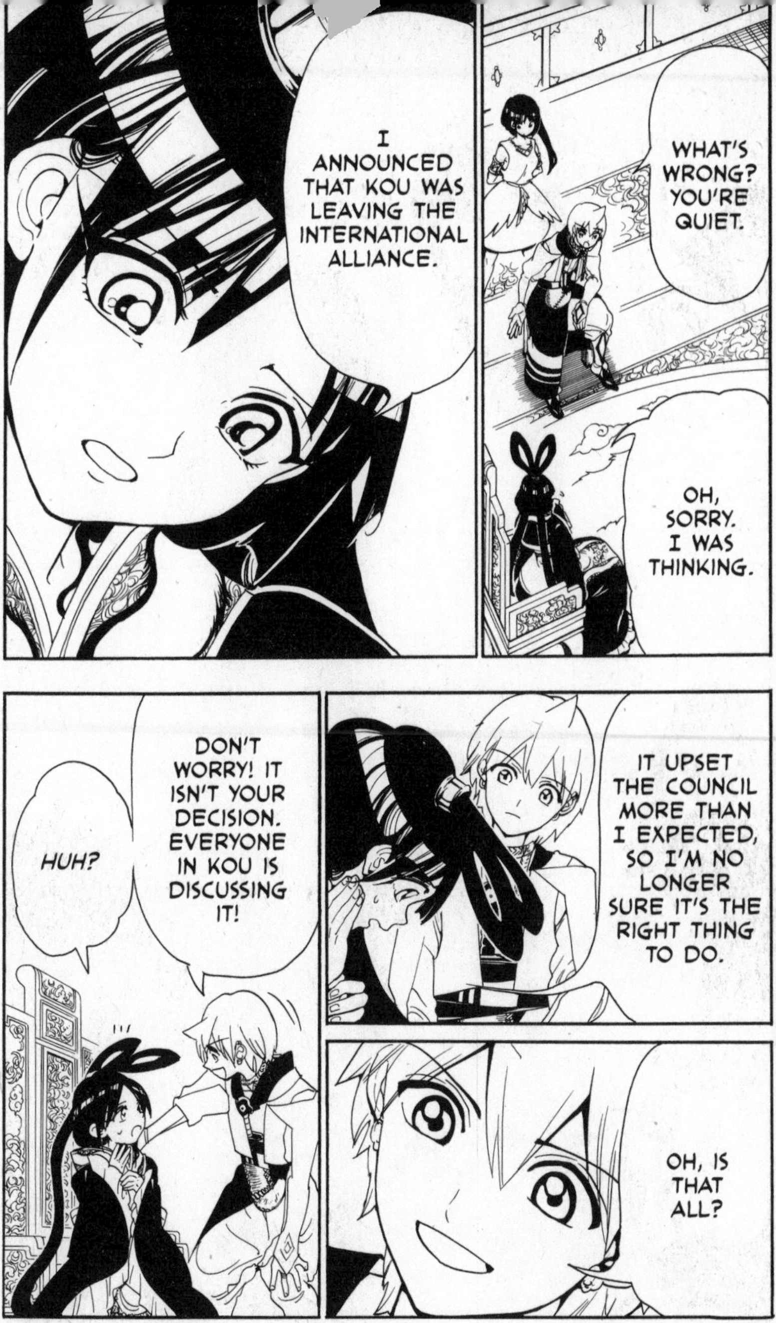
WHAT'S WRONG? YOU'RE QUIET.
OH, SORRY. I WAS THINKING.
I ANNOUNCED THAT KOU WAS LEAVING THE INTERNATIONAL ALLIANCE.
IT UPSET THE COUNCIL MORE THAN I EXPECTED, SO I'M NO LONGER SURE IT'S THE RIGHT THING TO DO.
OH, IS THAT ALL?
DON'T WORRY! IT ISN'T YOUR DECISION. EVERYONE IN KOU IS DISCUSSING IT!
HUH?

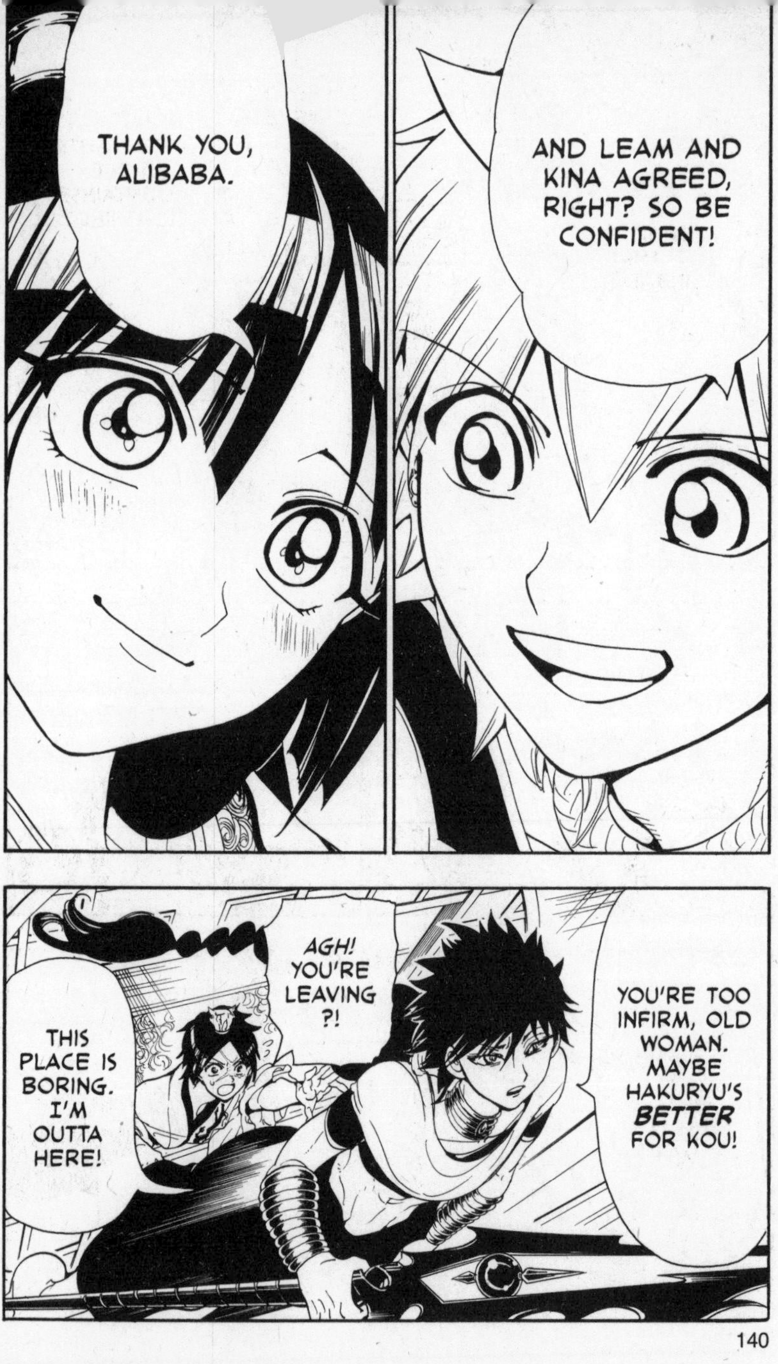
AND LEAM AND KINA AGREED, RIGHT? SO BE CONFIDENT!
THANK YOU, ALIBABA.
YOU'RE TOO INFIRM, OLD WOMAN. MAYBE HAKURYU'S *BETTER* FOR KOU!
AGH! YOU'RE LEAVING?!
THIS PLACE IS BORING. I'M OUTTA HERE!

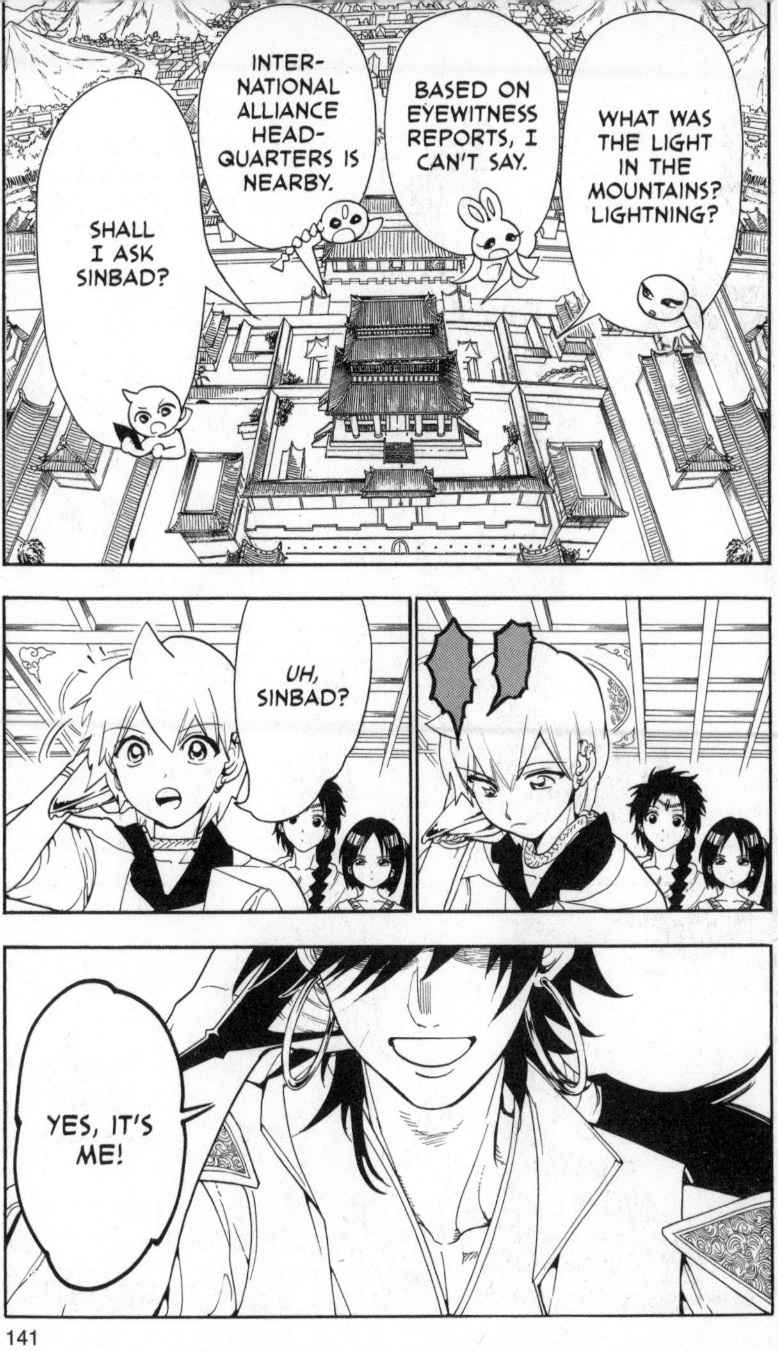
WHAT WAS THE LIGHT IN THE MOUNTAINS? LIGHTNING?
BASED ON EYEWITNESS REPORTS, I CAN'T SAY.
INTER-NATIONAL ALLIANCE HEAD-QUARTERS IS NEARBY.
SHALL I ASK SINBAD?
UH, SINBAD?
YES, IT'S ME!

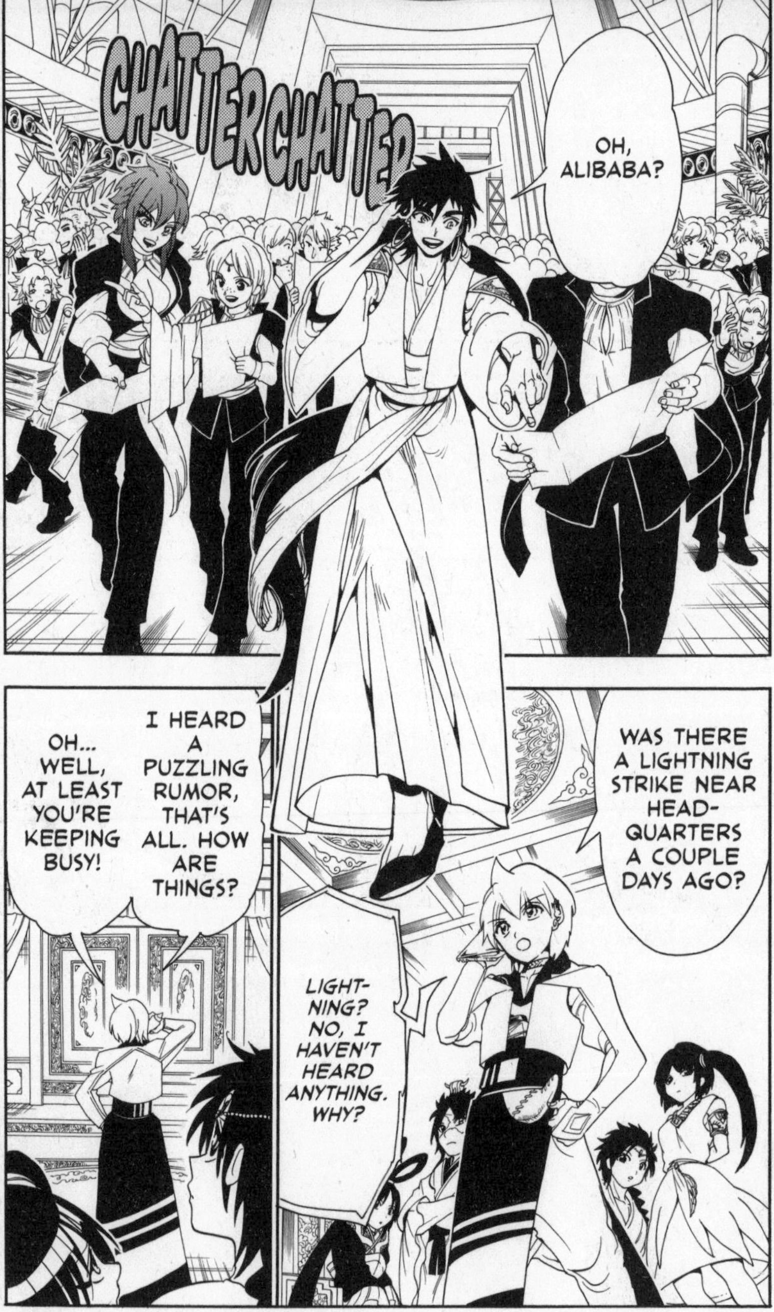
OH, ALIBABA?
CHATTER CHATTER
WAS THERE A LIGHTNING STRIKE NEAR HEAD-QUARTERS A COUPLE DAYS AGO?
LIGHT-NING? NO, I HAVEN'T HEARD ANYTHING. WHY?
I HEARD A PUZZLING RUMOR, THAT'S ALL. HOW ARE THINGS?
OH... WELL, AT LEAST YOU'RE KEEPING BUSY!

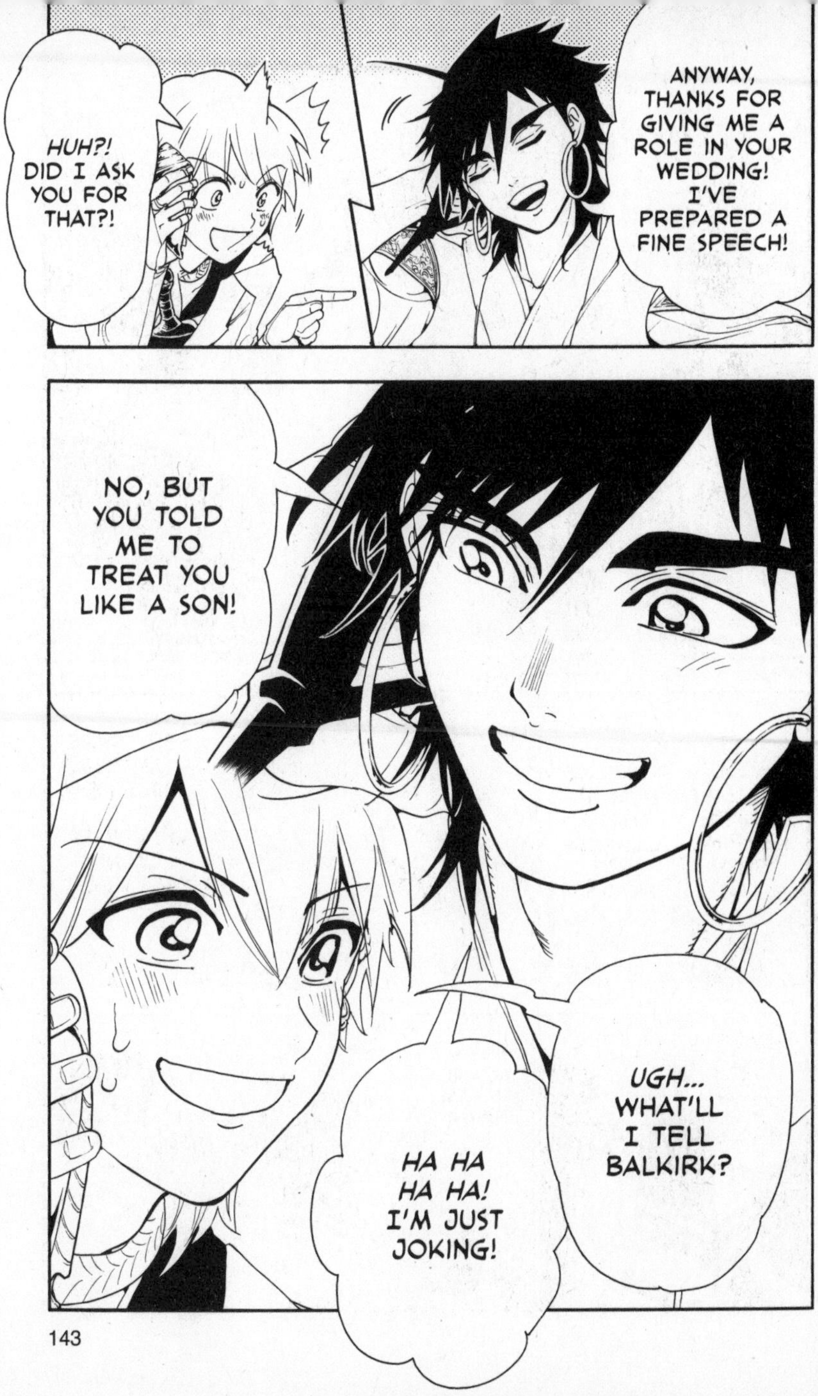
ANYWAY, THANKS FOR GIVING ME A ROLE IN YOUR WEDDING! I'VE PREPARED A FINE SPEECH!
HUH?! DID I ASK YOU FOR THAT?!
NO, BUT YOU TOLD ME TO TREAT YOU LIKE A SON!
UGH... WHAT'LL I TELL BALKIRK?
HA HA HA HA! I'M JUST JOKING!

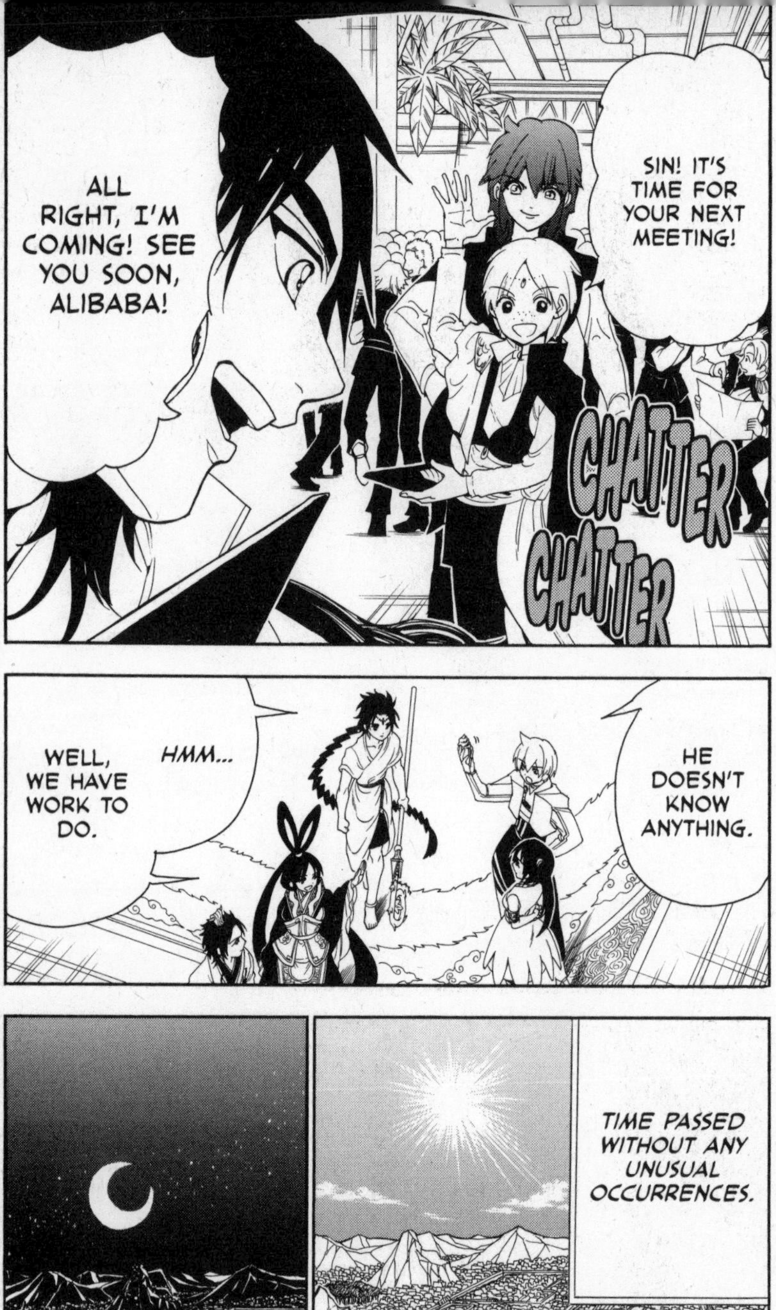
SIN! IT'S TIME FOR YOUR NEXT MEETING!
ALL RIGHT, I'M COMING! SEE YOU SOON, ALIBABA!
CHATTER
CHATTER
HE DOESN'T KNOW ANYTHING.
HMM...
WELL, WE HAVE WORK TO DO.
TIME PASSED WITHOUT ANY UNUSUAL OCCURRENCES.

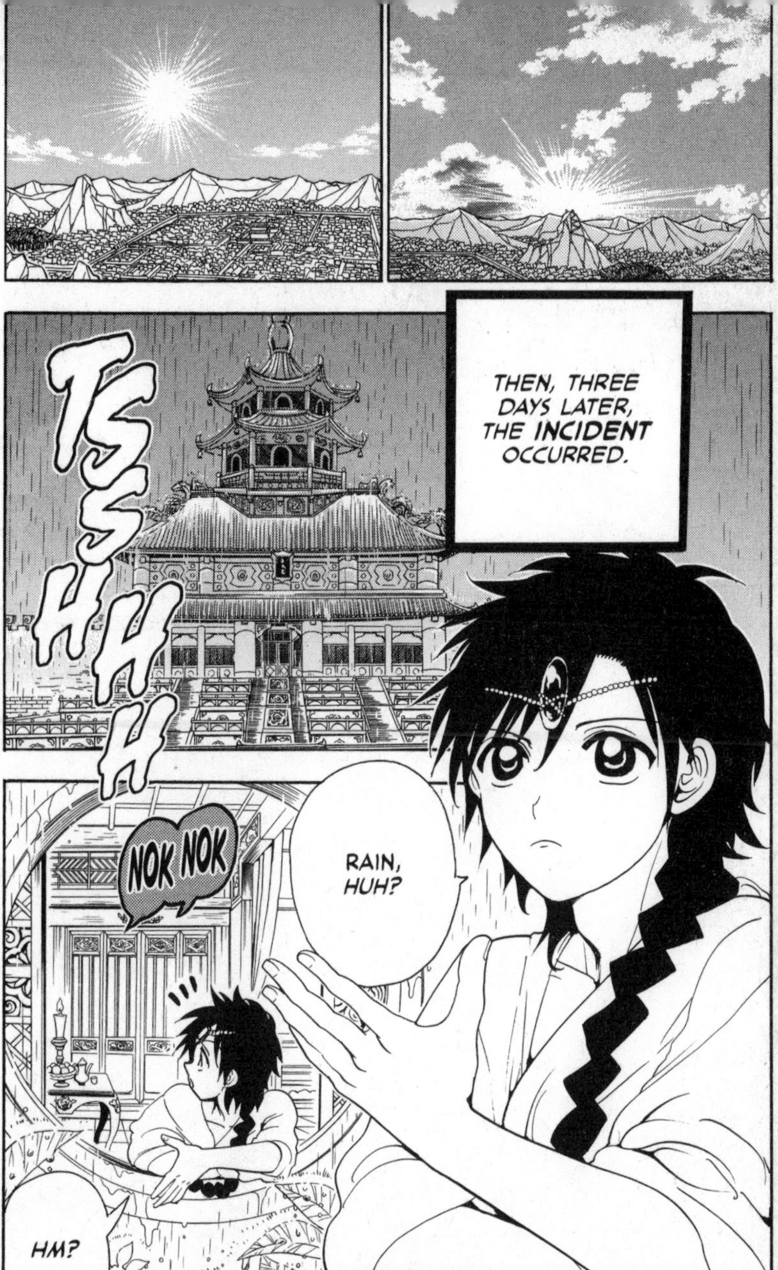
THEN, THREE DAYS LATER, THE INCIDENT OCCURRED.
TSSHHH
RAIN, HUH?
NOK NOK
HM?

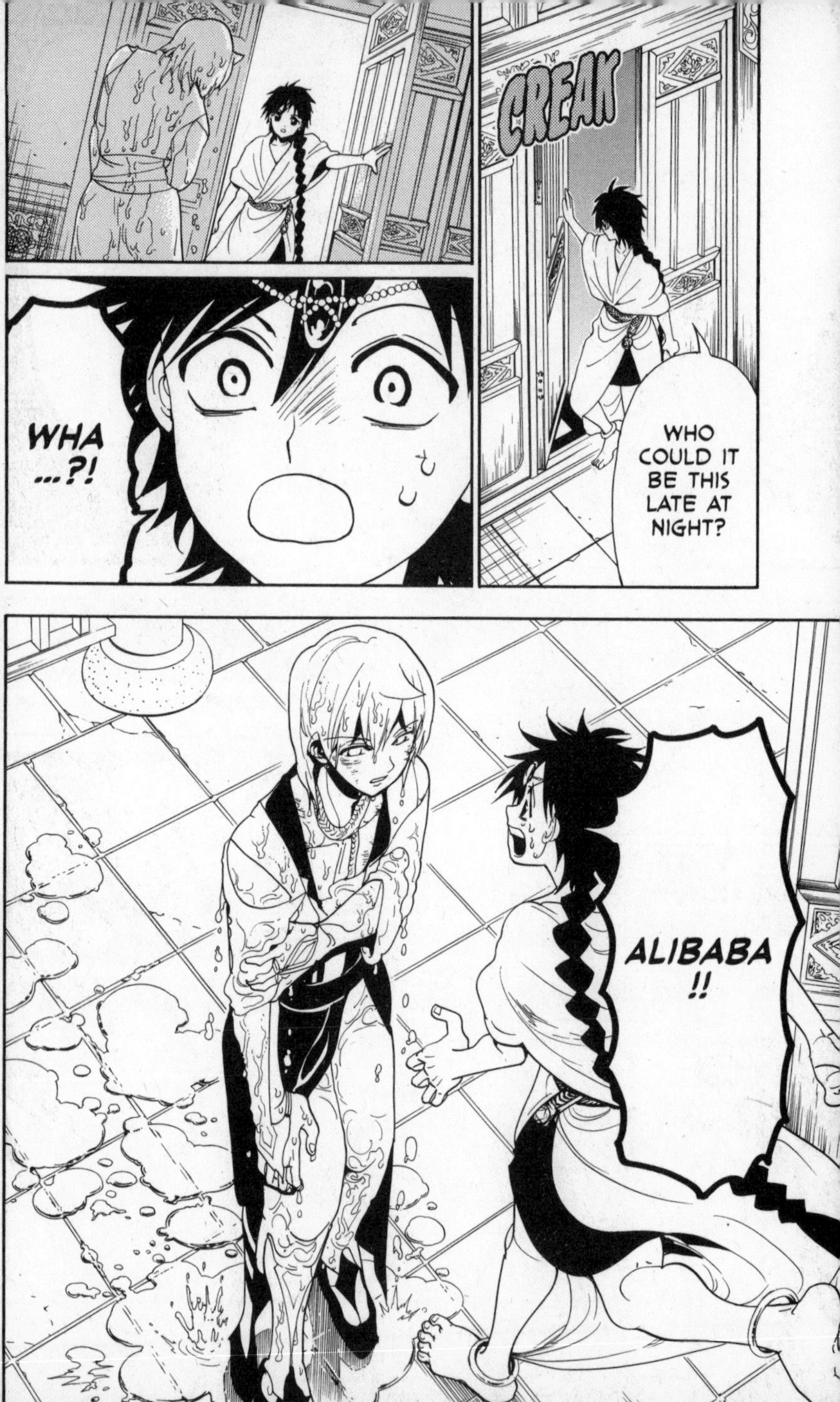
CREAK
WHO COULD IT BE THIS LATE AT NIGHT?
WHA ...?!
ALIBABA !!

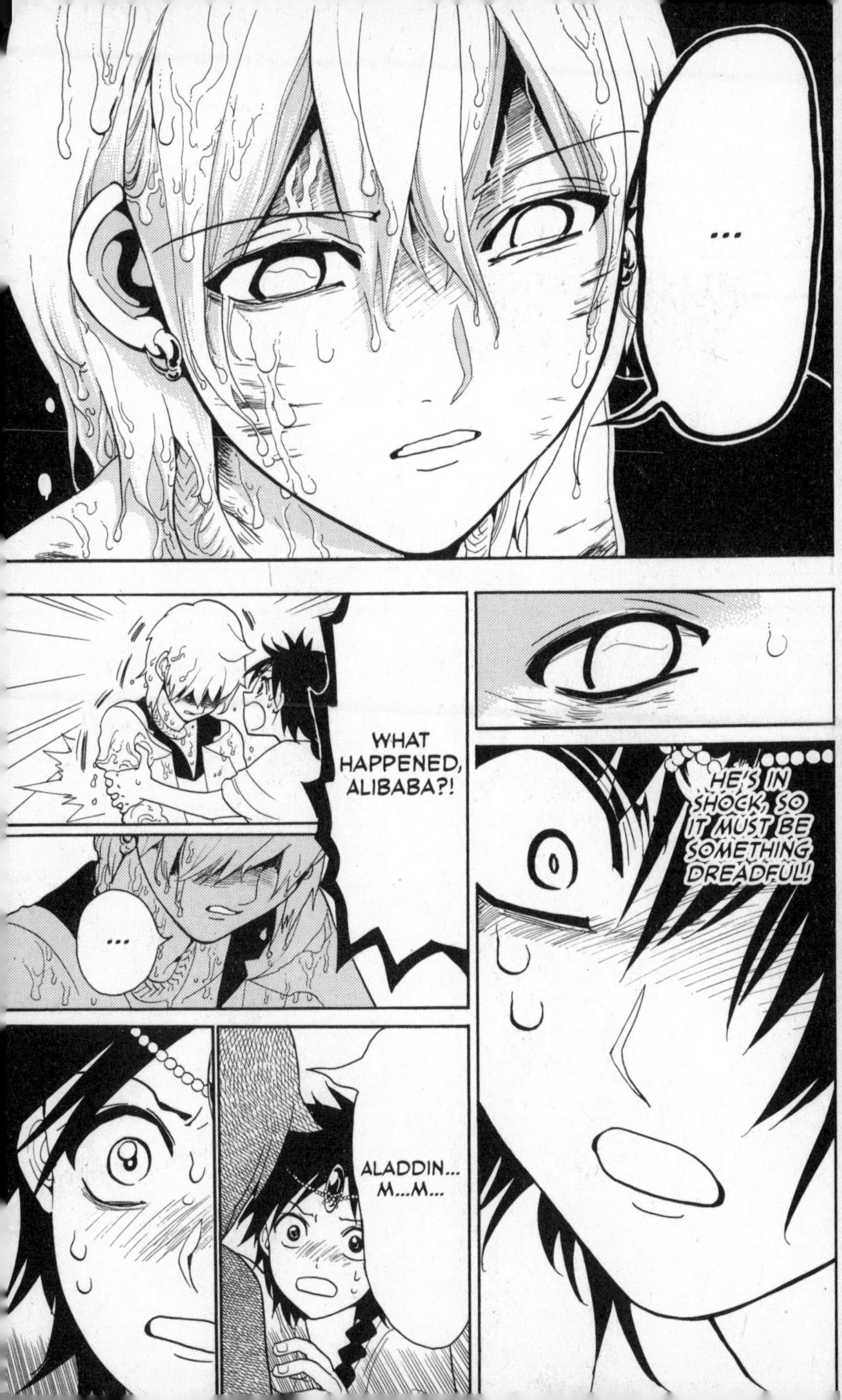
...
WHAT HAPPENED, ALIBABA?!
...
HE'S IN SHOCK, SO IT MUST BE SOMETHING DREADFUL!
ALADDIN... M...M...

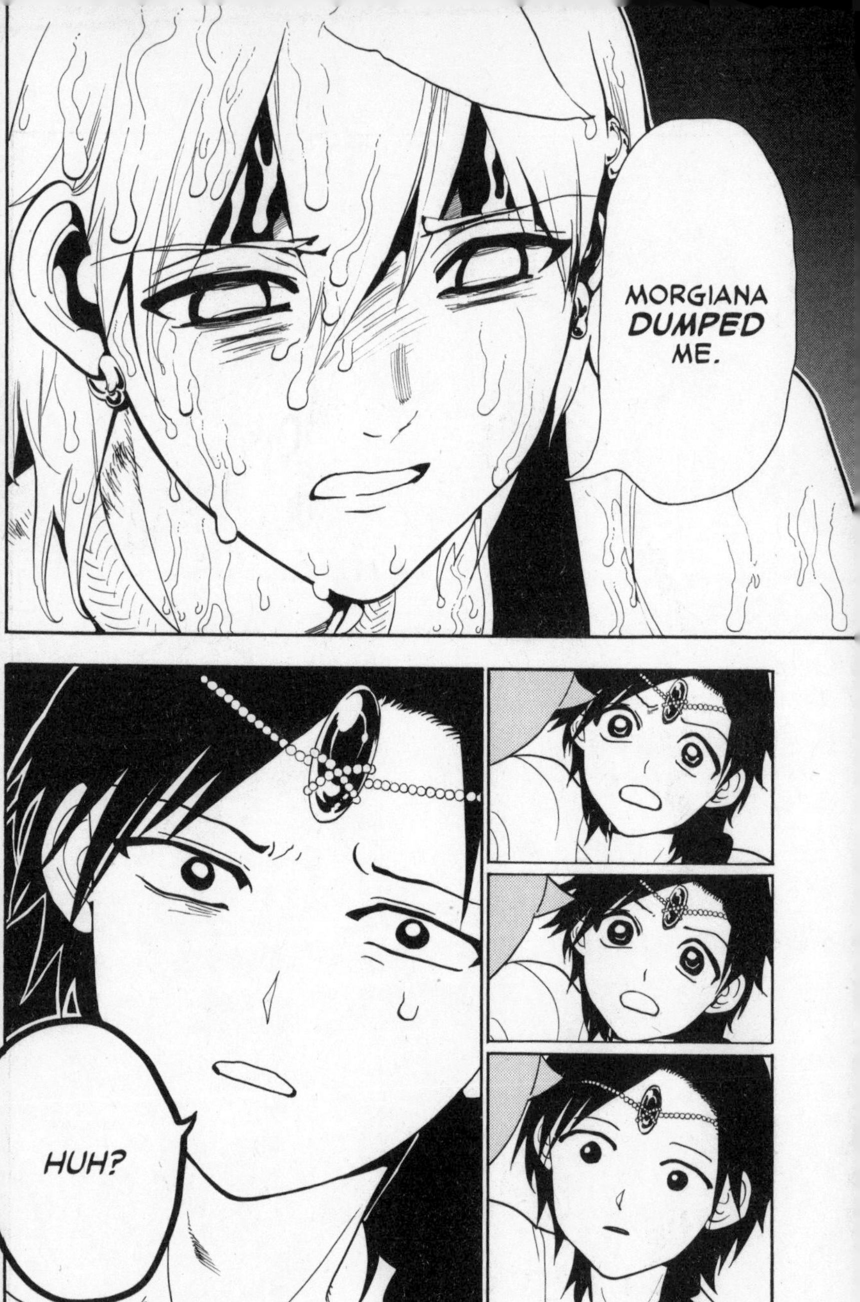
MORGIANA DUMPED ME.
HUH?

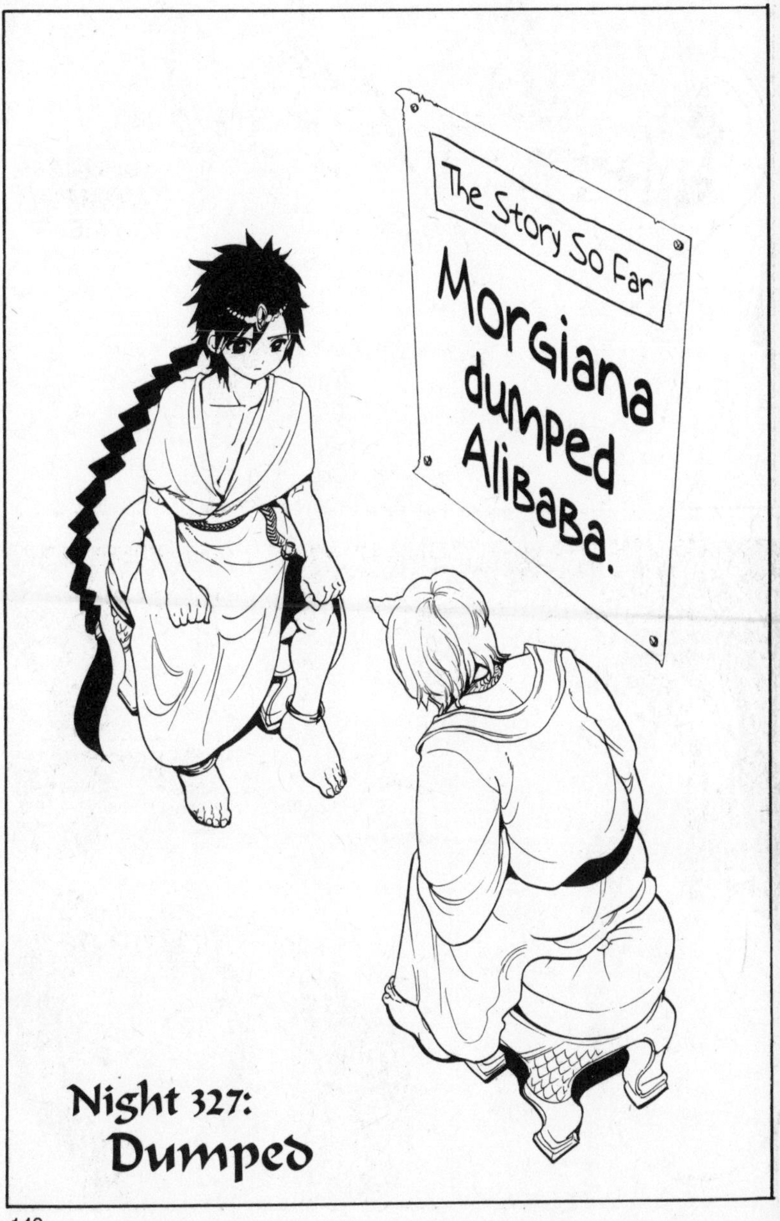
The Story So Far
Morgiana dumped Alibaba.
Night 327:
Dumped

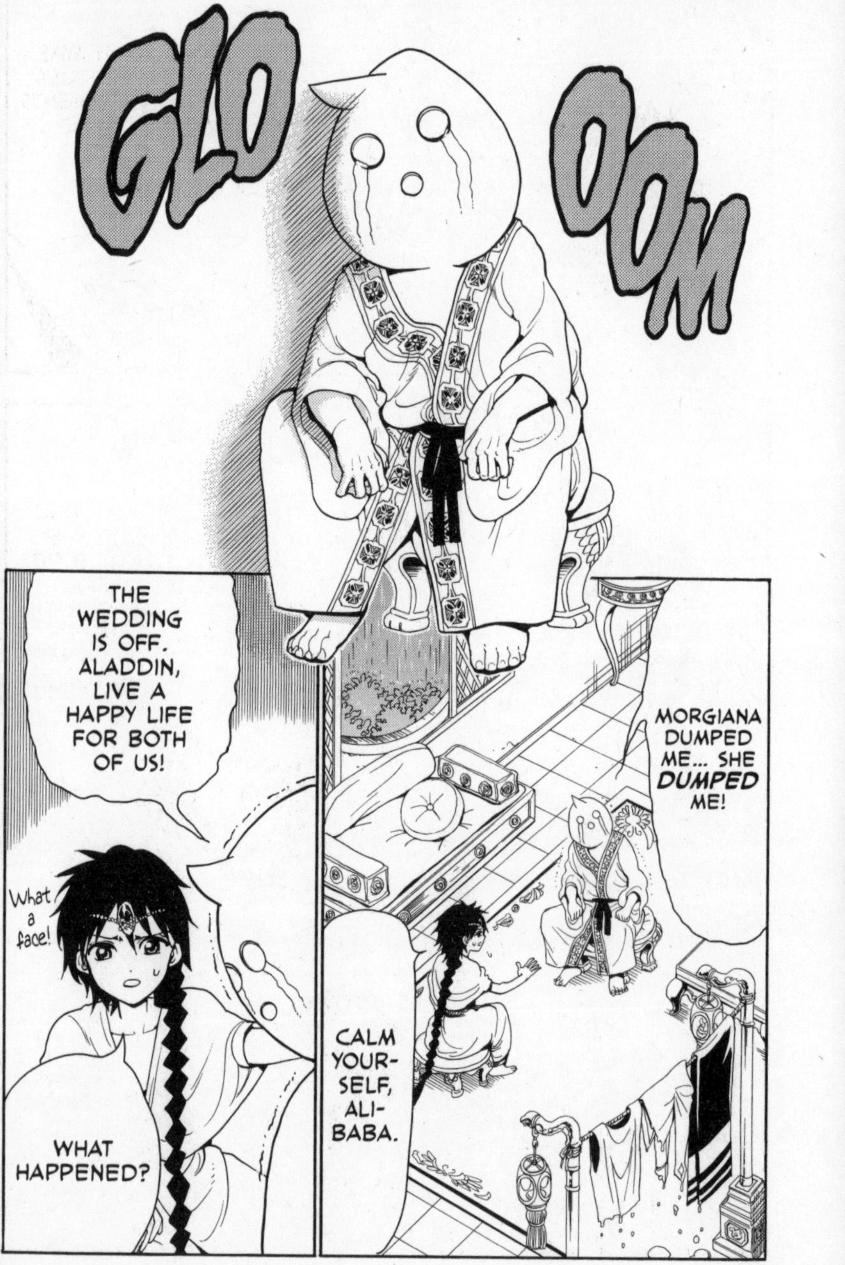
GLOOOM
MORGIANA DUMPED ME... SHE *DUMPED* ME!
CALM YOURSELF, ALI-BABA.
THE WEDDING IS OFF. ALADDIN, LIVE A HAPPY LIFE FOR BOTH OF US!
What a face!
WHAT HAPPENED?

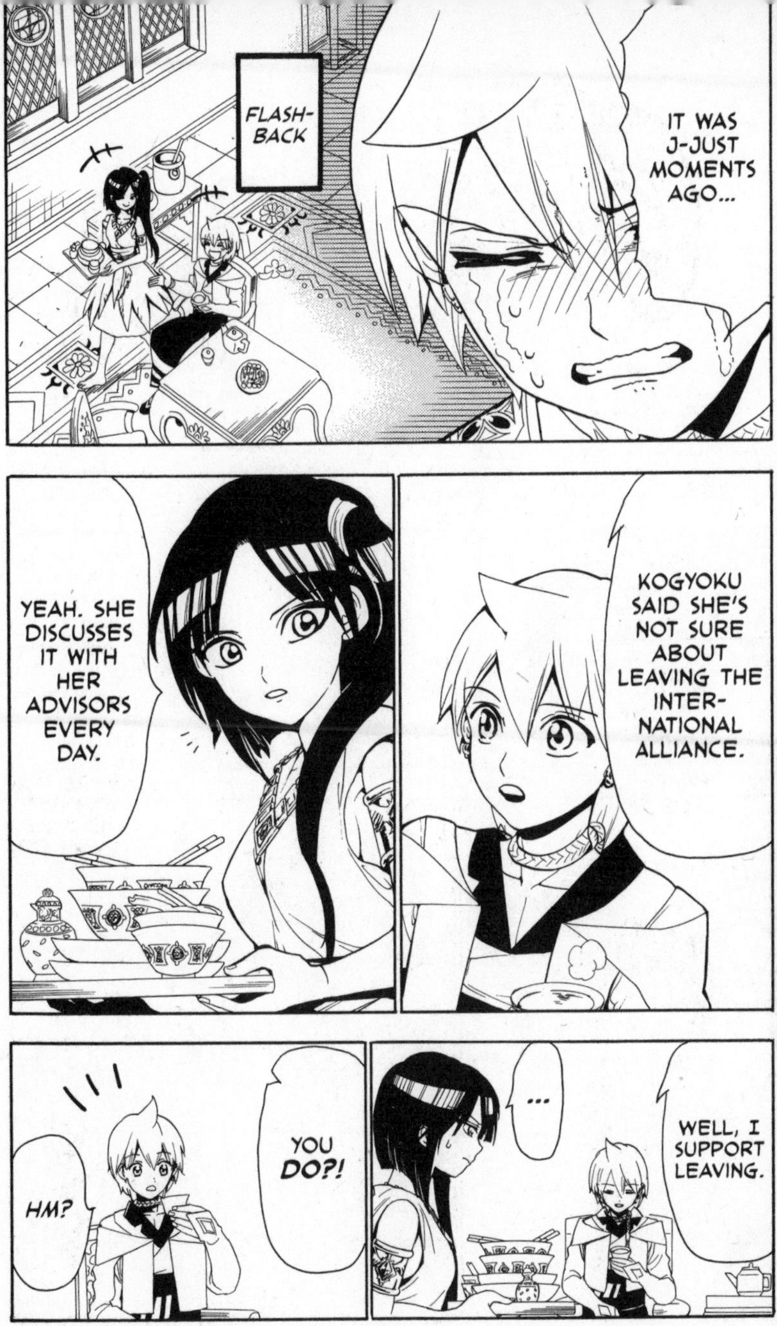
IT WAS J-JUST MOMENTS AGO...
FLASH-BACK
KOGYOKU SAID SHE'S NOT SURE ABOUT LEAVING THE INTER-NATIONAL ALLIANCE.
YEAH. SHE DISCUSSES IT WITH HER ADVISORS EVERY DAY.
WELL, I SUPPORT LEAVING.
...
YOU *DO?!*
HM?

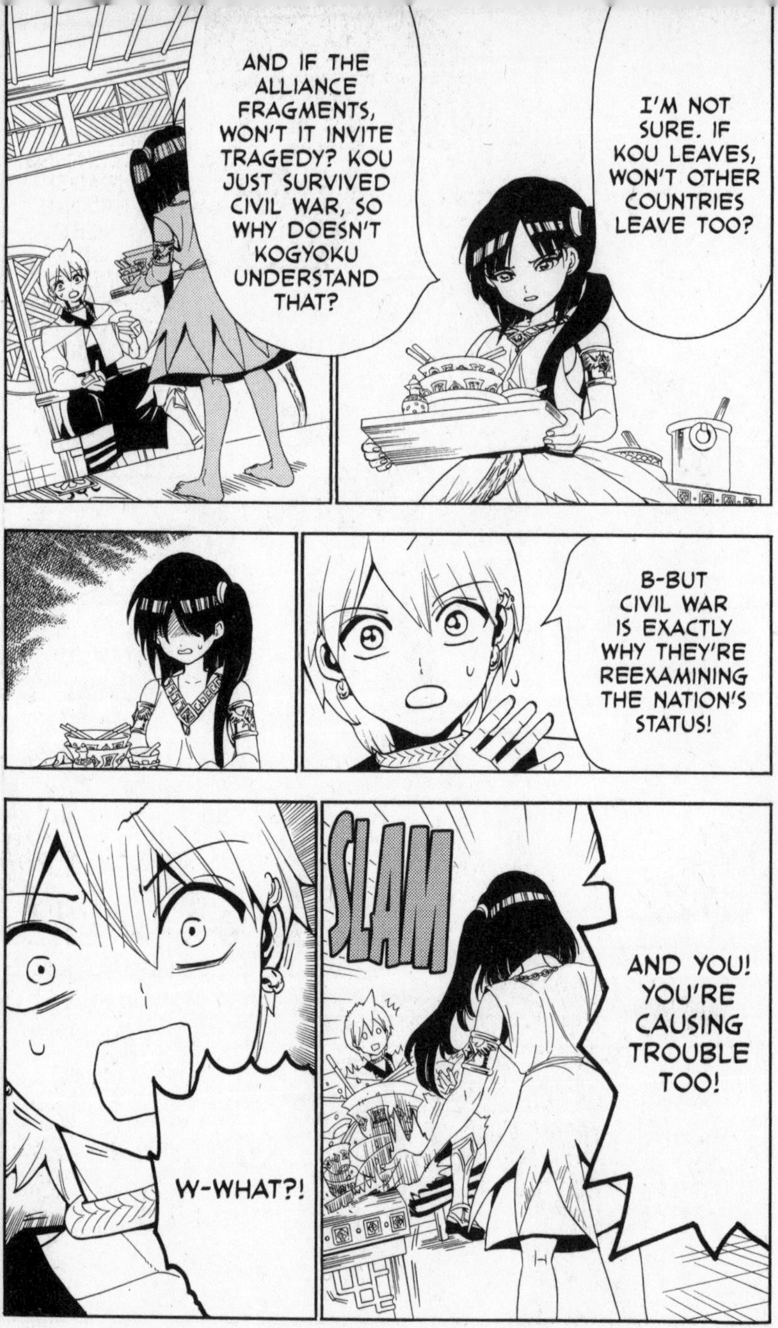
I'M NOT SURE. IF KOU LEAVES, WON'T OTHER COUNTRIES LEAVE TOO?
AND IF THE ALLIANCE FRAGMENTS, WON'T IT INVITE TRAGEDY? KOU JUST SURVIVED CIVIL WAR, SO WHY DOESN'T KOGYOKU UNDERSTAND THAT?
B-BUT CIVIL WAR IS EXACTLY WHY THEY'RE REEXAMINING THE NATION'S STATUS!
SLAM
AND YOU! YOU'RE CAUSING TROUBLE TOO!
W-WHAT?!

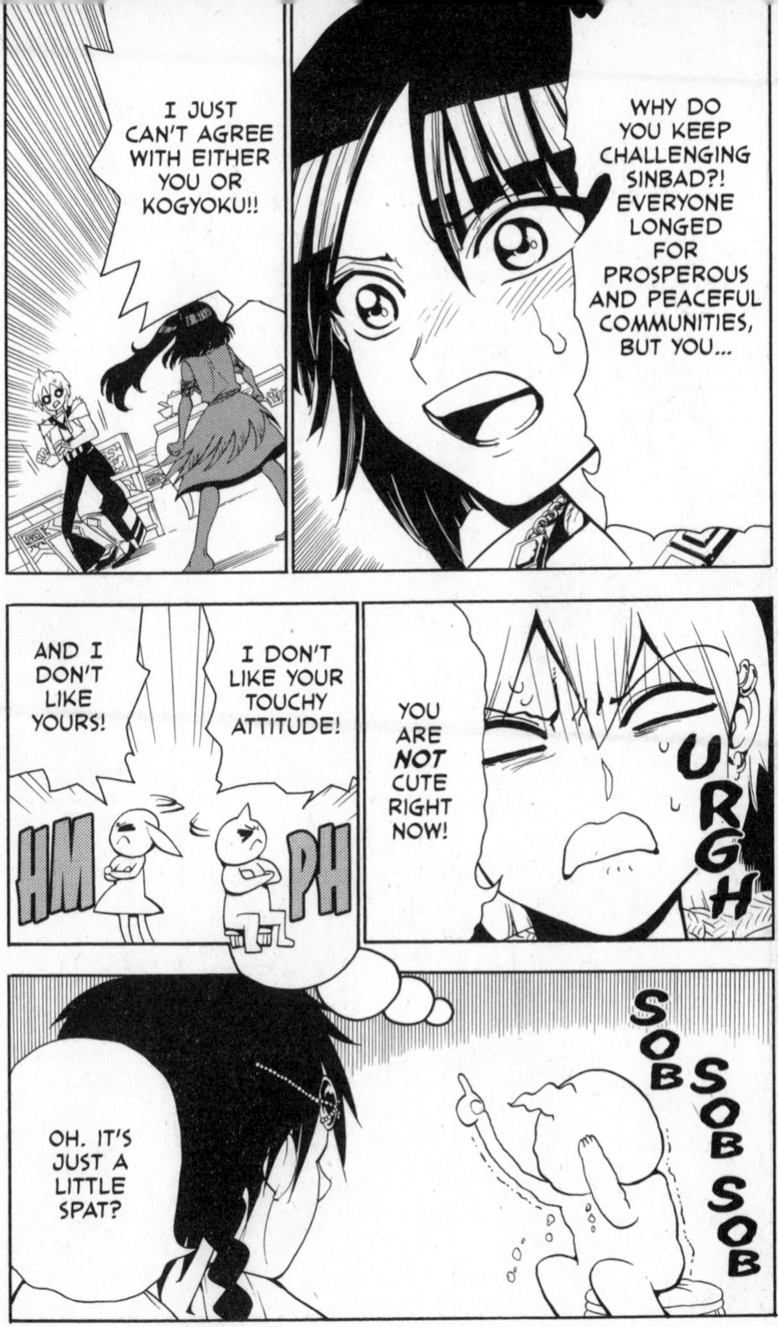
WHY DO YOU KEEP CHALLENGING SINBAD?! EVERYONE LONGED FOR PROSPEROUS AND PEACEFUL COMMUNITIES, BUT YOU...
I JUST CAN'T AGREE WITH EITHER YOU OR KOGYOKU!!
URGH
YOU ARE NOT CUTE RIGHT NOW!
I DON'T LIKE YOUR TOUCHY ATTITUDE!
AND I DON'T LIKE YOURS!
HMPH
SOB SOB SOB SOB
OH. IT'S JUST A LITTLE SPAT?

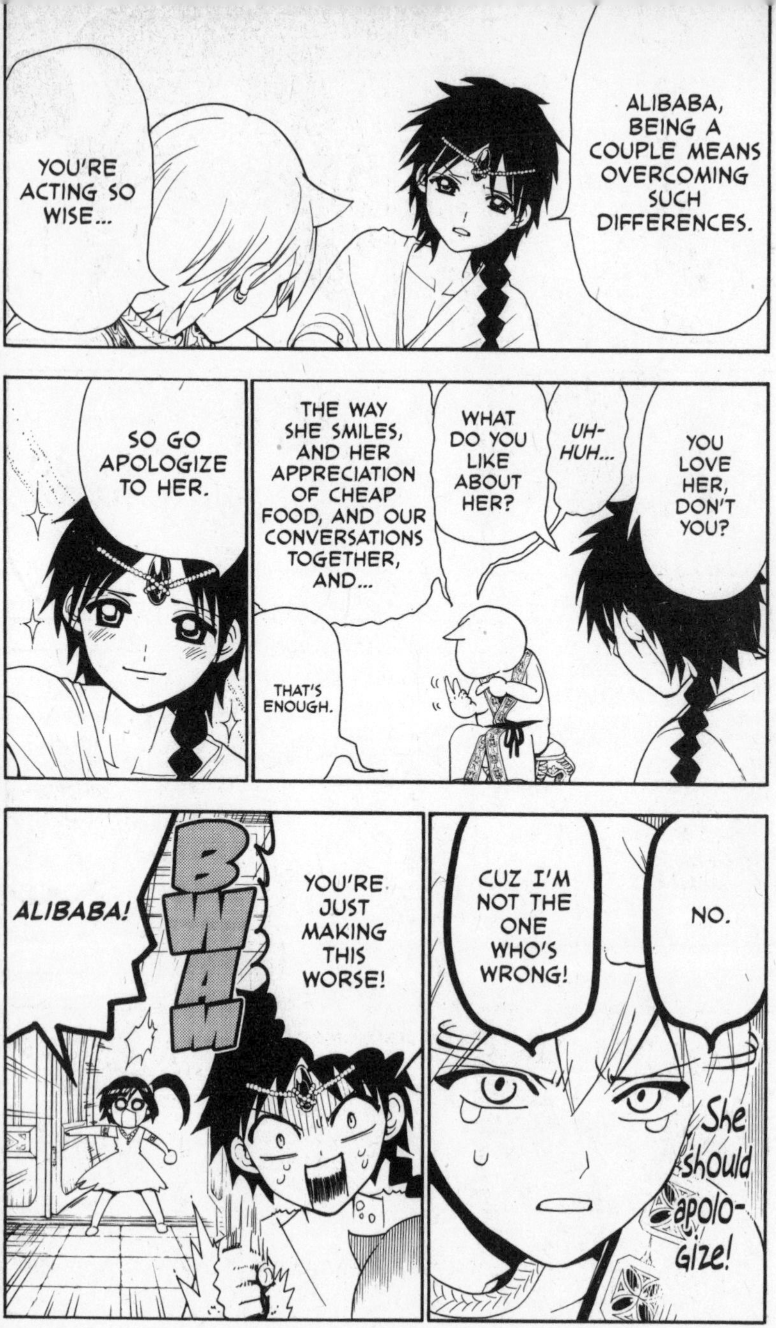
ALIBABA, BEING A COUPLE MEANS OVERCOMING SUCH DIFFERENCES.
YOU'RE ACTING SO WISE...
YOU LOVE HER, DON'T YOU?
UH-HUH...
WHAT DO YOU LIKE ABOUT HER?
THE WAY SHE SMILES, AND HER APPRECIATION OF CHEAP FOOD, AND OUR CONVERSATIONS TOGETHER, AND...
THAT'S ENOUGH.
SO GO APOLOGIZE TO HER.
NO.
CUZ I'M NOT THE ONE WHO'S WRONG!
She should apolo-gize!
YOU'RE JUST MAKING THIS WORSE!
BWAM
ALIBABA!

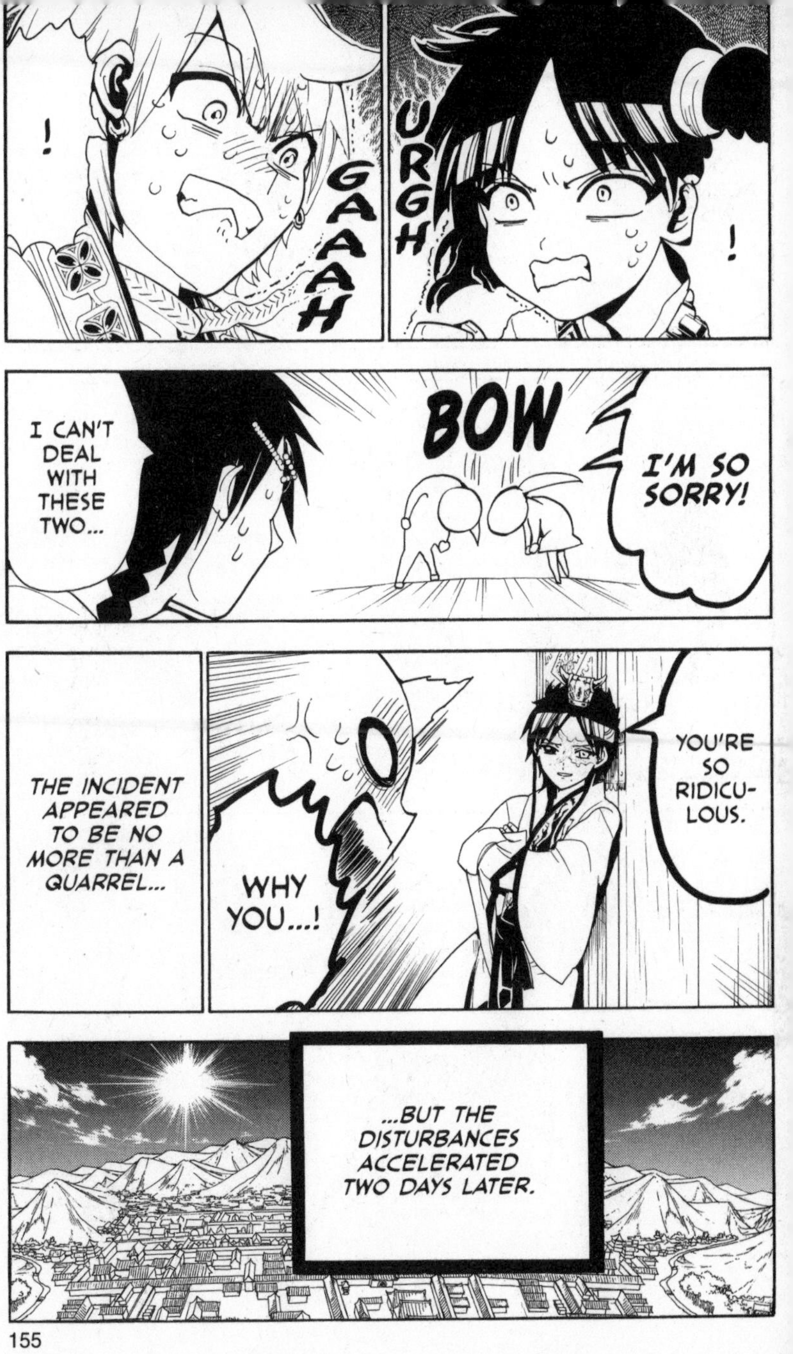
URGH
!
!
GAAAH
I'M SO SORRY!
BOW
I CAN'T DEAL WITH THESE TWO...
YOU'RE SO RIDICULOUS.
WHY YOU...!
THE INCIDENT APPEARED TO BE NO MORE THAN A QUARREL...
...BUT THE DISTURBANCES ACCELERATED TWO DAYS LATER.

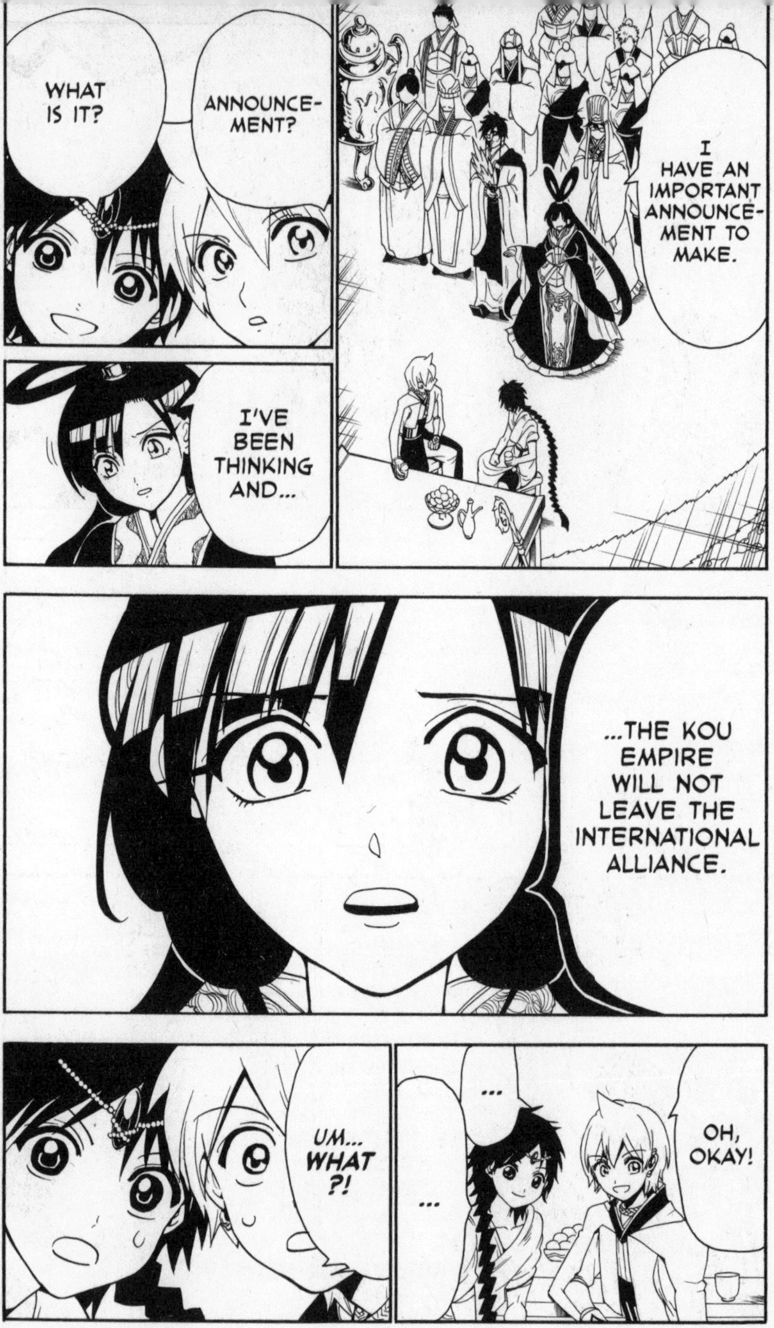
I HAVE AN IMPORTANT ANNOUNCEMENT TO MAKE.
ANNOUNCEMENT?
WHAT IS IT?
I'VE BEEN THINKING AND...
...THE KOU EMPIRE WILL NOT LEAVE THE INTERNATIONAL ALLIANCE.
OH, OKAY!
...
...
UM... WHAT?!

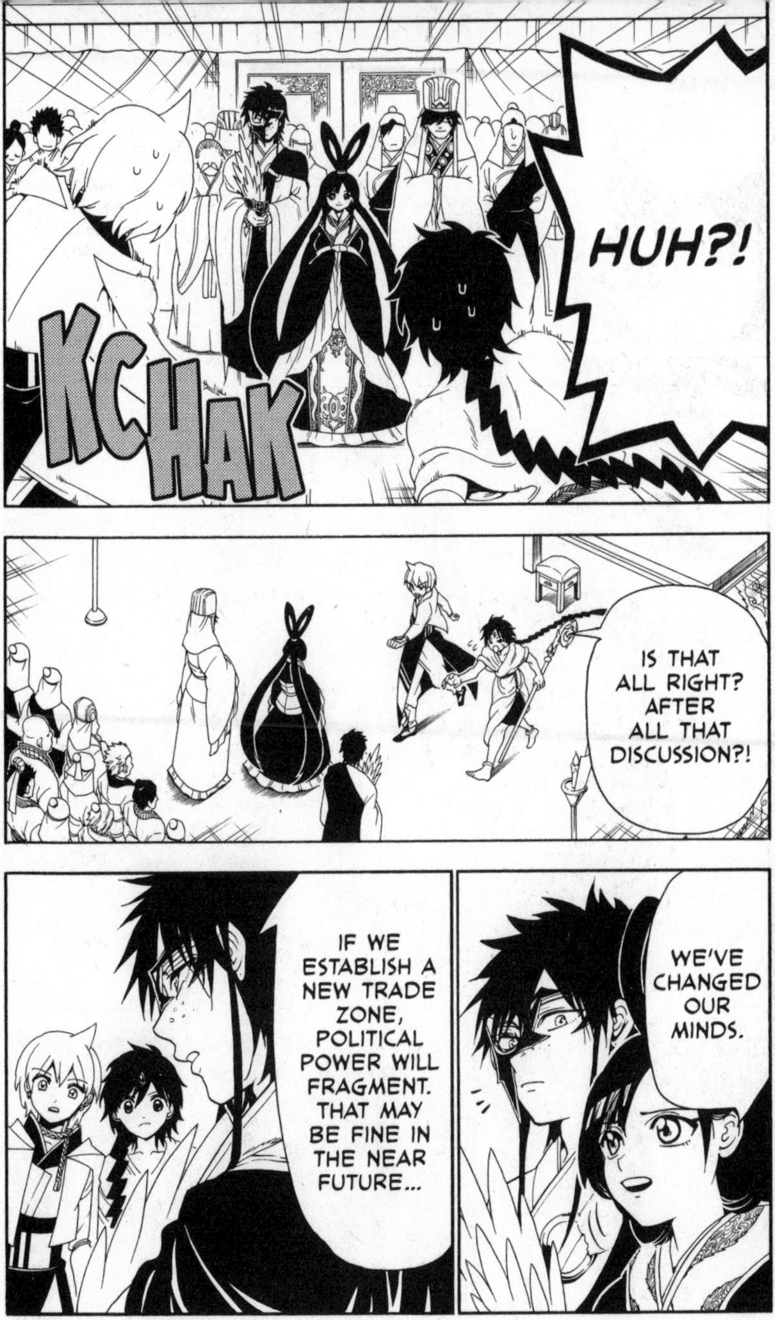
HUH?!
KCHAK
IS THAT ALL RIGHT? AFTER ALL THAT DISCUSSION?!
WE'VE CHANGED OUR MINDS.
IF WE ESTABLISH A NEW TRADE ZONE, POLITICAL POWER WILL FRAGMENT. THAT MAY BE FINE IN THE NEAR FUTURE...

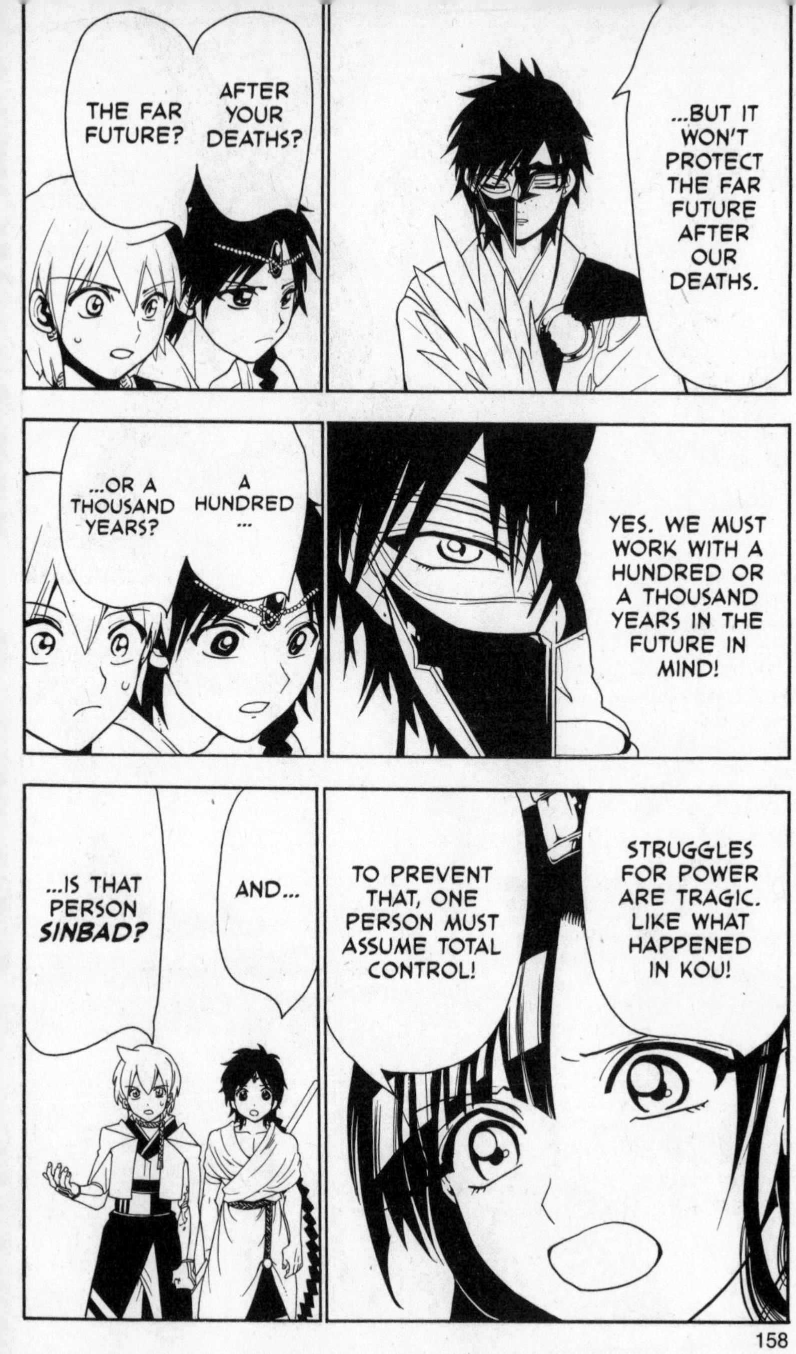
...BUT IT WON'T PROTECT THE FAR FUTURE AFTER OUR DEATHS.
AFTER YOUR DEATHS?
THE FAR FUTURE?
YES. WE MUST WORK WITH A HUNDRED OR A THOUSAND YEARS IN THE FUTURE IN MIND!
A HUNDRED...
...OR A THOUSAND YEARS?
STRUGGLES FOR POWER ARE TRAGIC. LIKE WHAT HAPPENED IN KOU!
TO PREVENT THAT, ONE PERSON MUST ASSUME TOTAL CONTROL!
AND...
...IS THAT PERSON *SINBAD?*

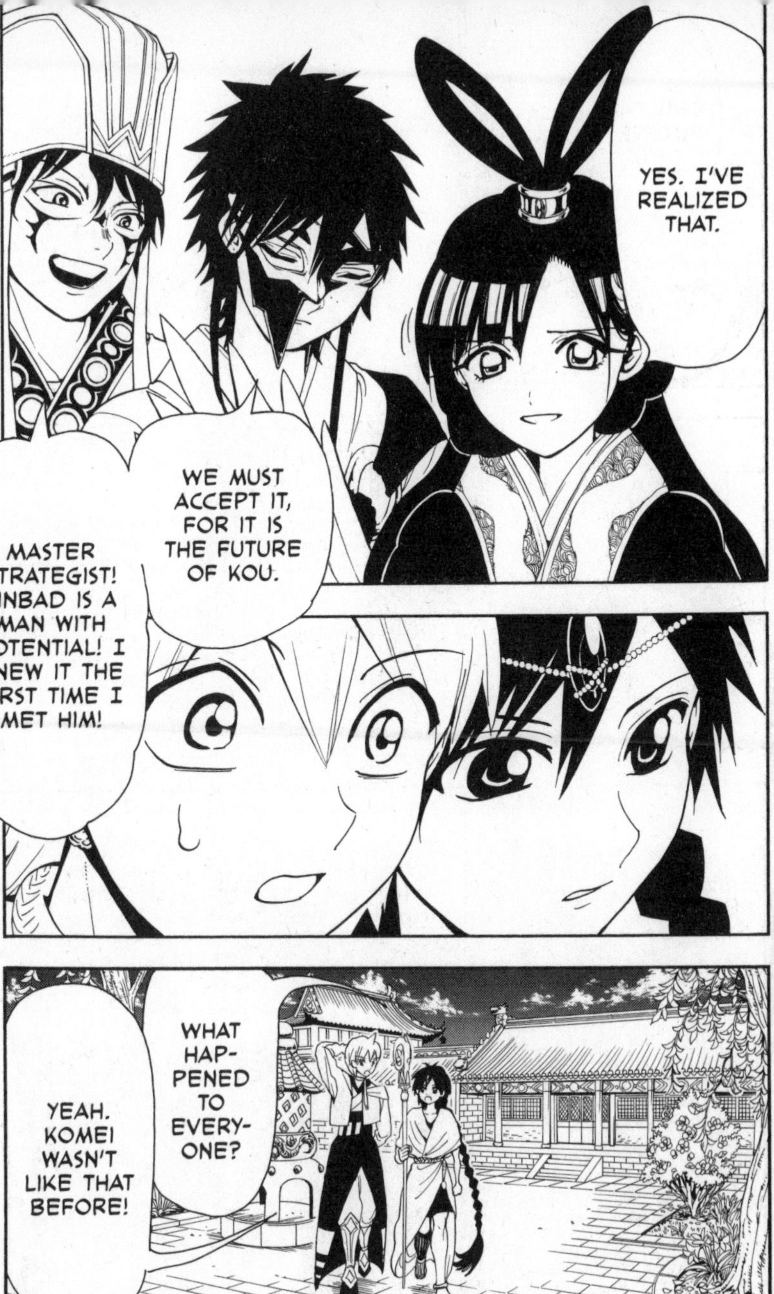
YES. I'VE REALIZED THAT.
WE MUST ACCEPT IT, FOR IT IS THE FUTURE OF KOU.
MASTER STRATEGIST! SINBAD IS A MAN WITH POTENTIAL! I KNEW IT THE FIRST TIME I MET HIM!
WHAT HAP-PENED TO EVERY-ONE?
YEAH. KOMEI WASN'T LIKE THAT BEFORE!

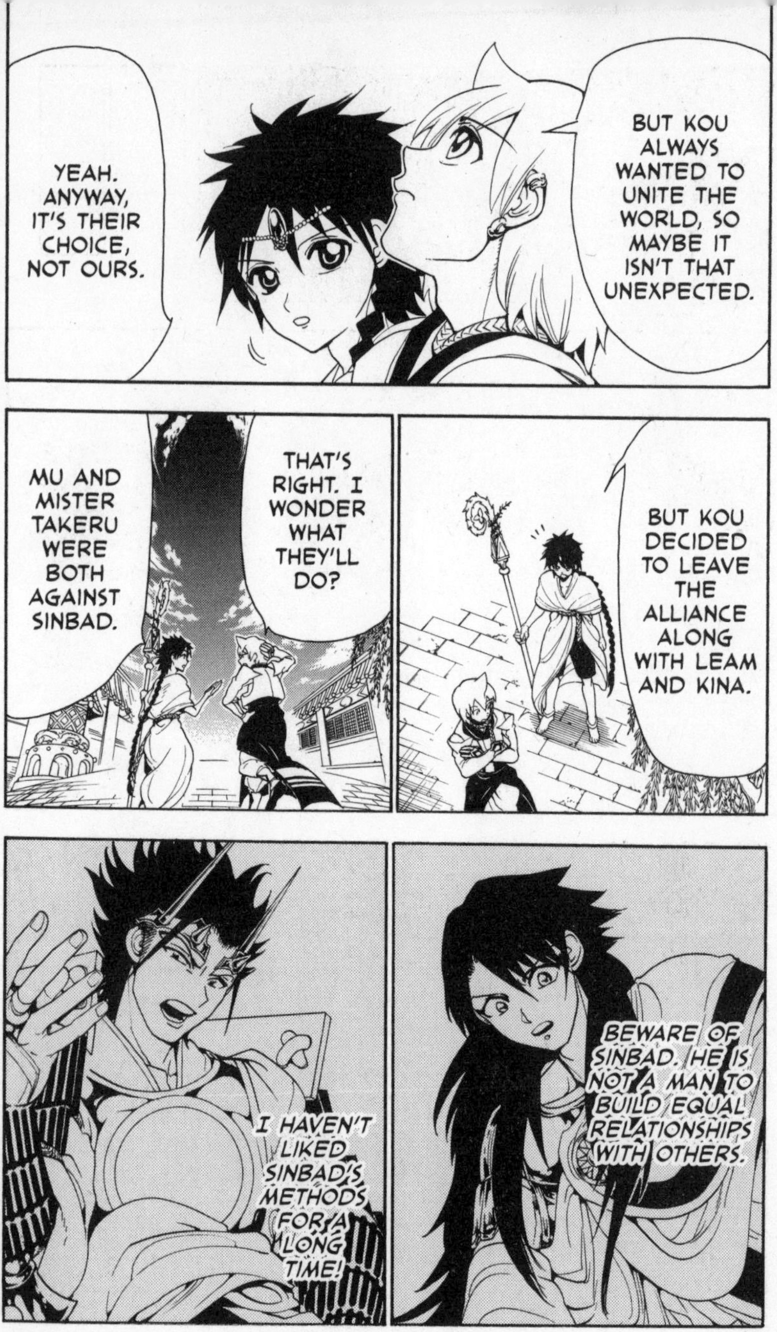
BUT KOU ALWAYS WANTED TO UNITE THE WORLD, SO MAYBE IT ISN'T THAT UNEXPECTED.
YEAH. ANYWAY, IT'S THEIR CHOICE, NOT OURS.
BUT KOU DECIDED TO LEAVE THE ALLIANCE ALONG WITH LEAM AND KINA.
THAT'S RIGHT. I WONDER WHAT THEY'LL DO?
MU AND MISTER TAKERU WERE BOTH AGAINST SINBAD.
BEWARE OF SINBAD. HE IS NOT A MAN TO BUILD EQUAL RELATIONSHIPS WITH OTHERS.
I HAVEN'T LIKED SINBAD'S METHODS FOR A LONG TIME!

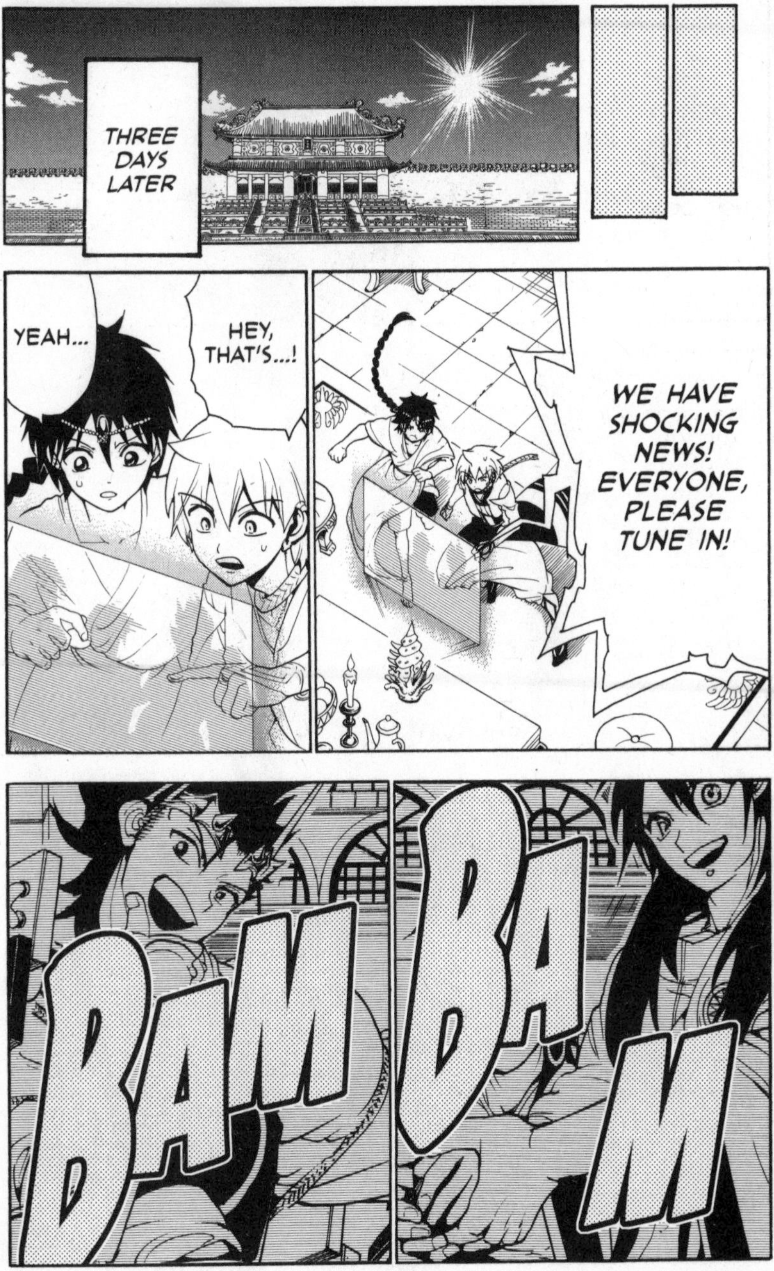
THREE DAYS LATER
WE HAVE SHOCKING NEWS! EVERYONE, PLEASE TUNE IN!
HEY, THAT'S...!
YEAH...
BAM
BAM

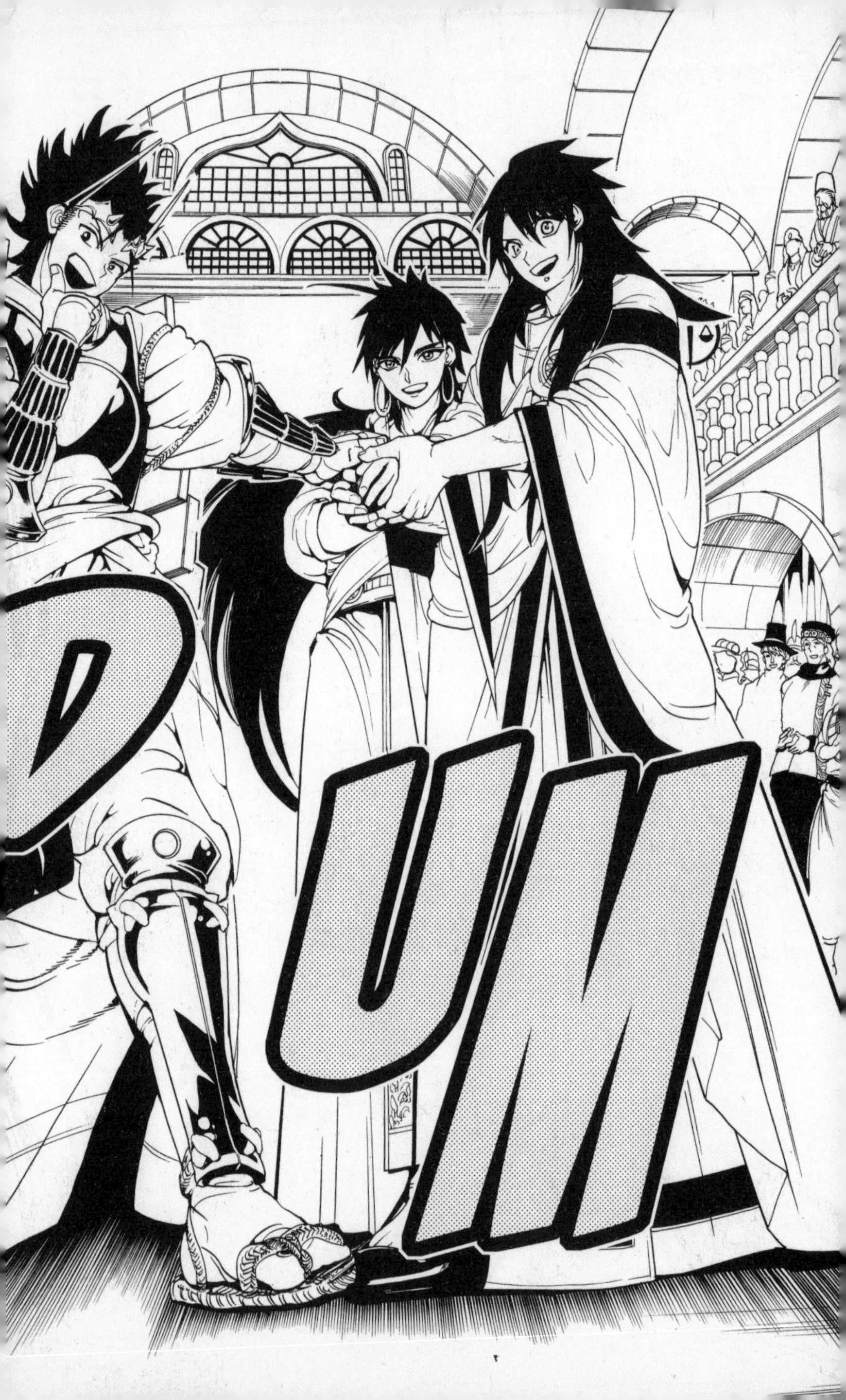
DUM

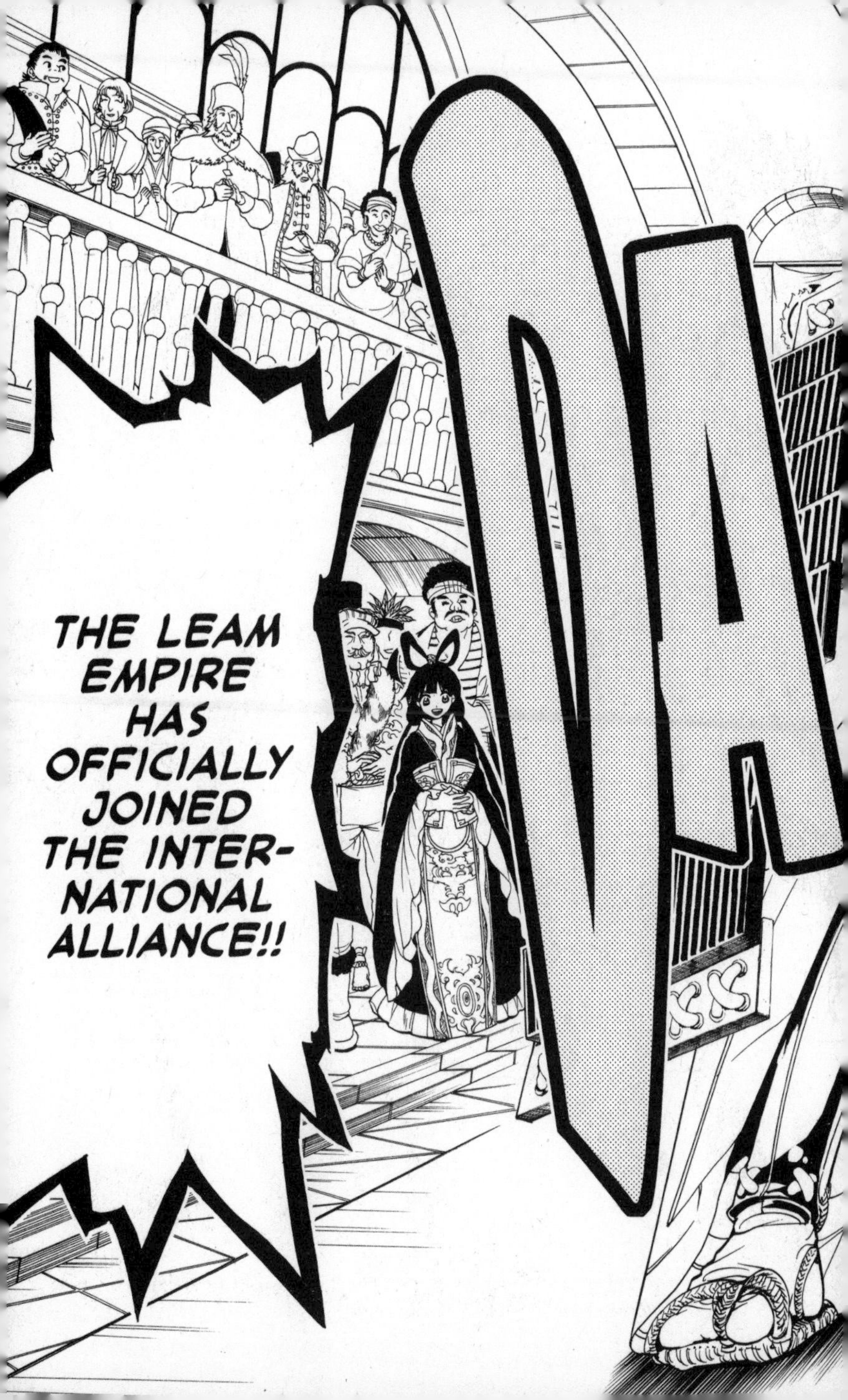
THE LEAM EMPIRE HAS OFFICIALLY JOINED THE INTER-NATIONAL ALLIANCE!!

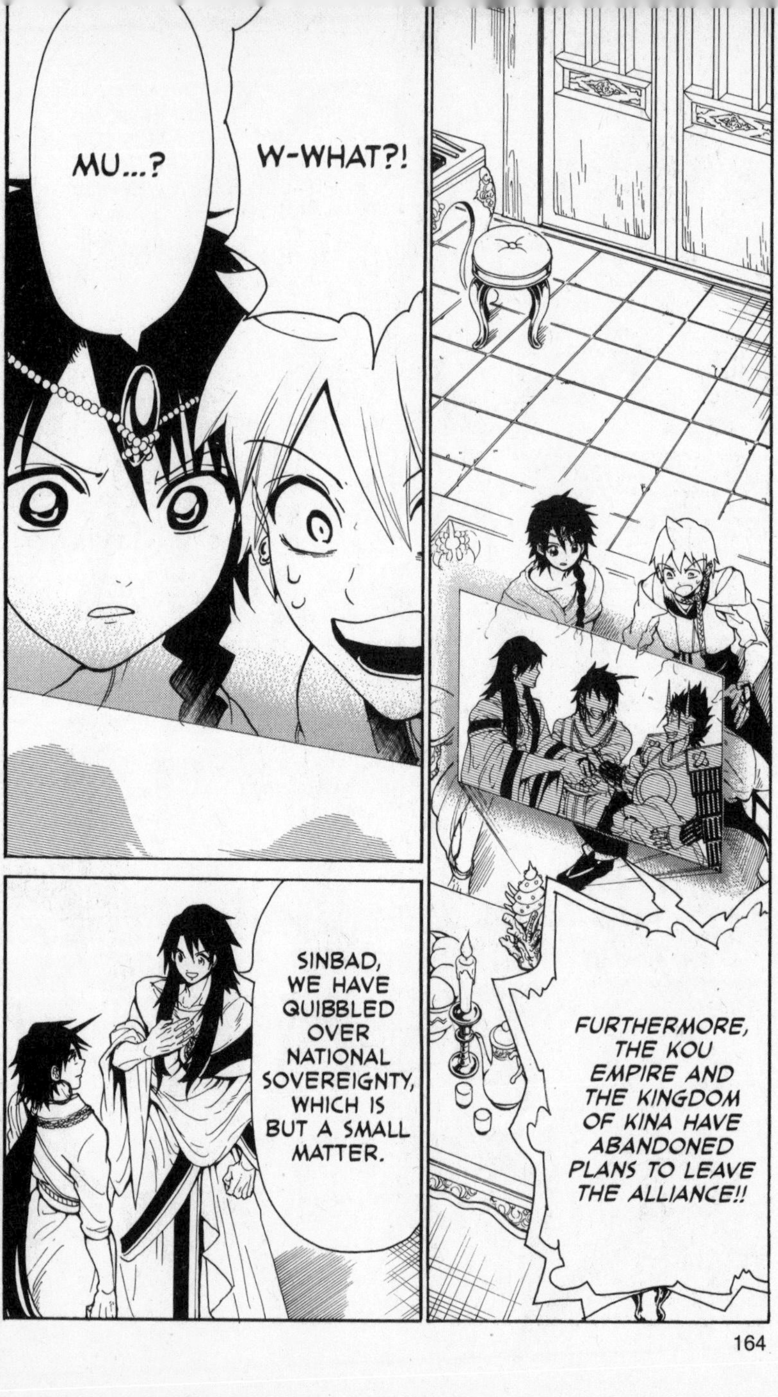
FURTHERMORE, THE KOU EMPIRE AND THE KINGDOM OF KINA HAVE ABANDONED PLANS TO LEAVE THE ALLIANCE!!
W-WHAT?!
MU...?
SINBAD, WE HAVE QUIBBLED OVER NATIONAL SOVEREIGNTY, WHICH IS BUT A SMALL MATTER.

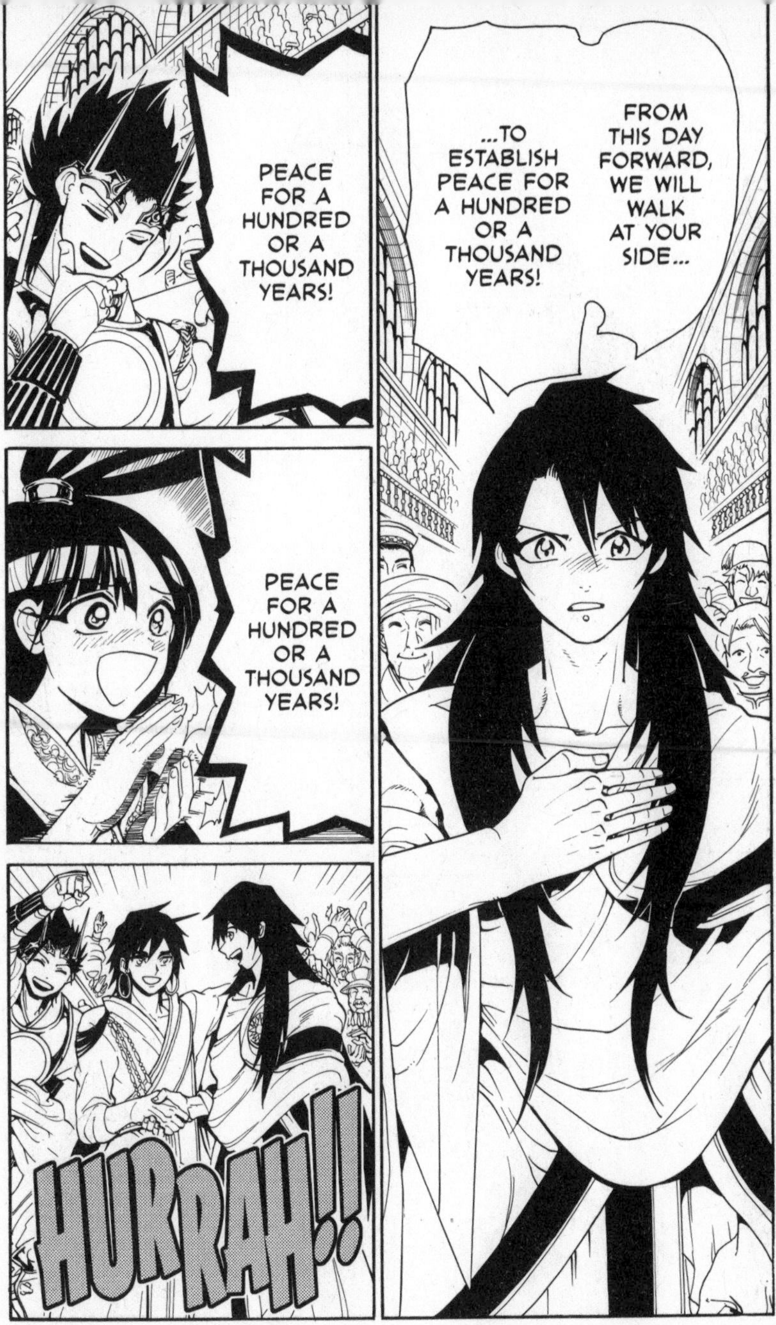
FROM THIS DAY FORWARD, WE WILL WALK AT YOUR SIDE...
...TO ESTABLISH PEACE FOR A HUNDRED OR A THOUSAND YEARS!
PEACE FOR A HUNDRED OR A THOUSAND YEARS!
PEACE FOR A HUNDRED OR A THOUSAND YEARS!
HURRAH!!

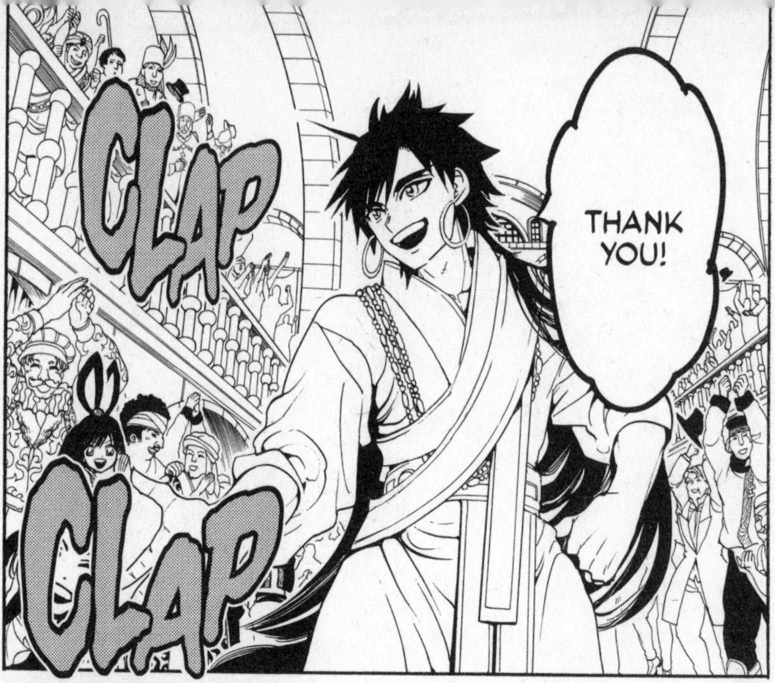
THANK YOU!
CLAP
CLAP

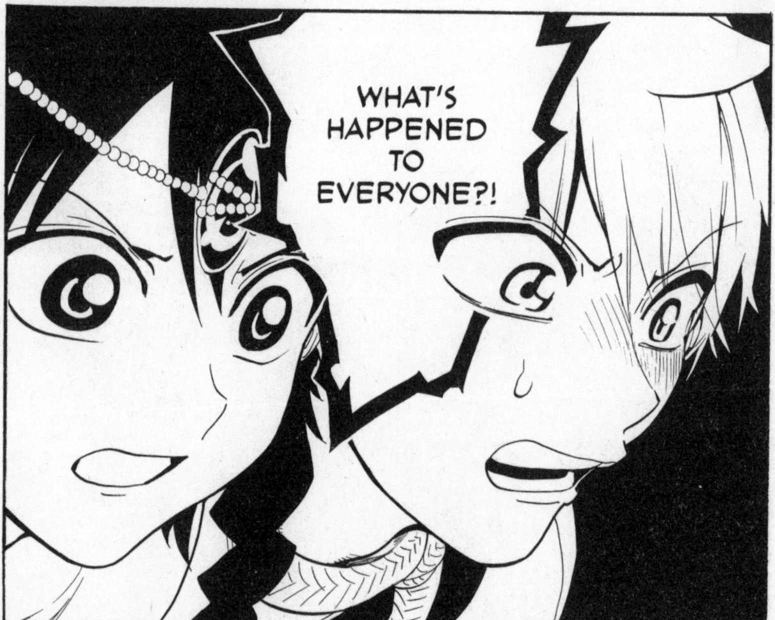
WHAT'S HAPPENED TO EVERYONE?!

Night 328: Common Hope

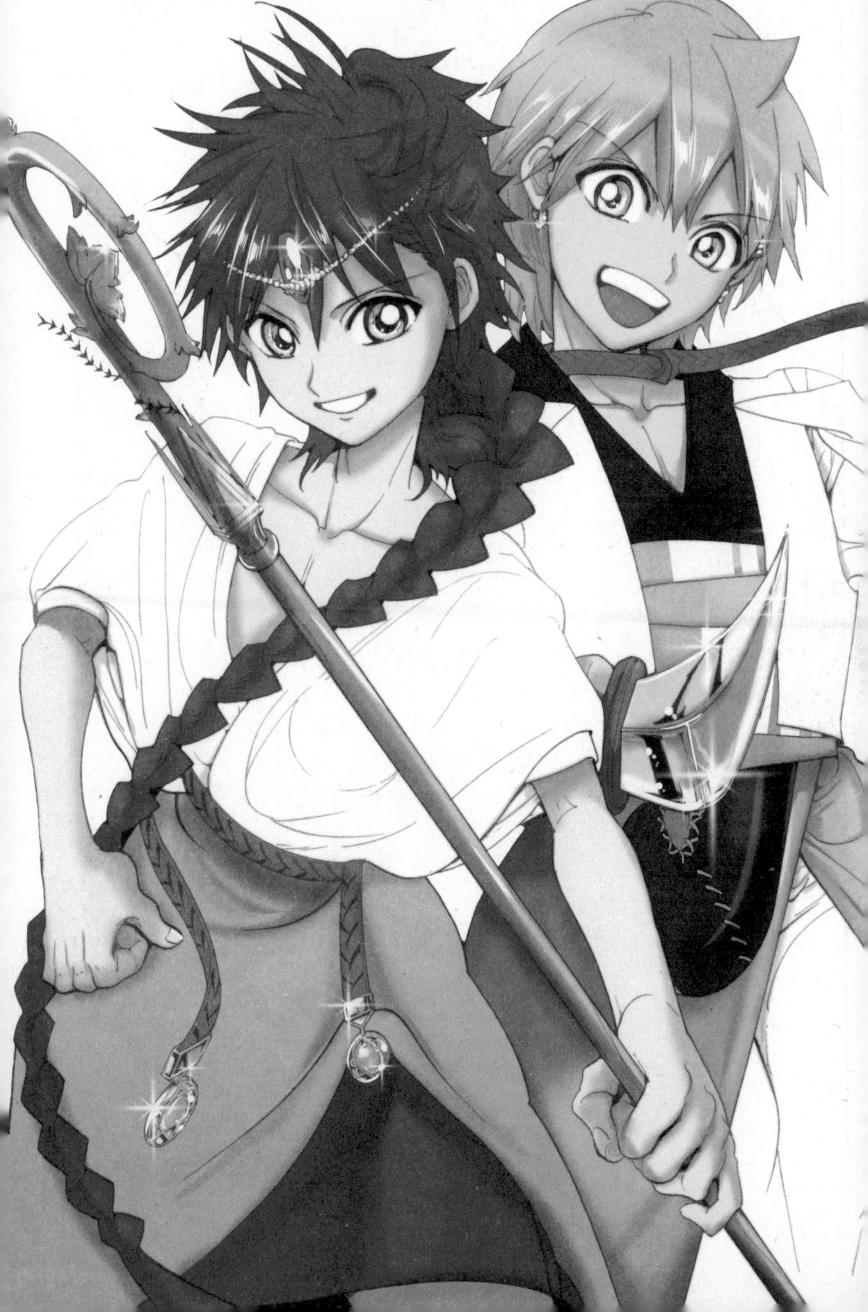

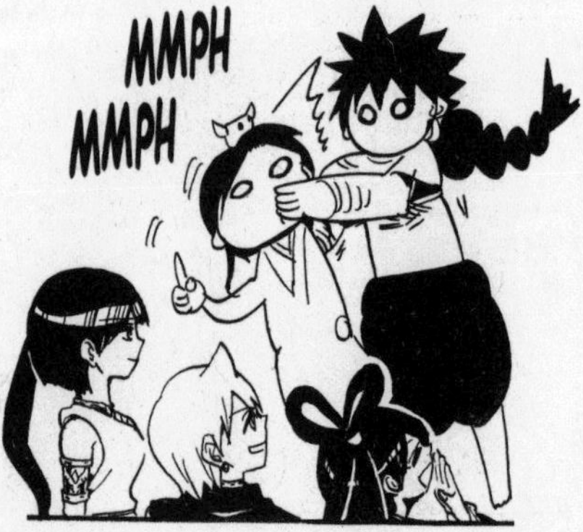
MMPH
MMPH

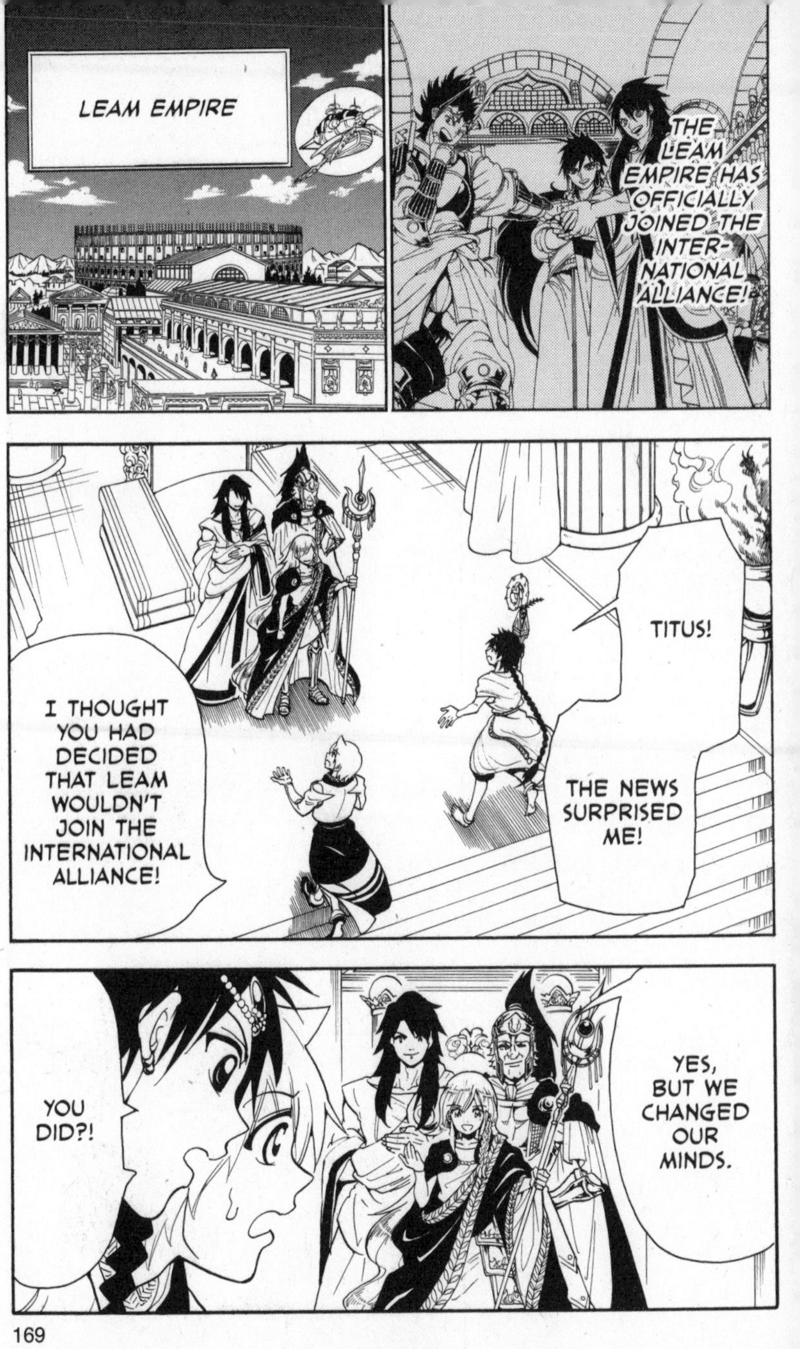
THE LEAM EMPIRE HAS OFFICIALLY JOINED THE INTER-NATIONAL ALLIANCE!
LEAM EMPIRE
TITUS!
THE NEWS SURPRISED ME!
I THOUGHT YOU HAD DECIDED THAT LEAM WOULDN'T JOIN THE INTERNATIONAL ALLIANCE!
YES, BUT WE CHANGED OUR MINDS.
YOU DID?!

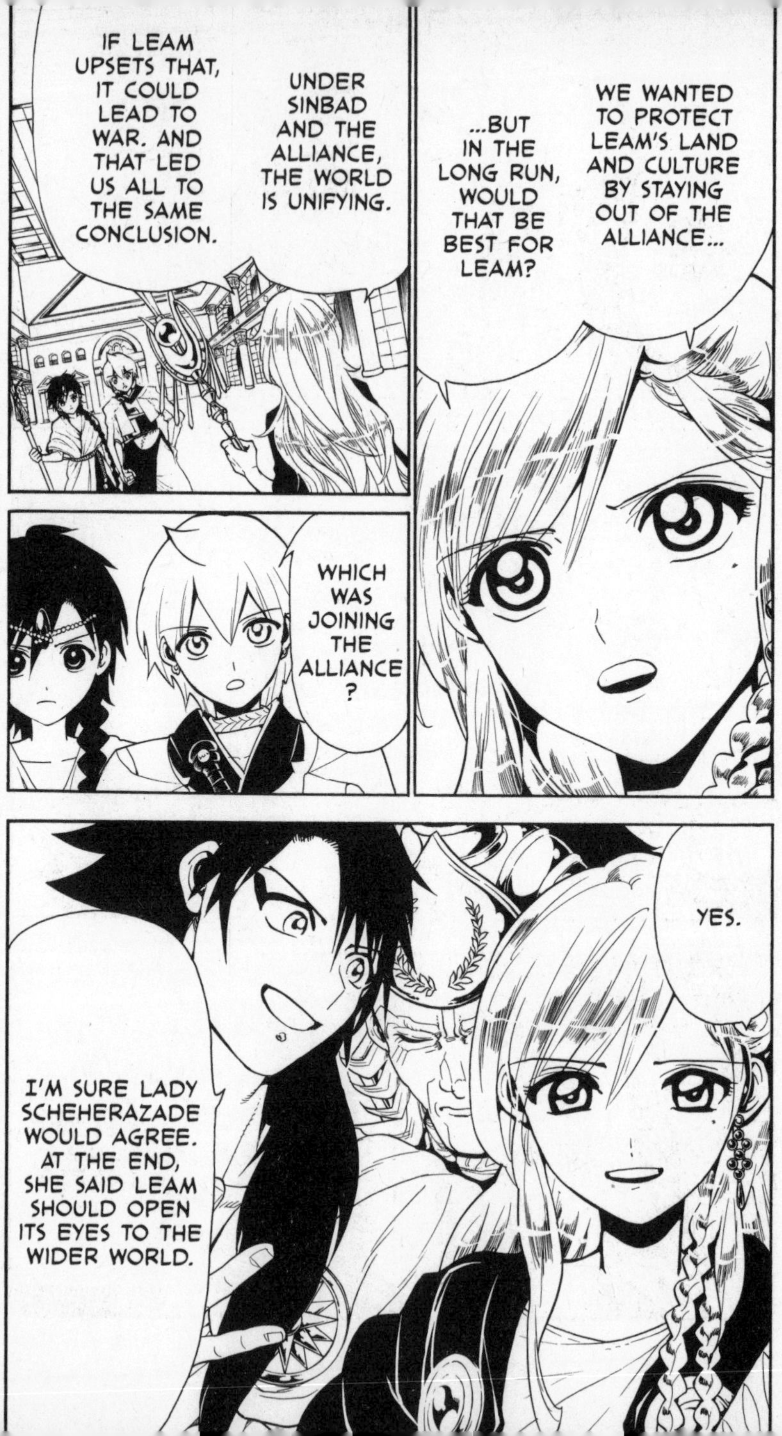
WE WANTED TO PROTECT LEAM'S LAND AND CULTURE BY STAYING OUT OF THE ALLIANCE...
...BUT IN THE LONG RUN, WOULD THAT BE BEST FOR LEAM?
UNDER SINBAD AND THE ALLIANCE, THE WORLD IS UNIFYING.
IF LEAM UPSETS THAT, IT COULD LEAD TO WAR. AND THAT LED US ALL TO THE SAME CONCLUSION.
WHICH WAS JOINING THE ALLIANCE?
YES.
I'M SURE LADY SCHEHERAZADE WOULD AGREE. AT THE END, SHE SAID LEAM SHOULD OPEN ITS EYES TO THE WIDER WORLD.

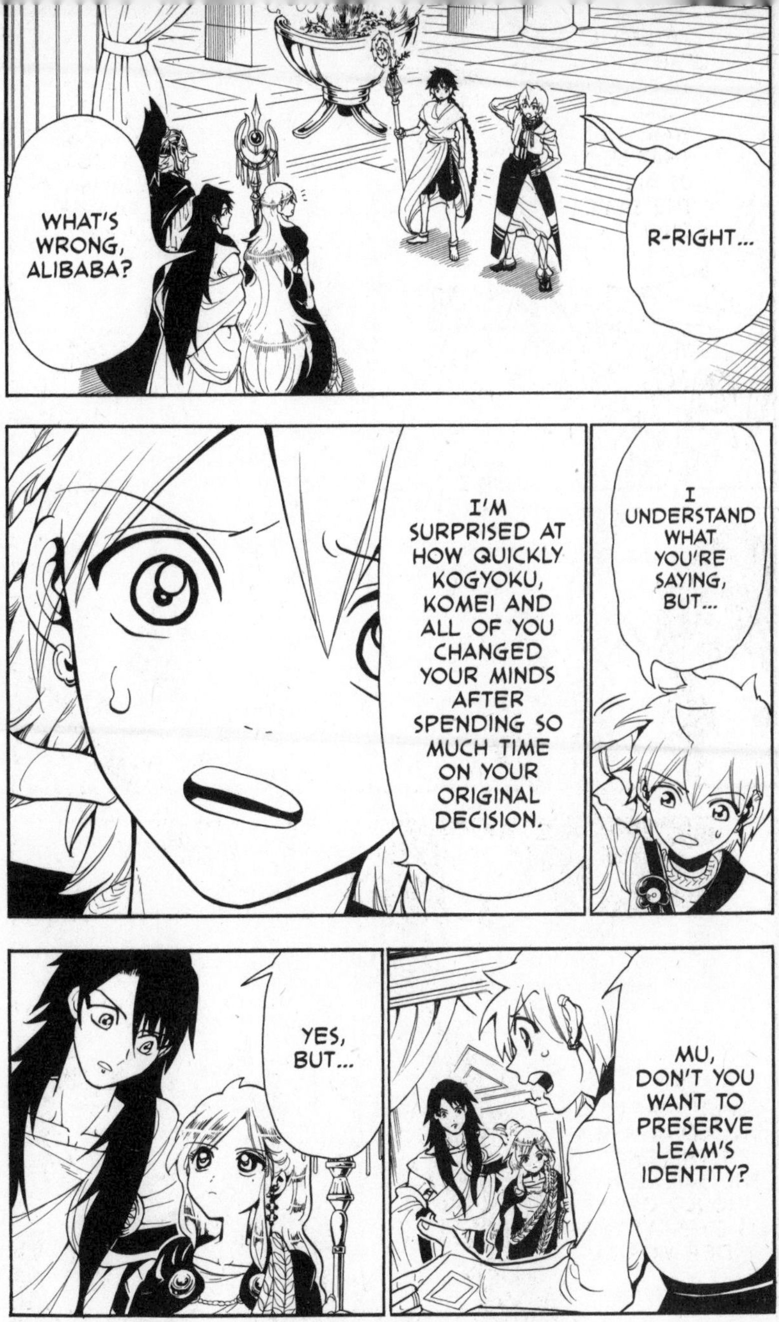
WHAT'S WRONG, ALIBABA?
R-RIGHT...
I UNDERSTAND WHAT YOU'RE SAYING, BUT...
I'M SURPRISED AT HOW QUICKLY KOGYOKU, KOMEI AND ALL OF YOU CHANGED YOUR MINDS AFTER SPENDING SO MUCH TIME ON YOUR ORIGINAL DECISION.
MU, DON'T YOU WANT TO PRESERVE LEAM'S IDENTITY?
YES, BUT...

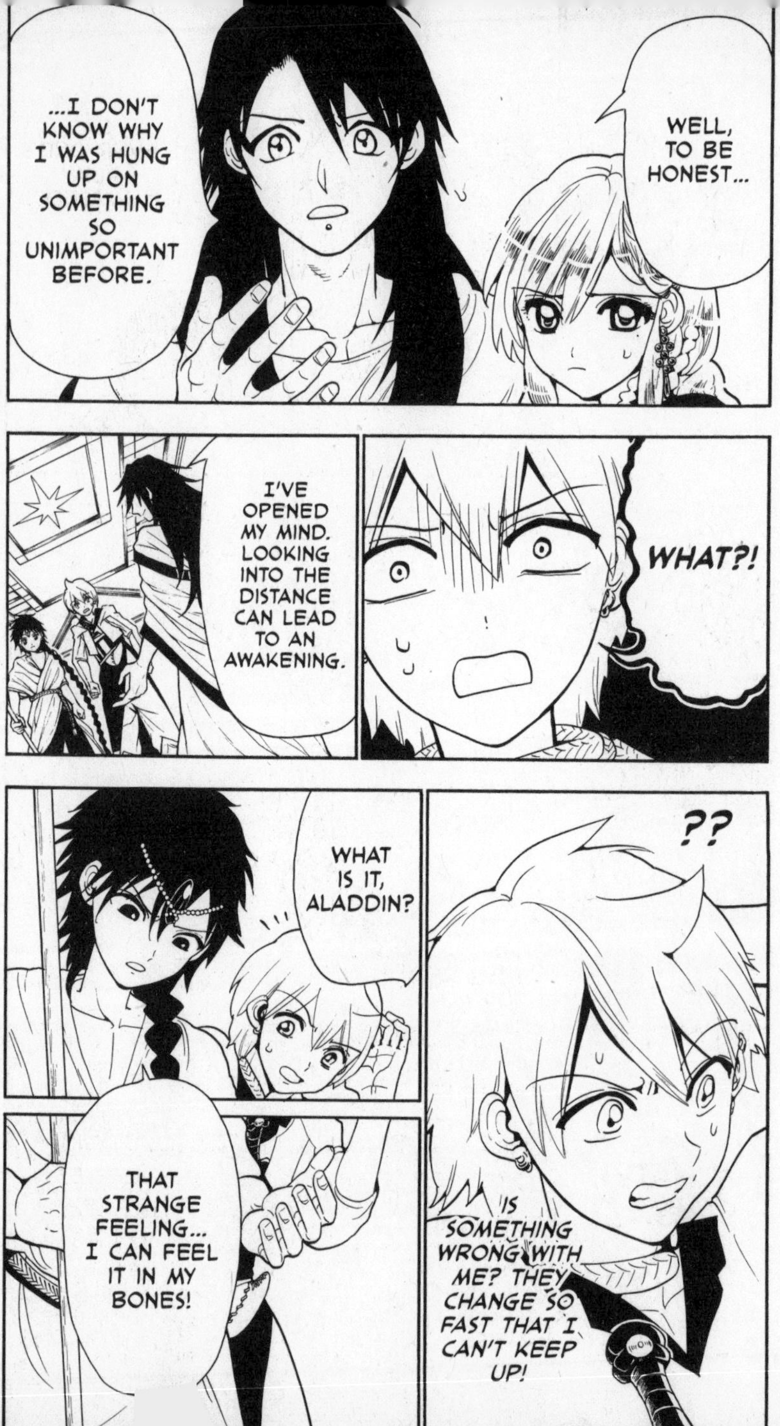
WELL, TO BE HONEST...
...I DON'T KNOW WHY I WAS HUNG UP ON SOMETHING SO UNIMPORTANT BEFORE.
WHAT?!
I'VE OPENED MY MIND. LOOKING INTO THE DISTANCE CAN LEAD TO AN AWAKENING.
??
IS SOMETHING WRONG WITH ME? THEY CHANGE SO FAST THAT I CAN'T KEEP UP!
WHAT IS IT, ALADDIN?
THAT STRANGE FEELING... I CAN FEEL IT IN MY BONES!

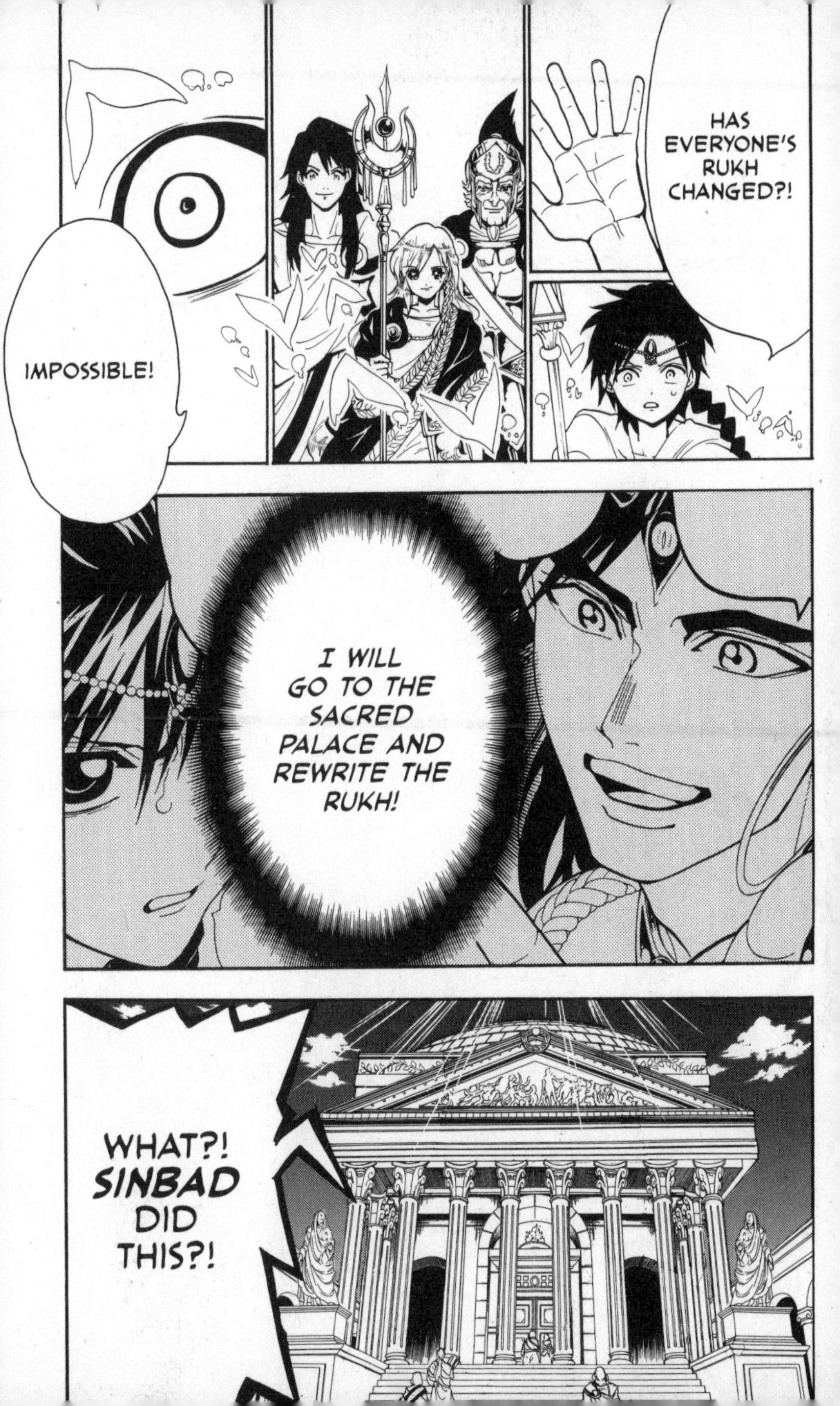
HAS EVERYONE'S RUKH CHANGED?!
IMPOSSIBLE!
I WILL GO TO THE SACRED PALACE AND REWRITE THE RUKH!
WHAT?! SINBAD DID THIS?!

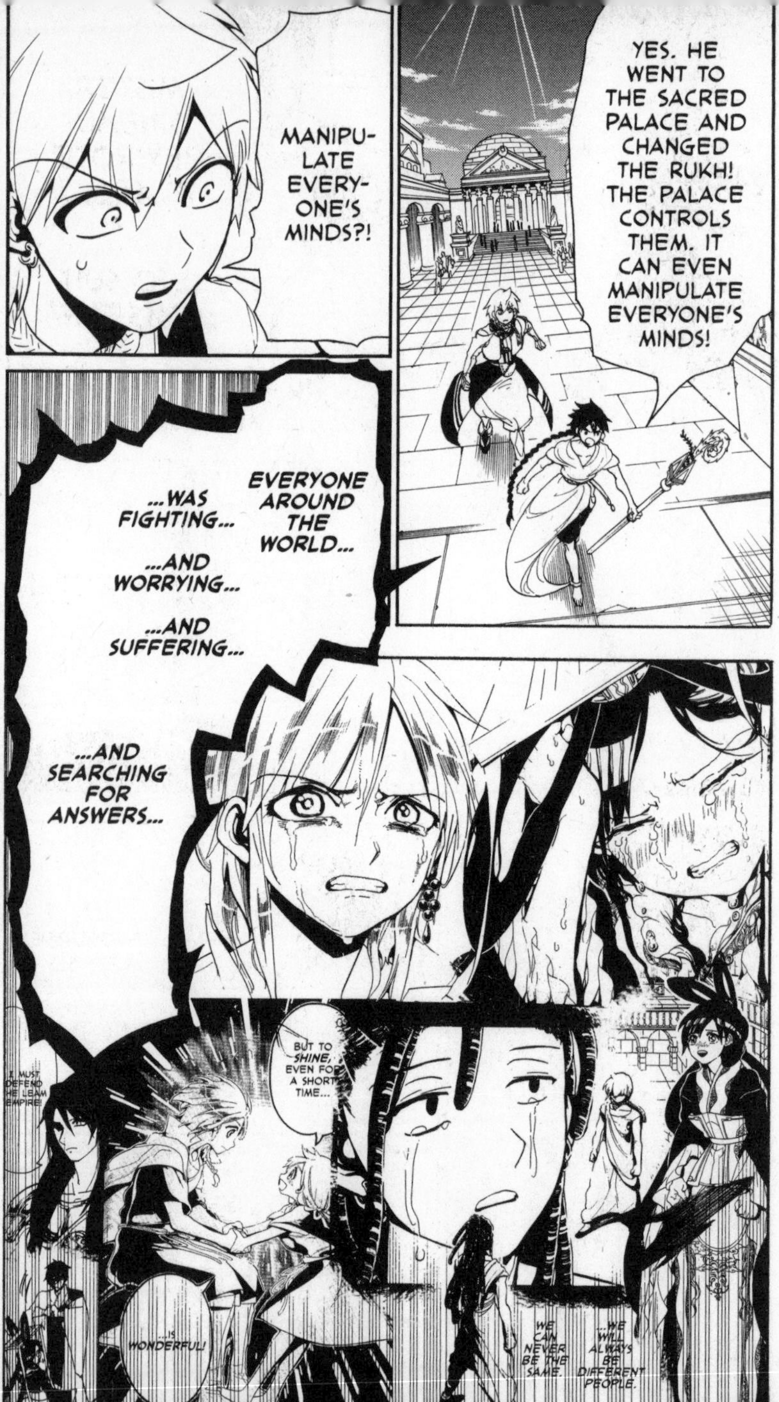
YES. HE WENT TO THE SACRED PALACE AND CHANGED THE RUKH! THE PALACE CONTROLS THEM. IT CAN EVEN MANIPULATE EVERYONE'S MINDS!
MANIPU-LATE EVERY-ONE'S MINDS?!
EVERYONE AROUND THE WORLD...
...WAS FIGHTING...
...AND WORRYING...
...AND SUFFERING...
...AND SEARCHING FOR ANSWERS...
WE CAN NEVER BE THE SAME.
...WE WILL ALWAYS BE DIFFERENT PEOPLE.
BUT TO SHINE, EVEN FOR A SHORT TIME...
...IS WONDERFUL!
I MUST DEFEND HE LEAM EMPIRE!

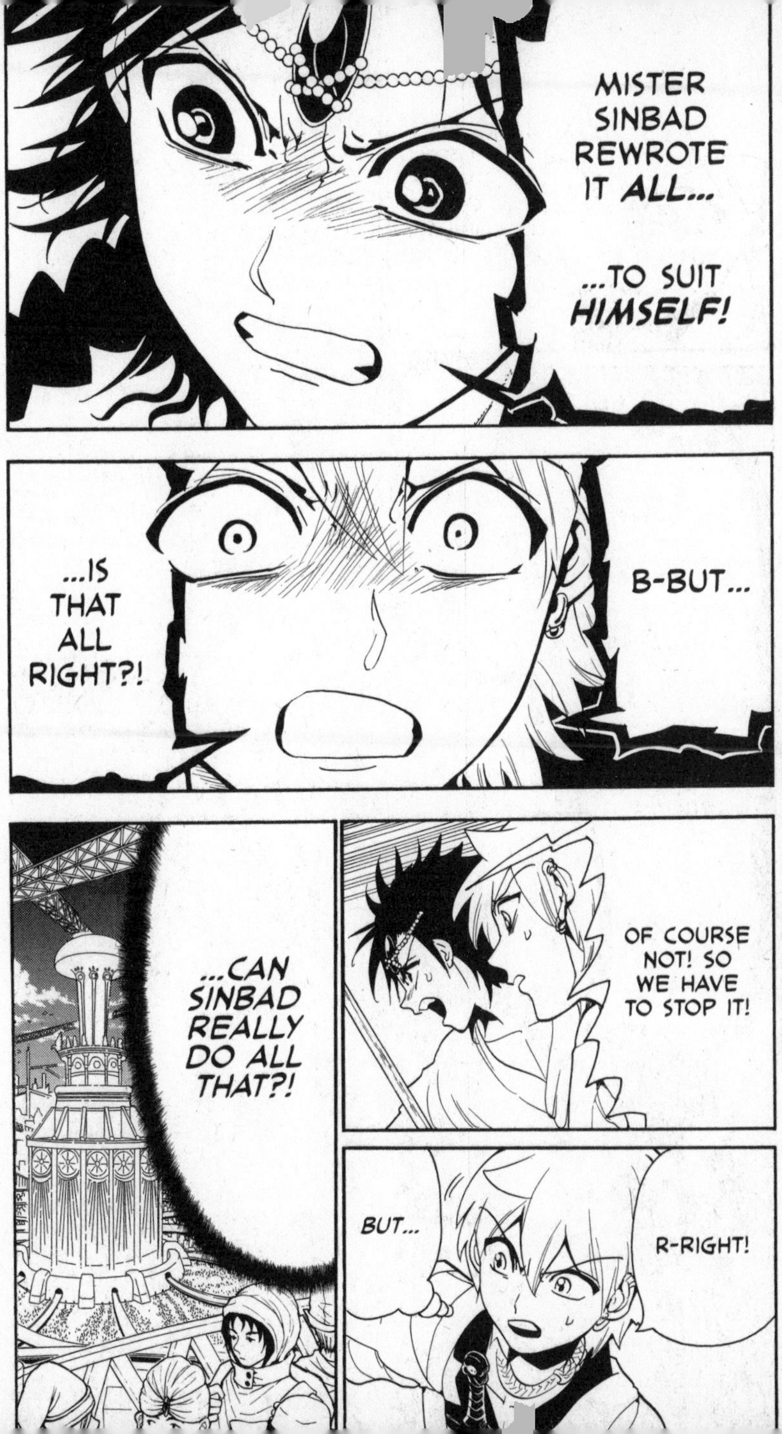
MISTER SINBAD REWROTE IT ALL...
...TO SUIT HIMSELF!
B-BUT...
...IS THAT ALL RIGHT?!
OF COURSE NOT! SO WE HAVE TO STOP IT!
R-RIGHT!
BUT...
...CAN SINBAD REALLY DO ALL THAT?!

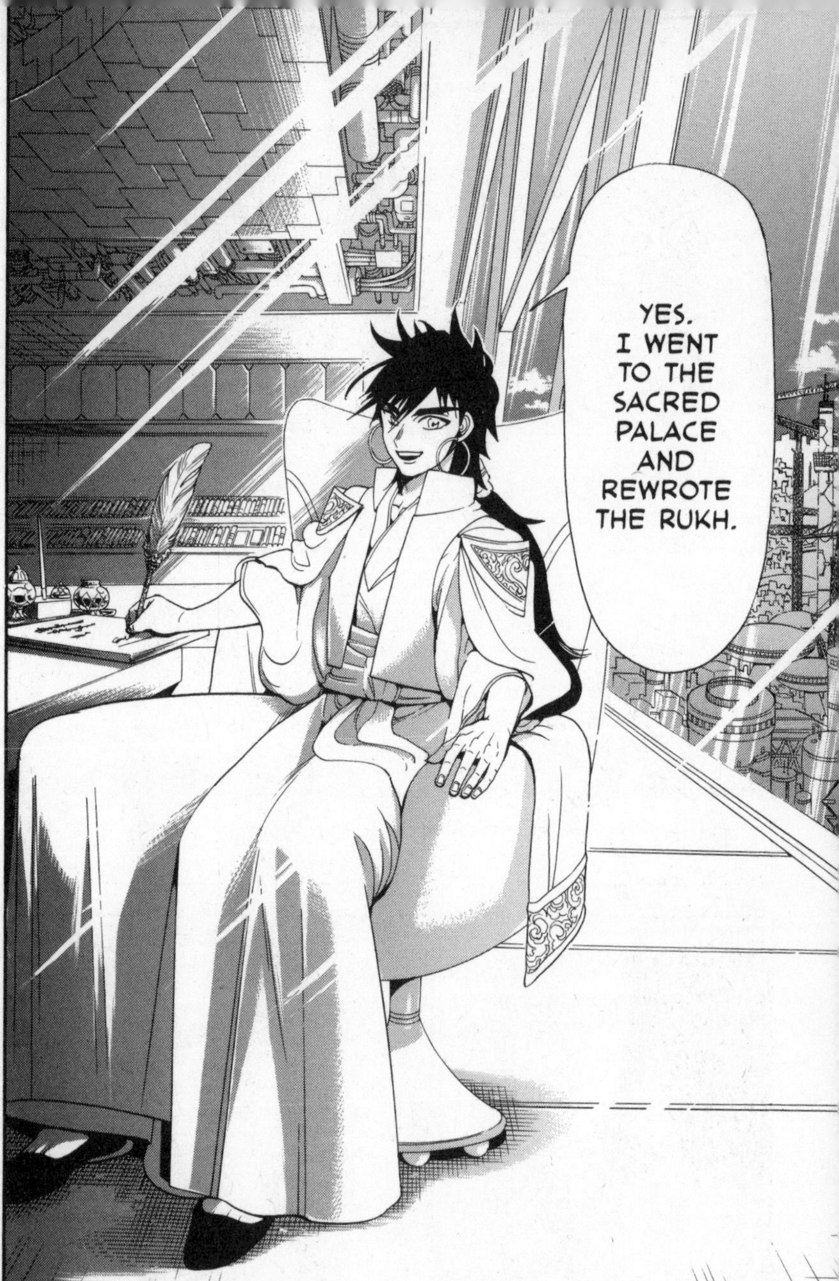
YES. I WENT TO THE SACRED PALACE AND REWROTE THE RUKH.

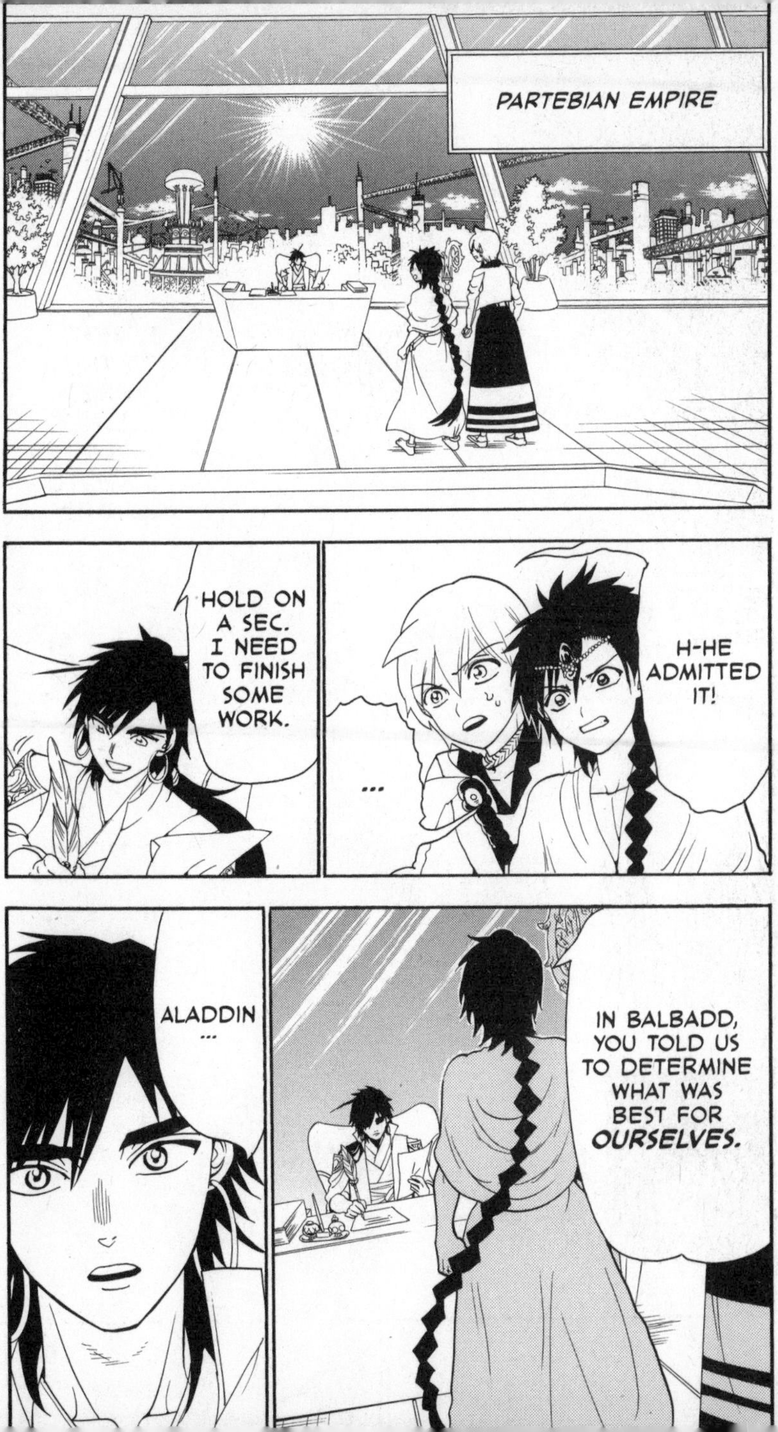
PARTEBIAN EMPIRE
H-HE ADMITTED IT!
...
HOLD ON A SEC. I NEED TO FINISH SOME WORK.
IN BALBADD, YOU TOLD US TO DETERMINE WHAT WAS BEST FOR *OURSELVES.*
ALADDIN ...

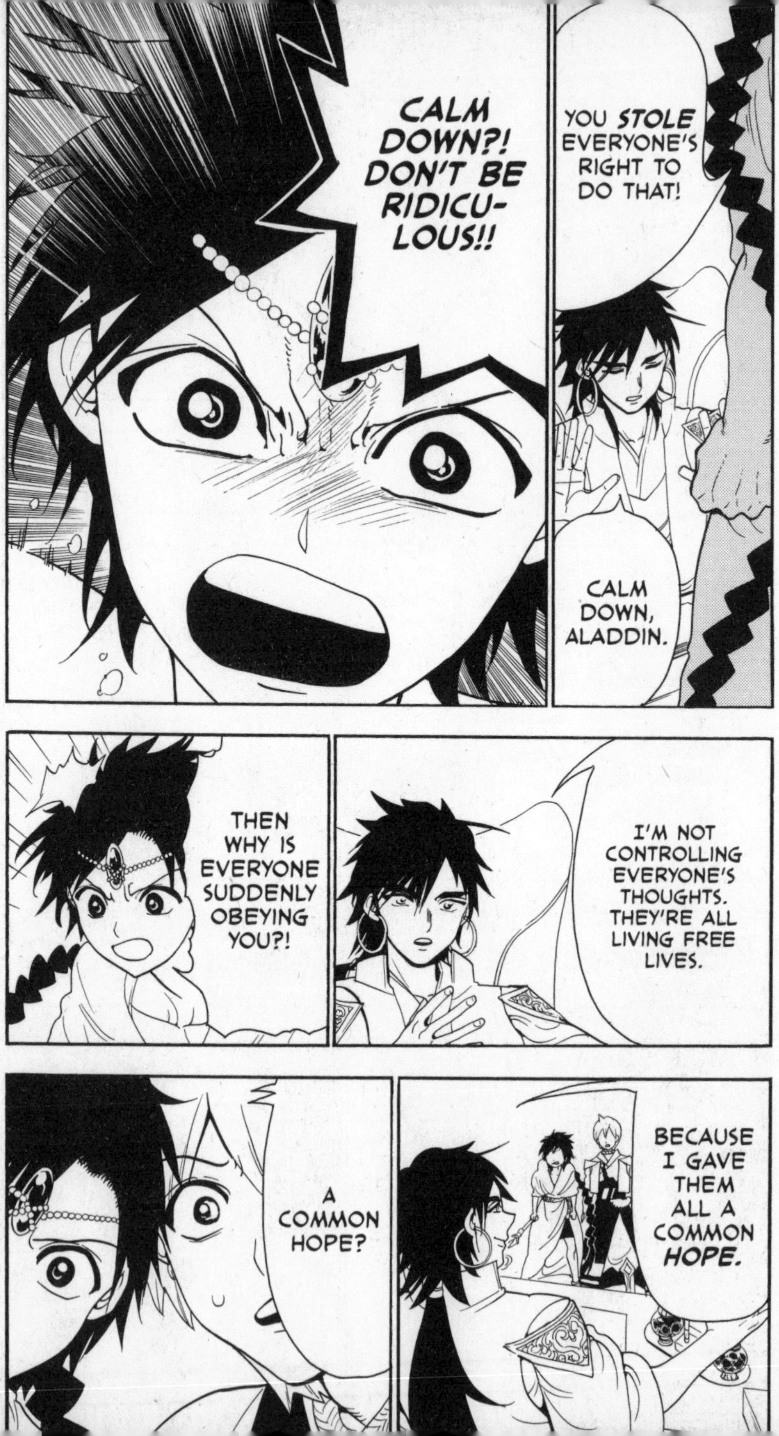
YOU STOLE EVERYONE'S RIGHT TO DO THAT!
CALM DOWN, ALADDIN.
CALM DOWN?! DON'T BE RIDICU-LOUS!!
I'M NOT CONTROLLING EVERYONE'S THOUGHTS. THEY'RE ALL LIVING FREE LIVES.
THEN WHY IS EVERYONE SUDDENLY OBEYING YOU?!
BECAUSE I GAVE THEM ALL A COMMON HOPE.
A COMMON HOPE?

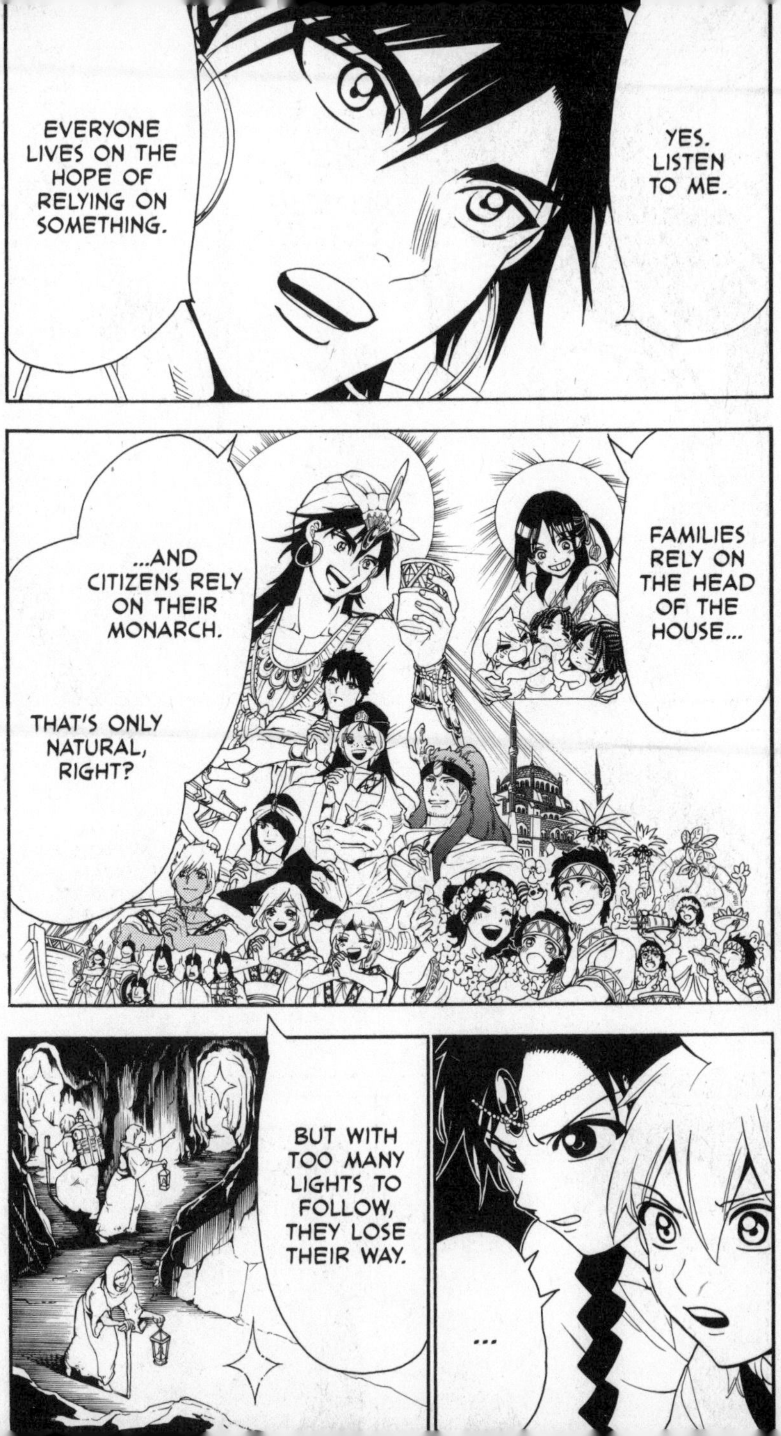
YES. LISTEN TO ME.
EVERYONE LIVES ON THE HOPE OF RELYING ON SOMETHING.
FAMILIES RELY ON THE HEAD OF THE HOUSE...
...AND CITIZENS RELY ON THEIR MONARCH.
THAT'S ONLY NATURAL, RIGHT?
...
BUT WITH TOO MANY LIGHTS TO FOLLOW, THEY LOSE THEIR WAY.

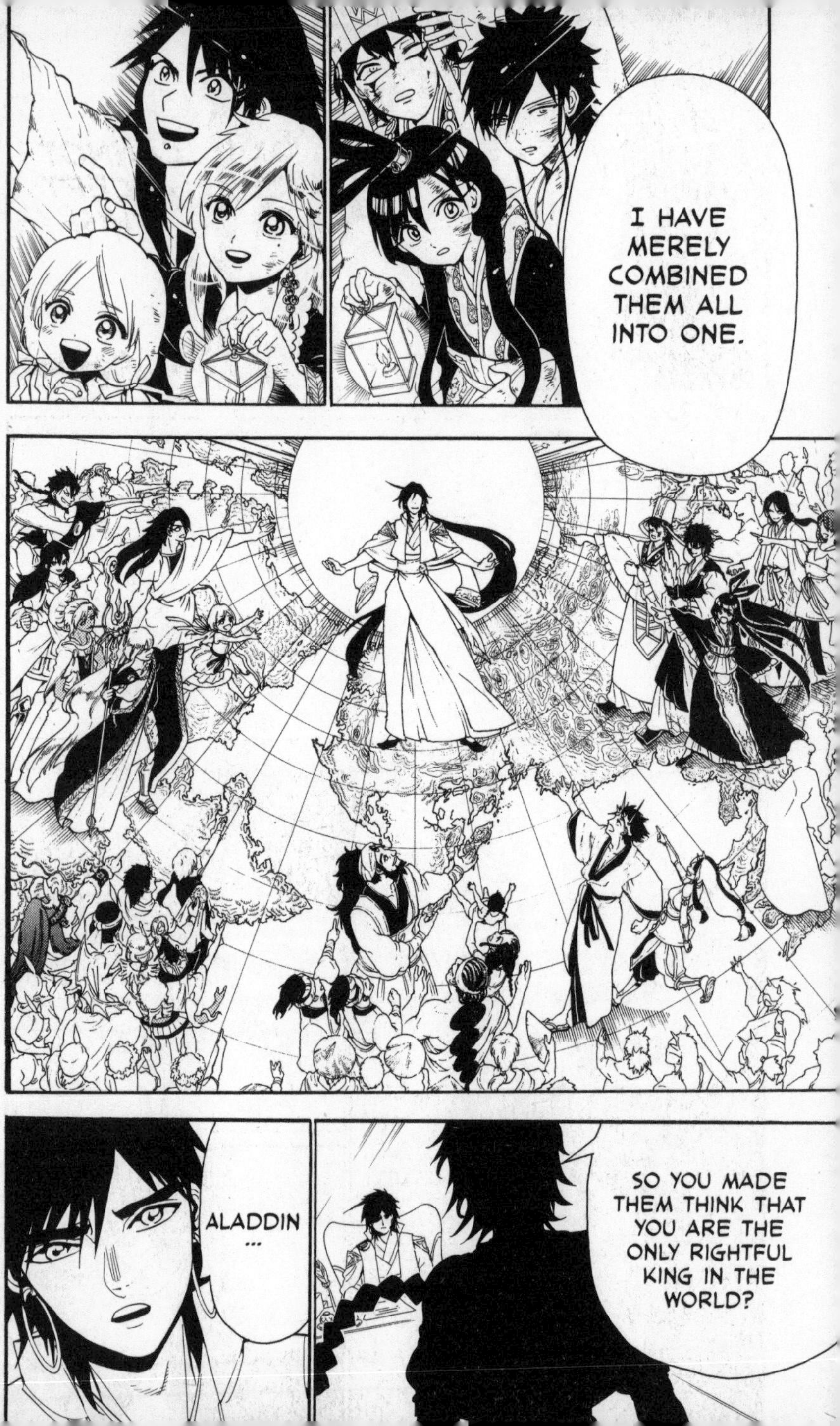
I HAVE MERELY COMBINED THEM ALL INTO ONE.
SO YOU MADE THEM THINK THAT YOU ARE THE ONLY RIGHTFUL KING IN THE WORLD?
ALADDIN ...

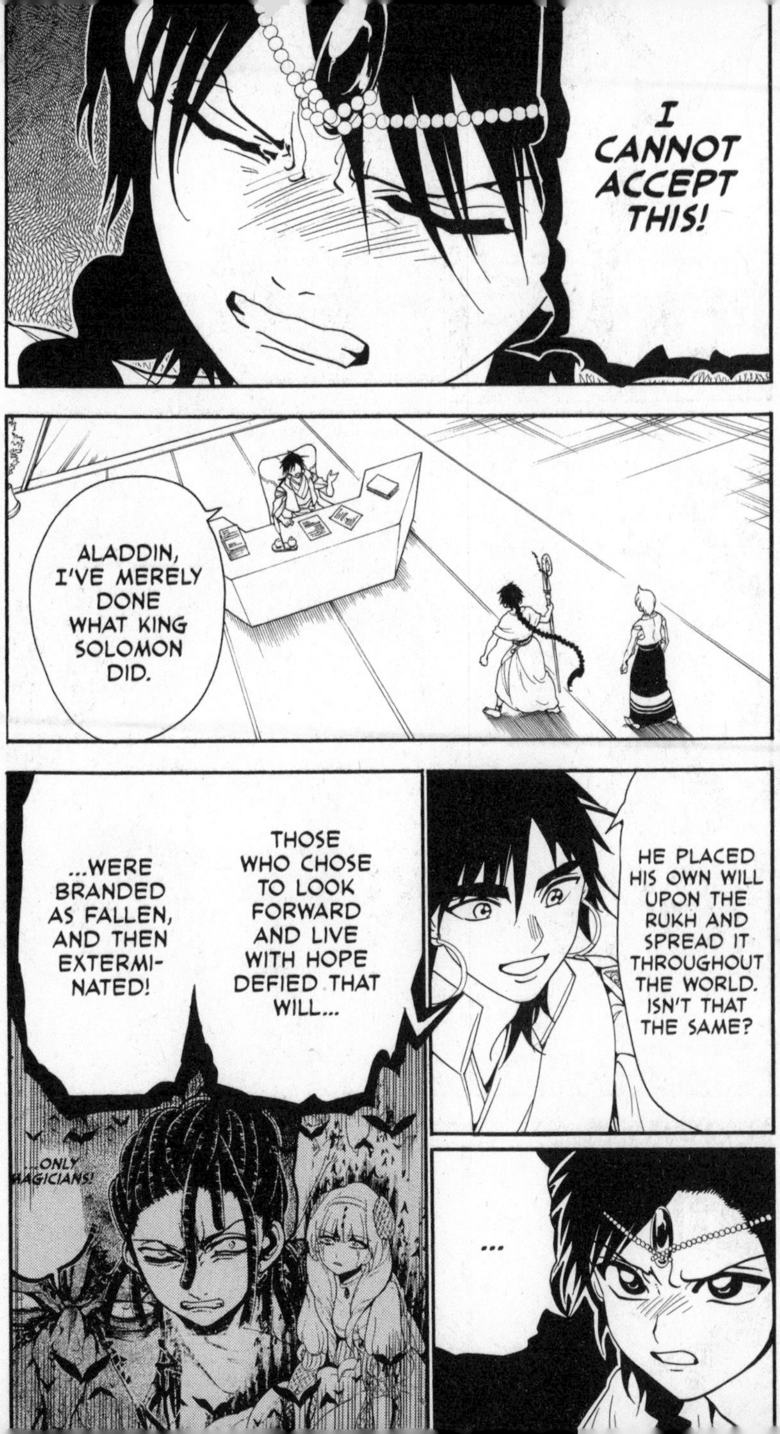
I CANNOT ACCEPT THIS!
ALADDIN, I'VE MERELY DONE WHAT KING SOLOMON DID.
HE PLACED HIS OWN WILL UPON THE RUKH AND SPREAD IT THROUGHOUT THE WORLD. ISN'T THAT THE SAME?
THOSE WHO CHOSE TO LOOK FORWARD AND LIVE WITH HOPE DEFIED THAT WILL...
...WERE BRANDED AS FALLEN, AND THEN EXTERMI-NATED!
...ONLY MAGICIANS!
...

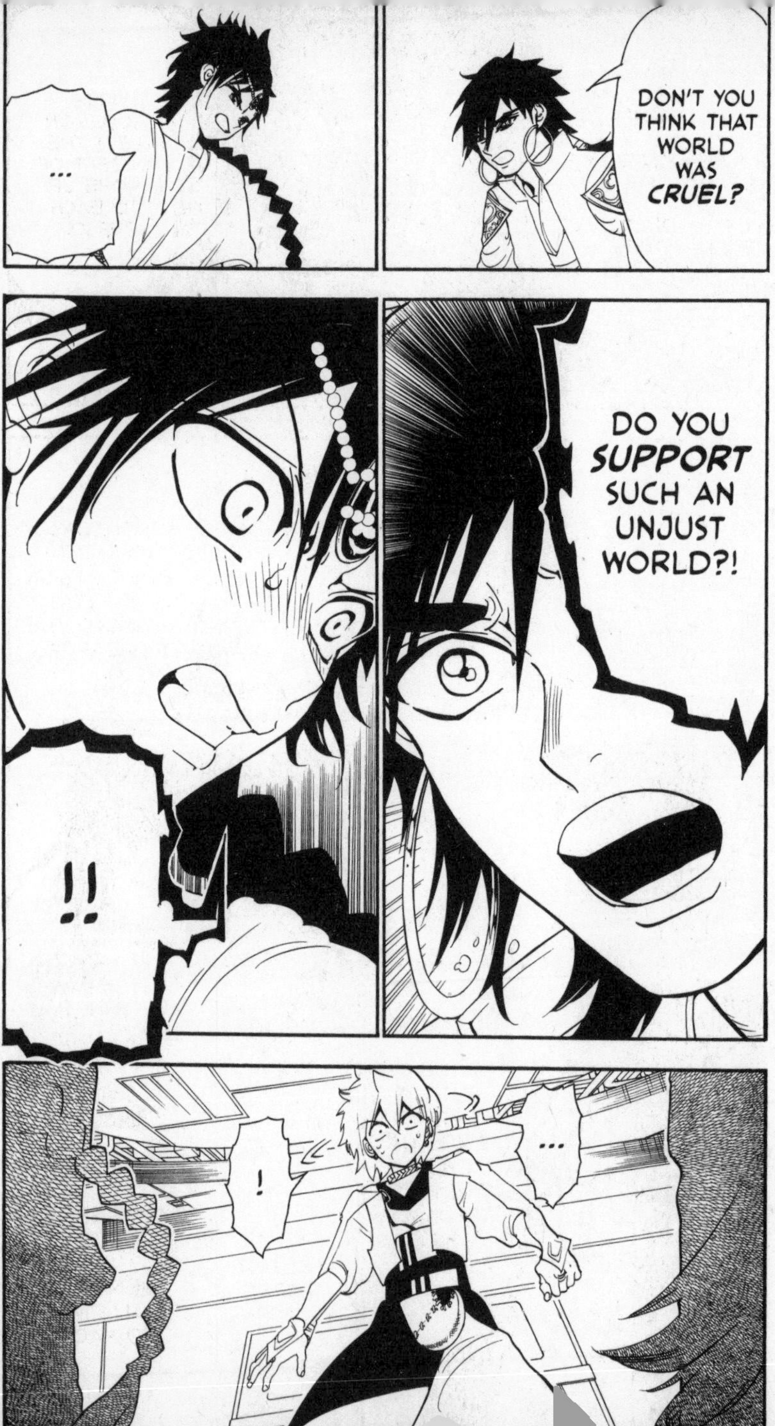
DON'T YOU THINK THAT WORLD WAS CRUEL?
...
DO YOU SUPPORT SUCH AN UNJUST WORLD?!
!!
...
!

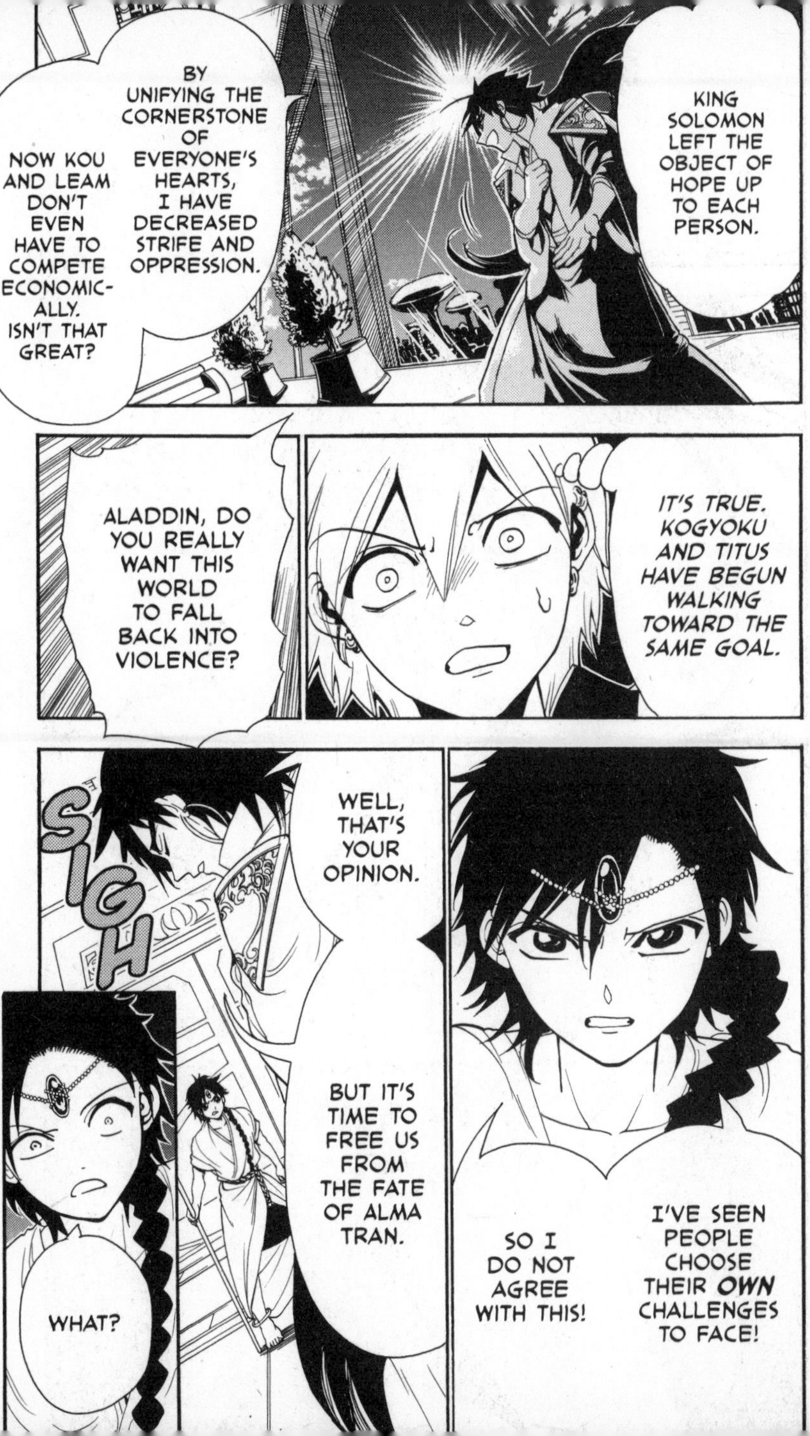
KING SOLOMON LEFT THE OBJECT OF HOPE UP TO EACH PERSON.
BY UNIFYING THE CORNERSTONE OF EVERYONE'S HEARTS, I HAVE DECREASED STRIFE AND OPPRESSION.
NOW KOU AND LEAM DON'T EVEN HAVE TO COMPETE ECONOMIC-ALLY. ISN'T THAT GREAT?
IT'S TRUE. KOGYOKU AND TITUS HAVE BEGUN WALKING TOWARD THE SAME GOAL.
ALADDIN, DO YOU REALLY WANT THIS WORLD TO FALL BACK INTO VIOLENCE?
I'VE SEEN PEOPLE CHOOSE THEIR *OWN* CHALLENGES TO FACE!
SO I DO NOT AGREE WITH THIS!
SIGH
WELL, THAT'S YOUR OPINION.
BUT IT'S TIME TO FREE US FROM THE FATE OF ALMA TRAN.
WHAT?

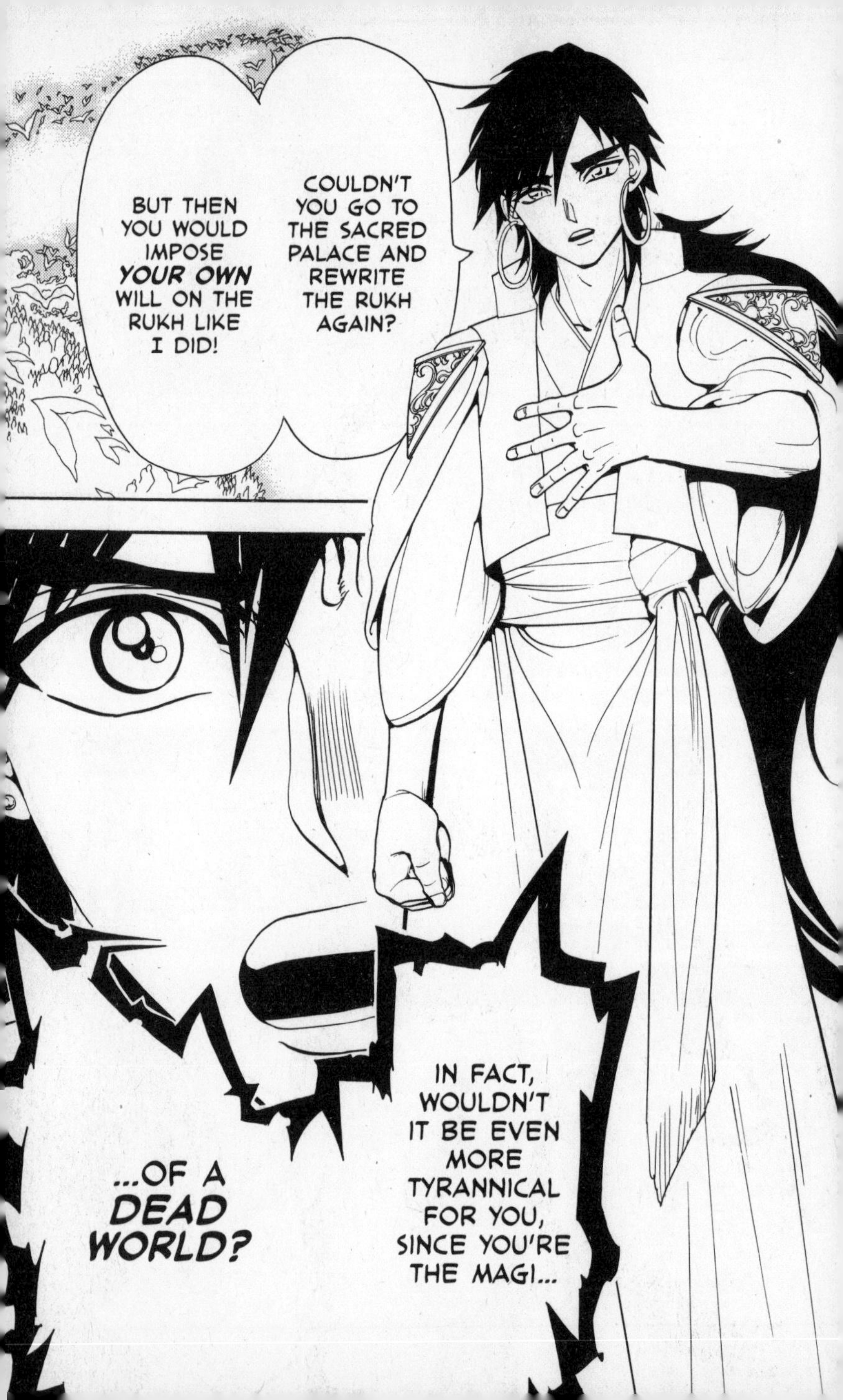
COULDN'T YOU GO TO THE SACRED PALACE AND REWRITE THE RUKH AGAIN?
BUT THEN YOU WOULD IMPOSE *YOUR OWN* WILL ON THE RUKH LIKE I DID!
IN FACT, WOULDN'T IT BE EVEN MORE TYRANNICAL FOR YOU, SINCE YOU'RE THE MAGI...
...OF A *DEAD WORLD?*

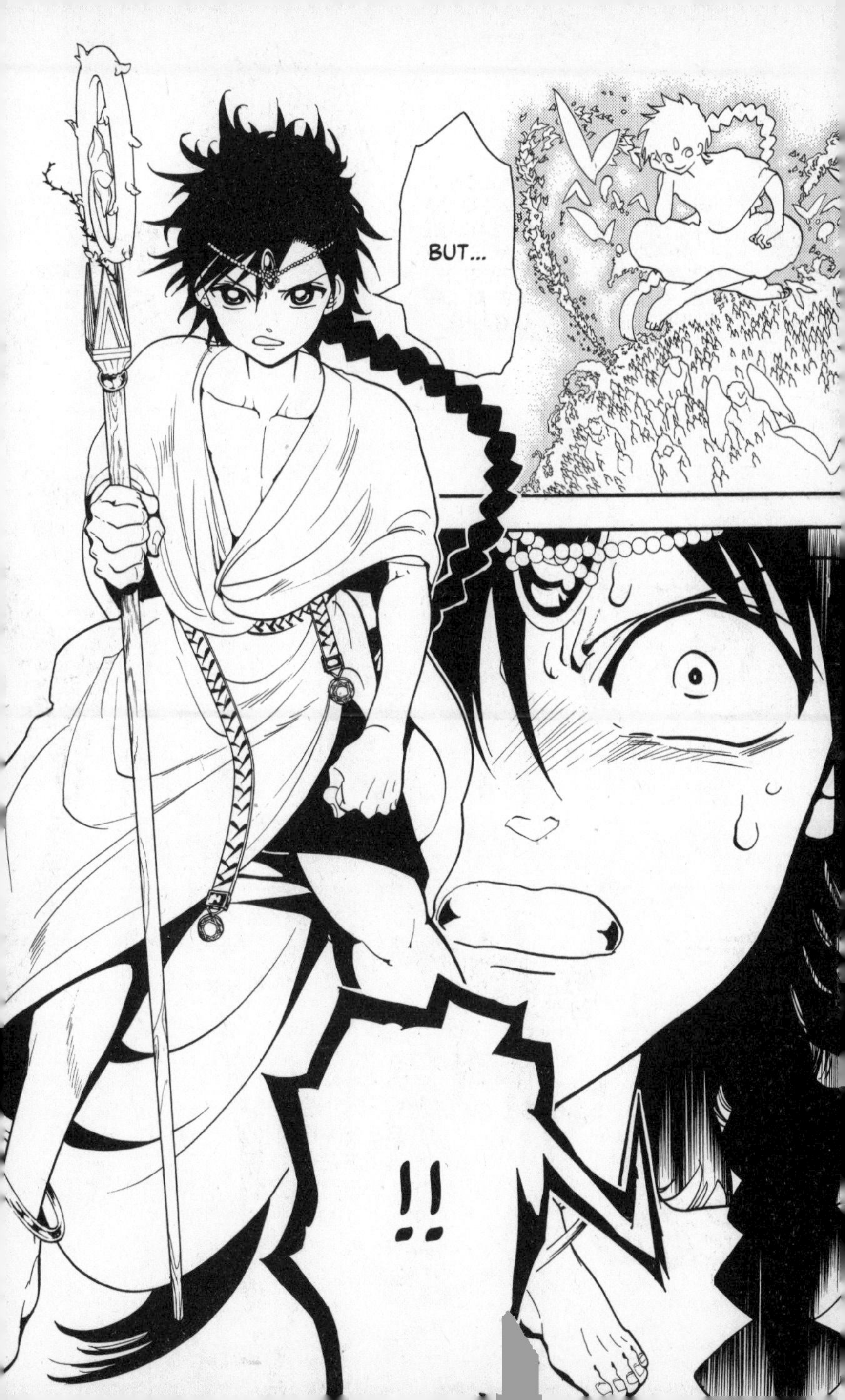
BUT...
!!

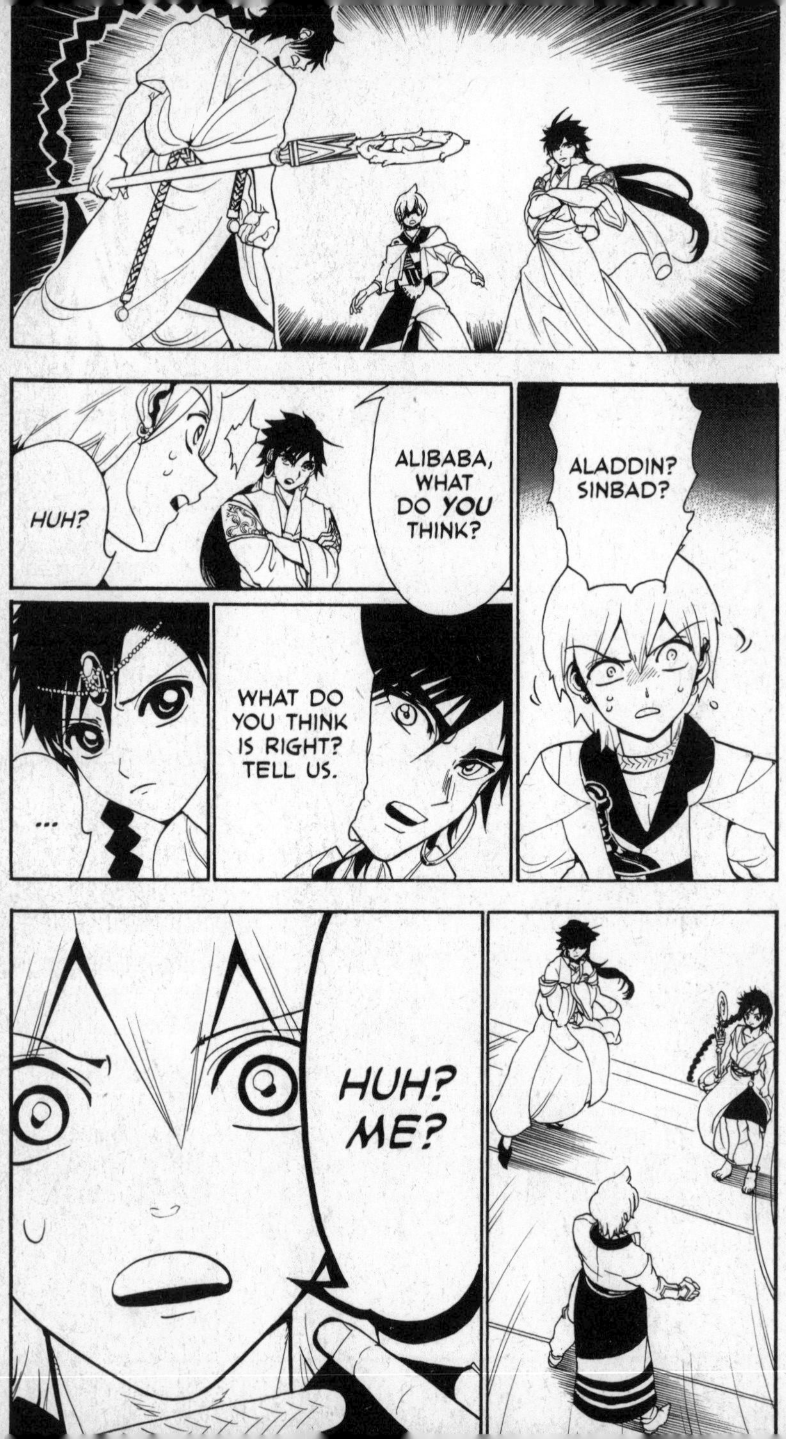
ALADDIN? SINBAD?
ALIBABA, WHAT DO YOU THINK?
HUH?
WHAT DO YOU THINK IS RIGHT? TELL US.
...
HUH? ME?

MAGI
The labyrinth of magic
33

Staff

■ **Story & Art**

Shinobu Ohtaka

■ **Regular Assistants**

Hiro Maizima

Yuiko Akiyama

Megi

Aya Umoto

Mami Yoshida

Yuka Otsuji

Chidori Ishigo

■ **Editors**

Kazuaki Ishibashi

Makoto Ishiwata

Katsumasa Ogura

■ **Sales & Promotion**

Tsunato Imamoto

Yuta Uchiyama

■ **Designer**

Hajime Tokushige + Bay Bridge Studio

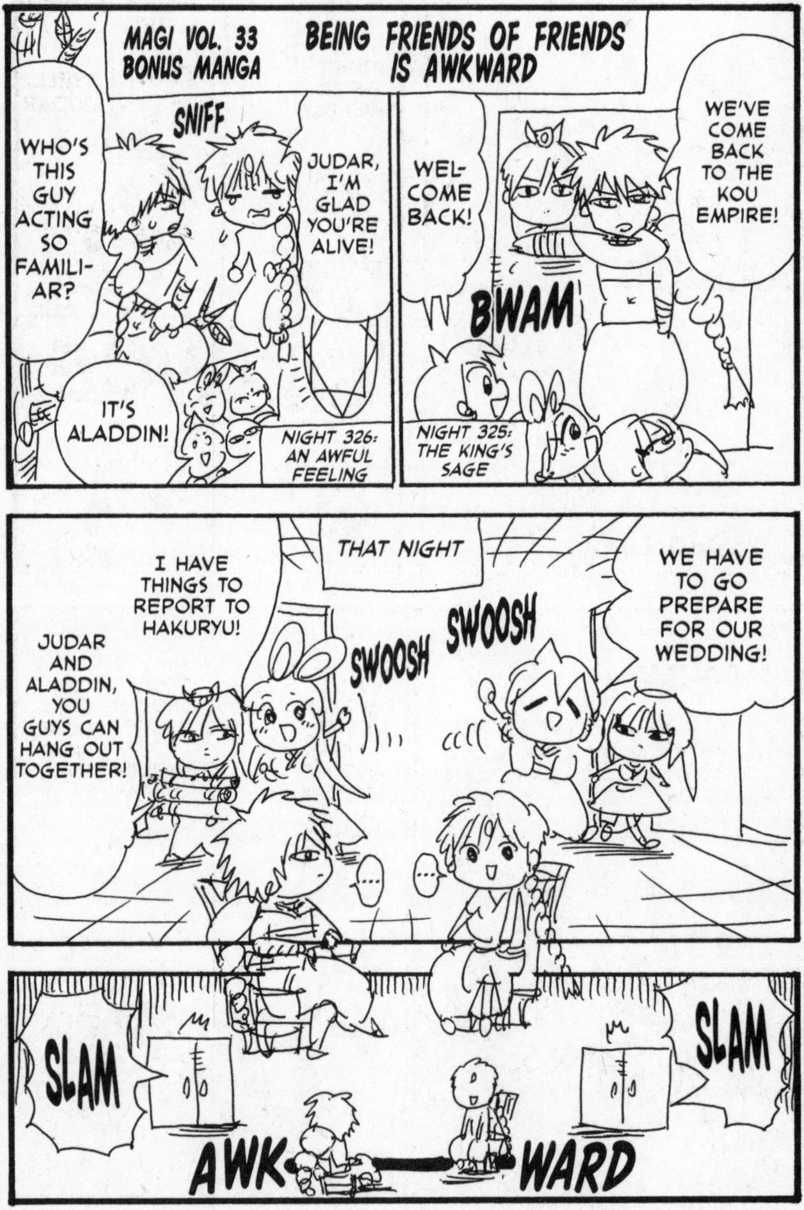

MAGI VOL. 33 BONUS MANGA
BEING FRIENDS OF FRIENDS IS AWKWARD
WE'VE COME BACK TO THE KOU EMPIRE!
WEL-COME BACK!
BWAM
NIGHT 325: THE KING'S SAGE
JUDAR, I'M GLAD YOU'RE ALIVE!
SNIFF
WHO'S THIS GUY ACTING SO FAMILI-AR?
IT'S ALADDIN!
NIGHT 326: AN AWFUL FEELING
THAT NIGHT
WE HAVE TO GO PREPARE FOR OUR WEDDING!
SWOOSH
SWOOSH
I HAVE THINGS TO REPORT TO HAKURYU!
JUDAR AND ALADDIN, YOU GUYS CAN HANG OUT TOGETHER!
....
....
SLAM
SLAM
AWK—WARD

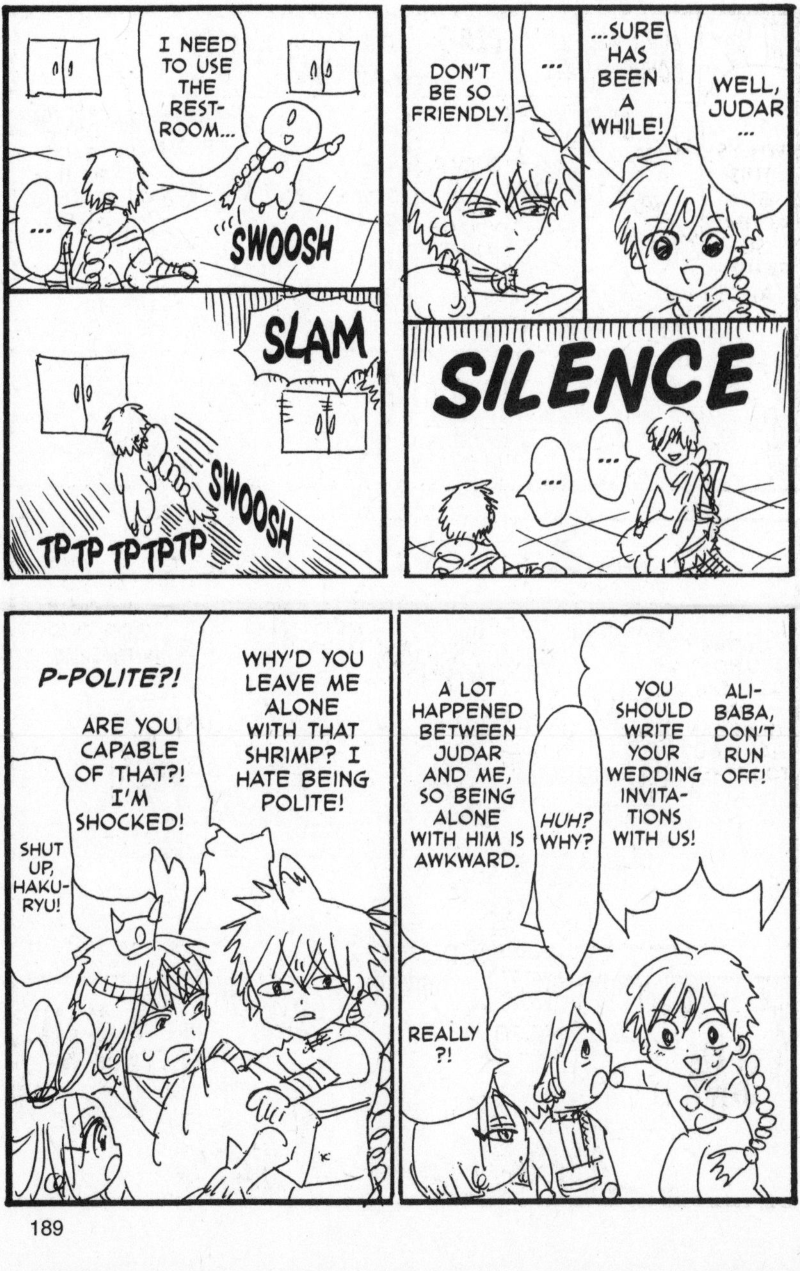
WELL, JUDAR ...
...SURE HAS BEEN A WHILE!
...
DON'T BE SO FRIENDLY.
I NEED TO USE THE REST-ROOM...
...
SWOOSH
SILENCE
...
...
SLAM
SWOOSH
TPTP TPTPTP
ALI-BABA, DON'T RUN OFF!
YOU SHOULD WRITE YOUR WEDDING INVITA-TIONS WITH US!
HUH? WHY?
A LOT HAPPENED BETWEEN JUDAR AND ME, SO BEING ALONE WITH HIM IS AWKWARD.
REALLY ?!
WHY'D YOU LEAVE ME ALONE WITH THAT SHRIMP? I HATE BEING POLITE!
P-POLITE?!
ARE YOU CAPABLE OF THAT?! I'M SHOCKED!
SHUT UP, HAKU-RYU!

TUG TUG
IT'S AWKWARD!! AW, PSHAW! HA HA HA!
TUG TUG
TAKE MY PLACE.
DON'T BE PATHETIC! YOU HAVE THINGS TO SAY TO HIM, RIGHT? THEN BE BOLD AND FACE HIM!
TOSS
TOSS
SLAM
SLAM
AWK—WARD
...
...
NOPE! NO WAY! CAN'T DO IT!
It's really awkward!
IN QISHAN, YOU TALKED TO ALIBABA LIKE NORMAL!
WHAT?!
BUT IT'S MORE COMPLICATED NOW!!

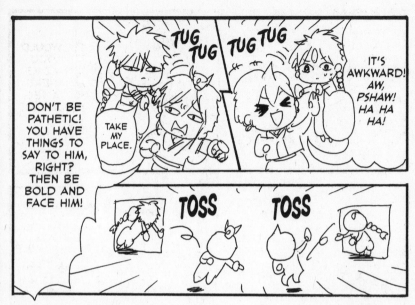

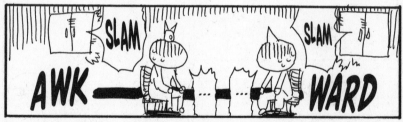

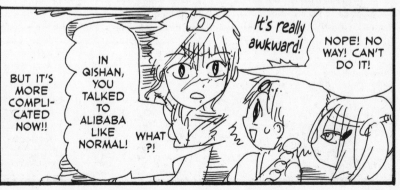

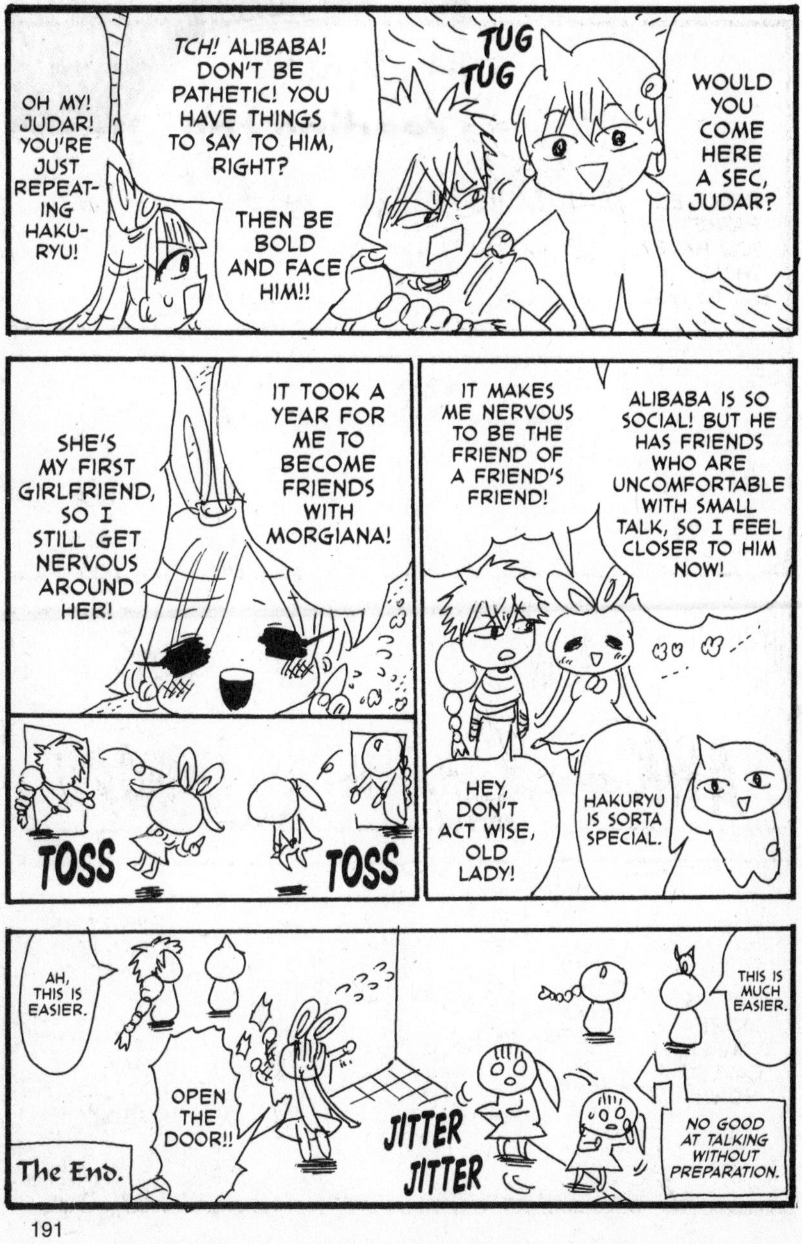
WOULD YOU COME HERE A SEC, JUDAR?
TUG TUG
TCH! ALIBABA! DON'T BE PATHETIC! YOU HAVE THINGS TO SAY TO HIM, RIGHT?
THEN BE BOLD AND FACE HIM!!
OH MY! JUDAR! YOU'RE JUST REPEAT-ING HAKU-RYU!
ALIBABA IS SO SOCIAL! BUT HE HAS FRIENDS WHO ARE UNCOMFORTABLE WITH SMALL TALK, SO I FEEL CLOSER TO HIM NOW!
IT MAKES ME NERVOUS TO BE THE FRIEND OF A FRIEND'S FRIEND!
HAKURYU IS SORTA SPECIAL.
HEY, DON'T ACT WISE, OLD LADY!
IT TOOK A YEAR FOR ME TO BECOME FRIENDS WITH MORGIANA!
SHE'S MY FIRST GIRLFRIEND, SO I STILL GET NERVOUS AROUND HER!
TOSS
TOSS
THIS IS MUCH EASIER.
NO GOOD AT TALKING WITHOUT PREPARATION.
JITTER JITTER
OPEN THE DOOR!!
AH, THIS IS EASIER.
The End.

You're reading the
WRONG WAY

MAGI reads from right to left, starting in
the upper-right corner. Japanese is read
from **right** to **left**, meaning that action,
sound effects, and word-balloon order are
completely reversed from English order.

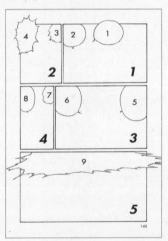